ESSENTIAL EXPERIMENTS
for
CHEMISTRY

Duncan Morrison
B.Sc., M.Sc. (Chemistry), Victoria University of Wellington, New Zealand
Career Chemistry Teacher, Vancouver, BC
Science Faculty Advisor, Faculty of Education, University of British Columbia, Vancouver, BC

Darrel Scodellaro
B.A.Sc. (Chemical Engineering), M. Ed., University of British Columbia, Vancouver, BC
Career Chemistry Teacher, Delta, BC

SMG
Lab Books

ESSENTIAL EXPERIMENTS FOR CHEMISTRY

For additional information
Email: *smg_info@smglabbooks.com*
Fax: 1-800-201 4587
Phone: 1-800-201 4587
Website: *www.smglabbooks.com*

ISBN: 0-9735707-0-9

2   3   4   5   FR   0   9   8   7   6   5   4

Printed and bound in Canada

Library and Archives Canada Cataloguing in Publication
Morrison, Duncan.
    Essential experiments for chemistry : students edition / Duncan Morrison, Darrel Scodellaro.
ISBN 0-9735707-0-9

    1. Chemistry--Experiments. I. Scodellaro, Darrel. II. Title.

QD33.2.M67 2004   540'.78   C2004-905451-1

Authors
Duncan Morrison
Darrel Scodellaro

Reviewers
Dr. Jim Hebden, Kamloops, BC
Cheri Smith, Abbotsford, BC
Dr. Marian deWane, Boise, Idaho

Publisher
Martin Goldberg, President, SMG Lab Books Ltd.

Produced by First Folio Resource Group, Inc.
Managing Editor: David Hamilton
Copy Editor: Linda Watson
Production Manager: Tom Dart
Design: Greg Duhaney
Illustrations: Adam Wood

Preface

Building on our years of experience as chemistry educators, members of chemistry curriculum and assessment teams and writing experiments for high school chemistry students, we have responded to the many requests from fellow teachers to develop a revised chemistry laboratory textbook. As a result, *Essential Experiments for Chemistry* provides all experiments required to meet high school and Advanced Placement programs in a single source. In developing this lab book, we have student-tested the experiments, and ensured they use materials that are easy to acquire, store, and maintain. In addition, we have selected an experiment format that is clear and easy to follow so that students will have a model from which to format their completed lab reports. Ultimately, by performing these experiments, students will get hands-on experience relating to all major chemical concepts associated with high school and Advanced Placement Chemistry courses of study.

In developing *Essential Experiments for Chemistry*, we want to thank Martin Goldberg who has led us in establishing SMG Lab Books Ltd. His role has been pivotal in converting our vision into an actual publication. In addition, Cheri Smith, Jim Hebden and Marian DeWane have been invaluable in reviewing our manuscript and providing insights related to the needs of students enrolled in chemistry programs in North America.

We wish to extend special thanks to Jim Hebden for allowing us to use and modify some of the experiments he designed and wrote up for his own students. Also thanks to Cheri Smith and Glenn Disney for providing us with recommendations for suitable experiments for the Advanced Placement program. We also would like to acknowledge the support and counsel provided by colleagues Bill Ferraro and Darryl Barber.

Duncan Morrison
Darrel Scodellaro

Contents

SAFETY IN THE CHEMISTRY LABORATORY   vii

SECTION 1   INTRODUCTION TO CHEMISTRY

Experiment 1A	Making Measurements and Working in the Chemistry Laboratory	1

SECTION 2   MATTER AND ITS CHANGES

Experiment 2A	Making Observations	9
Experiment 2B	Heating and Cooling Curves of a Pure Substance	13
Experiment 2C	Chemical and Physical Change	18
Experiment 2D	Graphing as a Means of Seeking Relationships	21
Experiment 2E	Determining Aluminum Foil Thickness	25

SECTION 3   ATOMS, MOLECULES, AND IONS

Experiment 3A	Recognizing Elements, Compounds, and Mixtures	28
Experiment 3B	Separation of a Mixture by Paper Chromatography	32

SECTION 4   THE MOLE CONCEPT

Experiment 4A	Counting Atoms in a Chemical Reaction	38
Experiment 4B	Determining the Empirical Formula of a Compound	41
Experiment 4C	Formula of a Hydrate	45

SECTION 5   CHEMICAL REACTIONS

Experiment 5A	Investigating Mass Changes in Chemical Reactions	49
Experiment 5B	Types of Chemical Reactions	52

SECTION 6   STOICHIOMETRY (CALCULATIONS INVOLVING REACTIONS)

Experiment 6A	Stoichiometric Analysis of an Iron-Copper Single Replacement Reaction	56
Experiment 6B	Predicting and Measuring the Mass of NaCl Produced	60
Experiment 6C	Mole Ratios in a Copper-Silver Replacement Reaction	65
Experiment 6D	Determining the Limiting Reactant and Percent Yield in a Precipitation Reaction	70
Experiment 6E	Using a Reactant in Excess in an Aluminum-Copper Replacement Reaction	74

SECTION 7 GASES

| Experiment 7A | The Gas Laws | 78 |
| Experiment 7B | Measuring and Reporting the Molar Volume of Hydrogen Gas | 83 |

SECTION 8 THERMOCHEMISTRY

Experiment 8A	Heat of Fusion of Ice	89
Experiment 8B	Molar Heats of Reaction and Hess's Law	93
Experiment 8C	Comparing Molar Heats of Combustion of Two Fuels	100

SECTION 9 THE PERIODIC TABLE AND CHEMICAL BONDING

| Experiment 9A | The Periodic Table | 106 |
| Experiment 9B | Model Building with Covalent Molecules | 112 |

SECTION 10 SOLUTION CHEMISTRY

Experiment 10A	Polar and Non-Polar Solutes and Solvents	116
Experiment 10B	Spectrophotometric Analysis	121
Experiment 10C	Factors Affecting Solubility and Rate of Dissolving	127
Experiment 10D	Solubility Trends and Precipitate Formation	132
Experiment 10E	An Introduction to Qualitative Analysis	136

SECTION 11 REACTION RATES

Experiment 11A	Factors That Affect Reaction Rates	141
Experiment 11B	The Iodine Clock Reaction	149
Experiment 11C	Measuring Reaction Rate Using Volume of Gas Produced	154
Experiment 11D	Order of a Reaction	159

SECTION 12 CHEMICAL EQUILIBRIUM

Experiment 12A	Investigating Chemical Equilibrium	163
Experiment 12B	The Quantitative Relationship of a Reaction at Equilibrium	171
Experiment 12C	Determination of a Solubility Product Constant	176
Experiment 12D	Applications of Solubility Product Principles	180

SECTION 13   ACIDS, BASES, AND SALTS

Experiment 13A	Introduction to Acids and Bases	187
Experiment 13B	Brönsted-Lowry Acid and Base Equilibria	191
Experiment 13C	Acid-Base Titration	195
Experiment 13D	Hydrolysis–The Reaction of Ions With Water	200
Experiment 13E	Acid-Base Trends of Metal and Non-Metal Hydroxides	206
Experiment 13F	Buffer Solutions of Weak Acids and Weak Bases	211
Experiment 13G	Using a Primary Standard to Analyze Acid and Base Solutions	216
Experiment 13H	Titration Curves	225

SECTION 14   ELECTROCHEMISTRY (OXIDATION-REDUCTION)

Experiment 14A	Oxidation-Reduction Reactions of Elements and Their Ions	230
Experiment 14B	Redox Titrations Involving Iodine	236
Experiment 14C	Redox Titrations Involving the Permanganate Ion	244
Experiment 14D	Electrochemical Cells	250
Experiment 14E	Electrolytic Cells	256
Experiment 14F	Corrosion of Iron	262

SECTION 15   ORGANIC CHEMISTRY

Experiment 15A	Making Models of Some Carbon Compounds	267
Experiment 15B	Preparation of Esters	271
Experiment 15C	Preparation of a Soap	276
Experiment 15D	Oxidation of Alcohols	281
Experiment 15E	Synthesis, Purification, and Analysis of an Organic Compound	286

SECTION 16   CHEMICAL ANALYSIS AND SYNTHESIS

Experiment 16A	Predictions Involving Precipitation, Acid-Base, and Redox Reactions	292
Experiment 16B	Molar Mass by Freezing Point Depression	296
Experiment 16C	Identifying a Volatile Liquid by Determining its Molar Mass	301
Experiment 16D	Gravimetric Analysis: Phosphorus Content in Fertilizer	306
Experiment 16E	Preparation and Testing of a Coordination Compound (Complex Salt)	310

APPENDICES

315

Safety in the Chemisty Laboratory

General Safety Precautions

1. Follow all instructions carefully and as written, unless instructed otherwise. Read the instructions before you start an experiment and ask your instructor if you are uncertain of any directions.

2. Never perform unauthorized experiments. Do only those experiments assigned or approved by your instructor.

3. A mature attitude is essential. Never run, push, or engage in horseplay or practical jokes. Do not throw objects in the laboratory. Consider the laboratory a place for serious work.

4. Never eat, drink, chew gum, or apply cosmetics in the laboratory.

5. Always carry objects carefully to their destinations. Do not try to carry an armful.

6. Always sit properly on your stool or chair — do not lean backwards. Never sit on work tables or a side bench.

7. Keep your work area clean and uncluttered. Store items such as books, packs, etc. away from your work area.

8. Dispose of chemicals as directed by the lab manual and/or your instructor.

9. Do not use the sink to discard filter paper or other solid wastes.

10. Turn off electrical equipment, water, and gas when not in use, and check that it is off at the end of the period.

11. Know the location of and how to operate all safety equipment in the classroom, including the fire extinguisher, fire blanket, sand, eyewash fountain, first-aid kit, and chemical-spill kit.

12. Know the evacuation route to be followed on exiting the classroom. In the event of an emergency, leave the building immediately in a quiet orderly manner, even if your instructor is not present.

13. In the case of an earthquake, immediately take cover under your work table and stay there until the shaking has stopped and it is safe to evacuate the building.

Laboratory Apparel Precautions

1. Do not wear loose-fitting sleeves, bulky outer-wear, or open-toe shoes. Proper footwear is required at all times.

2. Tie back long hair. Tuck neckties inside your shirt.

3. Wear safety goggles when using chemicals, hot liquids, lab burners, or hot plates

4. Wear lab aprons to protect clothing as directed.

5. Wear plastic gloves when working with preserved specimens or with poisonous, corrosive, or irritating chemicals.

Precautions for Working with Chemicals

1. Never touch or taste substances in the laboratory unless directed by your instructor.

2. Never drink from laboratory glassware or put any food item in glassware. Never pipet chemicals by mouth.

3. Never smell substances in the laboratory without specific instructions. When required to smell a substance, do not inhale fumes directly; waft the air above the substances toward your nose and sniff carefully.

4. Never use any chemical from an unlabeled bottle.

5. Read bottle labels carefully and be familiar with safety precautions for each chemical being used. Different countries use different systems for identifying safe-handling requirements for chemicals so it is important to have an understanding of the particular system that is used.

6. Know the special precautions when handling any chemical labeled *Flammable, Poison,* or *Corrosive*. Know what these terms mean.

7. Never return unused chemicals to the stock containers. Use only the supplied dispensing tool provided (dropper, spoon, etc.) and do not exchange it with another. Use only the suggested amount of a chemical — do not take excess.

Precautions for Working with a Lab Burner or Hot Plate

1. Wear safety goggles, tie back long hair, and roll up long, loose-fitting sleeves when working with a lab burner.

2. Learn how to light a lab burner correctly. Keep your head well back and use a proper gas-lighter.

3. If a burner does not light, or if the flame keeps going out, turn off the gas and ask your instructor for help.

4. Never allow flammable chemicals or materials near a flame.

5. Never leave a lighted lab burner, hot plate, or any hot object unattended.

6. Never reach over an exposed flame or heat source.

7. Use tongs, test tube holders, or oven mitts to handle hot equipment.

8. When you heat something in an open container such as a test tube, point the open end of the container away from yourself and others.

9. Use only heat-resistant glassware (e.g., Pyrex) for heating substances. Place a wire gauze under the glassware when heating it on a ring stand. Clamp flasks when heating them on a ring stand.

10. Allow ample time for heated objects to cool before touching them. Severe burns can result from handling hot objects that appear to be cool. Never place hot objects on the lab bench. Always place them on a heat-resistant mat.

Precautions for Working with Glassware and Other Lab Equipment

1. Use only the equipment specified in the laboratory instructions unless the instructor directs otherwise.

2. Never use chipped or cracked glassware — bring it to your instructor for disposal.

3. Make sure glassware is clean before you use it, and clean before you store it.

4. Keep your hands away from the sharp or pointed ends of equipment such as scalpels, dissecting probes, etc.

5. Do not force glass tubing or thermometers into rubber stoppers by pushing down on them with your hand. Use a lubricant and rotating motion, while applying gentle pressure. Ask your instructor for special instructions on this topic.

6. Dispose of broken glassware or tubing in the special "Broken Glass" container — NOT the waste basket.

Precautions for Working with Electrical Equipment

1. Never use equipment with frayed insulation or with loose or broken wires.

2. Make sure the area under and around the electrical equipment is dry and free of flammable materials.

3. Never touch electrical equipment with wet hands.

4. Turn off all power switches before plugging an appliance into an outlet or unplugging it. Dangerous sparking results when an appliance is unplugged before it is turned off.

5. Disconnect electrical equipment from the outlet by pulling on the plug — never jerk plugs from outlets by pulling on the cord.

6. Do not poke or place anything into electrical outlets.

Accident Procedures

1. Report all accidents or injuries to your instructor, no matter how minor.

2. Report all equipment breakage and chemical spills to your instructor.

3. If a chemical spills on your skin or clothing, wash it off immediately with plenty of cool water and notify the instructor as soon as possible.

4. If a chemical gets into your eyes or on your face, wash immediately at the eyewash fountain for at least 10 min and notify the instructor.

5. Clean up spills immediately using a wet sponge. If a hazardous chemical is spilled, notify the instructor before attempting to clean it up — a chemical spill kit may be needed.

6. Use a dustpan and a brush to pick up broken glass — do not attempt to pick it up with your bare hands.

7. Smother small fires, or use an approved fire extinguisher. Do not use water on chemical or electrical fires.

8. Extinguish clothing fires by smothering the flames with a fire blanket.

9. For a large or out-of-control fire, evacuate the building immediately — do not attempt to put the fire out!

Basic Instructions for Laboratory Work

1. Read the experiment before coming to the laboratory so that you have a general understanding of the activities you will perform.

2. It is common to perform experiments in small groups so it is important that you are able to work cooperatively.

3. Work conscientiously (and look after your partners) to avoid accidents.

4. To avoid confusion, do NOT use the Equipment and Chemical Reagents list as a shopping list to go around the lab and gather equipment and chemicals. Instead, read the Procedure and obtain equipment and chemicals ONLY WHEN DIRECTED.

5. When weighing, do not place chemicals directly on the balance since they may harm the balance.

6. Do not weigh hot or warm objects. Hot objects can actually create air currents that may interfere with the balance's ability to provide accurate readings. Therefore, allow hot objects to cool to room temperature before weighing.

Making Measurements and Working in the Chemistry Laboratory

The purpose of this experiment is to familiarize you with the techniques of working with common equipment in the chemistry laboratory and to gain an understanding of the role of measurement and precision in using that equipment. Specifically, you will be measuring length, mass, liquid volume, and temperature. Results you obtain will be compared with those of other students in order to show the amount of uncertainty in a measurement. This will be expressed in terms of the number of significant figures in the measurement. You will also practice methods of making solutions, heating, and filtering.

All measurements inherently have some uncertainty, which is determined by the piece of equipment you are using and your ability to take its readings. The most common method of expressing uncertainty in a value is to use significant figures. The number of significant figures in a value consists of all the digits in a measurement that you can definitely read, plus the first digit of which you are uncertain. For example, if a student measures and records a mass of 86.2 g, it is understood that the last digit (in this case, 2) is uncertain. Furthermore, if four students measured the mass of this object and came up with readings of 86.2 g, 86.3 g, 86.1 g, and 86.3 g, the average mass is 86.225 g. However the readings show that it is the tenths of a gram we are not sure of, and therefore any digits after that position are not valid or meaningful. The average mass should be quoted as 86.2 g, which has three significant figures to match what was originally measured. The uncertainty can be quoted as ± 0.1 g, which shows that the measured values show variation from the average by 0.1 g above and below the quoted value.

Also, the terms precision and accuracy are commonly used in describing measurements. Precision refers to how consistent measured values are. The greater the number of significant figures obtained, the better the likelihood for more precision. Accuracy on the other hand refers to how close a value is to the commonly accepted "correct" value. For instance, a series of values such as 1.98 g, 1.97 g, and 1.98 g show a high degree of precision. However, if the correct value is 1.85 g, then the results obtained are not accurate, perhaps because there is some source of error unaccounted for.

Using the centigram balance is the most typical way of measuring mass in a chemistry laboratory. It is important to check that the balance reads zero when no object is on the pan before beginning to use it. If an adjustment is necessary, check with your instructor before proceeding. Since balances can be put out of adjustment when moved, it is better if possible that the balances stay in one location in the lab and that you go to the balance rather than bringing it to your bench. It is good technique when weighing chemicals to weigh them on a piece of paper or other object such as a watch glass or beaker to prevent damage to the pan.

When measuring the volume of a liquid, you will notice the surface of the liquid is curved. This is called the *meniscus*. The correct way to take a volume reading is to position your eyes level with the bottom of the meniscus, and read the value at that point.

When making solutions, chemists refer to the substance that gets dissolved as the *solute* and the substance (usually water) that does the dissolving as the *solvent*. Furthermore, a solute that dissolves reasonably well is said to be *soluble*. In this experiment, calcium hydroxide is the solute and water is the solvent.

OBJECTIVES

1. to measure the length of some items and use combined class results to understand how to express the precision of those measurements

2. to measure the mass of various items and use combined class results to understand how to express the precision of those mass measurements

3. to measure the mass of a certain volume of water measured with three different pieces of equipment and use combined class results to understand how to express the precision of the volume measurements

4. to obtain practice in the techniques of dissolving, heating, and filtering

SUPPLIES

Equipment
centimetre ruler
centigram balance
graduated cylinder (25 mL)
volumetric pipet (25 mL)
pipet filler
plastic measuring spoon
2 beakers (250 mL)
beaker (100 mL)
ring stand
ring clamp
bunsen burner and wire
   gauze (or hot plate)
thermometer

filter funnel
filter paper
stirring rod
test tube (18 mm × 150 mm)
wash bottle
heat resistant pad
straw
paper "stickie" approximately
   7–8 cm square
30 pins (≤ 2.5 cm long)
lab apron
safety goggles

Chemical Reagents
calcium hydroxide, $Ca(OH)_2$

PROCEDURE

Part I: Measuring Length

1. Measure the length of the side of a square "stickie" provided to the nearest 0.1 mm and record this value in your copy of Table 1.

Part II: Measuring Thickness

1. Measure the total thickness of all the sheets of paper making up this book, excluding the cover, to the nearest 0.1 mm. Exclude the covers and the very first and last pages which are slightly thicker than the rest.

2. Determine the number of sheets of paper you measured (numbered pages divided by two and additional sheets not part of the regular numbering).

3. Record your results in your copy of Table 2 and in the manner suggested by your instructor to compare results with the rest of the class in order to obtain the class average.

Part III: Measuring Mass

1. Obtain at least 30 pins in a small beaker.

2. Using a centigram balance, measure the mass of one pin. (For this part of the experiment, it is permissible to weigh items directly on the pan).

3. Count out 30 pins and measure the total mass of them.

4. Record your results in your copy of Table 3 and in the manner suggested by your instructor to compare results with the rest of the class to obtain the class average.

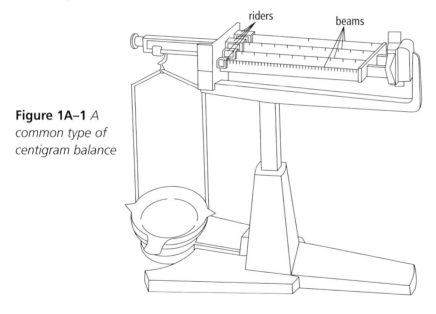

Figure 1A–1 *A common type of centigram balance*

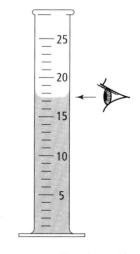

Figure 1A–2 *Reading a graduated cylinder. Your eye should be level with the top of the liquid. Take the reading at the bottom of the meniscus, the curved surface of the liquid. The correct reading for the volume shown in the figure is 17.5 mL.*

Part IV: Measuring Liquid Volume

1. Determine the mass of a clean, dry 100 mL beaker and record this value in Table 4.

2. Using the graduations on the side of the beaker, add water until you have added 25 mL, then determine and record the mass of beaker and water.

3. Empty and dry the beaker. Measure 25 mL of water as measured in a 25 mL graduated cylinder and add it to the beaker. Determine and record the mass of beaker and water.

4. Empty and dry the beaker. Using a 25 mL volumetric pipet and a pipet filler, measure 25 mL of water and add it to the beaker. Your instructor

will give directions for the type of pipet filler available to you. Determine and record the mass of beaker and water.

5. Also record your results in the manner suggested by your instructor to compare results with the rest of the class and obtain the class average.

Part V: Preparing a Solution

1. Put on your lab apron and safety goggles.

2. Using a plastic measuring spoon, obtain about 10 mL (2 teaspoons) of calcium hydroxide, $Ca(OH)_2$ and transfer it to a 250 mL beaker.

3. Add approximately 150 mL of water and stir to mix thoroughly to begin the dissolving process.

4. Since the calcium hydroxide is not very soluble, you will need to heat up the solution to increase the rate of dissolving. If using a bunsen burner, set up the beaker on a ring stand with ring and gauze as shown in Figure 1A-3, or use a hot plate if available. Heat the beaker until the temperature of the contents reaches approximately 60°C. Do not let the thermometer rest against the bottom of the beaker, but instead hold it in the middle of the solution.

Figure 1A-3 *Heating the calcium hydroxide and water*

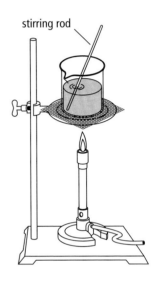

stirring rod

5. Maintain this temperature for about 10 min, stirring occasionally with a stirring rod, never with the thermometer. It is to be expected that some of the calcium hydroxide will be left undissolved. Then turn off the burner (or hot plate), remove the beaker to a heat resistant pad and proceed to Part VI.

Part VI: Filtering a Solution

1. Obtain a piece of filter paper and fold it in half, then in half again. Separate the still-folded paper to make one thickness on one side and three on the other so that the shape becomes a cone, as shown in Figure 1A-4.

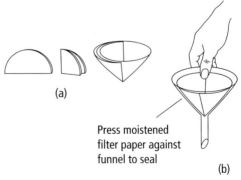

(a)

Press moistened filter paper against funnel to seal

(b)

Figure 1A-4 *(a) Folding the filter paper into a cone (b) After adding a small portion of water to moisten the paper, press to seal it to the funnel*

2. Place the paper cone in a filter funnel and use a wash bottle to wet it slightly to hold it in place. Place the funnel in the ring clamp on the ring stand, in such a way that the tip of the funnel touches the side of a clean, dry 250 mL beaker.

3. Carefully pour the contents of the beaker a portion at a time into the filter funnel and allow it to drain through. Pour it down a stirring rod as shown in Figure 1A-5. Keep the funnel about three-quarters full to increase the speed of filtration. It is not necessary to wash the last of the precipitate into the funnel since you are discarding the retained solid anyway. Adding water would then dilute the saturated solution.

4. When the filtering is complete, discard the filter paper and contents. The clear liquid obtained through the process of filtering is called the *filtrate*. It is a calcium hydroxide solution, also known as limewater.

5. Half fill a test tube with your limewater and bubble your exhaled breath through a straw into it until a change occurs. Observe and record the change.

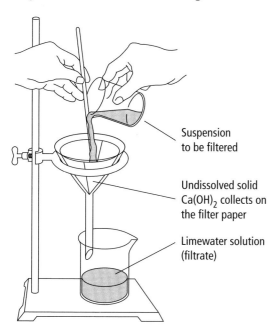

Suspension to be filtered

Undissolved solid Ca(OH)$_2$ collects on the filter paper

Limewater solution (filtrate)

Figure 1A-5 *Use a glass stirring rod and pour the liquid down it. This makes a more even flow and avoids splashes. Ensure that the stem of the funnel touches the side of the beaker.*

REAGENT DISPOSAL

Place the leftover limewater solution in the container designated by your instructor. Discard the filter paper and contents.

POST LAB CONSIDERATIONS

It is important for you to submit your results for Parts I to IV so that class averages can be obtained and you can see the variability of measurements of the same quantity. The mass of your empty beaker in Part IV should also be reported, not to obtain an average mass, but to show how the masses of apparently identical pieces of glassware can be considerably different. Students often make the erroneous assumption that, for example, all 100 mL beakers will have the same mass.

When measurements are used in calculations such as multiplication or division, the number of significant figures quoted in the calculated result is determined by the number of significant figures in the least precise quantity used.

The limewater solution you prepared is important in a chemistry laboratory since it is used as a test for carbon dioxide, CO_2. When CO_2 is blown into limewater or shaken with it, a white precipitate of calcium carbonate ($CaCO_3$) is formed, which gives the solution a milky appearance. If a solution of limewater is left in an open beaker, a white layer appears on the surface as CO_2 from the air reacts with it. For this reason, limewater must always be kept in closed containers.

EXPERIMENTAL RESULTS

Part I: Measuring Length

Table 1 (Remember to use the correct number of significant figures.)

Length of "Stickie" (cm)	Class Average
COMPLETE IN YOUR NOTEBOOK	

Part II: Measuring Thickness

Table 2

Thickness of This Book (cm)	Class Average	Number of Sheets of Paper
COMPLETE IN YOUR NOTEBOOK		

Part III: Measuring Mass

Table 3

Mass of One Pin (g)	Class Average	Mass of 30 Pins (g)	Class Average
COMPLETE IN YOUR NOTEBOOK			

Copying the experiment is prohibited.

Part IV: Measuring Liquid Volume

Table 4

Mass of 100 mL beaker =		g
Mass of Beaker + 25 mL Water (Measured in Beaker)	Mass of 25 mL Water (Measured in Beaker)	Class Average
COMPLETE IN YOUR NOTEBOOK		
Mass of Beaker + 25 mL Water (Graduated Cylinder)	Mass of 25 mL Water (Graduated Cylinder)	Class Average
COMPLETE IN YOUR NOTEBOOK		
Mass of Beaker + 25 mL Water (Volumetric Pipet)	Mass of 25 mL Water (Volumetric Pipet)	Class Average
COMPLETE IN YOUR NOTEBOOK		
List of masses of 100 mL beakers used by all other laboratory groupings:		

Part VI: Result of blowing exhaled air into the limewater solution:

ANALYSIS OF RESULTS

1. Refer to your measurements of your "stickie" in Table 1.
   a. After comparing the length of your "stickie" to those of other members of the class, express the length of the side in centimetres to the correct number of significant figures.
   b. Calculate the area of the square "stickie" in square centimetres and quote the answer to the correct number of significant figures, which is the same as the number in the length measurement.

2. Refer to your measurements of the paper thickness in Table 2.
   a. After comparing the thickness of the paper in this book to those of other members of the class, express the thickness in centimetres to the correct number of significant figures.
   b. Using the number of pages of paper comprising the book, calculate the thickness of one sheet of paper, to the correct number of significant figures.

3. Refer to your pin masses in Table 3.
   a. After comparing your mass of one pin to those of other members of the class, express the mass to the correct number of significant figures.
   b. After comparing your mass of 30 pins to those of other members of the class, express the mass to the correct number of significant figures.
   c. From this value, calculate the mass of one pin to the correct number of significant figures.

4. Refer to your mass and volume measurements in Table 4.
   a. Observe all the values for the masses of an empty 100 mL beaker. Which is the greatest? Which is the smallest?
   b. Given the fact that 1 mL of water has a mass of 1 g, convert the masses you obtained for the three different ways of measuring 25 mL to a volume in millilitres.
   c. Calculate the class average for each of the three methods and state the value to the correct number of significant figures. Which value is closest to the desired volume of 25 mL? Which piece of equipment gives the most precise results?

FOLLOW-UP QUESTIONS

1. A strip of copper is 15.2 cm long, 2.8 cm wide, and 0.2 mm thick. What is its volume in cubic centimetres, to the correct number of significant figures?

2. Magnesium metal is usually sold to chemistry labs as long strips of ribbon in a flat roll. If you required the mass of a 5 cm piece of magnesium ribbon and found it had a mass of 0.04 g, how could you obtain a more accurate mass reading for this 5 cm piece?

3. Arrange the three pieces of equipment you used to measure volume in order of increasing accuracy. Recall their shape and explain the reason for the increasing accuracy.

4. A student forgot to measure the mass of an empty 100 mL beaker before adding about 2 g of a chemical to it, and decided to simply obtain the mass of another empty 100 mL beaker instead. Would this be a satisfactory alternative? Refer to Analysis of Results 4a and determine the maximum amount the error in mass could be using the beakers in your class, expressed as a percentage of the required mass of 2 g.

5. In Part V, you dissolved a solute in some water to make a solution. If you had needed to know how much solute dissolved, how could you have determined this?

CONCLUSION

1. Generally state how you decided how many significant figures you must record when making measurements.

2. State how you should round off answers from calculations involving significant figures.

Making Observations

Observations are an important component of the scientific method, a means whereby scientists solve problems. The scientific method is cyclical in nature. First, a scientist makes observations and analyzes them in a search for patterns or relationships. Having discovered a relationship, the scientist checks it by making predictions of the outcomes of further tests. In doing these further tests, the scientist naturally makes more observations, and so on.

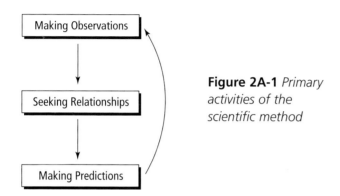

Figure 2A-1 *Primary activities of the scientific method*

In chemistry, you will constantly be checking for changes when you do experiments. Sometimes you will observe that no change occurs. This type of observation is just as important as one in which a change does occur.

"Observing" is often associated only with "seeing" – that is, "using your eyes." However, in science, "observing" implies using any or all of the senses of sight, touch, smell, hearing, and taste. Obviously, in a chemistry lab no unauthorized observations, particularly those involving touch, smell, or taste, should be conducted. Since the unaided senses are limited, scientists rely on special laboratory equipment such as thermometers and balances to extend their senses. Scientific equipment is used extensively in homes to monitor and control temperatures in ovens, refrigerators, and rooms, as well as in industries such as chemical processing and services such as health care.

Observations are classed as one of two types: qualitative and quantitative. Qualitative observations tend to be rather general and use words, not numbers, to describe an object or event. An example of a qualitative observation would be, "A car drove quickly down the street." Quantitative observations are more specific and usually describe something in terms of numbers. The observation above is quantitative when expressed as, "A car drove down the street at 50 km/h." Because quantitative observations are more specific than qualitative ones, they are generally more useful in science.

In this experiment, you will practice making both qualitative and quantitative observations while doing two activities: combining two different metals with water (Part I), and placing aluminum foil in copper(II) chloride solution (Part II).

OBJECTIVES

1. to make observations while watching materials interact and undergo change

2. to record and classify these observations as qualitative or quantitative

SUPPLIES

Equipment
3 beakers (250 mL)
2 test tubes (16 mm × 150 mm)
thermometer
centigram balance
metric ruler
tweezers
lab apron
safety goggles

Chemical Reagents
mossy zinc
calcium metal
phenolphthalein solution
aluminum foil
1M copper(II) chloride solution

PROCEDURE

Part I: Combining Two Different Metals With Water

1. Put on your lab apron and safety goggles.

2. Obtain two 250 mL beakers and fill each of them with about 150 mL of tap water. Label one beaker A and the other B.

3. Next fill two test tubes (16 mm × 150 mm) with tap water. Fill them to the brim so that no air remains in them.

4. With your thumb covering the open end, invert each test tube one at a time. Place one in beaker A and one in beaker B. Leave each test tube filled with water upside down in the beaker; as in Figure 2A-2.

5. Place a piece of mossy zinc in beaker A and immediately shift the test tube over to cover the metal. Hold the test tube in place and record your observations in your copy of Table 1 in your notebook.

6. Add 2 drops of phenolphthalein to beaker A and record your observations in Table 1.

7. Repeat Steps 5 and 6, this time adding a chunk of calcium metal to beaker B. Do not touch the calcium; use tweezers to pick it up. Record your observations in Table 2.

8. Repeat any steps of your choice in order to obtain quantitative observations. Use any lab equipment that has been made available to you, as well as your imagination! Before going ahead, however, check your procedure with your instructor.

9. Refer to the section on reagent disposal which follows and clean up your equipment.

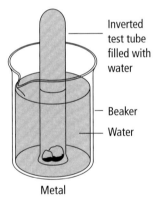

Inverted test tube filled with water

Beaker

Water

Metal

Figure 2A-2
Experimental setup for Part I

Part II: Aluminum Foil in Copper(II) Chloride Solution

1. Place 100 mL of copper(II) chloride solution in a clean 250 mL beaker, and record the temperature of the solution.

2. Cut a square of aluminum foil (approximately 15 cm × 15 cm) and roll it into a tube. To form the tube, you can roll the foil on a pencil.

3. Place the tube of aluminum foil in the beaker containing copper(II) chloride solution and immediately start recording your observations in your copy of Table 3.

Copper(II) chloride is poisonous. Wash away any spills or splashes with plenty of water.

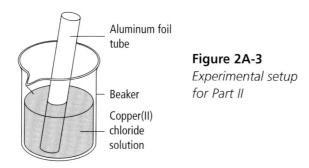

Figure 2A-3
Experimental setup for Part II

4. When no further changes appear, record the temperature of the remaining solution in Table 3.

5. Refer to the section on reagent disposal and clean up your equipment.

6. Before you leave the laboratory, wash your hands thoroughly with soap and water.

REAGENT DISPOSAL

After Part I, pour all liquids down the sink and follow with plenty of water. Place the remaining zinc and the remaining calcium into the designated containers. After Part II, place all liquids and the remaining solids in the designated container(s).

POST LAB CONSIDERATIONS

Because of the nature of this experiment, you might well have expected a variety of observations. Did you use all your senses? Where possible, you should have tried to obtain some quantitative observations to extend your qualitative observations.

An interesting activity at this point would be to compare your observations with those of another lab group.

EXPERIMENTAL RESULTS

Part I: Combining Two Different Metals with Water

Table 1 Zinc Metal in Water

Qualitative Observations	Corresponding Quantitative Observations (if any)
COMPLETE IN YOUR NOTEBOOK	COMPLETE IN YOUR NOTEBOOK

Table 2 Calcium Metal in Water

Qualitative Observations	Corresponding Quantitative Observations (if any)
COMPLETE IN YOUR NOTEBOOK	COMPLETE IN YOUR NOTEBOOK

Part II: Aluminum Foil in Copper(II) Chloride Solution

Table 3

Qualitative Observations	Corresponding Quantitative Observations (if any)
COMPLETE IN YOUR NOTEBOOK	COMPLETE IN YOUR NOTEBOOK

ANALYSIS OF RESULTS

1. In which of the tests did you observe a color change?

2. **a.** In which tests did you observe the formation of gas?
   b. Which observations allowed you to conclude that a gas was produced?

3. In which test(s) did you observe no change taking place?

FOLLOW-UP QUESTIONS

1. Suppose you want to collect and measure the volume of a gas produced in a chemical reaction. How would you do this?

2. Find out what phenolphthalein is and what it is commonly used for.

CONCLUSION

Report a significant qualitative and quantitative observation for each test you did.

Copying the experiment is prohibited.

Heating and Cooling Curves of a Pure Substance

Every pure substance has a *melting point*, a characteristic temperature at which it melts. This property of individual melting points can be used by chemists to identify substances. Likewise, when a liquid pure substance cools, it freezes at a characteristic temperature. Freezing points can therefore be used to differentiate between methanol and water, for example. Both of these are colorless liquids, but methanol freezes at –94°C, whereas water freezes at 0°C.

In this experiment, the pure substance to be studied is dodecanoic acid, also known as lauric acid. In Part I, you will first heat solid dodecanoic acid until it melts and forms a liquid, recording temperature values at regular intervals. In Part II, you will then investigate the cooling of this liquid until it solidifies, again recording temperature values at regular intervals. These temperature values will be graphed and analyzed after the experiment is complete.

OBJECTIVES

1. to investigate the heating process for solid dodecanoic acid

2. to investigate the cooling process for liquid dodecanoic acid

3. to determine and compare the melting and freezing points of dodecanoic acid

SUPPLIES

Equipment
ring stand
buret clamp
hot plate
test tube (18 mm × 150 mm)
    assembly (half full with solid
    dodecanoic acid with
    thermometer embedded)

beaker (400 mL)
thermometer for water bath
lab apron
safety goggles

Chemical Reagents
dodecanoic acid, $C_{11}H_{23}COOH$
    (in test tube apparatus)

PROCEDURE

Part I: The Heating Process

1. Put on your lab apron and safety goggles.

2. With your partner, decide in advance the role each of you will perform in Part I. As you carry out the heating process, one partner will act as observer, while the other will act as recorder. Later, in Part II, you can exchange roles. The recorder will be responsible for stating the 30 s intervals when temperature readings are to be taken, and then recording them when the observer has noted the temperature. To save time, Table 1 for the Experimental Results should be prepared ahead of time in your notebook.

3. Obtain a test tube assembly consisting of a thermometer embedded in solid dodecanoic acid from your instructor. Remove the cotton plug and save it for the end of the experiment.

4. Put 300 mL of tap water in a 400 mL beaker and place the beaker on the hot plate. Turn the hot plate on to high heat and raise the temperature of the water bath to between 55°C and 60°C. Monitor the water temperature with a thermometer. While the water is heating, set up a ring stand with a buret clamp to hold the test tube assembly as shown in Figure 2B-1.

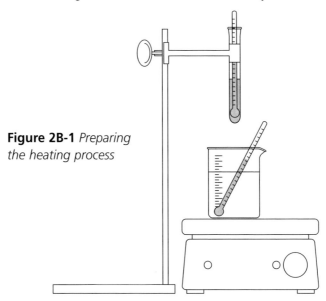

Figure 2B-1 *Preparing the heating process*

5. When the water bath has reached 55°C turn the hot plate to low heat. Lower the test tube assembly into the water bath and clamp in position so that all the dodecanoic acid is submerged below the water line. Record the temperature of the dodecanoic acid in your copy of Table 1, and every 30 s after that. During the heating process, the temperature of the water bath should be monitored with its thermometer to make certain that the water temperature remains above 55°C. (You may find it necessary to reheat the water bath with the hot plate.)

6. Temperature readings should continue to be taken every 30 s, until a temperature above 50°C is reached for the dodecanoic acid. As the dode-

canoic acid melts, stir it gently to mix the solid and liquid. Record the times when melting begins and ends, as well as any other observations.

7. Turn off the hot plate and move quickly to Part II.

Part II: The Cooling Process

1. Part II, like Part I, requires teamwork. You and your lab partner can exchange observing and recording duties at this point if you wish. Table 1 will be used for recording results from this part of the experiment as well.

2. Raise the test tube assembly out of the hot water bath and clamp it in position in a room temperature water bath as shown in Figure 2B-2. Just replace the hot water in the beaker with room temperature water.

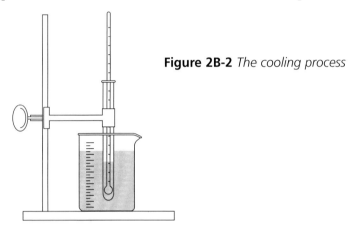

Figure 2B-2 *The cooling process*

3. Immediately start monitoring the cooling process. Record the temperature of the liquid dodecanoic acid.

4. Record the temperature of the dodecanoic acid every 30 s until a temperature near 25°C is attained. Record when solidification begins and ends, as well as any other observations.

5. When a temperature at or near 25°C has been attained you may stop recording temperature readings.

6. Reseal the test tube assembly with the cotton plug. Return the test tube assembly to your instructor and put away all your equipment.

7. Before you leave the laboratory, wash your hands thoroughly with soap and water.

REAGENT DISPOSAL

The test tube assembly containing the solidified dodecanoic acid with embedded thermometer is to be stored for future use.

POST LAB CONSIDERATIONS

The results you have collected can now be analyzed with graphs that will represent the heating and cooling curves of dodecanoic acid.

EXPERIMENTAL RESULTS

Table 1 Heating and Cooling of Dodecanoic Acid

Time (min)	Heating Process		Cooling Process	
	Temperature (°C)	Observations	Temperature (°C)	Observations
0				
0.5				
1.0				
1.5	*COMPLETE IN YOUR NOTEBOOK*	*COMPLETE IN YOUR NOTEBOOK*	*COMPLETE IN YOUR NOTEBOOK*	*COMPLETE IN YOUR NOTEBOOK*
2.0				
2.5				
etc.				

ANALYSIS OF RESULTS

Part I: The Heating Process

1. Using the results you obtained during the heating process, construct a graph of temperature versus time. Use small circles for these data points and sketch a smooth curve through these points.

2. Indicate on the graph where melting began and ended.

3. From your heating curve, determine the melting point of dodecanoic acid.

Part II: The Cooling Process

1. On the same graph as the heating curve, plot temperature versus time for the cooling process. Use small squares to distinguish these data points and sketch a smooth curve through these points.

2. Indicate on the graph where solidification began and ended.

3. From your cooling curve, determine the freezing point of dodecanoic acid.

4. Compare your melting and freezing points with each other and with those of two other lab groups. Explain any similarities or differences.

5. What can you conclude about the melting and freezing points of a pure substance?

Copying the experiment is prohibited.

FOLLOW-UP QUESTIONS

1. How would you explain the plateaus in your heating and heating curves?

2. Suppose that more dodecanoic acid had been used in Part I. What would be the change in appearance of the new heating curve? Sketch it.

CONCLUSION

State the results of Objective 3.

2C

Chemical and Physical Change

There are two types of change that are of particular interest to chemists: chemical change and physical change. A chemical change is one in which new substances are formed. A common example of a chemical change is the combustion of paraffin wax in a candle. The new substances formed as a result of this chemical change are carbon dioxide and water.

In a physical change, no new substance is formed. Sometimes physical changes are confused with chemical changes when heat and bubbles are involved. For example, when a liquid is heated to boiling, a physical (not a chemical) change occurs, since no new substance is formed. The liquid merely changes to a vapor with the same chemical composition. In the distillation of crude oil, the various components, which include gasoline, kerosene, and motor oils, have characteristic boiling points. Therefore, the individual components can be vaporized at a variety of temperatures and separated from the liquid mixture.

In this experiment, various chemical changes will be observed. Chemical changes are characterized by changes in such observable properties as color, odor, solubility, and the phase, among others. Learning to recognize chemical and physical changes is important in explaining the behavior of matter.

OBJECTIVES

1. to observe some changes in the laboratory

2. to infer whether each is a chemical or a physical change

3. to record some recognizable characteristics of chemical changes

CAUTION

Remember A, B, C, and D are unknowns; whether they are hazardous or not, it is always a good practice to minimize your contact with unknown chemicals. Some of these chemicals are corrosive to skin, eyes, or clothing. Wash spills and splashes off with plenty of water and notify your instructor.

SUPPLIES

Equipment
4 small test tubes
   (10 mm × 75 mm)
test-tube rack
4 medicine droppers

glass square
lab apron
safety goggles

Chemical Reagents
set of 4 unknown solutions

PROCEDURE

1. Put on your lab apron and safety goggles.

2. Label four test tubes A, B, C, and D. Obtain one third of a test tube of each of the unknown solutions.

3. Place a clean medicine dropper in each test tube. Set the test tubes in the test-tube rack on the lab bench.

4. Obtain a clean glass square. On a piece of white paper the size of the glass square, draw a grid like the one shown here, on which to conduct tests. Place the grid directly beneath the glass square.

	A	B	C	D
A				
B				
C				
D				

5. On each cell of the grid, combine the solutions as shown. Place just one drop of each solution on the glass square. There are only six different combinations.

6. Draw up a data table like the one below. Make brief comments in your table on any changes you observe. If no change occurs, record this as well.

7. Clean up, following the instructions for reagent disposal.

8. Before you leave the laboratory, wash your hands thoroughly with soap and water.

REAGENT DISPOSAL

All solutions can be rinsed down the sink with copious amounts of water.

POST LAB CONSIDERATIONS

As a review, note how the results of this experiment can be related to the discussion of physical and chemical changes in the introduction. If you observed in any instance that no change took place, you were probably overlooking the fact that mixing occurred, so the concentrations of the solutions changed. In such instances, a physical change has occurred.

EXPERIMENTAL RESULTS

Table 1

Unknown	A	B	C	D
A				
B				
C				
D				

ANALYSIS OF RESULTS

1. State whether a physical or a chemical change occurred for each combination of solutions.

FOLLOW-UP QUESTIONS

1. Describe (a) two chemical changes and (b) two physical changes that you might observe occurring in your everyday life.

CONCLUSION

State the results of Objective 3.

Graphing as a Means of Seeking Relationships

You will recall that the scientific method involves a cyclical process of making observations, seeking relationships, and making predictions. A scientist who looks for a relationship between two variables is often hoping to discover a mathematical relationship.

Just as people rely on language for communicating, scientists rely heavily on mathematics to better understand scientific concepts and communicate their ideas. While conducting an experiment, a scientist will typically produce a set of data as a part of the observations made, then will attempt to make sense of the data.

In this experiment, you will attempt to find a relationship between the mass and the volume of three liquids: water, methanol, and a salt solution. You will collect data on mass and volume, and then analyze the data by constructing and interpreting the graphs.

Quite often chemists discover certain relationships that turn out to be properties of substances and can be useful for identification purposes. An example of such a relationship will be determined in this experiment.

OBJECTIVES

1. to make measurements of mass and volume for three different liquids

2. to analyze the data by means of graphing techniques

3. to determine a mathematical relationship between mass and volume for each liquid

SUPPLIES

Equipment
burets (3 per class)
centigram balance
Erlenmeyer flask (250 mL)
lab apron
safety goggles

Chemical Reagents
water
methanol
salt (sodium chloride) solution

PROCEDURE

In order to make better use of lab time, you will be sharing your data with the other members of the class. You will therefore be depending on each other for

CAUTION

Methanol is highly flammable and toxic. Extinguish all flames in the area. Methanol is extremely poisonous if swallowed, and skin contact should be avoided.

good results. You will produce two data tables: one that consists of only your own lab station's data, and one that includes the data from the entire class. Your instructor will assign you a volume of liquid that you are to measure. Use this same volume for all three solutions.

1. Put on your lab apron and safety goggles.

2. Determine and record the mass of a clean, dry 250 mL Erlenmeyer flask. Since different flasks, although they appear to be identical, can have different masses, it is important that you use this same flask throughout this experiment.

3. Go to one of the burets that contains water, methanol, or salt solution (the order of the liquids is not important) and dispense your assigned volume into your Erlenmeyer flask as accurately as possible. If you do not obtain precisely your assigned volume, do not be concerned. What is important is that you accurately record the volume you do obtain in your copy of Table 1.

4. Measure the total mass of the liquid and the flask. Subtract the previous mass of the flask in order to determine the mass of the liquid. Record this figure in Table 1.

5. Now repeat Steps 2 and 3 for the other two liquids. Do not empty the flask each time you add a different liquid – just keep determining the mass of each volume by subtracting the previous balance reading.

6. A data table similar to Table 2 will be on the board. Copy your results from Table 1 onto the board.

7. When all lab stations have recorded their data on the board, copy the completed Table 2 in your notebook.

8. Before leaving the laboratory, wash your hands thoroughly with soap and water.

REAGENT DISPOSAL

Pour any leftover methanol into the designated waste container. Sodium chloride solution can be rinsed down the drain with plenty of water, as can the contents of the flask

POST LAB CONSIDERATIONS

A mathematical relationship can be expressed in the form of an equation. Graphs are extremely useful tools for scientists, since certain characteristic shapes of lines on graphs can lead to mathematical equations. For instance, any straight-line graph can be represented by a mathematical equation of the form $y = mx + b$. You may recall from mathematics courses that this equation is sometimes called the slope-intercept form.

Copying the experiment is prohibited.

A brief mathematics review might be helpful here.

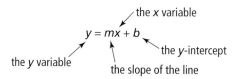

How is this equation related to the lab you just did? First, the y and x variables are defined by the terms "mass" and "volume" respectively. Second, the y-intercept will be zero because mass = 0 when volume = 0. Finally, the slope, m, must be calculated along with its appropriate units:

$$m = \frac{\Delta y}{\Delta x}$$

When reporting your mathematical relationship, you must ensure that it is meaningful. In other words, your final equation in the slope-intercept form would include the terms "mass" and "volume" rather than "y" and "x."

For the relationship between mass and volume the calculated slope of the graph has a specific meaning. This particular slope is more commonly known as *density* and is a very useful property of substances and mixtures.

EXPERIMENTAL RESULTS

Table 1 For Lab Station _____

Water		Methanol		Salt Solution	
Volume (mL)	Mass (g)	Volume (mL)	Mass (g)	Volume (mL)	Mass (g)
		COMPLETE IN YOUR NOTEBOOK			

Table 2 Class Results

	Water		Methanol		Salt Solution	
Lab Station	Volume (mL)	Mass (g)	Volume (mL)	Mass (g)	Volume (mL)	Mass (g)
1.						
2.						
3.						
continue	COMPLETE IN YOUR NOTEBOOK	COMPLETE IN YOUR NOTEBOOK	COMPLETE IN YOUR NOTEBOOK	COMPLETE IN YOUR NOTEBOOK	COMPLETE IN YOUR NOTEBOOK	COMPLETE IN YOUR NOTEBOOK
10.						
11.						
12.						

ANALYSIS OF RESULTS

Whenever a graph is constructed, the first question that arises is, "Which variable goes on the *y*-axis and which goes on the *x*-axis?" The answer is that, by convention, the dependent variable goes on the *y*-axis and the independent variable goes on the *x*-axis. The independent variable is the one over which you have control; it is the variable that you decided to measure. (Did you decide to obtain a certain volume or a certain mass of each liquid?)

1. Following the rules of good graphing, plot a graph showing mass vs. volume for each liquid. You should plot the results for all liquids on the same graph, but be careful to differentiate the results. For example, use circles for the data points of water, squares for those of methanol, and triangles for those of the salt solution.

2. If the lines on your graph illustrate straight-line relationships, determine the mathematical relationship between mass and volume for each liquid.

3. What is the density of each liquid? Consult your instructor for accepted values and compare your densities to these.

4. Use your graph to predict the mass of 6.5 mL of methanol.

5. Use your mathematical relationship from Analysis 2 to calculate the mass of 6.5 mL of methanol.

6. Compare your answers to Analysis 4 and 5 and explain why they might not be identical.

FOLLOW-UP QUESTIONS

1. Suppose you have a large supply of sponge balls with weights in the center, so that when the balls are piled on each other the bottom balls are flattened. Sketch a graph that generally describes mass vs. volume for these sponge balls.

2. Would weighted sponge balls represent a good model for liquid molecules such as water or methanol? Use the shapes of your graphs to support your answer.

3. Use your density value of methanol to predict the mass of 45.0 mL of methanol.

4. A sample of one of the chemical reagents from this experiment lost its label. A student tests the sample and notes that 68.0 mL weighs 85.23 g. What is the identity of the sample? Explain.

CONCLUSION

State the results of Objective 3.

Determining Aluminum Foil Thickness

In chemistry, we often use large and small quantities and sometimes these values are indirectly determined. An example of indirect measurement will be used in this experiment to determine the thickness of a piece of aluminum foil. Normally, a specialized tool called a micrometer would be used to directly measure the thickness of very thin materials but it is assumed that this tool is unavailable.

Two common concepts will be combined and used to measure the thickness of a small rectangular piece of aluminum foil:

1. Volume of a rectangular solid $V = LWH$ (length × width × height)

2. Density of a substance $D = m/V$ (mass / volume)

Imagine that your sheet of aluminum foil is a rectangular solid where the height is actually the sheet's thickness. Therefore, in this experiment, when you determine height from the volume equation, you will actually be measuring thickness.

Starting with the density formula, volume can be calculated since:

1. mass can be measured

2. density is known for aluminum

Now that volume is known, height (thickness) can be calculated from $V = LWH$ since:

1. volume is known

2. length and width can be measured

Even thinner than aluminum foil is the hard layer of aluminum oxide that forms on the surface of aluminum exposed to the air. This tenacious coating prevents further corrosion and can be given a constant thickness and a variety of bright colors in a commercial plating process known as *anodizing*.

OBJECTIVES

1. to calculate the thickness of a sheet of aluminum foil and express the answer in terms of proper scientific notation and significant figures

SUPPLIES

Equipment
3 rectangular pieces of aluminum foil (minimum 15 cm × 15 cm)
metric ruler
centigram balance

PROCEDURE

1. Obtain three rectangular pieces of aluminum foil that are at least 15 cm on each side and number these pieces 1, 2, and 3 with a pencil.

2. Use a metric ruler to measure the length and width of each piece of foil. Record the measurements (using significant figures) in your copy of Table 1.

3. Use a centigram balance to find the mass of each piece of aluminum foil. Record the masses (again, using significant figures).

4. Take a moment to compare and discuss your use of significant figures with those of another lab group.

REAGENT DISPOSAL

Place the used aluminum foil in the wastepaper basket.

POST LAB CONSIDERATIONS

In this experiment, the terms *accuracy* and *precision* are important and you need to understand the difference. Accuracy refers to how well a measured value compares to an accepted value. Precision, on the other hand, refers to how close your individual measurements are to one another. How accurate is your measured thickness of the aluminum foil? This will require you to compare your value to a value either listed on the box of foil or to one provided by your instructor. How precise are your measurements? This will simply depend on how similar they are to one another.

Scientific notation is used in the calculations because of the magnitude of the thickness measurements. Whenever very large or very small numbers are encountered in scientific work, it is best to express those numbers in scientific notation. Common sense usually dictates when to use fixed notation (0.1 cm) or scientific notation (1.0×10^{-6} cm).

EXPERIMENTAL RESULTS

Table 1

Sheet	Length (cm)	Width (cm)	Mass (g)
1	COMPLETE IN YOUR NOTEBOOK	COMPLETE IN YOUR NOTEBOOK	COMPLETE IN YOUR NOTEBOOK
2			
3			

ANALYSIS OF RESULTS

1. Refer to the introduction and use the formulas provided to calculate the thickness of each sheet of aluminum foil. The density of aluminum is 2.70 g/cm³. Show all of your work and results. Your answers should have the correct number of significant figures and be expressed in scientific notation.

2. Determine the average thickness of your sheets of aluminum foil.

3. Refer to the Post Lab Considerations. How does your thickness compare to the accepted value as provided by your instructor? In other words, how accurate is your measured thickness? How precise were your thickness values?

FOLLOW-UP QUESTIONS

1. A rectangular metal tray that measured 22.55 cm by 15.33 cm was plated with a very thin layer of gold. (The density of gold is 19.32 g/cm³.) The gold plating had a mass of 0.0538 g. Calculate the thickness of the plating using scientific notation and the correct number of significant figures.

2. By mistake, 1000.0 cm³ of oil was dumped into a pond with a surface area of 850.0 m². The density of the oil was 0.850 g/cm³. How thick was the resulting oil slick? Remember to use significant figures and scientific notation.

CONCLUSION

State the results of Objective 1.

3A

Recognizing Elements, Compounds, and Mixtures

In simple terms, chemistry can be defined as the study of the composition and interaction of matter. Matter is anything that has mass and occupies space. The universe is made up of many types of matter — water, rock, plants, air, people, to name just a few. It is quite easy to think of examples of matter, but it is more important to be able to organize them into groups. In order to better understand matter, chemists have developed a classification scheme for it. See Figure 3A-1 below.

Figure 3A-1
Classification of matter

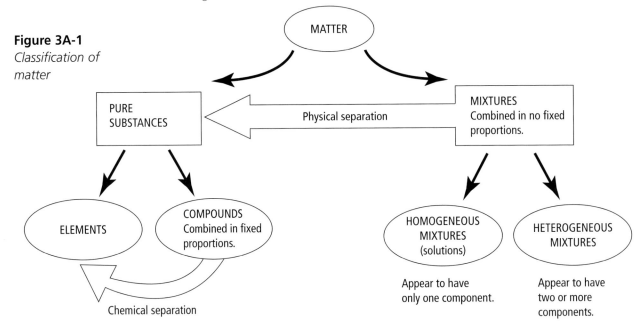

Among the many people who can appreciate the importance of classifying matter are workers in the mining industry. For example, the process for the production of the element copper often begins with the mining of a heterogeneous mixture called "copper ore." See Figure 3A-2 below.

Figure 3A-2 *Copper and sulfur can be recovered from copper ore*

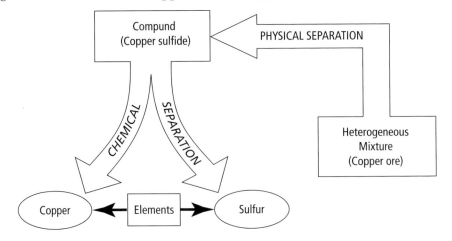

©SMG Lab Books Ltd.

In this experiment, you will act like a chemist by classifying matter. You will be given a number of unknown samples that you will test in various ways. You must decide whether a given sample is an element, a compound, or a mixture. As you know, mixtures consist of two or more substances physically combined in any proportion. Therefore, you will find that mixtures can be separated by physical means such as picking apart the components, selective dissolving, filtration, or evaporation. Compounds, on the other hand, can only be separated into elements by chemical means that are beyond the scope of this experiment.

OBJECTIVES

1. to use simple laboratory procedures to test a set of unknown samples of matter

2. to classify unknown samples of matter as elements, compounds, or mixtures

SUPPLIES

Equipment
tripod magnifier
stereomicroscope (if available)
tweezers
plastic spoon
3 test tubes (13 mm × 100 mm)
test-tube rack
lab burner

evaporating dish
crucible tongs
ring stand and ring support
filter paper and funnel
beaker (250 mL)
lab apron
safety goggles

Chemical Reagents
set of 5 unknown samples

PROCEDURE

1. Put on your lab apron and safety goggles.

2. Obtain a sample of each unknown from your instructor. Take care to number your samples according to your instructor's numbering system. If the unknown is solid, place about one half spoonful on a piece of paper. If the unknown is liquid, fill a test tube half full.

3. Use a data table similar to Table 1 to help organize your observations in your notebook.

4. Observe the unknowns carefully and record their properties.

5. Of the three solid unknowns, one is an element, one is a compound and one is a mixture. Devise a method to separate the components from the mixture then try it.

6. Of the two liquid unknowns, one is a compound and one is a mixture. Devise a means (other than tasting) of classifying them and try it.

CAUTION

You must not taste any of the unknowns as some are poisonous.

7. Clean up according to the reagent disposal instructions.

8. Before leaving the laboratory, wash your hands thoroughly with soap and water.

REAGENT DISPOSAL

Any remaining liquids can be rinsed down the sink with copious amounts of water. Any solid waste should go into the designated waste container.

POST LAB CONSIDERATIONS

Distinguishing between a mixture and a pure substance is fairly straightforward. If the unknown can be separated by physical means such as those available in this experiment, then it is a mixture. However, if the unknown is a pure substance, further tests may be required to determine whether it is an element or a compound.

EXPERIMENTAL RESULTS

Table 1

Unknown	Properties Observed	Possibilities		
		Element	Compound	Mixture
1				
2				
3	COMPLETE IN YOUR NOTEBOOK	COMPLETE IN YOUR NOTEBOOK	COMPLETE IN YOUR NOTEBOOK	COMPLETE IN YOUR NOTEBOOK
4				
5				

ANALYSIS OF RESULTS

1. Classify each of the solid unknowns as an element, compound, or mixture, and explain your decisions. If you are uncertain about any of the unknowns, explain why.

2. Which of the liquids was the compound and which was the mixture? How did you determine this?

FOLLOW-UP QUESTIONS

1. Give one example of each of the following. (Do not use any of the samples from this experiment.)
   a. homogeneous mixture
   b. heterogeneous mixture
   c. solid that is (i) an element (ii) a compound (iii) a mixture
   d. liquid that is (i) an element (ii) a compound (iii) a mixture
   e. gas that is (i) an element (ii) a compound (iii) a mixture

2. In some countries, desalination plants are used to separate salt from seawater. Consult a reference source and describe the process used in these plants. (Use the terms elements, compounds, and mixtures where appropriate in your description.)

3. In this experiment, one of the solids you tested was a compound and one was an element. What further tests would you perform to tell them apart?

CONCLUSION

State the results of Objective 2.

3B

Separation of a Mixture by Paper Chromatography

Chromatography is one technique used by chemists to separate mixtures of chemical compounds in order to identify or isolate their components. In chromatography, mixtures are separated according to the different solubilities of the components in liquids, or their adsorption on solids.

Chromatography has many applications, including the detection and measurement of pesticides in foods, and drugs in urine specimens. It is also used extensively in biological research to separate alcohols, amino acids, and sugars in plants, for example. In addition, the pharmaceutical industry relies on chromatography for the production of high-purity chemicals.

There are a variety of chromatographic techniques, but all share two features: a moving carrier phase and a stationary phase. In the stationary phase of paper chromatography, the sample to be analyzed is spotted onto a piece of filter paper. The sample is carried along this stationary phase by a solvent that acts as the moving carrier. The components of the sample are carried different distances along the paper, depending on their individual solubilities. (See Figure 3B-1.) After a length of time, therefore, the original spot is spread out into a series of bands. These bands are then analyzed, to determine their identities.

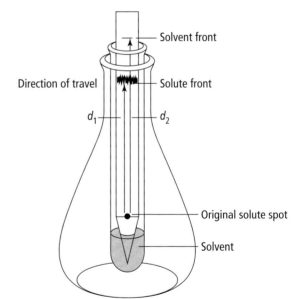

Figure 3B-1 *A typical paper chromatogram*

In paper chromatography, one method of identifying these separated components of a mixture is to calculate the R_f value of each. ("R_f" stands for "ratio of fronts".) An R_f value is simply the ratio of the distance traveled by the solute to the distance traveled by the solvent:

$$R_f = \frac{d_1}{d_2}$$

where d_1 = distance traveled by solute
d_2 = distance traveled by solvent

The R_f value of a substance is characteristic of that substance for a specific solvent. A substance having a high solubility in the moving phase will be carried further and consequently will have a high R_f value. By definition, R_f values vary from 0 to 1.

In this experiment, you will become acquainted with paper chromatography. In Part I, you will assemble a paper chromatography apparatus. In Part II, you will examine chromatographic results for a variety of food colorings. Then in Part III, you will separate two mixtures of these colorings and study the significance of the R_f values. Unfortunately, many chromatography tests on substances present two problems for the school chemistry lab:

1. The solvents required are often classified as hazardous and are therefore not recommended for school use.

2. In many cases, the time required for the separation of the mixture is too long for a typical laboratory period.

For these reasons, this experiment is restricted to the analysis of food colorings, which are readily soluble in water.

OBJECTIVES

1. to assemble and operate a paper chromatography apparatus

2. to study the meaning and significance of R_f values

3. to test various food colorings and to calculate their R_f values

4. to compare measured R_f values with standard R_f values

5. to separate mixtures of food colorings into their components

6. to identify the components of mixtures by means of their R_f values

SUPPLIES

Equipment
per class:
5 glass stirring rods
several pairs of scissors
per lab station:
3 large test tubes
    (25 mm × 200 mm)
3 Erlenmeyer flasks (250 mL)
metric ruler
pencil
chromatography paper strips
    (2.5 cm wide × 66 cm long)

Chemical Reagents
set of food colorings (yellow,
    green, blue, red)
unknown mixture of food
    colorings

PROCEDURE

Part I: Setting Up

1. Obtain three large test tubes and three Erlenmeyer flasks. (The sizes of these pieces of apparatus are important to the rest of the procedure.) Place a test tube in each of the flasks and label the test tubes A, B and C.

2. Obtain a 66 cm length of chromatography paper and cut it into three strips of 22 cm each. Using a *pencil*, lightly draw a line across each strip 4.0 cm from one end. (See Figure 3B-2). Use a pair of scissors to trim this end of the strip into a point, as shown in the drawing.

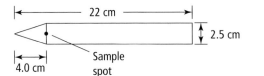

Figure 3B-2 *Preparing the chromatography strip*

3. Place some water (the solvent for this experiment) in each test tube so that it is 2.0 cm deep.

Part II: R_f Values of Individual Food Colorings

1. You will be assigned one food coloring to test: red, yellow, or blue. Take one strip of chromatography paper over to the station of food colorings. Using a glass stirring rod, spot the strip with the color assigned to you. (Refer again to Figure 3B-2). Be careful not to make too large a sample spot; it should not exceed 0.5 cm in diameter. (The smaller the spot, the better.) Write the color at the top of the strip.

2. Insert the strip in test tube A. Be very careful not to push the strip down too far; its tip should just touch the bottom of the test tube, and the water should cover about one half of its point. (See Figure 3B-3). Do not allow the flat surface of the strip to rest against the walls of the test tube. (Achieving this should not be difficult, since the width of the paper and the inside diameter of the test tube are almost the same.)

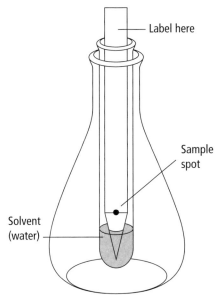

Figure 3B-3 *The final arrangement of the apparatus*

Copying the experiment is prohibited. ©SMG Lab Books Ltd.

3. Observe what happens to your sample spot as the water moves slowly up the paper as a result of capillary action.

4. Continue to make observations for the next 10 min. Try to identify two fronts as they move up the paper. One is the solute front (the food coloring) and should be easy to identify in this experiment. The other is the solvent front (water) and can only be seen upon close examination.

5. Since the movement of fronts is a rather slow process, you could start Part III of the experiment at this point. However, once you have begun Part III, you should return to Part II and complete it.

6. After about 20 min have elapsed, when you are satisfied that no further separation of color will occur, remove the strip from the test tube. Immediately draw a pencil line across the top edge of the solvent front, before it evaporates!

7. Referring to Figure 3B-4, measure d_2 and d_1 on your strip as precisely as possible. Record these values in Tables 1 and 2. Calculate the R_f value for your sample and record it as well.

8. Your instructor will have a data table similar to Table 2 on the board for the class results. Place your own results on this table and copy it into your notebook when it is complete.

9. Clean up according to the reagent disposal instructions.

Part III: Separation of Mixtures into Their Components

1. Take your second strip of chromatography paper and spot it with a sample of green food coloring. Spot the third strip with a sample of the unknown mixture of food colorings. Remember to label both spots at the top.

2. Insert the strips in test tubes B and C, and follow the same procedures as in Part II, Steps 2 to 7.

3. When you have finished, record your data in a copy of Table 3.

4. Clean up according to the reagent disposal instructions.

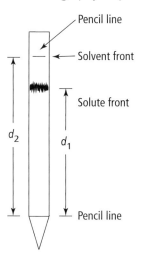

Figure 3B-4 *Making measurements on the chromatography strip*

REAGENT DISPOSAL

The dried chromatography paper can be placed in the designated container, or saved and placed in your lab report.

POST LAB CONSIDERATIONS

The separation of a mixture of food colorings is a good introduction to paper chromatography, because the components can be seen clearly spread out on the strip. Each component color has a characteristic R_f value that can be compared to a table of standard R_f values. The list of values provided in Table 4 is a partial list and may not correspond to your R_f values if the dyes used by the manufacturers of the food colorings are not identical. Therefore, the measured R_f averages (Table 2) will be more reliable than those in Table 4 when you are identifying the component colors of your mixtures.

EXPERIMENTAL RESULTS

Part II: R_f Values of Individual Food Colorings

Table 1 Results for Lab Station

Color Tested	
Distance solute traveled (d_1)	COMPLETE IN YOUR NOTEBOOK
Distance solvent traveled (d_2)	
Ratio of fronts (R_f)	

Table 2 Class Results

Lab Station	Colors Tested		
	Red R_f	Yellow R_f	Blue R_f
1			
2			
3	COMPLETE IN YOUR NOTEBOOK	COMPLETE IN YOUR NOTEBOOK	COMPLETE IN YOUR NOTEBOOK
Average R_f Values			

Part III: Separation of Mixtures into Their Components

Table 3 R_f Comparisons for Component Colors

	Component Colors	d_1 (cm) d_2 (cm)	Calculated R_f	Component R_f (From Table 2)
Green Coloring	COMPLETE IN YOUR NOTEBOOK	COMPLETE IN YOUR NOTEBOOK	COMPLETE IN YOUR NOTEBOOK	COMPLETE IN YOUR NOTEBOOK
Unknown Mixture				

Table 4 Some of the Dyes Approved for Food Coloring

Dye	Red #2	Red #3	Red #4	Yellow #5	Yellow #6	Blue #1	Blue #2
R_f	0.81	0.41	0.62	0.95	0.77	1.0	0.79

ANALYSIS OF RESULTS

1. **a.** Which of the colors you tested in Part II of the experiment appeared to contain one or more of the approved dyes listed in Table 4?
   b. Which, if any, of the colors you tested did not correspond to any of the approved dyes?

2. From your results in Part III, what are the components of the green food coloring? Support your answer both qualitatively and quantitatively.

3. What can you conclude about the identity of the components in the unknown mixture? What qualitative and quantitative evidence supports your answer?

4. What might happen if ink, rather than pencil, were used to mark the sample line on the chromatography paper?

5. Why should green food coloring be classified as a mixture, whereas yellow, blue, or red should not?

FOLLOW-UP QUESTIONS

1. Identify the dyes that appear on the chromatogram in Figure 3B-5. (Consult Table 4 for R_f values). The original sample was orange food coloring.

2. A pharmaceutical chemist runs a chromatography test on a substance and identifies two of its components by comparing their R_f values against certain standards. If the two components have R_f values of 1.0 and 0.41 and the solvent front has traveled 12.0 cm from the sample's origin, what is the separation distance on the chromatogram?

3. A chemist performs an R_f calculation, obtains a value of 1.2, and decides that the answer is unacceptable. Why?

CONCLUSION

State the results of Objective 6.

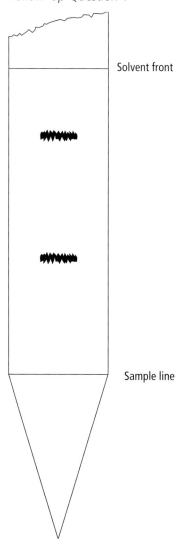

Figure 3B-5
Chromatogram for Follow-Up Question 1

Solvent front

Sample line

Counting Atoms in a Chemical Reaction

The mole is a very important concept since it allows chemists to determine the number of atoms or molecules of substances involved in chemical reactions. As you know, in chemistry, the mole represents a very large number (6.02×10^{23}) of atoms or molecules. In this experiment, you will react a sample of zinc metal with a solution of hydrochloric acid and determine the number of atoms of zinc that react. As you have learned in class, this "counting of atoms" is achieved by measuring the mass of an element then converting that mass first into moles then into atoms.

In this experiment, your goal is to react a sample of zinc metal with a solution of hydrochloric acid. The balanced chemical equation for this reaction is:

$$Zn(s) + 2HCl(aq) \rightarrow ZnCl_2(aq) + H_2(g) + heat$$

Hence, the progress of the reaction will be evidenced by bubbles of hydrogen gas produced. When the bubbles stop, the reaction is finished.

This experiment is intentionally designed so that some zinc will remain when the reaction ends. Therefore, by simply weighing the zinc sample before and after the reaction, the mass of zinc that has reacted can be easily determined. Knowing this value, you will be able to convert it to the actual number of atoms of zinc reacted.

Metals commonly react with acids and in some instances such reactions are intentionally performed. For instance, artists often use acid to etch designs in metal art and mechanics sometimes use acid to etch their names into metal tools.

OBJECTIVES

1. to determine the number of moles of atoms of zinc reacted

2. to determine the number of atoms of zinc reacted

SUPPLIES

Equipment
beaker (250 mL)
graduated cylinder (100 mL)
beaker tongs
hot plate
crucible tongs

centigram balance
stirring rod
lab apron
safety goggles

Chemical Reagents
mossy zinc
3M hydrochloric acid, HCl

PROCEDURE

1. Put on your lab apron and safety goggles.

2. Use a centigram balance to weigh a clean, dry 250 mL beaker. Record its mass in your copy of Experimental Results. This mass will be needed before and after the reaction.

3. Add one piece of dry mossy zinc to the beaker. Weigh and record the mass of the beaker and zinc. A piece of zinc between 1.0 g and 2.0 g is optimum.

4. Add approximately 50 mL of 3M HCl to the beaker and make and record qualitative observations about the reaction.

5. Allow the reaction to continue for 15 to 20 min.

6. To stop the reaction slowly add 100 mL of water to the beaker to dilute the acid solution. Carefully decant (pour just the solution) into a sink without dumping out the zinc. Add another 100 mL of water to the beaker and decant again.

7. Use the tongs to remove the zinc from the beaker and place it on a piece of paper towel.

8. Pour any remaining solution down the sink and rinse the sink with water. Also rinse out the beaker and return it to your lab station.

9. Put the wet zinc back into the beaker and place the beaker on a hot plate set at low heat. Periodically inspect the zinc by using tongs to remove it, then return it to the beaker. When the beaker and zinc appear to have slowly dried, remove the combination from the hotplate and allow it to cool.

10. Once again weigh the beaker and zinc and record this mass.

11. Clean up all of your materials.

REAGENT DISPOSAL

Rinse all solutions down the sink with copious amounts of water. Any solid waste should go into the designated waste container.

POST LAB CONSIDERATIONS

The chemical reaction in this experiment has been:

$$Zn(s) + 2HCl(aq) \rightarrow ZnCl_2(aq) + H_2(g) + heat$$

The fact that bubbles were produced is evidence that a gas was given off. Further tests would reveal that this gas was hydrogen. The mass of zinc should have decreased during the reaction making it possible to determine the number of atoms of zinc that reacted.

EXPERIMENTAL RESULTS

Before the reaction:

    Mass of dry beaker

    Mass of dry beaker + zinc

After the reaction:

    Mass of dry beaker + zinc

Qualitative Observations

ANALYSIS OF RESULTS

1. Use your data to determine the mass of zinc that reacted.

2. Calculate the number of moles of atoms of zinc reacted.

3. Calculate the number of atoms of zinc reacted.

4. Compare your answer to Analysis #3 to that of another lab group. Suggest an obvious reason for any difference.

FOLLOW-UP QUESTIONS

1. Suggest a reason why the reaction started very slowly then increased after a few minutes.

2. How would the results compare if twice the mass of zinc were used in this experiment?

3. **a.** How would the results compare if twice the amount of acid were added?
   b. How would this affect the amount of hydrogen gas produced?

CONCLUSION

State the results of Objectives 1 and 2.

   Copying the experiment is prohibited.

Determining the Empirical Formula of a Compound

A compound you will recall is a substance composed of two or more elements that have been chemically united. In this experiment you will form an iron-oxygen compound by chemically uniting the element iron with the element oxygen. You will use steel wool, which is primarily iron, and react it with the oxygen in the air. (Remember that air is about 20% oxygen.)

The reaction of iron with oxygen is very common; you are probably familiar with this process in the form of rusting. Rusting is a slow process and, under normal lab conditions, the steel wool might take several years to rust. Therefore, to enhance the rusting process, you will dip the steel wool in an ammonium chloride solution, which creates conditions that speed up the reaction.

You will observe that, even with the addition of ammonium chloride, the rusting process still takes time. The experiment cannot be completed in one lab period – in fact, you may not be able to complete the experiment for a week or so. Some forethought is necessary on your part so that you can plan your activities. By the end of the experiment (Part III) you will have collected data that will enable you to determine the empirical formula of the compound which has formed.

In most cases in daily life, the rusting process is considered undesirable and billions of dollars are spent on rust prevention. Chemists regularly conduct experiments such as this one in their search for improved methods of slowing rust formation. Such experimenting has lead to the development of new protective coating materials for iron as well as more sophisticated techniques such as cathodic protection. Cathodic protection is a technique that prevents the iron atoms from transferring their electrons to oxygen, thus preventing the rust reactions from occurring.

OBJECTIVES

1. to form a compound from the elements iron and oxygen

2. to determine the empirical formula of the compound produced in this chemical reaction

SUPPLIES

Equipment

ring stand	pipestem triangle
ring support	heat resistant mat
lab burner	centigram balance
crucible	lab apron
crucible tongs	safety goggles
water-soluble marker	medicine dropper

Chemical Reagents

steel wool, fine

$1M$ ammonium chloride solution, NH_4Cl

PROCEDURE

Part I: (First Day)

CAUTION

Ammonium chloride solution is mildly corrosive. Keep it off your skin and clothing and out of your eyes. Wash away any spills with plenty of water.

1. Put on your lab apron and safety goggles.

2. Obtain a clean, dry crucible (without a lid) and accurately determine its mass. Enter this value in your copy of Table 1.

3. Place a clump of steel wool on the balance pan and add or remove steel wool until you have 3.00 g.

4. Compress the 3.00 g of steel wool into a tight ball and place it in your crucible. Reweigh the crucible and contents, and enter the relevant information in your data table.

5. Take the crucible and contents to the "dunking station" that your instructor has set up. Here you will find the ammonium chloride solution in a large beaker.

6. Remove the ball of steel wool from the crucible and, using crucible tongs, gently submerge the steel wool in the ammonium chloride solution. Wait until the steel wool is thoroughly soaked, then remove it and carefully squeeze out any excess solution.

7. Replace the moistened steel wool in the crucible. Label the crucible with a water soluble marker; indicating your name and class.

8. Place your crucible, uncovered, in the designated storage location. Now the waiting begins!

Part II: (Next Several Days)

CAUTION

Objects that have been heated may appear to have cooled when, in fact, they are still hot. Serious burns can result.

1. Over the next week, check your crucible each day to observe any changes.

2. Each day, use a medicine dropper to add a few drops of ammonium chloride solution so that the steel wool is remoistened.

3. Continue these activities for as long as your instructor advises. The time required usually varies between four and seven days. Since Part II requires only a few minutes during each class, you can expect to carry on with activities other than this experiment during the waiting period.

Part III: (Final Day)

1. Retrieve your crucible from the storage location.

2. Set the crucible in a heating apparatus, as shown in Figure 4B-1. The crucible will sit inside a pipestem triangle which is connected to a ring support.

3. Heat the crucible and contents with the lab burner adjusted to a high temperature. The outside of the crucible will glow a dull red when it becomes very hot. Continue to heat the crucible at red heat for at least ten more minutes, and then turn off the burner.

4. Let the crucible cool so that you can touch it. CAUTION: The ring stand and accessories can burn you even after several minutes. If you are in doubt about the ring stand, you can test how hot it is by touching it with a piece of wet paper towel.

5. Determine the mass of the crucible and contents (a compound) and record this in your data table.

6. Clean up your materials according to the reagent disposal instructions and wash out and dry the crucible.

7. Before you leave the laboratory, wash your hands thoroughly with soap and water.

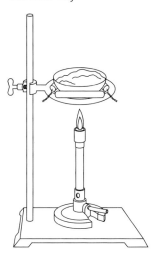

Figure 4B-1 *Apparatus for heating the steel wool on the final day*

REAGENT DISPOSAL

The ammonium chloride solution can be rinsed down the sink with large amounts of water. The crucible's contents can be placed in a garbage can.

POST LAB CONSIDERATIONS

In order to find the empirical formula of the compound produced, you need to know how many moles of iron and oxygen atoms reacted. Since you know the mass of iron reacted (you must assume here that all 3.0 g reacted), you can convert "mass of iron" into "moles of iron." The mass of oxygen reacted can be determined by examining Table 1 and applying some common sense: mass of compound – mass of iron = mass of oxygen. Now, the mass of oxygen atoms can be converted to moles of oxygen atoms. (Note: The atomic mass of 0 is 16.0, not 32.0.)

The next step towards determining the empirical formula is to calculate the ratio

$$\frac{\text{moles of O atoms}}{\text{moles of Fe atoms}}$$

Finally, if this mole ratio contains decimals, convert it into a whole number ratio. An example is given in the chart which follows.

	Moles	Mole Ratio	Ratio Doubled	Ratio Tripled
Element X	2.42	1	2	3
Element Y	6.46	2.67	5.33	8.01

You double, triple, etc., the mole ratio until you end up with a value very close to a whole number. In the example being discussed, the whole number ratio is 3:8. Hence, the empirical formula of the compound would be X_3Y_8.

EXPERIMENTAL RESULTS

Table 1

Before the Reaction	
Mass of crucible + iron (steel wool)	
Mass of crucible	COMPLETE IN YOUR NOTEBOOK
Mass of iron	
After the Reaction	
Mass of crucible + compound	
Mass of crucible	COMPLETE IN YOUR NOTEBOOK
Mass of compound (iron + oxygen)	

ANALYSIS OF RESULTS

1. Calculate the number of moles of iron atoms that reacted. Enter Analysis 1–4 values in a table similar to the one in Post Lab Considerations.

2. Determine the mass of oxygen atoms that reacted.

3. Calculate the number of moles of oxygen atoms that reacted.

4. Calculate the smallest whole-number ratio of oxygen atoms to iron atoms.

5. Write the empirical formula for the compound.

6. Look up the ion charges for iron and oxygen, and predict two possible formulas for iron oxide.

7. How does your experimentally-determined formula compare with your predicted formulas?

FOLLOW-UP QUESTIONS

1. Potassium persulfate is used in photography to remove the last traces of unwanted chemicals from photographic papers and plates. A 0.8162 g sample was found to contain 0.2361 g of potassium, 0.1936 g of sulfur; the rest was oxygen. What is the empirical formula of this compound?

CONCLUSION

State the results of Objective 2.

Copying the experiment is prohibited.   ©SMG Lab Books Ltd.

Formula of a Hydrate

A *hydrate* is a compound that has a definite number of water molecules incorporated into its crystal structure. The crystals appear dry, but when these compounds are heated strongly, water is given off, leaving the *anhydrous* (without water) form of the compound. Usually the number of moles of water present in a hydrate is in a whole-number ratio to the moles of the anhydrous salt. One common example of a substance that forms a hydrate is calcium chloride, $CaCl_2$. The formula of its hydrate is $CaCl_2 \bullet 6H_2O$ and it is named calcium chloride hexahydrate. This formula indicates that six moles of water are bound to one mole of the calcium chloride. In this case the color of the hydrate and the anhydrous salt are the same, but many hydrates undergo a color change when the water is driven off. Granules of anhydrous calcium chloride are often used to take moisture out of the air of damp rooms by forming the hydrate. Chemical drying agents such as calcium chloride are called desiccants. There may be a desiccator in your laboratory which is a large glass jar with lid, in which chemicals are kept dry in the presence of anhydrous calcium chloride. Depending on the humidity in your area, your instructor may want you to use one in this experiment as a place to allow the crucible to cool.

You may have heard the term carbohydrate. This name was given to a class of organic compounds having the general formula $C_x(H_2O)_y$, e.g. table sugar (sucrose), $C_{12}H_{22}O_{11}$. It was originally thought that the substances somehow had water molecules in a crystal structure with carbon, but subsequent research showed this was not the case. The name, however, remained.

In this experiment, you will be assigned a hydrate of unknown composition and you will use heat to drive off the bound water molecules. By determining the mass before and after heating you will be able to calculate the percentage of water in the hydrate. Subsequent calculations will enable you to determine the empirical formula of the hydrate, if the molar mass of the anhydrous salt is given.

The crucible that you will use gets very hot, and care must be taken in handling it. Use crucible tongs, and make sure it has cooled sufficiently before weighing it. Errors can be induced from convection currents above a hot crucible exerting a force on the balance arm, making the mass lighter than it should be. Never put a hot crucible on a bench top or any combustible material.

OBJECTIVES

1. to determine the percentage of water in an unknown hydrate

2. to determine the moles of water present in each mole of this unknown hydrate, when given the molar mass of the anhydrous salt

3. to write the empirical formula of the hydrate

SUPPLIES

Equipment
lab burner
crucible and lid
crucible tongs
pipestem triangle

ring stand and ring
centigram or digital balance
lab apron
safety goggles

Chemical Reagents
approximately 5 g of a hydrate
water

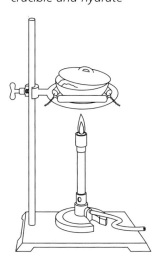

Figure 4C-1 *Set-up of equipment for heating the crucible and hydrate*

CAUTION

The major hazard in this experiment is being burned by handling a hot crucible that appears to be cool. Always use crucible tongs, and either allow the crucible to cool in the ring where it was heated or on a ceramic mat. Do not put a hot crucible on any combustible surface, including arborite and plastic.

PROCEDURE

1. Put on your lab apron and safety goggles.

2. Set up the pipestem triangle, iron ring, stand, and bunsen burner as shown in Figure 4C-1. The ring should be 5–6 cm above the top of the burner. Place a clean, dry crucible with lid on the pipestem triangle, and heat with the burner for approximately 3 min to make sure that the crucible is dry. The lid should be slightly off so that any moisture present may escape. Do not use a luminous flame on the burner as this may deposit carbon on it — make sure that the flame is blue.

3. Remove the burner and allow the crucible to cool for about 3 min. Check by bringing the back of your hand close to the crucible without touching it. If you can still feel the heat it is not yet cool enough.

4. Determine the mass of the empty crucible and lid. Record the mass in your copy of Table 1.

5. Place the hydrate that you are assigned into the crucible until it is approximately one-third full. Determine and record the mass of the crucible, lid and hydrate.

6. Place the crucible and contents on the pipestem triangle, arrange the lid slightly off, and begin heating. Gradually increase the heat until the bottom of the crucible is a dull red. Maintain this temperature for 5 min. To get the maximum heat, position the ring on the stand so that the crucible is just above the top of the light blue inner cone of the flame.

7. Turn off the burner and allow the crucible to cool for about 5 min. Check as before to make sure it is cool enough, then determine and record the mass of the crucible, lid and contents.

8. To make sure that all of the water is driven off you should reheat the crucible for another 5 min. Cool as before, then determine and record the mass. If the masses that you determine in Steps 6 and 7 do not agree within 0.03 g check with your instructor to see if there is time for one more heating. Use the lowest mass in your calculations.

9. After being satisfied with your final mass reading and the crucible has cooled, add a few drops of water to the contents of the crucible. Note any changes that occur.

REAGENT DISPOSAL

Place the contents of your crucible into the designated waste container, then rinse and dry your crucible.

POST LAB CONSIDERATIONS

Your instructor will give the mass of one mole of the anhydrous salt assigned to you. Using this, you can determine the empirical formula of the hydrate, as follows. Moles of the anhydrous salt in the sample can be obtained from the mass and molar mass, and moles of water in the sample can be obtained from the mass of water driven off and its molar mass. The ratio of moles of water to moles of anhydrous salt gives the whole number to be inserted in the empirical formula for the hydrate.

The purpose of adding water at the end of the experiment is to observe what happens as the anhydrous compound is rehydrated. There may be a noticeable change in appearance when the water is added or heat may be evolved.

EXPERIMENTAL RESULTS

Table 1

Mass of empty crucible and lid	
Mass of crucible, lid and hydrate	
Mass of hydrate	
Mass of crucible, lid and anhydrous salt (first heating)	
Mass of crucible, lid and anhydrous salt (second heating)	
Mass of anhydrous salt	
Mass of water given off	
Mass of one mole of anhydrous salt (from your instructor)	
Describe any changes that you observed when adding water to the crucible:	

ANALYSIS OF RESULTS

1. Calculate the percentage of water in the hydrate.

2. Calculate the number of moles of the anhydrous salt left behind.

3. Calculate the number moles of water removed by heat from your sample of hydrate.

4. Calculate the moles of water per mole of the anhydrous salt.

5. What is the empirical formula of the hydrate? (If you have not been told the formula for the anhydrous salt, give your answer as AB•xH$_2$O, where x is the answer to Analysis 4.)

FOLLOW-UP QUESTIONS

1. Suggest one or more reasons why the procedure used in this experiment may not give good results for some hydrates.

2. A hydrated substance was found to have the following percentage composition: Na = 16.1%, C = 4.2%, O = 16.8%, H$_2$O = 62.9%. What is the empirical formula of this compound?

3. A sample of 5.82 g of this substance was heated in a crucible as in this experiment. Calculate the mass of anhydrous compound that would remain in the crucible.

4. A hydrated substance was found to have the following percentage composition: Na = 18.53%, S = 25.87%, O = 19.34%, H$_2$O = 36.26%. What is the empirical formula of this compound?

CONCLUSION

State the result of Objective 3.

                                       ©SMG Lab Books Ltd.

Investigating Mass Changes in Chemical Reactions

5A

In the industrial manufacture of chemicals, it is important that the chemists know how much product to expect from a given reaction. In such reactions the substances reacting (the reactants) and those being produced (the products) are closely monitored.

In this experiment, you will investigate a fundamental law of chemical reactions. You will examine a reaction under controlled conditions to find out how much change in mass results. The reactants will be placed in a flask which is sealed to prevent any gain or loss of matter. The mass of the flask and its contents will be measured before and after the reaction.

OBJECTIVES

1. to observe a chemical reaction in a sealed flask

2. to determine the change in mass that occurs during a chemical reaction

SUPPLIES

Equipment
Erlenmeyer flask (250 mL)
rubber stopper for flask
2 test tubes (13 mm × 100 mm)
test-tube rack
crucible tongs
centigram balance
safety goggles
lab apron

Chemical Reagents
one of the following pairs of
    0.1M solutions:
    1. A) copper(II) sulfate
       B) sodium hydroxide
    2. A) lead(II) nitrate
       B) potassium iodide
    3. A) iron(III) nitrate
       B) potassium thiocyanate
    4. A) calcium chloride
       B) sodium carbonate

CAUTION

Many of these salts are poisonous. Keep your hands away from your face until you have washed thoroughly.

PROCEDURE

1. Put on your lab apron and safety goggles.

2. Obtain a test tube (13 mm × 100 mm) that will fit inside your flask as in Figure 5A-1. Label this test tube A.

3. Obtain a second test tube identical to the first test tube. Label it B.

4. Half fill test tube A with solution A and half fill test tube B with solution B.

5. Pour solution B into the flask.

6. Carefully lower test tube A into the flask, using a pair of crucible tongs if necessary. (If any of solutions A and B are allowed to mix you will have to start over.)

7. Place the stopper on the flask. At this point your assembled apparatus and contents should look like that depicted in Figure 5A-1.

8. Determine the mass of your assembled apparatus and record this value in your copy of Table 1.

9. After making certain that the stopper is secure, gently turn your apparatus upside down, allowing solutions A and B to mix and react.

10. Place the apparatus upright on the balance and measure its mass again. Record this value in Table 1.

11. Use your data to calculate the mass gained or lost during the reaction and record this value in Table 2, which will be on the board. Indicate a positive value for a gain and a negative value for a loss.

12. Copy Table 2 into your notebook when all members of the class have recorded their results.

13. Clean up according to the reagent disposal instructions. Use a test-tube brush to get glassware clean.

14. Before leaving the laboratory, wash your hands thoroughly with soap and water.

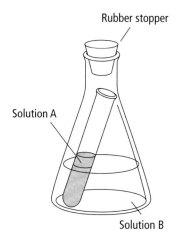

Figure 5A-1 *Apparatus assembled and ready for the reaction to start*

Rubber stopper

Solution A

Solution B

REAGENT DISPOSAL

All solutions and precipitates should be poured into the designated container.

POST LAB CONSIDERATIONS

When the class results are examined, keep in mind that there will always be some uncertainty in any measurement. The overall results should allow you to recognize any patterns and to draw some conclusions.

EXPERIMENTAL RESULTS

Table 1 Result for Lab Station _____

Identity of solution A
Identity of solution B
Mass of apparatus and contents before reaction
Mass of apparatus and contents after reaction

Table 2 Class Results

Lab Station	Solution A	Solution B	Mass Change (+ OR –) (g)
1.			
2.	COMPLETE IN YOUR NOTEBOOK	COMPLETE IN YOUR NOTEBOOK	COMPLETE IN YOUR NOTEBOOK
3.			
⋮			

ANALYSIS OF RESULTS

1. Why is it important that the flask be sealed for this experiment, even after the flask is returned to an upright position?

2. What observations lead you to believe that a chemical reaction occurred inside the flask?

3. In general, what overall mass change results from a chemical reaction?

FOLLOW-UP QUESTIONS

1. Suppose that a reaction was carried out in an open flask and the final mass was significantly greater than the initial mass. What would you conclude?

2. If a reaction was carried out in an open flask and the final mass was significantly less than the initial mass, what would you conclude?

3. What is "the law of conservation of mass" for chemical reactions? If necessary, use a reference book to find out.

CONCLUSION

State the results of Objective 2.

5B

Types of Chemical Reactions

There are many varieties of chemical reactions, some of them difficult to classify. However, the majority of chemical reactions fit into one of four main categories:

a. Synthesis (Combination): A + B → AB
   (Two substances combine to form a new substance.)

b. Decomposition: AB → A + B
   (The opposite of synthesis; one substance decomposes or breaks apart to form two new substances.)

c. Single Replacement: AB + X → A + XB
   (A single change of partners results.)

d. Double Replacement: AB + XY → AY + XB
   (Similar to single replacement, but a double exchange of partners occurs.)

In this experiment, you will first observe examples of each of the four types of chemical reactions. Next, you will write chemical equations that support your observations. Finally, you will classify each reaction as synthesis, decomposition, single replacement, or double replacement.

OBJECTIVES

1. to observe a variety of chemical reactions

2. to interpret and explain observations with balanced chemical equations

3. to classify each reaction as one of the four main types

CAUTION

Most of these solutions are poisonous, corrosive, or irritants. Wash any spills and splashes immediately with plenty of water. Notify your instructor.

SUPPLIES

Equipment	**Chemical Reagents**
lab burner	copper wire (bare)
6 test tubes (13 mm × 100 mm)	iron nail
one test tube will be flame heated	$0.5M$ copper(II) sulfate solution
test-tube clamp	solid copper(II) sulfate pentahydrate
dropping pipet	water
wood splints	$0.5M$ calcium chloride solution
crucible tongs	$0.5M$ sodium carbonate solution
steel wool	mossy zinc
safety goggles	$2M$ hydrochloric acid solution
lab apron	hydrogen peroxide solution (6%)
	manganese(IV) oxide

PROCEDURE

1. Put on your lab apron and safety goggles.
2. Make observations before, during, and after each reaction. Record your observations in your copy of Table 1 in your notebook.

Reaction 1

3. Adjust a burner flame to high heat.
4. Using crucible tongs, hold a 6 cm length of bare copper wire in the hottest part of the flame for a few minutes.

Reaction 2

5. Clean an iron nail with a piece of steel wool so the surface of the nail is shiny.
6. Place the nail in a test tube and add copper(II) sulfate solution so that one half of the nail is covered.
7. After approximately 15 min, remove the nail and note any changes in both the nail and the solution. (You should move onto Reactions 3 and 4 while you are waiting.)

CAUTION

Copper(II) sulfate is poisonous. Wash any spills and splashes immediately with plenty of water.

Reaction 3

8. Put some solid copper(II) sulfate pentahydrate in a test tube so that it is one third full. Note: Ensure that this test tube is heat resistant.
9. Using a test tube clamp, hold the test tube and contents at an angle away from yourself and your classmates. Heat the test tube, moving it back and forth gently over a burner flame.
10. Continue heating until no further change is observed. (Save the contents for Reaction 4.)

Reaction 4

11. Allow the test tube and contents from Reaction 3 to cool.
12. Use a dropping pipet to add 2 or 3 drops of water to the test tube.

Reaction 5

13. Fill a test tube one quarter full with calcium chloride solution. Fill a second test tube one quarter full with sodium carbonate solution.
14. Pour the calcium chloride solution into the test tube containing sodium carbonate solution.

CAUTION

Hydrochloric acid is corrosive to skin, eyes, and clothing. Wash any spills and splashes immediately with plenty of water.

Reaction 6

15. Place a piece of mossy zinc in a test tube.
16. Add hydrochloric acid solution to the test tube until the mossy zinc is completely covered.

Reaction 7

17. Half fill a test tube with hydrogen peroxide solution.

18. Add a small amount of manganese(IV) oxide. (Note: Manganese(IV) oxide acts as a catalyst in this reaction.)

19. Test the gas evolved by placing a glowing (not burning) splint into the mouth of the test tube.

20. Before leaving the laboratory, wash your hands thoroughly with soap and water.

REAGENT DISPOSAL

Place all liquid and solid waste into the designated waste containers.

POST LAB CONSIDERATIONS

To predict the products of a reaction, it is helpful to examine the chemical formulas of the reactants. Therefore, your first task is to determine which chemicals reacted in each case, then to write chemical formulas for these reactants.

Next, using a combination of logic and observations, predict the products for each reaction. Finally, balance each equation so that the number of atoms is conserved.

Classifying the reactions requires you to match each equation with one of the four types that were described in the introduction.

EXPERIMENTAL RESULTS

When making up the data table, leave spaces between each reaction.

Table 1

Reaction	Observations		
	Before	During	After
1			
2			
3			
4	COMPLETE IN YOUR NOTEBOOK	COMPLETE IN YOUR NOTEBOOK	COMPLETE IN YOUR NOTEBOOK
5			
6			
7			

Copying the experiment is prohibited.   ©SMG Lab Books Ltd.

ANALYSIS OF RESULTS

1. In Reaction 1, with which substance in the air did the copper react?

2. In Reaction 2, changes occurred in both the nail and the solution. What do the changes in the solution indicate?

3. What evidence did you see that the chemical changes took place in Reactions 3 and 4?

4. In Reaction 5, one of the products is sodium chloride (table salt), which, as you know, is highly soluble in water. What, therefore, would be the product that would account for the precipitate which formed?

5. How could you test the gas released in Reaction 6 to confirm its identity?

6. **a.** What does the glowing splint test suggest about the identity of the gas evolved in Reaction 7?
   b. The formula for hydrogen peroxide is H_2O_2. Two products are formed in Reaction 7, one of them is a common gas that you know from Analysis 6a and the other is a common liquid. What is the most likely identity of this common liquid?

FOLLOW-UP QUESTIONS

1. In some industrial processes, solutions have impurities removed by single replacement reactions. In electrolytic zinc processes, for instance, impurities of cadmium in the form of $CdSO_4$ are removed from the electrolyte by the addition of zinc dust. Write a balanced equation for this reaction.

2. Write the balanced equation for the electrolysis of water. What type of reaction is this?

CONCLUSION

For each of the seven reactions in this experiment, write a balanced equation and classify it as a synthesis, decomposition, single replacement, or double replacement reaction.

Stoichiometric Analysis of an Iron-Copper Single Replacement Reaction

Stoichiometry is an important field of chemistry that uses calculations to determine quantities such as the masses of reactants and products in chemical reactions. The word *stoichiometry* is derived from two Greek words: *stoicheion* (meaning "element") and *metron* (meaning "measure"). In other words, it is a very mathematical part of chemistry. We can find examples of its use in many chemical industries. Chemical engineers regularly use stoichiometry to estimate how much gold is present at a mine site or how much fertilizer can be manufactured from a given amount of polluting sulfur dioxide gas.

The reaction that occurs in this experiment is called a single replacement reaction and is described by the following balanced chemical equation:

$$Fe(s) + CuCl_2(aq) \rightarrow FeCl_2(aq) + Cu(s)$$

In this experiment, you will determine the moles of iron atoms reacted and moles of copper atoms produced, then calculate the corresponding mole ratio.

The mining industry often utilizes similar reactions to recover valuable metals from solutions that have formed in ponds at or near mine sites. Also, chemical analysis and calculation of ore content is vital to the industry. Even though iron and copper, along with gold, silver, lead, and antimony, were known metals in very early times, it has only been in modern times that chemists have been able to determine accurate analyses of their presence. Iron and copper occur naturally in the earth's crust typically as oxides or sulfides. Today an ore containing 4% copper is considered high-grade, while iron producers have little interest in ores containing less than 20-30% iron.

OBJECTIVES

1. to determine the number of moles of iron reacted

2. to determine the number of moles of copper produced

3. to calculate the ratio of moles of copper to moles of iron

SUPPLIES

Equipment		**Chemical Reagents**
2 beakers (250 mL)	wash bottle	copper(II) chloride
crucible tongs	sandpaper	crystals
centigram balance	hot plate	2 iron nails
plastic teaspoon	heat resistant mat	(approx. 5 cm)
stirring rod	lab apron	
	safety goggles	

PROCEDURE

Part I: Determining the Mass of Iron Reacted

1. Put on your lab apron and safety goggles.

2. Measure and record the mass of a clean, dry 250 mL beaker in your copy of Table 1 in Experimental Results. This mass will be needed at the end of the experiment.

3. Add one level scoop (plastic teaspoon) of copper(II) chloride crystals to the beaker. Add approximately 50 mL of water to the beaker and use a stirring rod to dissolve all the copper(II) chloride crystals.

4. Obtain two clean nails and use a piece of sandpaper to remove any coating from each nail's surface. Measure and record the combined mass of the nails.

5. Place the nails into the copper(II) chloride solution and let them sit for about 20 min. (See Figure 6A-1.) Observe what happens as the reaction proceeds. Look for solid copper forming while the iron nails react. Record your qualitative observations.

6. Use crucible tongs to hold one nail at a time above the beaker. Use water in a wash bottle to rinse off any remaining copper from the nails before removing them completely from the beaker. (See Figure 6A-2.) If necessary, use a stirring rod to scrape any excess copper from the nails and rinse the copper back into the beaker. Set the nails aside to dry on a paper towel. Also, wash and dry the metal tongs to prevent the tongs from reacting!

7. After the nails have completely dried, measure and record the mass of the nails.

Part II: Determining the Mass of Copper Produced

1. *Decant* means to pour off only the liquid and leave the solid behind from a container that is holding both solid and liquid. Carefully decant the liquid from the solid into a second 250 mL beaker. (See Figure 6A-3.) Rinse with water and decant again.

2. Place the beaker containing the wet copper on a hot plate set at medium. Heat gently until the copper appears to have dried. Set the beaker on a heat resistant mat to cool.

3. Measure and record the mass of the beaker containing the copper.

4. Clean up all of your materials.

5. Before leaving the laboratory, wash your hands thoroughly with soap and water.

CAUTION

Copper(II) chloride is poisonous. Wash any spills off skin or clothing with plenty of water.

Figure 6A-1 *Reacting the nails*

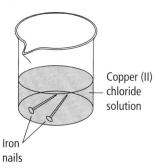

Copper (II) chloride solution

Iron nails

Figure 6A-2 *Rinsing the nails to remove remaining copper*

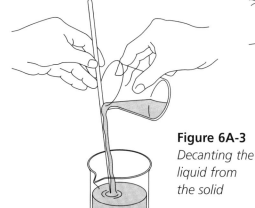

Figure 6A-3
Decanting the liquid from the solid

REAGENT DISPOSAL

Rinse all solutions down the sink with copious amounts of water. Any solid waste should go into the designated waste container.

POST LAB CONSIDERATIONS

The chemical reaction in this experiment has been:

$$Fe(s) + CuCl_2(aq) \rightarrow FeCl_2(aq) + Cu(s)$$

Therefore, it will be interesting to see if your ratio of copper produced to moles of iron reacted matches the mole ratio in the above balanced equation. These mole values will simply be calculated from the mass in grams of the chemicals consumed and produced.

EXPERIMENTAL RESULTS

Table 1

	Mass (g)
empty, dry beaker	
two iron nails (before the reaction)	
two iron nails (after the reaction)	
beaker + copper (dry)	

Qualitative observations

ANALYSIS OF RESULTS

1. Use your data to determine the mass of iron reacted.

2. Calculate the number of moles of atoms of iron reacted.

3. Use your data to determine the mass of copper produced.

4. Calculate the number of moles of atoms of copper produced.

5. Calculate the ratio of moles of copper produced to moles of iron reacted. Under ideal conditions, what should have been expected? (Hint: Refer to the equation in the Post Lab Considerations.)

FOLLOW-UP QUESTIONS

1. If the tongs used in the experiment were made of pure iron, what might happen if the tongs were allowed to remain in contact with the $CuCl_2$ solution?

2. A student carelessly allows some aluminum tongs to sit in a beaker containing $CuCl_2$ solution for a period of time and a reaction occurs.

Original mass of tongs	85.1 g
Final mass of tongs	73.2 g

   a. Write the balanced chemical equation for the reaction.
   b. Calculate the moles of atoms of aluminum that reacted.
   c. Calculate the number of atoms of aluminum that reacted.
   d. Calculate the moles of atoms of copper that are produced.
   e. Calculate the mass of copper that is produced.

CONCLUSION

State the results of Objective 3.

6B

Predicting and Measuring the Mass of NaCl Produced

Making predictions of the outcomes of chemical reactions is an integral part of the scientific process. Not only is it important to be able to predict the identity of chemicals that will be produced but you must also be able to predict the quantities of those chemicals. For the latter we use *stoichiometry* which involves performing calculations on chemical reactions. We can find examples of its use in many industrial applications. Stoichiometry allows chemists to determine how much iron is in a barge of iron ore, how much sulfur dioxide is in polluted air, or whether a new batch of fertilizer contains all of the nitrogen, phosphorus, and potassium listed on the label.

In this experiment, you will study two common reactions between acids and carbonates. In Reaction 1, hydrochloric acid (the acid present in stomach acid) and sodium hydrogen carbonate (sodium bicarbonate or baking soda) will be mixed. The reaction is immediate, impressive, and simple, yet it occurs in two steps. Two products initially result: table salt and carbonic acid, but the carbonic acid is quite unstable and instantly decomposes into water and carbon dioxide gas. It is the fizzing of the carbon dioxide gas that is most noticeable during the progress of this reaction. In the language of chemistry, this reaction can be best described as:

Reaction 1: $HCl(aq) + NaHCO_3(s) \rightarrow NaCl(aq) + H_2O(l) + CO_2(g)$

In Reaction 2, hydrochloric acid and sodium carbonate (washing soda) will be mixed. Reaction 2 should behave similarly to Reaction 1, but Reaction 2 is described by the following skeletal (unbalanced) equation:

Reaction 2: $HCl(aq) + Na_2CO_3(s) \rightarrow NaCl(aq) + H_2O(l) + CO_2(g)$

In both reactions, you will be using an excess of hydrochloric acid in order to ensure that the carbonates react completely. In each case, the excess hydrochloric acid solution can be easily boiled away, leaving only solid sodium chloride in the reaction vessel. At the end of the experiment, you will measure the final mass of the product. Boiling away the excess acid solution and obtaining the dry salt requires more time than is normally available in one lab period so this experiment will be typically carried out over two days.

It is interesting to note that Reaction 1 describes a way of neutralizing excess stomach acid (heartburn). Of course, this remedy should only be performed with the advice of a physician who would recommend proper substances and dosages. It is also interesting to note that such medically recommended dosages are determined through stoichiometry!

OBJECTIVES

1. to observe the reactions between hydrochloric acid and sodium hydrogen carbonate, then hydrochloric acid and sodium carbonate

2. to predict the mass of sodium chloride that should be produced in each reaction

3. to measure the actual mass of sodium chloride produced in each reaction

4. to determine the percent yield of sodium chloride in each reaction

SUPPLIES

Equipment
centigram balance
hot plates (for class use in fume hood)
2 Erlenmeyer flasks (250 mL)
beaker (250 mL)
plastic teaspoon
dropping pipet (1–3 mL)
safety goggles
lab apron

Chemical Reagents
1.0M hydrochloric acid, HCl
sodium hydrogen carbonate, $NaHCO_3$
sodium carbonate, Na_2CO_3

PROCEDURE

Part I: Reactions 1 and 2 (Day 1)

1. Put on your lab apron and safety goggles.

2. Obtain two clean, dry 250 mL Erlenmeyer flasks, identify them with your name, and then number them 1 and 2. Use the centigram balance to measure the empty flasks' masses. Record these values in your copy of Table 1 of Experimental Results in your notebook.

Reaction 1: HCl and $NaHCO_3$

3. Place about 1/2 level teaspoon of powdered sodium hydrogen carbonate in flask #1. Using too much powder will spoil your results. Find the combined mass of the flask and its contents and record this value.

4. Place about 150 mL of 1.0M hydrochloric acid in a 250 mL beaker. Using a dropping pipet, slowly add a pipet full of the acid to the flask containing the sodium hydrogen carbonate. Be careful to add the acid slowly so that the reaction bubbling does not force some the reactants out of the flask. Swirl the flask to ensure proper mixing. Do not add any more acid than is necessary since you will need to remove the excess acid solution later. Continue adding acid one pipet at a time until the bubbling stops and no white solid remains.

Reaction 2: HCl and Na_2CO_3

5. Repeat Steps 3 and 4 but this time use flask #2 with sodium carbonate.

Evaporating the Excess Hydrochloric Acid

6. Several hot plates will be set up in the fume hood. Place both Erlenmeyer flasks on one of the hot plates (See Figure 6B-1.) and leave them there. The hot plates will be shared with other students and the Erlenmeyer flasks will be monitored to dryness by your instructor. This activity will not be completed in this laboratory period.

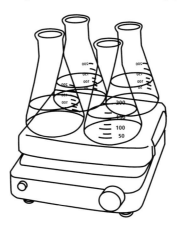

Figure 6B-1 *Evaporating solutions to dryness in a fume hood*

7. Clean up and put away all the other apparatus.

8. Before leaving the laboratory, wash your hands thoroughly with soap and water.

Part II: Measuring the Masses of NaCl Produced (Day 2)

1. Obtain your 2 Erlenmeyer flasks from your instructor and a centigram balance.

2. What remains in both Erlenmeyer flasks is now simply the dry NaCl(s) (table salt). Measure and record, in your copy of Table 2, the masses of both flasks containing the dry solid.

3. Wash out the flasks and put all equipment away.

4. Before leaving the laboratory, wash your hands thoroughly with soap and water.

REAGENT DISPOSAL

Rinse all solutions down the sink with copious amounts of water. Any solid waste should go into the designated waste container.

POST LAB CONSIDERATIONS

In each of the two reactions in this experiment, three products are formed: carbon dioxide, water, and sodium chloride. The only product that remains in the flask after heating is solid sodium chloride (table salt). Before attempting any stoichiometric calculations, you will need to determine the balanced equation for the reactions so that you can correctly predict the amounts of products that should have formed.

Chemists are often interested in how well they did in manufacturing a certain chemical. One way of measuring this is to calculate the percent yield of that particular chemical by using this formula:

$$\text{Percent yield} = \frac{\text{(actual mass produced)}}{\text{(theoretical mass produced)}} \times 100\%$$

EXPERIMENTAL RESULTS

Part I: Reactions 1 and 2 (Day 1)

Table 1

Part I, Reaction 1: HCl and NaHCO$_3$ (Day 1)		Part I, Reaction 2: HCl and Na$_2$CO$_3$ (Day 1)	
Mass of Erlenmeyer flask #1	COMPLETE IN YOUR NOTEBOOK	Mass of Erlenmeyer flask #2	COMPLETE IN YOUR NOTEBOOK
Mass of Erlenmeyer flask #1 + NaHCO$_3$		Mass of Erlenmeyer flask #2 + Na$_2$CO$_3$	

Part II: Measuring the Masses of NaCl Produced (Day 2)

Table 2

Part II: Measuring the Masses of NaCl Produced (Day 2)		
Reaction 1	Mass of Erlenmeyer flask #1 + dry solid NaCl (after the reaction)	COMPLETE IN YOUR NOTEBOOK
Reaction 2	Mass of Erlenmeyer flask #2 + dry solid NaCl (after the reaction)	

ANALYSIS OF RESULTS

Reaction 1

1. Copy the chemical equation for Reaction 1 from the introduction and check to see if it is balanced.

2. On Day 2, only NaCl(s) remained. What happened to the other two products?

3. From Part I Results determine the mass (in grams) of NaHCO$_3$ reacted.

4. Using the principles of stoichiometry you have learned in class, calculate the theoretical mass of NaCl that should have been produced from the mass of $NaHCO_3$ reacted.

5. From Part II Results determine the actual mass of NaCl that was produced.

6. Consult the Post Lab Considerations and calculate the percent yield of NaCl.

Reaction 2

1. Repeat Analyses 1 to 6 for Reaction 2.

2. What are some possible reasons for a yield that is not 100%?

FOLLOW-UP QUESTIONS

1. A similar reaction occurs between hydrochloric acid solution (HCl) and solid limestone (calcium carbonate). Write a balanced equation for this reaction.

2. If 6.00 g of limestone reacted above, what theoretical masses of the following would be produced?
   a. calcium chloride
   b. carbon dioxide
   c. water

3. In terms of stoichiometry, why was it important to have a balanced chemical equation for Follow-Up Question #2?

CONCLUSION

State the results of Objectives 2, 3, and 4.

Mole Ratios in a Copper-Silver Replacement Reaction

When working with chemical reactions, it is important not only to be able to predict the identity of the chemicals produced but also to be able to predict the quantities of those chemicals. For the latter we use *stoichiometry*, the act of performing calculations on chemical reactions. Each year throughout the world, the production of major chemicals is measured in the millions of tonnes so mistakes involving calculations of such large amounts could be very costly. Even small calculation errors involving rare chemicals could cost a company a lot of money. This experiment will familiarize you with the techniques of measuring and calculating various quantities in chemical reactions.

In this experiment you will react an excess amount of copper metal with a solution of silver nitrate in a single replacement reaction. The skeletal (unbalanced) equation for this reaction is:

$$Cu(s) + AgNO_3(aq) \rightarrow Cu(NO_3)_2(aq) + Ag(s)$$

This same reaction and similar ones are used in modern metal refining processes as one step in the production of pure metals from their ores.

Through the use of stoichiometric calculations you will determine the mass of silver that should be produced knowing the mass of copper that reacted. You will then compare this predicted silver value with the actual mass of silver produced. Finally, you will be able to determine the ratio of moles of silver produced to moles of copper used for the reaction.

It is important to note that you are producing pure silver metal from silver nitrate solution. As you know, the cost of silver is significant and consequently, so is the cost of silver nitrate. As a result, your instructor may wish to recycle the silver for future experiments. Alternatively, for obvious reasons, your instructor may choose to perform this experiment as a class demonstration.

OBJECTIVES

1. to observe the reaction between copper metal and silver nitrate solution

2. to measure the mass of copper that reacted in this experiment

3. to measure the mass of silver that was produced in this experiment

4. to determine the ratio of moles of silver to moles of copper

SUPPLIES

Equipment
centigram balance
wash bottle
filtering apparatus
beaker (250 mL)
glass stirring rod or wooden
    splint
plastic "cling" wrap
lab apron
safety goggles

Chemical Reagents
bare copper wire (16 gauge)
silver nitrate (powder or solution)

PROCEDURE

Part I: Starting the Reaction (Day 1)

1. Put on your lab apron and safety goggles.

2. Obtain a clean, dry 250 mL beaker and write your name on it.

3. Obtain a 50 cm length of bare copper wire. Form a coil by wrapping the wire around a cylinder such as a large test tube or 25 mL graduated cylinder. Leave a portion straight to use as a hanger. Weigh the copper coil and record the results in your copy of Table 1 in your notebook. Hang the coil from a stirring rod so that it will be suspended in the middle of the beaker and just above the bottom of the beaker. (See Figure 6C-1.) Remove the coil and stirring rod and set them aside for now. Your instructor will tell you whether to proceed with Option 1 or 2 in the next step.

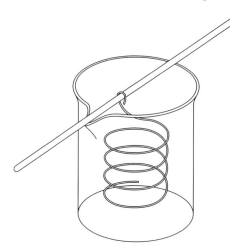

Figure 6C-1 *Setting up the apparatus*

4. Option 1: Using $AgNO_3$ Crystals
   Obtain a pre-measured sample of approximately 4 g of $AgNO_3$ crystals from your instructor. (Note: $AgNO_3$ crystals react with skin and stain it black. A delayed reaction occurs when exposed to light. This stain is harmless and will wear off in a few days. However, make every effort to avoid contact with skin or clothing.) Add about 150 mL of water to the beaker, then add the crystals. Stir with a stirring rod to dissolve the crys-

tals. Use the wash bottle to thoroughly rinse the stirring rod's coating back into the beaker. Set the stirring rod aside on a paper towel, then dry it.

Option 2: Using $AgNO_3$ Solution

Add about 150 mL of approximately $0.16M$ $AgNO_3$ solution to your beaker. (Note: $AgNO_3$ crystals react with skin and stain it black. A delayed reaction occurs when exposed to light. This stain is harmless and will wear off in a few days. However, make every effort to avoid contact with skin or clothing.)

5. Re-hang the copper coil on the stirring rod and suspend it in the solution. Make careful observations for the next few minutes.

6. Carefully cover the stirring rod and beaker with a piece of plastic "cling" wrap to minimize evaporation and contamination.

7. The reaction needs to continue for several hours so store your beaker containing all the chemicals in the assigned location until next lab period.

Part II: Separating and Recovering the Two Metals (Day 2)

The two metals are now to be separated and recovered. One metal is the excess copper that remains in the coil and the other is the silver that formed as crystals during the reaction.

1. Put on your lab apron and safety goggles.

2. Obtain your beaker from the storage location and make careful observations. Shake the crystals off the coil to allow them to sink to the bottom of the beaker. Next, lift the coil so that it hangs just above the solution. Now use a wash bottle to rinse the silver crystals off the coil. Use a combination of scraping with the stirring rod and rinsing to remove all of the crystals from the coil. (See Figure 6C-2.)

Figure 6C-2 *Rinsing any remaining silver crystals from the coil*

3. Place the copper coil on a piece of paper towel and set it aside to dry. Drying time should only take a few minutes but in the meantime proceed to Step 4.

4. Allow the silver crystals to settle to the bottom of the beaker, then carefully decant the liquid to another 250 mL beaker. (See Figure 6C-3.) Stop decanting if you notice any flecks of silver escaping. In the original beaker you may notice flecks of copper mixed with the silver crystals. These came off the coil when it was rinsed. If this is the case, see your

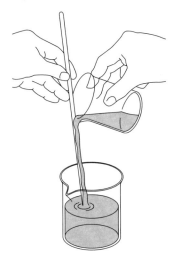

Figure 6C-3 *Decanting the liquid from the silver crystals*

instructor for a small amount of $AgNO_3$ solution to add to this mixture. Stir to ensure that these Cu flecks react.

5. Add 150 mL of water to the beaker, stir the crystals, and allow them to settle for a couple of minutes. This process is intended to remove as much remaining $Cu(NO_3)_2(aq)$ as possible. Decant for a second time.

6. Obtain a piece of filter paper and put your name on it in pencil. Weigh the filter paper and record this value. Set up a filtering apparatus and filter the silver crystals from the original beaker. Use the wash bottle to rinse all the crystals from the beaker onto the filter paper. When this first filtering is almost complete, perform one last rinsing of the crystals in the filter paper by gently spraying more water on them from the wash bottle. After the second filtering, place the wet filter paper containing silver crystals on a folded paper towel and store in the assigned location to dry.

7. Weigh the dried copper coil and record its mass. Do Analysis of Results 1–3 to prepare for the next day.

8. Clean up all your equipment.

9. Before leaving the lab, wash your hands thoroughly with soap and water.

Part III: Weighing the Silver (Day 3)

1. Weigh the filter paper with silver crystals and record the mass.

2. Note: During cleanup, place the silver crystals in the specially designated container.

REAGENT DISPOSAL

Rinse all solutions down the sink with copious amounts of water. Any solids should go into the designated containers.

POST LAB CONSIDERATIONS

A single replacement reaction was used to replace copper solid with silver solid. If the reaction was allowed sufficient time, then all of the Ag^+ ions in the solution should have changed to Ag atoms (Ag solid). One challenge in reactions such as this is to separate the solid (Ag) produced from the other product of the reaction. In this case that product is $Cu(NO_3)_2(aq)$ which will add to the mass of the Ag if it is not removed. That was the reason for the repeated rinsing of the Ag(s) during the Procedure.

After measuring the mass of Cu(s) reacted, you will use stoichiometric calculations to predict the mass of Ag(s) that should have formed. The actual mass of Ag(s) produced can then be compared to this stoichiometric prediction and the percent yield of Ag can be calculated.

$$\text{Percent yield} = \frac{\text{actual mass produced (grams)}}{\text{theoretical mass produced (grams)}} \times 100\%$$

EXPERIMENTAL RESULTS

Table 1

Copper Data	Mass (g)
Mass of copper wire (before the reaction)	
Mass of copper wire (after the reaction)	COMPLETE IN YOUR NOTEBOOK
Silver Data	
Mass of filter paper	
Mass of filter paper + silver crystals	COMPLETE IN YOUR NOTEBOOK

ANALYSIS OF RESULTS

1. Copy the chemical equation for the reaction from the introduction and balance it.

2. From your data, determine the mass of copper reacted.

3. Use stoichiometric calculations to determine the theoretical mass of silver metal that should be produced.

4. From the data collected, determine the actual mass of silver metal produced.

5. Calculate the percent yield of silver.

6. What is the value of the ratio of $\dfrac{\text{actual moles of silver produced}}{\text{actual moles of copper reacted}}$? What <u>should</u> this value be?

FOLLOW-UP QUESTIONS

1. What chemical species causes the solution to change color as the reaction proceeds?

2. One step in the refining of Zn(s) involves adding Zn dust to a solution containing impurities of $CdSO_4$ to remove the cadmium from the solution and replace it with Zn^{2+}.
   a. Write a balanced chemical equation for this reaction.
   b. How many grams of zinc would have to be added to remove 956.5 g of cadmium metal?

CONCLUSION

State the results of Objective 4.

6D

Determining the Limiting Reactant and Percent Yield in a Precipitation Reaction

One example of a double replacement reaction is the mixing of two solutions resulting in the formation of a precipitate. In solution chemistry, the term *precipitate* is used to describe a solid that forms when a positive ion (cation) and a negative ion (anion) are strongly attracted to one another. In this experiment, a precipitation reaction will be studied. Stoichiometry will then be used to investigate the amounts of reactants and products that are involved. The word *stoichiometry* is derived from two Greek words: *stoicheion* (meaning "element") and *metron* (meaning "measure"). Stoichiometry is an important field of chemistry that uses calculations to determine the quantities (masses, volumes) of reactants and products involved in chemical reactions. It is a very mathematical part of chemistry.

In this experiment, you will react a known amount of sodium carbonate solution with a known amount of calcium chloride solution. The skeletal (unbalanced) equation for the resulting double replacement reaction is:

$$Na_2CO_3(aq) + CaCl_2(aq) \rightarrow NaCl(aq) + CaCO_3(s)$$

Note that three of the chemicals have their states or phases designated as (*aq*) and one is designated as (*s*). The (*aq*) represents the term *aqueous* which means that the substance is soluble and dissolved in water. The (*s*) means that the substance is a *solid* (in this case, it is a precipitate). Precipitate formation is easily observed as the mixed solutions turn cloudy and, if desired, the precipitate can be easily separated from the solution by filtering. Since your precipitate will be separated and weighed, this experiment will require a second lab period to allow time for the precipitate to dry. Stoichiometry will then be used to determine the amount of precipitate that should be formed in the reaction.

It is often difficult as well as impractical to combine just the right amount of each reactant that is required for a particular reaction to occur. Given this fact, this experiment is designed so that only one of the reactants will be completely used up. This is called the *limiting reactant* because it limits the amount of products formed. Since the other reactant will have a quantity remaining, it is called the *excess reactant*. One of your tasks will be to determine which of your reactants is limiting and which is in excess.

The two chemical reactants in this experiment have common uses in our lives. In one solid form, sodium carbonate is known as "washing soda" and is used to enhance the effectiveness of laundry soap. Calcium chloride solid can act as a *desiccant* (drying agent) and is used by recreational vehicle owners to remove moisture from the air in the vehicle during winter storage.

OBJECTIVES

1. to observe the reaction between solutions of sodium carbonate and calcium chloride

2. to determine which of the reactants is the limiting reactant and which is the excess reactant

3. to determine the theoretical mass of precipitate that should form

4. to compare the actual mass with the theoretical mass of precipitate and calculate the percent yield

SUPPLIES

Equipment

centigram balance
2 graduated cylinders (25 mL)
beaker (250 mL)
wash bottle
filtering apparatus (ring with stand, Erlenmeyer flask (250 mL) + funnel)
filter paper
lab apron
safety goggles

Chemical Reagents

0.70M sodium carbonate solution, Na_2CO_3
0.50M calcium chloride solution, $CaCl_2$

PROCEDURE

Part I: The Precipitation Reaction (Day 1)

1. Put on your lab apron and safety goggles.

2. Obtain two clean, dry 25 mL graduated cylinders and one 250 mL beaker.

3. In one of the graduated cylinders measure 25 mL of the Na_2CO_3 solution. In the other graduated cylinder measure 25 mL of the $CaCl_2$ solution. Record these volumes in your copy of Experimental Results in your notebook.

4. Pour the contents of both graduated cylinders into the 250 mL beaker and observe the results. Record these qualitative observations in your notebook. Allow the contents of the beaker to sit undisturbed for 5 min to see what happens to the suspended solid particles. Meanwhile, proceed to Step 5.

5. Obtain a piece of filter paper and put your name on it using a pencil. Weigh and record the mass of the filter paper, then use it to set up a filtering apparatus as shown in Figure 6D-1.

6. Use the wash bottle to lightly wet the filter paper in the funnel to keep the filter paper in place. Swirl the beaker and its contents to suspend the precipitate in the solution, then pour it carefully and slowly into the filter funnel. It takes time to complete the filtering process so plan to do it in stages. Use the wash bottle to rinse the remaining precipitate from the beaker.

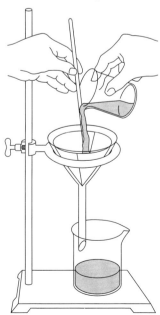

Figure 6D-1 *Filtering the solid from the liquid*

7. Use the wash bottle one last time to rinse the precipitate in the filter paper. This will remove any residual NaCl(aq) that remains with the precipitate.

8. After the filtering is complete, remove the wet filter paper containing $CaCO_3$ precipitate and place it on a folded paper towel. Put your filter paper in the assigned location to dry.

9. Clean up all your apparatus.

10. Wash your hands thoroughly with soap and water before leaving the laboratory

Part II: Weighing the Dried Precipitate (Day 2)

1. Weigh and record the mass of the dry filter paper containing the $CaCO_3$ precipitate.

REAGENT DISPOSAL

Rinse all solutions down the sink with copious amounts of water. Any solids should go into the designated containers.

POST LAB CONSIDERATIONS

The double replacement reaction in this experiment formed two chemicals which are commonly known to you. The NaCl(aq) is salt water and the $CaCO_3$(s) is a component of some classroom chalks.

Using the data collected, you will be able to calculate the moles of each of the chemicals that are added together to react. Then using the principles of stoichiometry you will be able to determine which chemical is the limiting reactant and thereby predict how much precipitate should form. This stoichiometric determination will then be compared to the actual mass of $CaCO_3$(s) formed.

Chemists are often concerned with optimal yields in manufacturing a certain chemical. One way of measuring this is to calculate the percent yield of that particular chemical by using this formula:

$$\text{Percent yield} = \frac{\text{actual mass produced (grams)}}{\text{theoretical mass produced (grams)}} \times 100\%$$

EXPERIMENTAL RESULTS

Part I: The Precipitation Reaction (Day 1)

Qualitative Observations

Quantitative Observations

Volume of 0.70M Na_2CO_3 solution

Volume of 0.50M $CaCl_2$ solution

Part II: Weighing the Dried Precipitate (Day 2)

Mass of filter paper + dry solid $CaCO_3$

Mass of filter paper

ANALYSIS OF RESULTS

1. Copy the chemical equation for the reaction from the introduction and balance it.

2. From your Part I Results, calculate the moles of Na_2CO_3 that were added to the beaker.

3. From your Part I Results, calculate the moles of $CaCl_2$ that were added to the beaker.

4. Use your answers from Analysis 1–3 above and stoichiometric principles to determine which chemical is the limiting reactant.

5. Use stoichiometric calculations to determine the theoretical mass of $CaCO_3$ precipitate that should have formed.

6. From your Part II Results, calculate the actual mass of $CaCO_3(s)$ precipitate that formed.

7. Calculate the percent yield of $CaCO_3(s)$.

FOLLOW-UP QUESTIONS

1. If you were to evaporate the filtered solution to dryness, would you be left with only solid NaCl? Explain.

2. What theoretical volume of the Na_2CO_3 solution used in this experiment would result in no excess reactant?

3. A precipitation reaction occurs when 50.0 mL of 0.50M $BaCl_2$(aq) is mixed with 75.0 mL of 0.75M Na_2CO_3(aq). The only precipitate is the $BaCO_3(s)$ formed.
   a. Write the balanced equation that describes this reaction.
   b. Which chemical is the limiting reactant?
   c. Predict the theoretical mass of $BaCO_3(s)$ that should form.
   d. This experiment was conducted and the percent yield was found to be 82%. What was the actual mass of $BaCO_3(s)$ that formed?

CONCLUSION

State the results of Objectives 2, 3, and 4.

6E

Using a Reactant in Excess in an Aluminum-Copper Replacement Reaction

Certain metallurgical situations require the addition of a pure metal to an electrolytic solution in order to remove impurities of a different metal. One example is found in the manufacturing process of pure zinc metal. In one stage of the process, zinc dust is added to a $ZnSO_4$(aq) solution which contains impurities of $CdSO_4$(aq). This addition of zinc dust causes a single replacement reaction in which the Cd^{2+} ions are replaced by Zn^{2+} ions and metallic Cd is removed as an impurity. In such instances chemists rely on stoichiometry to predict the amount of the zinc metal required.

In this experiment, stoichiometry will be used to predict the required amount of solid copper(II) chloride that should be dissolved in water in order to completely react with a known amount of aluminum metal. It is difficult as well as impractical to combine just the right amounts of each reactant that are required for a particular reaction to occur. Given this fact, this experiment is designed so that the aluminum is the limiting reactant and copper(II) chloride will be used in excess. The skeletal (unbalanced) equation for the resulting single replacement reaction is:

$$Al(s) + CuCl_2(aq) \rightarrow AlCl_3(aq) + Cu(s)$$

You will start with a known mass of aluminum foil and predict an excess amount of copper(II) chloride crystals required for the foil to react completely. In addition, you will be able to weigh the copper produced and determine the mole ratio of copper to aluminum that was involved in the reaction.

OBJECTIVES

1. to observe the reaction between aluminum metal and a solution of copper(II) chloride

2. to predict the mass of copper(II) chloride required to completely react a known amount of aluminum

3. to measure the mass of copper produced

4. to compare the moles of copper produced with the moles of aluminum reacted (as a whole number ratio)

SUPPLIES

Equipment

centigram balance	plastic spoon	filtering apparatus
beaker (100 mL)	stirring rod	lab apron
2 beakers (250 mL)	wash bottle	safety goggles

   ©SMG Lab Books Ltd.

Chemical Reagents

aluminum foil, Al

copper(II) chloride crystals, $CuCl_2$

PROCEDURE

Part I: Predicting the Required Amount of $CuCl_2$(s) (Day 1)

1. Obtain a piece of aluminum foil that measures approximately 15 cm × 15 cm. Exact size is not critical.

2. Weigh the aluminum foil and record its mass in your copy of the Experimental Results.

3. Do Prediction Questions 1–5 now. You will need this information in the steps that follow.

Part II: Reacting the Aluminum with the $CuCl_2$

1. Put on your lab apron and safety goggles.

2. Obtain a 100 mL beaker and add one full scoop (plastic teaspoon) of $CuCl_2$ crystals to the beaker.

3. Measure and record the mass of a clean, dry 250 mL beaker. With the 250 mL beaker still on the centigram balance, add $CuCl_2$ crystals until you reach your predicted excess mass. (Refer to your answer to Prediction Question #5.) Return any unused $CuCl_2$ crystals to the designated container provided by your instructor.

4. Carefully add 150 mL of water to the 250 mL beaker containing the $CuCl_2$ crystals and stir until all the crystals are dissolved.

5. Loosely roll the aluminum foil into a tube and place the tube into the solution in the beaker. Make qualitative observations over the next 5 min and record these.

6. Over the next 10 min stir the mixture regularly to ensure that all the aluminum reacts.

Part III: Determining the Mass of Copper Produced

1. *Decant* means to pour off only the liquid and leave the solid behind from a container that is holding both solid and liquid. Carefully decant the liquid from the solid into a second 250 mL beaker. (See Figure 6E-1.)

2. Add 150 mL of water, stir, allow the slurry to settle 2 min, and decant a second time. This is an important step as you attempt to rinse away as much of the $AlCl_3$ residue as possible.

3. Set up a filtering apparatus, then weigh and record the mass of your filter paper. Put your name on the filter paper in pencil.

4. Pour the beaker contents into the filter funnel and use a wash bottle to rinse all particles of copper from the beaker.

5. When the filter has drained, use the wash bottle to gently spray water on the copper residue to rinse it once again.

CAUTION

$CuCl_2$ is poisonous. Wash any spills with plenty of water then notify your instructor.

Figure 6E-1 *Decanting the liquid from the solid*

6. Remove the drained, wet filter paper and copper from the funnel and place it on a folded paper towel. Place all this material in the assigned location to dry.

7. Clean up all of your equipment and wash your hands thoroughly before leaving the lab.

Part IV: Weighing the Dried Copper (Day 2)

1. Obtain your sample of dried filter paper and copper and weigh it. Record this mass.

2. Clean up all of your equipment and wash your hands thoroughly before leaving the lab.

REAGENT DISPOSAL

Rinse all solutions down the sink with copious amounts of water. Any solid waste should go into the designated waste container.

POST LAB CONSIDERATIONS

The chemical reaction in this experiment has been:

$$Al(s) + CuCl_2(aq) \rightarrow AlCl_3(aq) + Cu(s)$$

Note that this equation is unbalanced. It will be interesting to see if your ratio of moles of copper produced to moles of aluminum reacted agrees with the mole ratio in the balanced equation. These mole values will simply be calculated from the masses (in grams) of the chemicals that have been consumed or produced.

One challenge in reactions such as this is to separate the solid Cu produced from the other product of the reaction. In this case that product is $AlCl_3(aq)$ which will add to the mass of the Cu if it is not removed. That was the reason for the repeated rinsing of the Cu(s) after the reaction.

Sometimes an unexpected secondary chemical reaction occurs. In this experiment, you will have noticed bubbles of a gas forming yet there is no suggestion of a gas being produced in the above equation. Tests show that the gas being produced is hydrogen gas. The explanation for this is beyond the scope of this experiment but this secondary reaction occurs to a small degree so it will not significantly affect your results.

EXPERIMENTAL RESULTS

Mass of aluminum

Mass of empty 250 mL beaker

Qualitative observations of the reaction

Mass of filter paper

Mass of filter paper + copper

   ©SMG Lab Books Ltd.

ANALYSIS OF RESULTS

Prediction Questions: Predicting the Excess Mass of $CuCl_2$(s) Required

1. Copy the chemical equation from the introduction and ensure that it is balanced.

2. Use your Results (mass of aluminum) to calculate the moles of aluminum to be reacted.

3. Calculate the moles of $CuCl_2$(s) required for a complete reaction with the aluminum.

4. Calculate the mass (in grams) of $CuCl_2$(s) that is required for a complete reaction with the aluminum.

5. Calculate a 50% excess of $CuCl_2$(s) required. To obtain this, simply take your answer from Analysis 4 and multiply it by a factor of 1.5.

Determining the Moles of Copper Produced

6. Use your Results to determine the mass of copper produced.

7. Calculate the number of moles of copper produced.

8. Calculate the ratio of moles of copper produced to moles of aluminum reacted. Under ideal conditions, what should have been expected? (Hint: Refer to your balanced equation in Analysis 1.)

FOLLOW-UP QUESTIONS

1. In this experiment, what evidence suggests that copper ions were removed from the solution?

2. A student carelessly allows some aluminum tongs to sit in a beaker containing $CuCl_2$ solution overnight and a reaction occurs. In the morning the solution is colorless.

   Original mass of tongs   85.1 g
   Final mass of tongs   73.2 g

   a. Write the balanced chemical equation for the reaction.
   b. Calculate the moles of aluminum that reacted.
   c. Calculate the mass of $CuCl_2$ that must have reacted.
   d. Which reactant was in excess and by how much?

CONCLUSION

State the results of Objective 4.

7A

The Gas Laws

The gas laws state relationships between pressure, volume, temperature, and quantity of a gas. Several prominent pioneering scientists investigated and quantified the relationships between gas variables. As a result, the gas laws have been attributed to people like Robert Boyle, Jacques Charles, Joseph Gay-Lussac, and Amadeo Avogadro. In this experiment, you will confirm the findings of Boyle and Charles.

Robert Boyle (1627–1691) was an Irish chemist and physicist who investigated the relationship between pressure and volume of a gas. He discovered that, as the pressure of a gas increases, volume decreases accordingly.

Jacques Charles (1746–1823) was a French scientist who first quantified the relationship between gas volume and temperature. He discovered that all gases change volume to the same extent when temperature is changed by a fixed amount. Simply stated, volume increases as temperature increases.

One application of Boyle's Law can be found in the storage of gases. Gases such as oxygen (for medical use) and helium (for party balloons) are stored under high pressure so that their containers take up relatively small volumes, which make them portable. The expansion of gases when heated is described by Charles' Law and is one of the basic principles on which the workings of the internal combustion (automobile) engine rely. The hot gases produced by the ignition of gasoline vapor and air expand, forcing the piston down in the cylinder, which eventually is translated into motion of the vehicle.

OBJECTIVES

1. to determine the mathematical relationship between pressure and volume of a gas

2. to determine the mathematical relationship between volume and temperature of a gas

SUPPLIES

Equipment

Boyle's Law apparatus (syringe with pressure gauge)	thermometer
	thermometer clamp
Charles' Law apparatus (syringe with end cap)	buret clamp
	stirring rod
barometer (classroom)	hot plate
ring stand	lab apron
beaker (1000 mL)	safety goggles

PROCEDURE

Part I: Boyle's Law

1. Put on your lab apron and safety goggles.

2. Read the room barometer and record the atmospheric (room) pressure in kilopascals (kPa) in your Experimental Results.

3. Assemble the 20 mL syringe and pressure gauge (0–100 kPa) as shown in Figure 7A-1. Note: The syringe may indicate that its units are "cc" which is equivalent to "mL."

4. With the pressure gauge disconnected, set the volume of air in the syringe to 20 mL. Reconnect the pressure gauge and the gauge should read 0 kPa. Record these two values in your copy of Table 1.

5. With the apparatus lying safely on the lab table, reduce the volume of the syringe to 19 mL, then take another pressure reading and record it.

6. Repeat Step 4 in 1 mL increments until you reach a volume of 11 mL. Past experience has shown that the pressure gauge readings become distorted and unreliable after this volume. (In total you will end up with 10 readings {20, 19, 18, 17, 16, 15, 14, 13, 12, 11}.)

Figure 7A-1 *Boyle's Law Apparatus*

Part II: Charles' Law

1. Remove the pressure gauge from the syringe and fill the syringe to a volume of 5 mL with air.

2. Place the closed valve on the tip of the syringe and clamp the syringe with a buret clamp. Note: The volume scale should not be obscured by the clamp.

3. Obtain a thermometer and thermometer clamp.

4. Add approximately 900 mL of water at room temperature to a 1000 mL beaker.

5. Assemble the apparatus as shown in Figure 7A-2. Lower the syringe far enough into the water so that 10 mL of volume in the syringe is under water. With the thermometer in its clamp, adjust the thermometer so that it sits at about the same level as the air column in the syringe. The syringe and the thermometer should not touch each other nor should they touch any part of the beaker.

Figure 7A-2 *Charles' Law Apparatus*

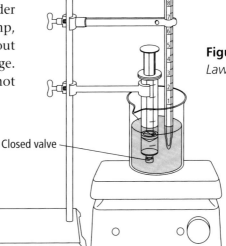

Closed valve

6. Wait 2 min and record the gas volume and temperature in your copy of Table 2. (Note: It is assumed here that the water bath temperature is equal to the syringe gas temperature.)

7. Turn the hot plate on to medium and gradually heat the water bath. Occasionally stir the water to minimize hot spots.

8. For approximately every 25°C rise in water temperature, record the temperature and gas volume. (Note: When you are ready to take a reading, friction within the syringe may prevent the piston from properly moving to a new volume. To overcome this, grasp the syringe and lift the piston slightly, then release it. The piston will then spring back to indicate the new volume.) Continue until the boiling temperature is reached and record the final volume of the air in the syringe. (In total you will end up with 4 readings {for example, 20°C, 45°C, 70°C, 95°C }.)

9. Allow the apparatus to cool to a safe handling temperature, then put away all of your equipment.

POST LAB CONSIDERATIONS

Part I: Boyle's Law

From your data, a pressure versus volume graph will first be constructed and examined. Then a second graph will be drawn in order to seek a linear relationship and a mathematical formula that describes Boyle's Law.

In Boyle's era, syringes were certainly not available, plastic or otherwise. For his apparatus, Boyle used a glass tube bent in the shape of the letter "J" with the short end sealed and the long end open. By pouring mercury into the open end, it was possible to trap an air bubble at the closed end. The pressure on the air bubble was directly proportional to the height of the mercury column and the volume of the air bubble was proportional to the length of its column. Thus, it was possible to measure the volume occupied by a fixed sample of air at a measured pressure. To obtain more pressure, Boyle simply added more mercury.

Part II: Charles' Law

Kelvin scale temperatures must be used to properly illustrate numerical temperature relationships in gas laws. For instance, in the relationship between gas volume and temperature, Kelvin temperatures allow for a direct proportion in which a temperature of zero (absolute zero) results in zero volume (or zero pressure) for an ideal gas. By definition, an ideal gas has gas molecules that occupy zero volume. In theory, at absolute zero temperature (0 K), molecules should have no kinetic energy or molecular motion. (When writing temperatures in the Kelvin scale, it is the convention to omit the degree symbol and merely use the letter K.)

From your data, a volume versus temperature graph can be constructed. This graph can be used to confirm two relationships. First, the graph will be extrapolated to zero volume in order to estimate absolute zero (0 K). Then, using that as the origin of the graph, the mathematical formula representing Charles' Law will be derived, with temperatures expressed on the Kelvin scale.

Part I: Boyle's Law

Room Pressure (kPa)

Table 1 Volume and Pressure Readings for a Gas Syringe

Volume (mL)	Pressure Gauge Reading (kPa)	Pressure (kPa) (Pressure Gauge Reading + Room Pressure)
20		
19	COMPLETE IN YOUR NOTEBOOK	COMPLETE IN YOUR NOTEBOOK
continue		
11 (last reading)		

Part II: Charles' Law

Table 2 Temperature and Volume Readings for a Gas Syringe

Temperature (°C)	Volume (mL)
COMPLETE IN YOUR NOTEBOOK	COMPLETE IN YOUR NOTEBOOK

ANALYSIS OF RESULTS

Part I: Boyle's Law

1. On graph paper provided by your instructor, plot a graph of pressure versus volume of gas (from Table 1). Be sure to choose scales that create the largest graph possible (while still using simple quantities for the size of a unit on the graph).

2. What type of relationship does this graph illustrate?

3. Make another data table similar to Table 1 but replace your Volume (V) values with calculated 1/V values. Then, on a second sheet of graph paper, plot a graph of pressure versus 1/volume. Again, choose suitable scales.

4. What type of relationship does this P versus 1/V graph illustrate? Determine your mathematical relationship between P and 1/V.

Part II: Charles' Law

1. On a third sheet of graph paper, plot a graph of volume of gas versus temperature (from Table 2). Make your temperature scale span from –300°C to +100°C. (Leave room below your Celsius scale for a later Kelvin scale.) At 0°C construct your y-axis (Volume). After plotting your data on the graph paper, draw a line of best fit and extrapolate it to intersect the Temperature axis at 0 mL of Volume. How close did you come to estimating Kelvin's absolute zero (–273°C)?

2. Add the Kelvin scale below your Celsius scale on your graph. Now, with temperature in Kelvin, determine your mathematical relationship between V and T.

FOLLOW-UP QUESTIONS

1. Explain what will eventually happen to a helium-filled balloon that is released at the earth's surface. Which gas law applies here?

2. Explain why aerosol spray cans should never be thrown into fires or disposed of in incinerators. Which gas law applies here?

CONCLUSION

State the results of Objectives 1 and 2.

Measuring and Reporting the Molar Volume of Hydrogen Gas

A variety of gases are commercially prepared by the chemical process industries. For instance, hydrogen and oxygen gases are produced as a result of the electrolysis of water. Both of these gases are converted to liquid form and are used to launch the space shuttle. Another gas, chlorine, is manufactured from electrolysis of an aqueous solution of common salt (sodium chloride). Its derivatives are used for water sterilization and as bleaching agents in pulp and paper and household laundry detergents. Thus, the manufacture, collection, and measurement of gases are important and deserve special consideration.

Chemists are concerned not only with the identities of the chemicals in a reaction, but also with the relative amounts of these chemicals. The chemists need to be able to count the number of molecules that are both reacting and being produced. When solids and liquids are measured, it is usually convenient to determine their masses and calculate their respective moles of molecules. While the mass of a gas cannot easily be measured, the volume occupied by a gas is a convenient measurement. This volume is affected by the temperature, pressure, and number of molecules of the gas. As the moles of molecules of gas increase, the volume increases; as the temperature increases, the volume increases; as the pressure increases, the volume decreases.

The volume of a gas occupied by one mole of a substance at a given temperature and pressure is called its molar volume. Furthermore, Avogadro's hypothesis implies that, regardless of the type of gas, the molar volumes of gases are the same if their temperatures and pressures are the same. Consequently, it is important to remember that reporting the molar volume of a gas is meaningless unless its temperature and pressure are also included.

In this experiment, you will measure the volume of hydrogen gas produced in a single replacement reaction. You will react a known mass of magnesium metal with an excess of hydrochloric acid and collect the generated hydrogen gas over water in a gas-measuring tube. The evolved gas will rise to the top of the water-filled tube, displacing an equal volume of water. The chemical reaction will be:

$$Mg(s) + 2HCl(aq) \rightarrow MgCl_2(aq) + H_2(g)$$

As hydrogen gas forms over the water and displaces the water downward, water vapor is also formed so that both gases are present. As a result, the pressure produced is a combination of the partial pressures of each of these two gases and this will have to be taken into account.

OBJECTIVES

1. to observe a reaction in which hydrogen gas is produced and collected over water

2. to measure the molar volume of the hydrogen gas produced at room temperature and pressure

3. to report the measured volume of the hydrogen gas as a standard molar volume and compare it to the accepted value

SUPPLIES

Equipment

thermometer (classroom)
barometer (classroom)
ring stand
buret clamp
gas-measuring tube (50 mL)
funnel
graduated cylinder (25 mL)
beaker (400 mL)
one-hole stopper (to fit gas measuring tube)

500 mL or 1000 mL glass graduated cylinder, or deep glass container
metric ruler
copper wire, bare, thin (eg. 22 gauge), approximately 20 cm
room temperature water
lab apron
safety goggles

Chemical Reagents

magnesium ribbon
6M HCl

Figure 7B-1 *Building a copper cage*

Figure 7B-2 *Gas-measuring tube in position to add acid*

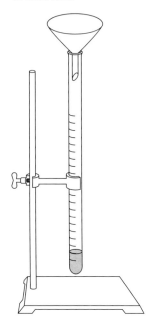

PROCEDURE

1. Put on your lab apron and safety goggles.

2. Record the barometric (room) pressure and the room temperature in your copy of Table 1 in your notebook.

3. Find out the mass of 1.000 m of magnesium ribbon from your instructor and record this value.

4. Obtain a piece of magnesium ribbon approximately 4 cm long (or as directed by your instructor). Carefully measure the length of the ribbon as accurately as you can, then record this value in your copy of Table 1 in your notebook.

5. See Figure 7B-1 to aid your understanding of this step. Obtain a piece of fine copper wire approximately 20 cm in length. Use a pen or pencil to form the copper wire into a conical cage by wrapping the wire towards the end of the pen tip. Leave 5 cm of wire unwrapped to act as a means to hook the cage over the end of the gas-measuring tube. Fold the magnesium ribbon so that it fits in the copper wire cage. Note: It is important to close the cage completely around the magnesium so that the magnesium cannot escape as it reacts. Set this cage aside for Step 10.

6. Add about 300 mL of room-temperature water to a 400 mL beaker.

7. Assemble a ring stand and buret clamp apparatus that will support a gas-measuring tube. (See Figure 7B-2.)

8. Obtain 10 mL of 6M HCl in a graduated cylinder. Use a funnel to carefully add this HCl to the gas-measuring tube. Remove the funnel and rinse it and the graduated cylinder out with water to remove any remaining acid.

9. Remove the gas-measuring tube from the clamp and tilt it on an angle. Fill it with water from the 400 mL beaker slowly, so that you do not disturb the acid layer. Fill the tube almost to the top, then replace it in the clamp.

10. Hang the copper cage inside the top of the gas-measuring tube by folding the end of the handle over the end of the tube. The cage should hang about 4 cm from the top of the tube. (See Figure 7B-3.)

11. Add enough water now to completely fill the tube, then insert a one-hole stopper. A small amount of water should squeeze out when the stopper is added. This will ensure that no air remains in the tube.

12. Place the 400 mL beaker on the base of the ring stand, then once again remove the gas-collection tube from the clamp. With one finger, cover the stopper hole, turn the tube upside down, and submerge it in the beaker of water. Reclamp the tube in its new position. (See Figure 7B-4.) If you watch carefully you will be able to see the more dense acid working its way down towards the trapped magnesium strip.

13. When the acid contacts the magnesium a reaction will occur. Observe this reaction until it stops, then wait about 5 min for the solution and gases to reach room temperature. Remember, two gases are inside the tube at this point: hydrogen gas and water vapor.

14. This step will adjust the gas volume to room pressure. Reach into the water in the beaker and once again cover the stopper hole with one finger. Transfer the tube to a large container filled with room temperature water as in Figure 7B-5. Now, move the tube up or down in the water until the water level inside the tube lines up with the water level outside the tube. (This ensures that the pressure inside the tube is the same as room pressure.) Record this gas volume.

15. Rinse out the gas-measuring tube with water and put away all equipment.

16. Before leaving the laboratory, wash your hands thoroughly with soap and water.

REAGENT DISPOSAL

Dispose of the copper wire cage into the designated waste container. Rinse all solutions down the sink with copious amounts of water.

POST LAB CONSIDERATIONS

Normally the mass of reacting magnesium would be directly weighed on a centigram balance. However, in this case, the mass of a short strip of magnesium ribbon is so small that weighing it would be unreliable. Therefore, a long strip was weighed and the mass of the short strip can be proportionally determined.

Figure 7B-3 *Hang the cage in the tube*

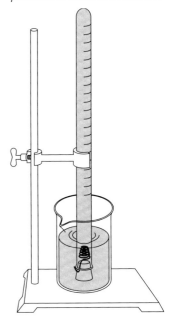

Figure 7B-4 *Apparatus in position to start the reaction*

Figure 7B-5 *Adjusting the pressure inside the tube to room pressure*

The balanced equation for the single replacement reaction in this experiment is:

$$Mg(s) + 2HCl(aq) \rightarrow MgCl_2(aq) + H_2(g)$$

From the mass of Mg(s) consumed, you can use stoichiometry to predict the moles of $H_2(g)$ produced. You can use your measured volume of $H_2(g)$ to determine the volume occupied by one mole of hydrogen (molar volume) at room temperature and pressure. The accepted value for molar volume at room temperature and pressure (25°C and 101.3 kPa) is 24.5 L/mol.

Further Analysis of Results

It will be interesting to compare your results with another accepted value, namely the *standard* molar volume of a gas. Avogadro's hypothesis states that "equal volumes of gases at the same temperature and pressure contain equal moles of molecules." A modern extension of this hypothesis is described by the standard molar volume for gases, which is the same for all ideal gases. Standard molar volume is the volume occupied by one mole of any gas at STP, which stands for Standard Temperature and Pressure (0°C and 101.3 kPa). The accepted value for standard molar volume is 22.4 L/mol.

To determine the standard molar volume of the $H_2(g)$ produced in this experiment you must use your collected data and make a few adjustments and conversions:

1. The pressure measured must be first adjusted to partial pressure of $H_2(g)$, then this partial pressure converted to standard pressure.

2. The room temperature (in Kelvin) must be converted to standard temperature.

Since the collected hydrogen gas was mixed with water vapor, an adjustment must be made to the measured pressure since this pressure is caused by both gases. In other words, this measured gas pressure represents a total pressure. In Step 14, this total pressure was measured inside the tube by equalizing it to the atmospheric pressure in the room ($P_t = P_{atm}$). The total pressure of the gas mixture is also equal to the sum of the component partial pressures of each gas:

$$P_t = P_{H_2} + P_{H_2O}$$

So, by consulting a data table for the partial pressure exerted by water (P_{H_2O}), the above equation can be solved for the partial pressure exerted by hydrogen gas (P_{H_2}).

This pressure value and the room temperature can then be substituted into the combined gas laws to convert the molar volume into a *standard* molar volume that would be occupied by this gas at STP.

EXPERIMENTAL RESULTS

Table 1

Atmospheric (room) pressure (kPa)	
Room temperature (°C)	
Mass of 1.000 m of Mg ribbon (g)	*COMPLETE IN YOUR NOTEBOOK*
Length of Mg ribbon used (cm)	
Volume of collected gas (mL)	

ANALYSIS OF RESULTS

(Refer to the Post Lab Considerations as necessary.)

1. Copy the balanced equation from the Post Lab Considerations.
   a. What mass of Mg(s) reacted? (Convert the length of your magnesium strip into grams.)
   b. Use stoichiometry to determine the moles of H_2(g) that should be produced when your mass of magnesium completely reacts.

2. Convert your measured volume (mL) of H_2(g) first into litres (L), then calculate the molar volume (L/mol). How does your value (measured at room temperature and pressure) compare to 24.5 L/mol?

Further Analysis of Results (Standard Molar Volume)

3. Use Data Table 2 to look up the partial pressure of water vapor (P_{H_2O}), then calculate the partial pressure of hydrogen gas (P_{H_2}).

Table 2: Vapor Pressure Data for H_2O

Temperature (°C)	P_{H_2O} (kPa)	Temperature (°C)	P_{H_2O} (kPa)
11	1.31	21	2.49
12	1.40	22	2.64
13	1.50	23	2.81
14	1.60	24	2.99
15	1.71	25	3.17
16	1.82	26	3.36
17	1.94	27	3.57
18	2.06	28	3.78
19	2.20	29	4.01
20	2.34	30	4.25

4. Determine the standard molar volume of H_2(g) by adjusting your molar volume to conditions of STP. Apply the gas law relationships as follows:

$$\text{Molar Volume} \times \left(\frac{P_{H_2}}{101.3 \text{ kPa}} \right) \times \left(\frac{273 \text{ K}}{T_{room}} \right)$$

FOLLOW-UP QUESTIONS

1. Use a labeled diagram to explain how Step 14 allows you to determine that the total gas pressure inside the tube is the same as room pressure.

2. Why was it necessary to have a hole in the stopper? What problem might occur if the cage is positioned too close to the stopper?

3. How would the volume of hydrogen gas produced differ if twice the length of magnesium ribbon had been used? How would this affect the molar volume?

4. Would changing the molarity of the hydrochloric acid affect the final results? Explain.

5. At STP, one mole of any gas occupies 22.4 L. What volume would one mole of He gas occupy at 202.6 kPa and 50°C?

6. Calculate the percentage error in your experimental value of standard molar volume, assuming that 22.4 L is the correct value.

CONCLUSION

State the results of Objectives 2 and 3.

Heat of Fusion of Ice

In an earlier experiment (Experiment 2B) you learned that temperature stays constant during a phase change of a substance while the heat is either absorbed or released during the phase change. In this experiment you will determine the actual amount of heat required for a phase change of a substance, namely the melting of ice. The experiment will be done in a simple calorimeter, an apparatus that contains the material undergoing the temperature change and enables the temperature to be recorded easily.

The *temperature* of a substance is a measure of the average amount of kinetic energy per particle of the substance. The higher the temperature, the higher the average kinetic energy, and the faster the molecules are moving. *Heat,* on the other hand, is a measure of the *total* amount of energy contained by a substance and depends not only on the temperature, but what the substance is and how much of it you have. The quantity of heat (q) required to raise the temperature of a substance in one phase is given by the equation:

$$q = m \times c \times \Delta T$$

where q = quantity of heat (kJ)

m = mass of substance (kg)

c = specific heat capacity (kJ/kg•°C)

ΔT = temperature change (°C)

Water has one of the highest specific heat capacities of any substance, at 4.18 kJ/kg•°C. Iron, for example, has a value approximately one tenth of that of water, at 0.450 kJ/kg•°C. In other words, water requires a relatively high quantity of heat to change its temperature. Another way of looking at this concept is to consider that if the same amount of heat is supplied to equal amounts of two different materials, the one with the lower specific heat capacity undergoes a much larger increase in temperature. This explains why a very rapid temperature rise occurs if an iron saucepan is inadvertently left on a heating element without any water in it. Furthermore, the large specific heat capacity of water is the reason why climate is much less extreme in locations near an ocean or another large body of water such as one of the Great Lakes. Summers are not as hot and winters are not as cold, compared to locations well away from a large body of water. Similarly, the large amount of water in our bodies also helps us to withstand temperature extremes.

When a solid is heated, the molecules eventually possess enough energy to overcome the intermolecular forces of attraction in the solid and break free from one another. This is the process of *melting* or *fusion*, and the temperature at which it occurs is the *melting point* of the substance. The substance remains at this temperature until all of it has melted, and the energy required for this change of state is called the heat of fusion, and is usually quoted with the units of kJ/kg.

In this experiment you will determine the heat of fusion of ice. Ice cubes at 0°C will be placed in warm water at a measured temperature and the final temperature will be recorded when the system has come to thermal (temperature) equilibrium. The heat lost by the warm water in cooling to the final temperature will be equal to the heat required to melt the ice and then raise the temperature of the resulting water to the final temperature. The calorimeter you will use is simply comprised of a stirring rod and thermometer in a covered styrofoam cup. Styrofoam has a very low specific heat capacity and, consequently, is an excellent heat insulator which minimizes heat loss to the surroundings and heat absorption by the cup itself.

OBJECTIVES

1. to calculate the energy absorbed by a mass of ice as it melts

2. to calculate the heat of fusion of ice in kJ/kg

SUPPLIES

Equipment
centigram or digital balance
styrofoam cup (large, approx. 300 mL)
lid for styrofoam cup (with two holes, one in middle, one close to edge)
400 mL beaker

source of warm water (kettle, or hot water tap)
thermometer
stirring rod
lab apron
safety goggles

Chemical Reagents
ice cubes

PROCEDURE

CAUTION

Your thermometer is made of glass and breaks easily, leaving sharp edges that cut. Handle your thermometer gently. Do not use it to crush or stir ice. If your thermometer breaks, call your instructor. If it contains mercury, be aware that mercury liquid and vapor are very poisonous.

1. Put on your lab apron and safety goggles.

2. Determine the mass of a clean, dry styrofoam cup and lid and enter it and all future readings in your copy of Table 1 in your notebook.

3. Using the method given by your instructor, obtain about 200 mL of warm water in your beaker. Adjust the temperature to about 40°C with cold water if necessary.

4. Pour the water into your styrofoam cup, add the lid, and record the mass of the cup, lid, and water.

5. Obtain two medium-sized ice cubes and dry them with a paper towel.

6. Record the temperature of the water in the cup to the nearest 0.1°C.

7. Quickly remove the lid from the cup, add the two ice cubes, and replace the lid. Insert a thermometer in the side hole, letting it go to the bottom of the cup, and insert a stirring rod in the center hole. Stir the cup's contents slowly and constantly with the stirring rod and measure the temperature as soon as the ice has melted. (You will have to peek under the lid occasionally.) Continue to monitor the temperature for another minute, to make sure the contents reach a constant temperature.

8. Remove the thermometer and stirring rod. Record the new mass of the cup, lid, and contents, in order to be able to determine the mass of ice added.

9. Empty your containers of water and wash your hands thoroughly with soap and water before leaving the laboratory.

REAGENT DISPOSAL

No chemicals other than water are used in this experiment.

POST LAB CONSIDERATIONS

In this experiment, the heat lost by the warm water equals the heat gained by the ice. The heat gained by the ice is used in two ways: first the ice melts and then the water produced by the melting of the ice has its temperature raised from 0°C to the final temperature of the mixture. In other words,

$$q_{(temp\ loss)} = q_{(melting)} + q_{(temp\ gain)}$$

The measured masses in grams must be converted to kilograms in order to calculate the heat values. Remember that the specific heat capacity of water is 4.18 kJ/kg•°C

EXPERIMENTAL RESULTS

Table 1

Mass of empty cup and lid	g	kg
Mass of cup, lid, and warm water	g	kg
Mass of warm water	g	kg
Temperature of warm water, T_{warm}(°C)		
Final temperature after melting T_{final}(°C)		
ΔT(loss) = T_{warm} – T_{final} (°C)		
ΔT(gain) = T_{final} – 0°C = T_{final} (°C)		
Final mass of cup, lid, and contents	g	kg
Mass of ice added	g	kg

ANALYSIS OF RESULTS

If necessary, consult the Introduction and Post Lab Considerations for formulas (relationships) required.

1. Calculate the quantity of heat lost, $q_{(temp\ loss)}$, by the warm water solution, in kilojoules.

2. Calculate the quantity of heat absorbed, $q_{(temp\ gain)}$, by the melted ice, in going from 0°C to the final equilibrium temperature, in kilojoules.

3. Calculate the amount of heat, $q_{(melting)}$, that must have been absorbed in the melting process.

4. Calculate the heat of fusion for ice, H_{fus}, in kJ/kg.

FOLLOW-UP QUESTIONS

1. The accepted value for the heat of fusion of ice, H_{fus}, is 334 kJ/kg. By what percentage does your value vary from the accepted value?

2. Suggest any possible assumptions or sources of error that could account for any difference observed for your value of H_{fus} and whether they would make your answer larger or smaller than the accepted value.

3. Heat is given off in the process in which a liquid solidifies to form a solid. The heat of solidification has the same numerical value as the heat of fusion but is opposite in sign. When water is frozen into ice cubes in a refrigerator, where does the released heat go?

CONCLUSION

State the result of Objective 2.

Copying the experiment is prohibited.

Molar Heats of Reaction and Hess's Law

When a chemical reaction takes place, bond breaking occurs in the reactant molecules and new bonds are formed in the product molecules. The process of breaking bonds always requires energy input (endothermic) and the process of forming bonds always releases energy (exothermic). Whether an overall reaction is endothermic or exothermic depends on which of these processes involves the greater amount of energy.

The term enthalpy (also called heat content) represents the total amount of energy contained in a substance, and is given the symbol H. Chemists use the term ΔH to represent the overall change in the enthalpy as a reaction proceeds, where $\Delta H = H_{products} - H_{reactants}$. If a reaction is exothermic, energy is released from the reactant molecules to the surrounding environment and consequently, the heat content of the products is less than that of the reactants. Hence, ΔH is a negative quantity. An example of such a reaction is the burning of gasoline. Conversely, if a reaction is endothermic, energy is absorbed from the surrounding environment into the reactant molecules as they form products and consequently, the heat content of the products is greater than that of the reactants. Hence, ΔH is a positive quantity. An example of such a reaction is the electrolysis of water to produce hydrogen and oxygen.

If an amount other than one mole of reactant is used, the energy change during the reaction is given the symbol "q". If "n" moles of a reactant are used in the reaction, the *Molar* Enthalpy of Reaction, ΔH, is the enthalpy change per mole of reactant, calculated as q/n.

This experiment is designed to measure the ΔH in kJ/mol for three different but related reactions and determine if there is a relationship involving these ΔH values. The three reactions to be studied are shown by the following equations:

1) $\qquad\qquad NaOH(s) \rightarrow Na^+(aq) + OH^-(aq)$

2) $\qquad NaOH(s) + H^+(aq) + Cl^-(aq) \rightarrow H_2O(l) + Na^+(aq) + Cl^-(aq)$

3) $Na^+(aq) + OH^-(aq) + H^+(aq) + Cl^-(aq) \rightarrow H_2O(l) + Na^+(aq) + Cl^-(aq)$

The first reaction just involves the dissolving of NaOH to form a solution, so the heat term of that reaction is called the *Heat of Solution*. The other two are chemical reactions, so each of the heat terms is called a *Heat of Reaction*. The experiment will be performed in a simple calorimeter consisting of a styrofoam cup and lid.

OBJECTIVES

1. to determine the amount of heat energy released in three separate reactions, using a simple calorimeter

2. to calculate the molar heat of reaction (ΔH, in kJ/mol) for each reaction performed

3. to determine the relationship existing between the three ΔH values obtained and the three reaction equations given in the introduction

SUPPLIES

Equipment
2 graduated cylinders (100 mL)
styrofoam cup (200 mL)
lid for cup with two holes in it (one in the center, one at the side)
weighing paper or weighing boat
centigram or digital balance

thermometer
   (preferably –10°C to +50°C)
stirring rod
lab apron
safety goggles
plastic gloves

Chemical Reagents
solid NaOH (pellets or granules)
1.0*M* NaOH
1.0*M* HCl

PROCEDURE

Part I: Heat of Solution of Solid Sodium Hydroxide

1. Put on your lab apron, safety goggles, and plastic gloves.

2. Obtain exactly 100 mL of water in a graduated cylinder and pour it into a dry styrofoam cup.

3. Measure the temperature of the water to the nearest 0.1°C and record it and subsequent measurements from Part I in your copy of Table 1 in your notebook. Between readings, lay your thermometer on a piece of paper towel in a safe place.

4. You need a mass of between 1.9 g and 2.1 g of NaOH. Your instructor will tell you how to obtain this mass, which will depend on whether the NaOH is in the form of pellets or granules, and whether you are weighing it onto a piece of weighing paper, into a weighing boat, or some other container. Record the exact mass of the NaOH.

5. As soon as the mass has been recorded, transfer the NaOH to the water in the styrofoam cup and place the lid on the cup. (NaOH absorbs water and carbon dioxide from the air as soon as it is exposed to air, and this is why you must get the NaOH into the cup as quickly as possible.)

6. Insert a thermometer in the side hole of the lid, allowing it to reach the bottom of the cup, and insert a stirring rod into the center hole. Stir the cup's contents slowly and constantly with the stirring rod.

7. Approximately every 30 s check the progress of the dissolving and monitor the thermometer for temperature changes. As soon as all the NaOH has dissolved, watch the thermometer carefully and record the highest temperature reached.

8. Place the solution of NaOH in the designated waste container and rinse and dry your cup in readiness for Part II.

CAUTION

Your thermometer is made of glass and can easily break, leaving sharp edges that cut. Handle your thermometer gently. Do not use it to stir the solution. If your thermometer breaks, call your instructor. If it contains mercury, be aware that mercury liquid and vapor are very poisonous.

CAUTION

Solid sodium hydroxide is very corrosive to skin, eyes, and clothing; if any gets in your mouth or is swallowed, it will cause serious damage. Wear lab apron, safety goggles, and gloves. Do not touch any of the solid, even when wearing gloves. Use a spatula or other method given by your instructor for handling this chemical. If any is spilled, do not attempt to pick it up or move it. Wash any spilled material off your skin or clothing immediately with plenty of water. Call your instructor.

Part II: Heat of Reaction between Hydrochloric Acid and Solid Sodium Hydroxide

1. Measure 50 mL of 1.0*M* hydrochloric acid, HCl, into your graduated cylinder and add water to dilute it to the 100 mL mark. (You now have 100 mL of 0.50*M* HCl.) Pour the solution into your dry styrofoam cup.

2. Measure the temperature of the HCl solution and record it and other measurements from Part II in Table 2 in your notebook.

3. In the same manner as in Part I, obtain approximately 2 g of NaOH and quickly record the exact mass.

4. Transfer the NaOH to the HCl solution in the styrofoam cup and stir gently to dissolve. Monitor the temperature in between stirrings.

5. As soon as all the NaOH has dissolved, observe the thermometer carefully until it reaches the highest temperature. Record this value.

6. Discard the solution down the sink, then rinse and dry your cup in preparation for Part III.

The hydrochloric acid solution is corrosive to skin, eyes, and clothing. Wear safety goggles and gloves. Wash any spills and splashes off your skin and clothing immediately with plenty of water. Call your instructor.

Part III: Heat of Reaction between Hydrochloric Acid and Sodium Hydroxide Solution

1. Measure exactly 50 mL of 1.0*M* HCl into a graduated cylinder and then pour it into the dry styrofoam cup.

2. Measure exactly 50 mL of 1.0*M* NaOH into another graduated cylinder.

3. Record the temperature of each solution to the nearest 0.1°C. Rinse and dry the thermometer before using it again in the second solution.

4. Pour the NaOH solution into the HCl solution in the styrofoam cup. Stir with a stirring rod to mix the solutions, then measure the temperature. Observe and record the highest temperature reached.

5. Pour the solution down the sink and clean up your apparatus. Wash your hands thoroughly with soap and water before leaving the laboratory.

The NaOH solution is corrosive to skin, eyes, and clothing. Wear safety goggles and gloves. Wash any spills or splashes immediately with plenty of water. Call your instructor.

REAGENT DISPOSAL

The NaOH solution produced in Part I, along with any NaOH and HCl solutions you have left over, should be returned to the waste containers designated by your instructor. The solutions resulting from Parts II and III should be close to neutral and can be discarded down the sink.

POST LAB CONSIDERATIONS

The heat produced in each of the three reactions was absorbed by the solutions in the styrofoam cup calorimeter. For each reaction, the heat absorbed (q) is calculated from the equation:

$$q = m \times c \times \Delta T$$

where m = mass of the solution (kg)
c = specific heat capacity of the solution (kJ/kg•°C)
ΔT = temperature change of the solution (°C)

In order to perform these calculations, some simplifying assumptions must be made. First, assume the heat lost to the styrofoam cup and to the surrounding air is negligible. Second, assume that the dilute solutions used have the same density as water, namely, 1.00 g/mL. This enables you to calculate the mass from the volume used. Third, assume the specific heat of the solutions is the same as that of water, namely 4.18 kJ/kg•°C. Note that masses of the solutions must be converted to kilograms.

The values calculated for q each have units of kJ, and refer to the differing amounts of chemicals used. In order to compare the heat terms properly, the value for the Heat of Solution (ΔH_1) and the two Heat of Reaction values (ΔH_2 and ΔH_3) must be expressed in units of kJ/mol. Therefore, you must calculate the number of moles of NaOH used in each part of the procedure and divide these values into the corresponding q values to obtain the molar heats of reaction. Finally, after considering what happens to the temperature of the surrounding solution as the reactions proceed, the appropriate sign is assigned to the values of ΔH_1, ΔH_2, and ΔH_3.

EXPERIMENTAL RESULTS

Part I: Heat of Solution of Solid Sodium Hydroxide
Table 1

Volume of water used (mL)	
Initial temperature of water (T_i)	
Mass of NaOH (g)	
Final temperature of NaOH solution (T_f)	

Part II: Heat of Reaction between Hydrochloric Acid and Solid Sodium Hydroxide
Table 2

Volume of HCl(aq) used (mL)	
Initial temperature of HCl(aq) (T_i)	
Mass of NaOH (g)	
Final temperature of resulting solution (T_f)	

Part III: Heat of Reaction between Hydrochloric Acid and Sodium Hydroxide Solution

Table 3

Initial temperature of HCl (aq)	
Initial temperature of NaOH(aq)	
Average initial temperature (T_i)	
Final temperature of resulting solution (T_f)	
Molarity of NaOH solution used	
Volume of NaOH solution used (mL)	

ANALYSIS OF RESULTS

1. Transfer your experimental results to the appropriate lines in each of the following tables.

2. By filling in all remaining lines in the tables, calculate q (in kJ) and ΔH (in kJ/mol) for each of the three reactions. If necessary, refer to the Post Lab Considerations for formulas.

Part I: Heat of Solution of Solid Sodium Hydroxide

Initial temperature of water (T_i)	
Final temperature of NaOH solution (T_f)	
Temperature change ($T_f - T_i = \Delta T$)	
Mass of 100.0 mL of water (g)	
Mass of 100.0 mL of water (kg)	
Heat produced (q)	
Mass of NaOH (g)	
Moles of NaOH	
Heat produced /mol NaOH (kJ)	
ΔH_1 (kJ/mol NaOH)	

Part II: Heat of Reaction between Hydrochloric Acid and Solid Sodium Hydroxide

Initial temperature of HCl(aq) (T_i)	
Final temperature of resulting solution (T_f)	
Temperature change ($T_f - T_i = \Delta T$)	
Mass of 100.0 mL of HCl (g)	
Mass of 100.0 mL of HCl (kg)	
Heat produced (q)	
Mass of NaOH (g)	
Moles of NaOH	
Heat produced /mol NaOH (kJ)	
ΔH_2 (kJ/mol NaOH)	

Part III: Heat of Reaction between Hydrochloric Acid and Sodium Hydroxide Solution

Initial temperature of HCl(aq)	
Initial temperature of NaOH(aq)	
Average initial temperature (T_i)	
Final temperature of resulting solution (T_f)	
Temperature change ($T_f - T_i = \Delta T$)	
Mass of resulting 100.0 mL solution (g)	
Heat produced (q)	
Molarity of NaOH solution used	
Volume of NaOH solution used (mL)	
Volume of NaOH solution used (L)	
Moles of NaOH	
Heat produced /mol NaOH (kJ)	
ΔH_3 (kJ/mol NaOH)	

Copying the experiment is prohibited.

3. Refer to the chemical equations shown in the introduction and write the net ionic equations for each of these three reactions. How are they related?

4. Write the appropriate calculated ΔH values beside your net ionic equations.

5. How does the value of ΔH_2 compare to the sum of ΔH_1 and ΔH_3?

6. Hess's Law states that if an overall reaction can be shown to be made up of a number of smaller steps, the ΔH for the overall reaction is equal to the sum of the ΔH's of the individual steps. Do your results confirm this?

7. Calculate the percentage deviation between ΔH_2 and the sum of ΔH_1 and ΔH_3. Assume ΔH_2 to be correct. Suggest some possible reasons for the observed difference, if any.

FOLLOW-UP QUESTIONS

1. The dissolving of ammonium nitrate in water is a highly endothermic process. How could this fact be utilized for the treatment of athletic injuries?

2. If a student repeated Part I of the experiment, but used twice as much NaOH, how would this affect the amount of heat produced? How would it affect the ΔH_1?

3. If double the amount of NaOH were used in Part II, without changing any other concentrations or volumes, would this double the amount of heat produced in this reaction? Explain the reasons for your answer.

CONCLUSION

State the results of Objectives 2 and 3.

8C

Comparing Molar Heats of Combustion of Two Fuels

A *calorimeter* is an apparatus that is designed to measure the heat change (enthalpy change) occurring during a chemical reaction. In this experiment you will carry out a combustion reaction, and the heat of such a reaction is usually described as the *heat of combustion*, ΔH. Although research labs have very sophisticated and expensive calorimeters, you can build a very simple one with just a tin can.

A calorimeter measures heat based on a very simple but important principle:

HEAT RELEASED = HEAT GAINED

The calorimeter we will use here is simply a tin can filled with water, with a thermometer in it. In the first part of this experiment, the combustion of a common fuel (candle wax) will be studied. A candle will burn directly under the can and we will assume that all of the heat released will go straight up into the water in the can. That is, we will assume:

HEAT RELEASED BY CANDLE = HEAT GAINED BY WATER

The chemical reaction involved is simply the combustion (burning) of candle wax (paraffin). Since paraffin is a mixture of organic compounds, we will assume it has the average chemical formula $C_{25}H_{52}$. The skeletal equation for the combustion of paraffin is:

$$C_{25}H_{52} + O_2 \rightarrow CO_2 + H_2O$$

It is obviously an exothermic reaction since it releases heat and it is the total amount of heat released that you will measure. This total amount of heat released can also be expressed as the enthalpy change (ΔH in kJ) or, in this case, heat of combustion. In order to compare the heat of one reaction with another, the heats will be compared on a per mole basis. Thus another quantity, the *molar* heat of combustion (ΔH in kJ/mol), must be used.

In Part II, another fuel will be studied: methyl alcohol, more properly known as methanol. You may be familiar with methanol as an additive to windshield washing solution to prevent winter freezing. Also, methanol appears as a blend in some gasoline and is even used as a fuel for some race cars. It will be interesting to compare the heat released by the methanol with the heat released by a candle.

The skeletal equation for the combustion of methanol is:

$$CH_3OH + O_2 \rightarrow CO_2 + H_2O$$

OBJECTIVES

1. to measure the heats of combustion or enthalpy changes (ΔH in kJ) for the combustion of paraffin wax and methanol

2. to determine the molar heats of combustion (ΔH in kJ/mol) and compare the two values

3. to write the equations for the exothermic reactions in two ways:
   a. using a thermochemical equation
   b. using ΔH notation

SUPPLIES

Equipment

calorimeter (tin can assembly with wire hanger)	alcohol lamp	centigram balance
	matches or equivalent	stirring rod
		lab apron
thermometer	base for candle (lid from tin can or jar lid)	safety goggles
thermometer clamp		

Chemical Reagents

paraffin wax (candle)
methanol

PROCEDURE

Part I: Measuring Heat Released by Paraffin

1. Put on your lab apron and safety goggles.

2. Obtain a candle which is made of paraffin wax and attach it to a base by dripping some wax on the base.

3. Weigh the candle and base. Record this mass in your copy of Table 1 in your notebook.

4. Weigh the empty calorimeter, but place a small piece of paper on the balance to protect it from soot on the bottom of the can (from previous experiments). Record this mass. Important: Keep the piece of paper for Step 5.

5. Half fill the calorimeter with cold water, reweigh as before, using the piece of paper under the can, and record.

6. Assemble the apparatus as shown in Figure 8C-1. The thermometer bulb should sit close to the middle of the water sample.

7. Accurately record the temperature of the water, then light the candle. Adjust the calorimeter so that it sits in the tip of the flame. Try to control drafts so that the flame is going straight up. You may find it necessary to shield the flame.

8. Allow the candle to burn for about 10 min. Occasionally, stir the water gently with a stirring rod to prevent hot spots. After the 10 min of heating, carefully blow out the flame. (You don't want to spray any molten paraffin off the top of the candle because it will affect your results.) Watch the temperature for about a minute and record the highest temperature that is reached.

9. Reweigh the candle and base.

CAUTION

Methanol is very poisonous and flammable. Do not spill any near an open flame.

Figure 8C-1 *A tin can calorimeter*

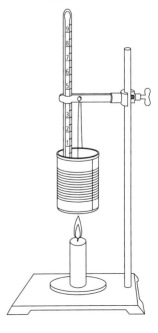

Part II: Measuring Heat Released by Methanol

1. Repeat Steps 3 to 9 but this time use an alcohol lamp (containing methanol) instead of a candle. Record all observations in Table 2.

2. Clean up all of your supplies.

3. Before leaving the laboratory, wash your hands thoroughly with soap and water.

REAGENT DISPOSAL

None required.

POST LAB CONSIDERATIONS

To find the heat released by each fuel you will use the formula $q = m \times c \times \Delta T$ as described below. However, in order to *compare* heats of combustion, you must also determine the amount of fuel that reacted and factor that into your calculated heat value. To do this you will calculate *molar* heats of combustion by simply dividing your ΔH values by moles of fuel consumed and thereby compare kJ/mol of each fuel.

Heat Calculations

To determine the total heat that was absorbed by the calorimeter, use the formula:

$$q = m \times c \times \Delta T$$

where q = quantity of heat absorbed by calorimeter (kJ)

m = mass of water in the can (kg)

c = specific heat capacity of water (a constant) = 4.18 kJ/kg•°C

ΔT = temperature change of water (°C)

Recall the calorimetric principle that the heat gained by the calorimeter is equal to the heat released by the combustion reaction. It then follows that:

• since q (in kJ) is the heat absorbed by the calorimeter, then

• ΔH (in kJ) is the total heat of combustion, so $\Delta H = -q$, and

• ΔH (in kJ/mol) is the *molar* heat of combustion.

Once the heat effects of a reaction have been determined, they can be commonly expressed in two ways. In a thermochemical equation, the heat value is written as part of the chemical equation. In this experiment, which involves exothermic reactions, the heat term is added on the right. If the ΔH notation is used, the ΔH term is written separate from the equation, and in exothermic reactions has a negative value.

EXPERIMENTAL RESULTS

Part I: Measuring Heat Released by Paraffin

Table 1 Heat Released by Paraffin

Candle (Paraffin)	
Initial mass of candle and base (g)	
Final mass of candle and base (g)	COMPLETE IN YOUR NOTEBOOK
Calorimeter	
Mass of empty calorimeter (g)	
Mass of calorimeter + water (g)	COMPLETE IN YOUR NOTEBOOK
Initial temperature of water (°C)	
Final temperature of water (°C)	

Part II: Measuring Heat Released by Methanol

Table 2 Heat Released by Methanol

Alcohol Lamp (Methanol)	
Initial mass of alcohol lamp (g)	
Final mass of alcohol lamp (g)	COMPLETE IN YOUR NOTEBOOK
Calorimeter	
Mass of empty calorimeter (g)	
Mass of calorimeter + water (g)	
Initial temperature of water (°C)	COMPLETE IN YOUR NOTEBOOK
Final temperature of water (°C)	

ANALYSIS OF RESULTS

Part I: Measuring Heat Released by Paraffin

1. Copy the equation for the combustion of paraffin from the introduction and balance it.

2. From Table 1 calculate the following:
   a. mass of paraffin (candle wax) that reacted
   b. mass of water in the calorimeter
   c. change in temperature of the water in the calorimeter

3. Total Heat of Combustion: Use the formula from the Post Lab Considerations to calculate the heat (q) gained by the water. Next calculate ΔH in kJ.

4. Paraffin Reacted: From the mass of paraffin reacted calculate the moles of paraffin reacted.

5. Molar Heat of Combustion: Calculate the molar heat of combustion which is the heat released per mole of paraffin burned, ΔH in kJ/mol.

Part II: Measuring Heat Released by Methanol

1. Repeat Analysis numbers 1–5 but use methanol (and Table 2) for all calculations. In this section, renumber 1–5 as 6–10.

11. Compare your molar heats of combustion for paraffin and methanol with one other lab group. Theoretically, these values should be identical. Give one reason why they may be different.

12. When comparing kJ/mol for different fuels, why does it not matter how long the different fuels had been burning?

FOLLOW-UP QUESTIONS

1. Another useful and more practical heat comparison is to compare kJ/g of fuel burned. To do this, convert your molar heats of combustion to kJ/g, then compare these values to the accepted values provided by your instructor. Suggest reasons for any differences from accepted values.

An "oxygen bomb" calorimeter (See Figure 8C-2.) is used by nutrition research labs to measure the energy content of foods as their heats of combustion. To determine the energy in a certain food, a weighed sample of that food is placed in the oxygen bomb and burned in a similar fashion to the fuels in this experiment. The "bomb" gets its name from its appearance and the possibility of explosion if conditions involving pure oxygen are not properly controlled!

2. A 1.50 g sample of sucrose (table sugar, $C_{12}H_{22}O_{11}$) was burned in an oxygen bomb calorimeter which was filled with 4.00 L of water. (Remember that the density of water is 1.00 g/mL.) As a result, the temperature of the water changed from 25.0°C to 29.6°C. Calculate the molar heat of combustion for sucrose.

Copying the experiment is prohibited.

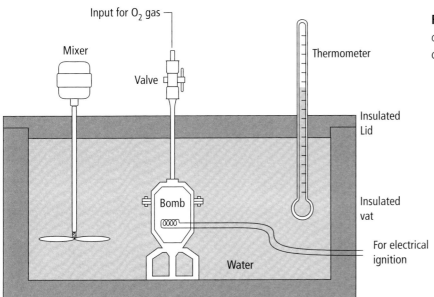

Input for O₂ gas

Mixer

Valve

Thermometer

Insulated Lid

Insulated vat

Bomb

For electrical ignition

Water

3. A reaction was carried out in an oxygen bomb calorimeter and 21.64 kJ of energy was released into 648 g of water. If the initial water temperature was 20.4°C, calculate the final temperature of the water.

4. A 0.650 mol sample of a fuel was burned in an oxygen bomb calorimeter. For the combustion of this fuel, $\Delta H = -35.5$ kJ/mol. The result was that the temperature of 3.00 kg of water was raised to 28.2°C. What was the water's initial temperature?

CONCLUSION

State the results of Objective 3 using molar heats of combustion.

THE PERIODIC TABLE AND CHEMICAL BONDING

The Periodic Table

In 1869, a Russian chemist named Dmitri Mendeleev realized that in order to advance knowledge of chemistry the elements needed to be organized in such a way as to show relationships between them. Accordingly, he placed elements with similar chemical properties in vertical columns or groups, arranged in order of increasing atomic mass. There were a number of gaps in his table, but he predicted there were elements yet to be discovered that would fit in those positions. Subsequent research soon led to these discoveries, therefore validating his classification. In 1871 he published a table showing 59 elements, which you will study in this activity.

The modern periodic table accommodates over 50 more elements (up to 116), with more being actively sought. Note that the form of the periodic table allows it to accommodate an unlimited number of extra elements. The table is arranged in order of increasing atomic number, which is a concept that had not been discovered at the time of Mendeleev. However, the arrangement of elements within the chart is similar in organization to the table he published in 1871. Trends in the chemical and physical properties of elements are now seen as a periodic function of electron configuration, which is determined by the atomic number.

In the three parts of this experiment, you will first determine the electronic configurations for a number of elements. Then, you will relate these configurations to observed trends in the properties of atomic radii and first ionization energies for these elements. Lastly, you will construct Mendeleev's periodic table from a list of clues, using the modern periodic table and other reference sources.

OBJECTIVES

1. to show the relationship between electron configuration and the location of an element within the periodic table

2. to examine and graph periodic trends in atomic radii and the first ionization energies for the first twenty elements in the periodic table

3. to construct the periodic table published by Mendeleev in 1871 by identifying the elements from a list of clues

SUPPLIES

Equipment
pencil
ruler
textbook and other reference materials
graph paper

PROCEDURE

Part I: Electron Configuration and the Periodic Table

1. Make a copy in your notebook of the section of the periodic table illustrated in Figure 9A-1. For each element shown, write its electron configuration within the appropriate box. As a check, remember that the sum of all the electrons (which are represented as superscripts after the shell and subshell designations) must equal the atomic number of the element.

Part II: Atomic Number, Atomic Radius, Ionization Energy, and the Periodic Table

1. Using the data listed in Table 1, plot a graph of the atomic radius of each element against increasing atomic number. The atomic radii shown here are given in nanometres. (1 nm = 1×10^{-9}m)

2. Using the data listed in Table 1, plot a graph of the first ionization energy of each element against increasing atomic number.

Table 1 Atomic Number, Atomic Radius, and Ionization Energies for Selected Elements

Element	Atomic Number	Atomic Radius (nm)	First Ionization Energy (kJ/mol)
Hydrogen	1	0.078	1312
Helium	2	0.128	2372
Lithium	3	0.152	513
Beryllium	4	0.113	899
Boron	5	0.083	801
Carbon	6	0.077	1086
Nitrogen	7	0.071	1402
Oxygen	8	0.066	1314
Fluorine	9	0.071	1681
Neon	10	0.070	2081
Sodium	11	0.186	496
Magnesium	12	0.160	738
Aluminum	13	0.143	577
Silicon	14	0.117	787
Phosphorus	15	0.093	1012
Sulfur	16	0.104	1000
Chlorine	17	0.099	1251
Argon	18	0.174	1520
Potassium	19	0.227	418
Calcium	20	0.197	590

Part III: Other Characteristics of Elements and the Periodic Table

1. The positions of the 59 elements found on Mendeleev's 1871 version of the periodic table are coded below for Figure 9A-2, first with a number representing the column number, followed by a letter indicating the position within that column. Use a text or other reference sources to find the name of the element corresponding to the clue given. Write the name in the correct position in your copy of Figure 9A-2 in your notebook.

1A has a nucleus containing just one proton.

1B is an alkali metal with two electrons in its +1 ion

1C is a highly reactive metal formed in the electrolysis of table salt.

1D has a first ionization energy of 418 kJ/mol.

1E has a major use as a conducting metal in electrical wiring.

1F is the first alkali metal with a completed 3d subshell.

1G has a symbol that was derived from its Latin name argentum.

1H is an alkali metal with atomic number 55.

1I has a Latin name aurum, derived from the Latin word for dawn, aurora.

2A is the first element in the alkaline earth group of elements.

2B burns with a bright white light and is used in flares and fireworks.

2C is the metallic component of the mineral marble.

2D is a metal used to galvanize iron to protect it from rusting.

2E has 36 electrons in its 2+ ion.

2F is used along with nickel in one type of rechargeable battery.

2G is a metal with an outermost electron configuration of $6s^2$.

2H is a liquid metal, which once went by the name of quicksilver.

3A is the first member of group 13 (IIIA) of the modern periodic table.

3B is a lightweight metal obtained from bauxite and used for making beverage cans.

3C is a transition metal with 39 protons in the nucleus.

3D has only 1 electron in the 5p subshell.

3E gives its name to the series of metals starting here that also go by the name rare earth metals.

3F has only 1 electron in its 6p subshell.

4A is the element whose compounds comprise the branch of chemistry called organic chemistry.

4B is the second most abundant element in the earth's crust.

4C has 2 electrons in the 3d subshell.

4D has a nuclear charge of 40+.

4E derives its symbol from the Latin word stannum.

4F is the stable metal that is the end product of the radioactive decay of uranium.

4G is the element formed when uranium gives off an alpha particle.

5A is the most abundant element in the atmosphere.

5B is a non-metallic element that ignites spontaneously when exposed to air.

5C has 23 protons in its nucleus.

5D is a very poisonous non-metal belonging to period 4 and group 15 (VA) in the modern periodic table.

5E is found between zirconium and molybdenum in the modern periodic table.

5F has a symbol derived from its Latin name stibium.

5G has an atomic number of 73.

5H is the heaviest member of group 15 (VA) in the modern periodic table.

6A is the most abundant element in earth's crust.

6B is a yellow non-metal, made as a byproduct in purification of natural gas.

6C is an ingredient along with iron and nickel in stainless steel.

6D has 4 electrons in its 4p subshell.

6E has a nuclear charge of 42+.

6F is a group 16 (VIA) element whose atomic mass is larger than the element after it in the periodic table.

6G has a major use as a filament in incandescent light bulbs because of its high melting point.

6H is the most abundant naturally occurring radioactive element, used in many nuclear reactors.

7A is a greenish-yellow diatomic gas, produced by electrolysis of common salt.

7B has a nuclear charge of 25+.

7C is the only non-metallic element that is a liquid at room temperature.

7D is a halogen whose crystals sublime, giving a violet vapor.

8A is the major metal used in construction.

8B is often used to make coins, and one coin is commonly called by this name.

8C has 7 electrons in its 3d subshell.

8D is located directly above osmium in the modern periodic table.

8E has a nuclear charge of 45+.

8F has 8 electrons in its 4d subshell.

8G has the greatest density of any known element at 22.57 g/cm^3.

8H has 77 protons in its nucleus.

8I is an inert metal often used in electrodes and jewelry, and is more valuable than gold.

EXPERIMENTAL RESULTS

Part I: Electron Configuration and the Periodic Table

Figure 9A-1

Representative elements of periods 1-4

Part II: Atomic Number, Atomic Radius, Ionization Energy, and the Periodic Table

On your own graph paper, choose the correct axes and appropriate scales for plots of atomic radii and first ionization energy versus atomic number.

Part III: Other Characteristics of Elements and the Periodic Table

Figure 9A-2

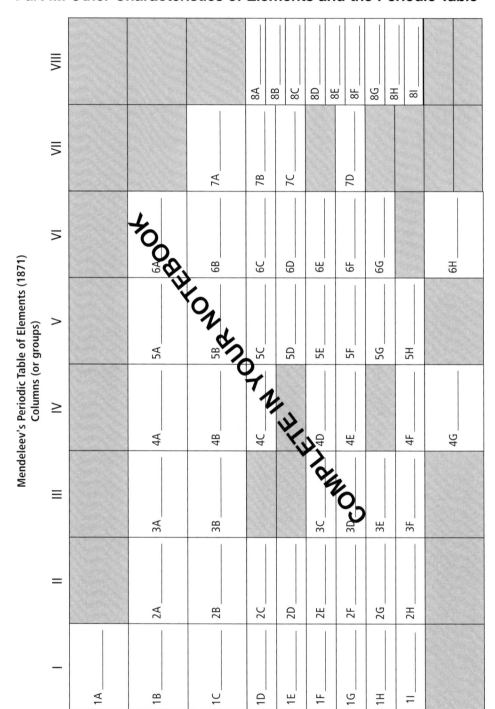

ANALYSIS OF RESULTS

1. Examine the placement of electron configurations in Figure 9A-1. What relationship exists between an element's placement within a group and its electron configuration?

2. Examine your graph of atomic radius plotted against increasing atomic number. Can a periodic tendency be observed (a) across each period and (b) down each group? If so, describe the indicated trends.

3. Which group has members of the largest atomic radii for a given period? Which group has the smallest?

4. Examine your graph of first ionization energy plotted against increasing atomic number. Can a periodic tendency be observed (a) across each period and (b) down each group? If so, describe the indicated trends.

FOLLOW-UP QUESTIONS

1. No members of group 18 (VIIIA) of the modern periodic table can be found on Mendeleev's version of the periodic table. Suggest a reason for their absence.

2. What factor may account for the observed trend in atomic radii as the atomic number increases across a period?

3. The observed general trend in ionization energies shows two slight discontinuities in each period. Examine the electron configuration at these points and explain why such a discontinuity may occur.

CONCLUSION

State the relationship between electron configuration and location of an element in the periodic table. Also, state the general trend in atomic radii and first ionization energy as the atomic number increases across a given period and down a given group of the table.

9B

Model Building with Covalent Molecules

The most common way that chemists represent structures of covalent molecules is in two dimensions. This is because of the need to show them on paper or another flat surface. There are two main methods for showing molecular structure in two dimensions. These are the electron-dot (Lewis) formula and the structural formula. The electron-dot formula shows a covalent bond as a pair of dots representing the two electrons in the bond, whereas the structural formula shows the covalent bond as a straight line joining the two atoms.

In order to understand the three-dimensional nature of a compound, we need to make a model and there are a number of different types that can be used. A ball-and-stick model shows the spatial arrangement of the atoms and the angles between the bonds. If a spring is used instead of a stick, this enables the stretching and bending of the bond to be visualized as well. The advantage of both of these is that the models can be easily taken apart and reassembled into other molecules. However, neither of these makes any attempt to show the relative sizes of the atoms. A space-filling model can show the relative sizes as well as the orientation of the atoms. Increasingly in recent years, chemists have been making excellent use of the advances in computer graphics technologies, to make computer simulations of the structure of many molecules. This is especially true with the very complicated three-dimensional structures of biological molecules such as proteins and deoxyribonucleic acid (DNA).

In making models in this experiment, you need to be aware that atoms which require more than one bond will sometimes have double or triple bonds between two atoms. In addition, sometimes molecular formulas may have a number of different structural formulas called isomers which represent completely different compounds. As an example, C_2H_6O is the molecular formula for both ethyl alcohol (ethanol) and dimethyl ether, which belong to two completely different classes of compounds.

OBJECTIVES

1. to construct molecular models of some simple and more complicated molecules, in order to visualize their shape

2. to construct all possible structures for some molecules that have different structural isomers

3. to draw structural formulas for all the molecules studied

SUPPLIES

Equipment

molecular model kit

PROCEDURE

1. Obtain a molecular model kit and separate the atoms by color. Using the chart below, decide which color to represent each atom by. Record them in your notebook.

Atom	Nnumber of Bonding Sites (Holes or Extensions)
hydrogen fluorine chlorine bromine iodine	1
oxygen sulfur	2
nitrogen phosphorus	3
carbon silicon	4

2. Make models of the following molecules. There is only one structural formula for each one. If you think you have another structure, try rotating the molecule to various different positions and you will find it is not in fact new. Sketch the structure of each model in your notebook.
   a. water H_2O
   b. methane CH_4
   c. methanol CH_4O
   d. ethane C_2H_6
   e. silicon tetrachloride $SiCl_4$
   f. ammonia NH_3
   g. hydrazine N_2H_4
   h. hydrogen sulfide H_2S

3. For the following molecular formulas there are two or more arrangements of the atoms. For each one, try to find all the different structural isomers that exist. Draw the structural formula for each isomer in your notebook.
   a. C_4H_{10}
   b. C_3H_8O
   c. $C_2H_4Br_2$
   d. $C_2H_3Cl_2Br$

4. Elements that have two or more bonding sites can sometimes form double or triple bonds. All the following molecules contain one or more double or triple bonds in their structure. Make a model of each and draw the structural formula in your notebook.

    a. carbon dioxide CO_2
    b. nitrogen N_2
    c. oxygen O_2
    d. ethene (ethylene) C_2H_4
    e. ethyne (acetylene) C_2H_2
    f. hydrogen cyanide HCN
    g. carbon disulfide CS_2
    h. methanal (formaldehyde) CH_2O

5. If you still have time available your instructor may suggest other molecules for you to try. Draw their structural formulas in your notebook.

POST LAB CONSIDERATIONS

Using models is a great aid in enabling you to visualize molecules in three dimensions. Often when using a two-dimensional representation it may appear that there are several possible structures for a molecule. However, when using a model that can be turned upside-down, end-over-end, or viewed from the opposite side, it soon becomes apparent that seemingly different structures are in fact identical. Models will be very useful later in your studies when you must learn how to name structures, especially the many possible structures of compounds of carbon (called organic compounds). When there are four single bonds attached to a carbon atom, the bonds arrange themselves as far away from one another a possible, in what is called a tetrahedral arrangement. The angle between adjacent bonds is 109.5°. For simplicity, single bonds in carbon compounds (especially larger ones) are often shown as though the molecule has been squashed flat. See Figure 9B-1(a) for an example, using carbon tetrafluoride, CF_4. Here, the bond angles appear to be 90°, but it is understood that they are at 109.5°. Diagrams like this are still very useful because they still indicate how the atoms are connected in the molecule. If an attempt at a three-dimensional diagram is required, it can be done as shown in Figure 9B-1(b):

Figure 9B-1 *Structural Formulas for CF₄.*
(a) two-dimensional
(b) three-dimensional

In the three-dimensional diagram, the ordinary line represents a bond in the plane of the paper, the solid wedge represents a bond coming forward from the plane of the paper, and the broken wedge represents a bond going backwards behind the plane of the paper.

EXPERIMENTAL RESULTS

Your observations in this experiment may be recorded in table form. However, it will be difficult to prepare the table for Procedure 3 in advance as you do not know how many structures there are for each substance. Just list the compound and then draw all of the structures you find for that compound.

ANALYSIS OF RESULTS

1. How many different structures did you write for (a) C_4H_{10} (b) C_3H_8O (c) $C_2H_4Br_2$ (d) $C_2H_3Cl_2Br$?

2. The class of carbon compounds that contain the hydroxyl group (O directly attached to H, –O–H) is called the alcohols. Review the structures that you sketched for C_3H_8O. How many have a hydroxyl group? (These are isomers of the alcohol propanol.) Any structures remaining are not alcohols and belong to a completely different class of compound. How many do you have?

FOLLOW-UP QUESTIONS

Using your new understanding of bonding and structural formulas, draw structural formulas for the following:

1. Br_2

2. HCl

3. H_2O_2

4. C_3H_6

5. Si_2H_6

6. S_2Cl_2

CONCLUSION

What is the advantage of representing molecules by means of three-dimensional models?

10A

Polar and Non-Polar Solutes and Solvents

Chemists have studied the differences between ionic and covalent compounds by investigating such characteristics as melting points and solubilities of the solids and electrical conductivities of their solutions. As a result, they discovered that ionic compounds have higher melting points than covalent compounds. They also found that solutions of ionic compounds are good conductors of electricity, whereas solutions of covalent compounds are poor conductors. Finally, they learned that ionic compounds tend to be more soluble in water, while covalent compounds tend to be more soluble in methanol. In the case of solubility, chemists also noted one obvious exception to this trend: sucrose (table sugar), a covalent compound, is highly soluble in water but only slightly soluble in methanol. From these results, it appears that not all covalent compounds are soluble in the same type of solvent.

People engaged in the drycleaning industry have learned that different stains on garments sometimes require different approaches to cleaning. A drycleaner will often ask a customer for information about a given stain and then make a cleaning decision based on that information. In many cases, the nature of the stain (solute) will determine the drycleaning solvent to be used.

Covalent compounds can be further classified as polar or non-polar. Although, as a result of the sharing of electrons between component atoms, all covalent compounds are bonded, this sharing is not necessarily an *equal* sharing of electrons. As a result, one side of a neutral molecule can end up with a net negative charge, while the other side is left with a net positive charge. (See Figure 10A-1.) It is this type of covalent compound which is said to be polar. It is more common than the non-polar type.

The classification of a covalent compound as polar or non-polar requires information about electron-sharing tendencies and molecular shapes. Since such a detailed study of compounds is beyond the scope of this experiment, you will simply be informed as to the classification of the compounds you will be using. It is important to remember that both the solute and the solvent have characteristics that can affect solubility. Therefore, in this experiment you will test the solubilities of a variety of solutes in a variety of solvents. The solutes to be tested are ionic, polar covalent, and non-polar covalent, while the solvents to be tested are polar covalent and non-polar covalent. (There are no typical ionic solvents.) In Part I, you will be doing solubility tests on known solutes and in Part II, you will be testing the solubility of unknown solutes. In Part III, you will be mixing liquids to study their solubilities.

Figure 10A-1 *A polar water molecule*

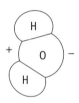

OBJECTIVES

1. to determine the type of solvent that generally dissolves ionic compounds

2. to determine the type of solvent that generally dissolves polar covalent compounds

3. to determine the type of solvent that generally dissolves non-polar covalent compounds

4. to investigate the effect of adding a polar liquid solute to a non-polar liquid solvent

SUPPLIES

Equipment
6 test tubes (13 mm × 100 mm)
6 stoppers to fit test tubes
test-tube rack
tweezers
lab apron
safety goggles

Chemical Reagents
sodium chloride (table salt) crystals
sucrose (table sugar) crystals
iodine crystals
3 unknown solid solutes
paint thinner (or varsol)
glycerin

PROCEDURE

Part I: Solubility Tests on Known Solutes

1. Put on your lab apron and safety goggles.

2. Obtain 6 clean, dry test tubes and place them in a test-tube rack so that you have two rows of test tubes with three test tubes in each row.

3. Half fill one set of three test tubes with water at room temperature and half fill the other set of three test tubes with paint thinner. Your test tubes should now form a grid that is similar to the grid in Table 1 in Experimental Results.

4. In the first pair of test tubes (one containing water, the other containing paint thinner), add enough crystals of salt with a pair of tweezers to cover the bottom of the test tubes.

5. Stopper one of these test tubes, then invert it to agitate the mixture. Turn the test tube over several times until you are convinced that no further change will take place. Carefully examine the inside of the test tube for crystals that may get trapped on the walls. Repeat this agitation process for the second test tube, then record your observations for both test tubes in your copy of Table 1 in your notebook. (Record whether or not the solute dissolves.)

6. Repeat Steps 3 and 4 with crystals of sugar in the second pair of test tubes.

7. Repeat Steps 3 and 4 with an iodine crystal in the remaining pair of test tubes. (Note: One iodine crystal gives better results than several crystals.)

8. Clean up your apparatus according to the reagent disposal instructions.

CAUTION

Paint thinner is poisonous. Wipe away any spills with paper towel.

CAUTION

Some of these unknown solutions can harm skin and clothing. Wash off spills and splashes with plenty of water. Call your instructor.

Part II: Solubility Tests on Unknown Solutes

1. Repeat Part I of this experiment, but refer to Table 2 and test the solubilities of unknown solutes A, B, and C.

Part III: Mixing Two Liquids

1. Fill a clean test tube one quarter full with water, then add twice as much paint thinner as water to the same test tube.

2. Stopper the open end of the test tube and agitate the liquids as in Part I.

3. Examine what happens to the liquids after agitation and record your observations in your copy of Table 3.

4. Add one iodine crystal to the test tube and agitate the contents. Make a labeled sketch of your test tube and its contents. Include this sketch in your observations.

5. Using a second test tube, repeat Steps 1 to 4, but use glycerin in place of paint thinner. Glycerin is also known as glycerol, or, as you will learn in organic chemistry, 1,2,3–propanetriol. It is a polar liquid.

6. Clean up all apparatus according to the reagent disposal instructions.

7. Before you leave the laboratory, wash your hands thoroughly with soap and water.

REAGENT DISPOSAL

Pour the contents of all test tubes into the container designated by your instructor. Wash out the test tubes with detergent and water, using a test tube brush if necessary. Be sure to thoroughly rinse out the detergent from the test tubes.

POST LAB CONSIDERATIONS

It is obvious from the results in Table 1 that certain types of solutes will dissolve only in certain types of solvents. Although there are exceptions to the results obtained in this experiment, you should now be able to propose a general rule for the type of solvent that will dissolve each type of solute.

©SMG Lab Books Ltd.

EXPERIMENTAL RESULTS

Part I: Solubility Tests on Known Solutes

Table 1 Known Solutes with Known Solvents

Solvents	Solutes		
	Salt (NaCl) (Ionic)	Sugar ($C_{12}H_{22}O_{11}$) (Polar Covalent)	Iodine (I_2) (Non-Polar Covalent)
Water (Polar covalent)	COMPLETE IN YOUR NOTEBOOK	COMPLETE IN YOUR NOTEBOOK	COMPLETE IN YOUR NOTEBOOK
Paint thinner (Non-polar covalent)			

Part II: Solubility Tests on Unknown Solutes

Table 2 Unknown Solutes with Known Solvents

Solvent	Solute		
	A	B	C
Water (Polar covalent)	COMPLETE IN YOUR NOTEBOOK	COMPLETE IN YOUR NOTEBOOK	COMPLETE IN YOUR NOTEBOOK
Paint thinner (Non-polar covalent)			

Part III: Mixing Two Liquids

Table 3

Combinations of Liquids	Covalent Types	Results
Water and paint thinner	COMPLETE IN YOUR NOTEBOOK	COMPLETE IN YOUR NOTEBOOK
Water and glycerin		

ANALYSIS OF RESULTS

1. **a.** What general trend appears in Table 1 with regard to which type of solute dissolves in which type of solvent?
   b. This general solubility trend is sometimes expressed as "Like dissolves like." Explain this expression.

2. Classifying the solutes:
   a. Attempt to classify each of the unknown solutes from Part II as ionic, polar covalent, or non-polar covalent.
   b. What problem do you encounter in making this classification?
   c. Explain what further tests you would perform to remove any doubts about your classification.

3. **a.** Compare the results from Part III with the general solubility trends observed in Part I.
   b. Using a reference, explain the meaning of the term "immiscible", then use this word to describe results from Part III.

4. How did the addition of iodine crystals help in identifying the layers of liquids in the water–paint thinner combination?

5. Explain how many layers you would expect to see if water, paint thinner, and glycerin were combined in one test tube.

FOLLOW-UP QUESTIONS

1. Explain which solvent from this experiment you would use to remove road salt stains from a pair of jeans.

2. Some people use gasoline (a non-polar covalent compound) to clean grease stains from clothing. Although it is an effective solvent for grease, explain why gasoline should never be used for this purpose. Suggest a suitable alternate solvent.

CONCLUSION

What general rule can be followed when choosing a type of solvent for a particular solute?

Spectrophotometric Analysis

One of the most important skills a chemist must acquire is knowing how to prepare a solution of a substance with a precise volume and molarity (concentration). In a wide variety of laboratories, including medical, teaching, research, manufacturing, and testing laboratories, solutions of known concentration are regularly required. Solutions whose concentrations are known are referred to as *standard* solutions. Another important skill is to be able to measure the unknown concentration of a solution quickly and easily.

In Part I of this experiment, you will prepare a solution of cobalt(II) nitrate hexahydrate, $Co(NO_3)_2 \bullet 6H_2O$, having a molarity of $0.160M$. In Part II, you will make several solutions of lower concentrations by making appropriate dilutions. Then in Part III, the known concentration solutions will be placed in an instrument called a spectrophotometer that will be used to determine their color intensities. Finally, you will use the spectrophotometer to analyze an unknown cobalt(II) nitrate solution in order to determine its molarity.

A spectrophotometer makes use of the fact that in any given colored solution, light of a particular frequency is absorbed. When a suitable frequency is selected, the light is passed through the solution (which should be in a special type of tube called a cuvette having walls of uniform thickness which is designed for this purpose) and detected by a photo cell. The intensity of the light is shown by a needle on a dial and can be read either as absorbance or as percent transmittance. The value of this reading depends upon the concentration of the colored material in the solution.

Your instructor may set up the spectrophotometer in advance or selected students may be asked to do it. (The instructions below refer to a Bausch and Lomb Spectronic 20® spectrophotometer. If your instrument is a different one, your instructor will advise you of any modifications to the procedure.) The procedure is as follows:

1. Turn on the instrument by the front left-hand knob. Allow it to warm up for 15 min.

2. Select an appropriate wavelength to use by rotating the dial on the top right of the instrument. In this experiment, use 510 nm.

3. With the receptacle lid closed, adjust the left-hand knob on the front of the instrument until the needle reads 0% transmittance.

4. Place a cuvette three quarters full of distilled water in the receptacle on top and close the lid. Adjust the right-hand knob on the front of the instrument until the needle reads 100% transmittance. The spectrophotometer is now ready for use.

The following are some important points to note regarding the use of this instrument:

a. Make sure the receptacle lid is always closed before taking any readings, since stray light will affect the results.

b. Don't touch any of the knobs unless specifically directed by your instructor to recheck the 0% and 100% transmittance calibration.

c. The scale may have a mirror behind it—make sure the needle and its mirror image are lined up with one another before taking the reading to ensure greater accuracy.

d. If you are using the special tubes (cuvettes) for the spectrophotometer, make sure that the lines marked on them line up with the mark on the receptacle.

Your instructor may tell you to read either of the two scales (percent transmittance or absorbance) or both. There are advantages and disadvantages to each type of reading. The percent transmittance scale is uniform and therefore easier to read, but the calibration graph produced will be a curve and a graph must be drawn in order to obtain the concentration of the unknown. The absorbance scale is more difficult to read; it increases as you go from right to left and the size of the unit changes across the scale. However, the resulting calibration graph will usually be a straight line in the range of concentrations used; therefore, the concentration of an unknown may be obtained by calculation as well as from the graph.

OBJECTIVES

1. to prepare a standard solution of known concentration of cobalt(II) nitrate

2. to prepare various dilutions of the standard solution

3. to measure the percent transmittance, or absorbance, or both, of the solutions using a spectrophotometer, and to construct a calibration graph from the data

4. to determine the concentration of an unknown cobalt(II) nitrate solution using the calibration graph

SUPPLIES

Equipment
beaker (100 mL)
centigram balance
volumetric flask (100 mL)
    or graduated cylinder
    (100 mL)
funnel
wash bottle
5 test tubes (18 mm × 150 mm)
test-tube rack

graduated cylinder (10 mL)
graduated cylinder (25 mL)
dropping pipet
spectrophotometer
5 cuvettes (use 13 mm × 100 mm
    test tubes instead if necessary)
lab apron
safety goggles

Chemical Reagents
cobalt(II) nitrate hexahydrate, $Co(NO_3)_2 \cdot 6H_2O$
solution of above substance of unknown concentration
distilled water

Part I: Preparation of a Standard Co(NO₃)₂ Solution

1. Before coming to the laboratory, calculate the mass of cobalt(II) nitrate hexahydrate $Co(NO_3)_2 \cdot 6H_2O$, needed to make 100.0 mL of a 0.160M solution. Check with other students or your instructor to make certain that you have calculated the correct mass before proceeding.

2. Put on your lab apron and safety goggles.

3. Obtain a centigram balance and measure the mass of a clean, dry 100 mL beaker. Next weigh out the precise amount of $Co(NO_3)_2 \cdot 6H_2O$ (calculated in Step 1 above) in the beaker.

4. Dissolve the compound in about 50 mL of water in the beaker.

5. Transfer the solution to a 100 mL volumetric flask by means of a funnel. Then, using a wash bottle, wash the beaker several times with small amounts of water, adding the washings to the flask. Be careful not to add so much water that you go beyond the mark. (Note: If you do not have a 100 mL volumetric flask, use a 100 mL graduated cylinder instead.)

6. Remove the funnel and add water from the wash bottle until the volume is exactly at the 100 mL mark. (Add the water drop by drop when you are close.)

7. Stopper the flask and shake to ensure thorough mixing. You now have a 0.160M Co(NO₃)₂ solution. Chemists refer to such an initially prepared solution of known molarity as a *stock solution*.

CAUTION

Cobalt(II) nitrate is toxic. Do not get any in your mouth.

Part II: Preparation of Dilute Solutions of Co(NO₃)₂

1. Obtain 5 test tubes (18 mm × 150 mm) and place them in a rack. Label them A to E.

2. In test tube A, place approximately 10 mL of your stock solution (0.160M).

3. Prepare a diluted solution by placing 12.0 mL of the stock solution in a 25 mL graduated cylinder and adding water until the solution is up to the 16.0 mL mark. Transfer this solution to test tube B.

4. Repeat Step 3 using 8.0 mL of stock solution and making it up to 16.0 mL. (If the graduated cylinder is wet from previous washings, rinse it out with about 4 mL of your stock solution first and discard the rinsing liquid.) Transfer the diluted solution to test tube C.

5. In the same manner, prepare a dilution with 4.0 mL of stock solution made up to 16.0 mL for test tube D and 2.0 mL of stock solution made up to 16.0 mL for test tube E.

6. Calculate the new molarities of the diluted solutions and enter them in your copy of Table 1 in your notebook.

Part III: Measuring the Concentration with a Spectrophotometer

1. Make sure you understand thoroughly how to use the spectrophotometer, as outlined in the introduction to this experiment.

2. Transfer solutions A to E into five cuvettes. (If cuvettes are not available, use 13 mm × 100 mm test tubes that are clean and scratch-free instead.) If the tubes are wet inside, rinse each with about 4 mL of the solution which will go into it, discard the rinsings, then fill each about three quarters full with the appropriate solution.

3. Make sure the tubes are clean and dry on the outside, place each in turn in the receptacle on top of the spectrophotometer, and then close the lid. Read off the value of either the percent transmittance or the absorbance, or both, as directed by your instructor. Enter the values in Table 1.

4. Obtain a $Co(NO_3)_2$ solution of unknown concentration from your instructor and note any identifying letter or number on it. Fill a tube three quarters full as before. Read either percent transmittance or absorbance, depending on which scale you read for your standards. Enter this value in Table 1 as well.

5. Before you leave the laboratory, wash your hands thoroughly with soap and water.

REAGENT DISPOSAL

Rinse all solutions down the sink with copious amounts of water, unless your instructor asks you to save them.

POST LAB CONSIDERATIONS

The accuracy of your answer for the concentration of the unknown molarity $Co(NO_3)_2$ solution will be a good measure of your experimental skills. It is important to have taken all your readings carefully and have double-checked them to be sure you had the correct values. Graphs must now be plotted carefully and accurately.

The spectrophotometer results from the known molarity solutions will be used to create a curved and/or straight calibration line for the $Co(NO_3)_2$ solution. Then, the unknown molarity of the given $Co(NO_3)_2$ solution can be determined from this calibration line. Your instructor may ask you to average the molarities determined from each of the two lines.

Copying the experiment is prohibited.   ©SMG Lab Books Ltd.

EXPERIMENTAL RESULTS

Table 1

Test Tube	Original Molarity	Dilution	New Molarity	Absorbance (A)	Percent Transmittance (%)
A	0.160M	—	0.160M		
B	0.160M	12 mL to 16 mL			
C	0.160M	8 mL to 16 mL	COMPLETE IN YOUR NOTEBOOK	COMPLETE IN YOUR NOTEBOOK	COMPLETE IN YOUR NOTEBOOK
D	0.160M	4 mL to 16 mL			
E	0.160M	2 mL to 16 mL			
	Unknown	—	—		

ANALYSIS OF RESULTS

1. Calculate the molarity of the Co^{2+} ion in each of solutions A–E. The new molarity is given by the molarity of the stock solution multiplied by the dilution factor (ratio of original volume to final volume).

2. Plot a graph of absorbance versus concentration using proper graphing techniques. (Substitute percent transmittance for absorbance if that is what you measured.) Your instructor may ask you to plot both graphs.

3. Determine the unknown concentration of your given solution by reading from your graph the concentration that is equivalent to the absorbance or percent transmittance you recorded. If your instructor asked you to plot both graphs, you may need to report the average of the two values. Be sure to state in your report which unknown you used if more than one was available.

FOLLOW-UP QUESTIONS

1. Why does a volumetric flask have the shape it does?

2. Looking at your results and the shape of your graph, do you think your results could have been improved by the use of graduated pipets instead of graduated cylinders?

3. Why is it a good idea to wash out the tubes with the solution you are using before refilling them to read in the spectrophotometer?

4. In order to analyze the waste water containing Co^{2+} from a manufacturing process, 1.0 L of water was evaporated to 10.0 mL and then placed in

a spectrophotometer tube. The absorbance was found to be 0.30 A (63% transmittance). Using your calibration curve, calculate the number of milligrams of Co^{2+} in 1.0 L of waste water.

CONCLUSION

State the results of Objective 4.

10C

Factors Affecting Solubility and Rate of Dissolving

Solutions are homogeneous mixtures containing a solute (the substance being dissolved) and a solvent (the substance doing the dissolving). Solutes and solvents can be any combination of solids, liquids, and gases. The most common solutions have liquid solvents. You can probably think of many solutions of this sort that you encounter regularly, such as fruit juices, soda pop, and salt water.

When a solute is dissolved by a solvent to form a solution, several characteristics of the process are of interest to chemists. One characteristic is the *rate* of dissolving, which depends upon the time required for a given amount of solute to dissolve in a given amount of solution. Another is *solubility*, a measure of the amount of solute that will dissolve in a given amount of solvent.

In Part I of this experiment, you will investigate the effect of temperature on the rate of dissolving of sodium chloride and potassium nitrate crystals in water. In Part II, you will investigate the effect of temperature on the solubilities of these substances in water.

OBJECTIVES

1. to determine the effect of temperature on rate of dissolving

2. to determine the effect of temperature on solubility

3. to determine whether a relationship exists between solubility and rate of dissolving

SUPPLIES

Equipment
6 test tubes (18 mm × 150 mm)
test-tube rack
test-tube holder
graduated cylinder (10 mL)
stopwatch or watch with second
    hand
thermometer
3 beakers (250 mL)

water-soluble marker
2 glass stirring rods
plastic spoon
hot plate
centigram balance
lab apron
safety goggles

Chemical Reagents
sodium chloride crystals (NaCl)
potassium nitrate crystals (KNO_3)
distilled water
ice cubes

PROCEDURE

Part I: Effect of Temperature on Rate of Dissolving

1. Put on your lab apron and safety goggles.

2. Use a hot plate to heat 150 mL of water in a 250 mL beaker to boiling. Set this water aside as your hot water bath. If you have a lab partner, one of you can proceed to Step 3 while the other monitors the boiling of the water.

3. Obtain one half spoonful of sodium chloride crystals and one half spoonful of potassium nitrate crystals on separate, labeled pieces of folded paper. Weigh out three 0.5 g samples of sodium chloride and three 0.5 g samples of potassium nitrate on six labeled pieces of folded paper.

4. Obtain six test tubes and label three of them A and three of them B, using a water-soluble marker. Make sure you label them near the top. Set the empty test tubes in a test-tube rack.

5. Add 10 mL of distilled water to each of the six test tubes.

6. Set up a water bath at room temperature by adding 150 mL of water to a second beaker. Set up a cold water bath by adding 150 mL of ice and water to a third beaker.

7. Set one A test tube and one B test tube in each of the three water baths. Allow these test tubes to sit in the water baths for about 3 min while you get organized for Step 8.

8. Record the temperature of the cold water bath in your copy of Table 1 in your notebook. Add a 0.5 g sample of the NaCl crystals to test tube A while it remains in the bath and start timing. Quickly cover the test tube with a thumb and immediately tilt the tube back and forth once to remove any crystals which might have stuck to the sides. Using a stirring rod, stir the contents of the test tube at a steady rate and time how long it takes the crystals to dissolve.

9. Repeat Step 8 for a 0.5 g sample of KNO_3 in test tube B.

10. Repeat Steps 8 and 9 for the other water baths. Reheat the hot water bath before use.

11. Clean up all test tubes according to the reagent disposal instructions. Save the three water baths as well as one test tube A and one test tube B for Part II of the experiment.

Part II: Effect of Temperature on Solubility

1. Readjust the temperatures of the three water baths from Part I. Reheat the hot bath and add more ice to the cold bath if necessary.

2. Obtain 3.0 g NaCl and 3.0 g of KNO_3.

3. Add 10 mL of water to a clean test tube labeled A and 10 mL of water to one labeled B.

4. Set the test tubes in the cold water bath and wait for about 3 min. Record the water temperature in your copy of Table 2 in your notebook. Put the

CAUTION

Potassium nitrate is harmful if swallowed. It is also a strong oxidizer — contact with combustible material may cause fire.

NaCl in test tube A and the KNO_3 in test tube B. Use two different, labeled stirring rods to stir each of the solutions for approximately 2 min. Record your observations in Table 2.

5. Move both test tubes to the water bath at room temperature and stir for approximately 2 min. Record your observations.

6. Repeat Step 5 for the hot water bath.

7. Add another 1.0 g of each solute to its respective test tube in the hot water bath and stir for approximately 2 min. Record these observations in Table 2.

8. Clean up all your apparatus according to the reagent disposal instructions.

9. Before leaving the laboratory, wash your hands thoroughly with soap and water.

REAGENT DISPOSAL

All solutions, as well as any remaining solid sodium chloride or potassium nitrate, may be rinsed down the sink with copious amounts of water.

POST LAB CONSIDERATIONS

A solution is considered to be saturated if it contains as much solute as can be possibly dissolved in a given amount of solvent at a given temperature. The solubility of a solid in a liquid is often expressed as the mass of solid dissolved in 100 mL of liquid to form a saturated solution.

The only factor that affects solubility is temperature. Other factors such as smaller solute particle size and stirring will cause a higher rate of dissolving, but they will not cause more solute to dissolve. Thus, solubility remains the same.

As you might expect, an increase in temperature can produce a higher rate of dissolving. However, when rates are compared between solids at different temperatures, some unexpected results are observed. One substance may dissolve faster than another at one temperature – but the reverse may be true at a different temperature. By examining your data in Table 1 and the information provided by Figure 10C-1, you can deduce a reason for this unusual phenomenon.

For the purposes of this experiment, rate of dissolving refers to the rate at which 0.5 g of solute dissolves in 10.0 mL of water at a specific temperature. Thus, rate of dissolving can be expressed as 1/time (s) or s^{-1}. For instance, if the time taken to dissolve is 40 s, the rate of dissolving is $1/40$ s $= 2.5 \times 10^{-2}$ s^{-1}.

EXPERIMENTAL RESULTS

Part I: Effect of Temperature on Rate of Dissolving
Table 1

Beaker	Temperature (°C)	Sodium Chloride		Potassium Nitrate	
		Time to Dissolve Sample (in s)	Rate of Dissolving (in s^{-1})	Time to Dissolve Sample (in s)	Rate of Dissolving (in s^{-1})
Cold					
Room Temp.	COMPLETE IN YOUR NOTEBOOK	COMPLETE IN YOUR NOTEBOOK	COMPLETE IN YOUR NOTEBOOK	COMPLETE IN YOUR NOTEBOOK	COMPLETE IN YOUR NOTEBOOK
Hot					

Part II: Effect of Temperature on Solubility
Table 2

Beaker	Temperature (°C)	Sodium Chloride	Potassium Nitrate
Cold			
Room Temp.	COMPLETE IN YOUR NOTEBOOK	COMPLETE IN YOUR NOTEBOOK	COMPLETE IN YOUR NOTEBOOK
Hot			
Hot (with more solute added)			

ANALYSIS OF RESULTS

1. For Part I, calculate the rate of dissolving for each solute at each temperature. Enter this information in Table 1 in your notebook.

2. Refer to your data in Table 1 in answering the following questions.
   a. How does temperature appear to affect the rate of dissolving?
   b. How does the rate of dissolving of KNO_3 compare to that of NaCl at the highest temperature?
   c. How do these rates compare at room temperature?
   d. How do these rates compare at the lowest temperature?

3. Refer to your data in Table 2 in answering the following questions.
   a. How does temperature appear to affect solubility?
   b. How does the solubility of KNO_3 compare to that of NaCl at the lowest temperature?

c. How do these solubilities compare at room temperature?

d. How do these solubilities compare at the highest temperature?

4. At certain temperatures, KNO_3 has a higher rate of dissolving than $NaCl$, but at other temperatures the opposite is true. Suggest a reason for this phenomenon. (If necessary, consult Figure 10C-1.)

5. Does rate of dissolving depend on temperature or on solubility? Explain your answer.

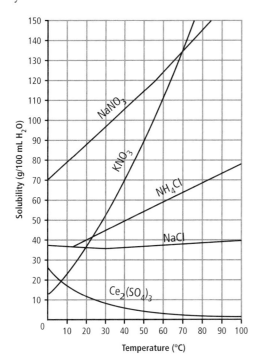

Figure 10C-1 *Each line illustrates the effect of temperature on the solubility of a different substance*

FOLLOW-UP QUESTIONS

1. a. Other than temperature, what other factors increase the rate of dissolving?

b. What effect do these additional factors have on solubility?

2. Cerium(III) sulfate, $Ce_2(SO_4)_3$, is an unusual substance in that its solubility decreases as the temperature increases. (See Figure 10C-1.) On the basis of this information and your experimental results, predict what will happen to the rate of dissolving as the temperature increases.

CONCLUSION

State the results of Objective 3.

10D Solubility Trends and Precipitate Formation

A precipitation reaction occurs when certain ions are allowed to interact in solution. The result of the interaction is that the force of attraction between a positive ion and a negative ion is so great that they join together to form a slightly soluble substance called a *precipitate*. Certain *lakes* (coloring pigments in inks and wallpapers) are produced by precipitation reactions. Chemists often analyze a precipitation reaction by writing a series of equations that enables them to understand how the precipitate resulted. A *formula equation* shows all of the compounds involved in the reaction and also identifies the precipitate that forms. For example, when solutions of lead(II) nitrate and potassium iodide are mixed, a yellow precipitate results. The initial fomula equation for the reaction would be:

$$Pb(NO_3)_2(aq) + 2KI(aq) \rightarrow 2KNO_3 + PbI_2$$

one of these products must be a solid
(the precipitate)

Further tests are required to deduce that the precipitate here is lead(II) iodide. Therefore, the final formula equation should be written as:

$$Pb(NO_3)_2(aq) + 2KI(aq) \rightarrow 2KNO_3(aq) + PbI_2(s)$$

The next equation used to analyze the reaction is a *complete ionic equation* which shows all compounds other than the precipitate in their dissociated form:

$$Pb^{2+}(aq) + 2NO_3^-(aq) + 2K^+(aq) + 2I^-(aq) \rightarrow 2K^+(aq) + 2NO_3^-(aq) + PbI_2(s)$$

A close examination of the above ionic equation reveals that K^+ ions and NO_3^- ions do not change in the reaction. Hence, they are known as *spectator ions*. When you eliminate all spectator ions from the ionic equation you are left with the *net ionic equation:*

$$Pb^{2+}(aq) + 2I^-(aq) \rightarrow PbI_2(s)$$

This net ionic equation shows only those ions which were actually involved in the reaction.

In this experiment, you will mix several solutions together; some will form precipitates and some will not. One of your tasks will be to deduce the identity of the precipitates by carefully examining all of your results. Having identified the precipitates, you will analyze the precipitation reaction by writing formula, complete ionic, and net ionic equations.

OBJECTIVES

1. to mix several pairs of solutions together and then note whether any precipitates form

2. to deduce, from the experimental results, which combinations of ions form precipitates

3. to write a balanced formula equation for each precipitation reaction

4. to write a complete ionic equation for each precipitation reaction

5. to determine and write the net ionic equation for each precipitation reaction

SUPPLIES

Equipment
6 small test tubes
   (10 mm × 75 mm)
test-tube rack
6 medicine droppers
glass square (10 cm × 10 cm)
lab apron
safety goggles

Chemical Reagents
one or more sets of 6 solutions

PROCEDURE

1. Put on your lab apron and safety goggles.

2. Obtain a sample of each solution in each of the 6 small test tubes, filling each test tube one quarter full and labeling it. Use one medicine dropper for each solution to avoid contaminating the others. Place the samples in the test-tube rack at your lab station.

3. Place a drop of one solution on the glass square and using the appropriate dropper, add a drop of second solution to it. All the drop tests can be done at one time by duplicating the patterns on Table 1. Your observations will be enhanced if you place the glass square over a dark (preferably black) surface.

4. If a precipitate forms, record this result in your copy of Table 1 in your notebook by placing "ppt" in the appropriate square, along with the color of the precipitate. If no precipitate forms, simply mark a dash (–) in the square.

5. Repeat Steps 2 and 3 until all possible combinations of solutions have been tested.

6. Follow the reagent disposal instructions, then rinse out all equipment and dry the glass square. Test another set of solutions (repeat Steps 1 to 4) if time permits.

7. Before you leave the laboratory, wash your hands thoroughly with soap and water.

CAUTION

Several of these solutions are poisonous. Wash any spills and splashes immediately with plenty of water.

Notify your instructor.

REAGENT DISPOSAL

Wash all solutions down the sink with copious amounts of water.

POST LAB CONSIDERATIONS

In each square of the data table, which shows that a precipitate forms, you will notice that there are two possible compounds that could be the precipitate. It is up to you, through a series of logical deductions based on all the data in the table, to determine the identity of the precipitate in each case.

If, for example, a precipitate was recorded in the Na^+, SO_4^{2-} / Al^{3+}, Cl^- square, then the precipitate would be either $NaCl$ or $Al_2(SO_4)_3$. Before you can conclusively choose either of these compounds, you will need to examine the possibilities in the other squares.

EXPERIMENTAL RESULTS

The table below is only a sample table. The actual solutions will depend on the set that is provided by your instructor.

Table 1

Solution	Al^{3+} Cl^-	Ba^{2+} NO_3^-	Ba^{2+} Cl^-	Sr^{2+} NO_3^-	Al^{3+} SO_4^{2-}	Na^+ SO_4^{2-}
Na^+ SO_4^{2-}						
Al^{3+} SO_4^{2-}						
Sr^{2+} NO_3^-						
Ba^{2+} Cl^-						
Ba^{2+} NO_3^-						
Al^{3+} Cl^-						

COMPLETE IN YOUR NOTEBOOK

ANALYSIS OF RESULTS

1. What observations led you to believe that precipitates formed?

2. How many precipitation reactions did you observe in total?

3. What are the formulas for the precipitates that formed? How many *different* precipitates formed?

4. Construct a table summarising your results similar to Table 2, which shows those combinations of ions that formed precipitates and those that did not.

Copying the experiment is prohibited.

Table 2

This negative ion	Plus these positive ions	Formed
e.g. S^{2-}	Na^+, Ca^{2+}	No precipitate
S^{2-}	Cu^{2+}	Precipitate

5. For each different precipitation, write the following:
   a. balanced formula equation
   b. complete ionic equation
   c. net ionic equation

FOLLOW UP QUESTIONS

1. Compare your table from Question 4 above to a table of solubilities. Describe any similarities or differences in results.

CONCLUSION

State the results of Objective 5.

10E

An Introduction to Qualitative Analysis

The term "qualitative analysis" in chemistry refers to a set of procedures used to identify a particular ion or ions in a given sample when it is not necessary to find out the quantity of any ion present. (Hence the term "qualitative" rather than "quantitative" is used.)

If the number of types of ions that could be in a sample is large, then the scheme to be followed in order to correctly identify a particular ion becomes very complex. A large number of reagents, many of which may give no result, is required. The quantities and concentrations of reagents involved are critical, since in many cases the separation of two ions depends upon relatively small differences in solubility. For these reasons a comprehensive treatment of qualitative analysis is beyond the scope of this experiment, but it is worthwhile for you to see the methods involved and to acquire enough knowledge of some reactions to enable you to identify some unknowns.

In Part I of this experiment, you will look at a scheme for identifying different metal ions belonging to Group 2 of the periodic table (the alkaline earth metals), namely magnesium, calcium, strontium, and barium ions. Then in Part II, you will look at a scheme for identifying four different anions, namely carbonate, sulfate, chloride, and iodide. In each case, after carrying out your reactions, you will be given at least one unknown containing one ion to be identified.

OBJECTIVES

1. to carry out tests on the ions Mg^{2+}, Ca^{2+}, Sr^{2+}, and Ba^{2+} that enable each to be identified separately and to use these tests to identify an unknown

2. to carry out tests on the ions SO_4^{2-}, CO_3^{2-}, Cl^-, and I^- that enable each to be identified separately and to use these tests to identify an unknown

SUPPLIES

Equipment
10 test tubes (13 mm × 100 mm)
test-tube rack
lab apron
safety goggles

Chemical Reagents

0.1M Mg(NO$_3$)$_2$

0.1M Ca(NO$_3$)$_2$

0.1M Sr(NO$_3$)$_2$

0.1M Ba(NO$_3$)$_2$

0.02M K$_2$CrO$_4$

0.1M (NH$_4$)$_2$C$_2$O$_4$

0.1M Na$_2$SO$_4$

0.1M NaOH

0.1M Na$_2$CO$_3$

0.1M NaCl

0.1M NaI

0.1M AgNO$_3$

1M HNO$_3$

6M NH$_3$

solution containing an unknown cation

solution containing an unknown anion

PROCEDURE

Part I: Qualitative Analysis of Group 2 Elements

1. Put on your lab apron and safety goggles.

2. Place 2 mL of each of 0.1M Mg(NO$_3$)$_2$, Ca(NO$_3$)$_2$, Sr(NO$_3$)$_2$, and Ba(NO$_3$)$_2$ respectively in four 13 mm × 100 mm test tubes.

3. To each tube, add 2 mL of 0.02M K$_2$CrO$_4$ and observe in which tubes a precipitate occurs. Note also the amount of precipitate as light or heavy, and whether it formed immediately or after a short time had elapsed. Record your observations in your copy of Table 1 in your notebook.

4. Repeat Steps 2 and 3, using 2 mL of 0.1M (NH$_4$)$_2$C$_2$O$_4$ as the added reagent. Record your observations in Table 1.

5. Repeat Steps 2 and 3, using 2 mL of 0.1M Na$_2$SO$_4$ as the added reagent. Again, record what you observe.

6. Repeat Steps 2 and 3, using 2 mL of 0.1M NaOH as the added reagent. Record your observations.

7. Obtain an unknown solution containing only one cation and carry out separate reactions on 2 mL of the sample with 2 mL of each of the four reagents. Identify the cation from your results.

Part II: Qualitative Analysis of Selected Anions

1. Place 2 mL of 0.1M Na$_2$CO$_3$, Na$_2$SO$_4$, NaCl, and NaI respectively in four 13 mm × 100 mm test tubes.

2. To each tube, add 2 mL of 1M HNO$_3$. Observe the results and record them in your copy of Table 2.

3. Repeat Step 1, then add to each tube 2 mL of 0.1M Ba(NO$_3$)$_2$ and note and record in which tubes a precipitate was formed.

4. To the tubes containing precipitates, add 1 mL of 1M HNO$_3$. Observe and record the results.

5. Repeat Step 1, then add to each test tube 2 mL of 0.1M AgNO$_3$. Note in which test tubes a precipitate results and record your results in Table 2.

6. Divide the contents of each test tube containing a precipitate in half, placing each half in a separate test tube.

CAUTION

Barium compounds are poisonous. Do not get any in your mouth, do not swallow any.

Chromates are poisonous and are skin irritants. Do not get any in your mouth, do not swallow any. Wash away any spills and splashes with plenty of water.

Oxalates are poisonous. Do not get any in your mouth, do not swallow any.

CAUTION

Nitric acid is corrosive to skin and clothing. Wash away any spills and splashes with plenty of water.

7. To one set of precipitates add 1 mL of 1M HNO$_3$. Observe the results and record them in Table 2.

8. To the other set of precipitates add 1 mL of 6M NH$_3$, observe, and record the results.

9. Obtain a sample containing a single unknown anion. Carry out each test that you used for the known anions and observe the results. Identify the anion from your results.

10. Wash your hands thoroughly with soap and water before leaving the laboratory.

REAGENT DISPOSAL

Test tubes containing silver compounds, barium compounds, and chromates should be emptied into the designated waste containers. All other waste material may be safely rinsed down the sink with copious amounts of water.

POST LAB CONSIDERATIONS

The reactions in Part I are all straight forward precipitation reactions. It is important to observe how much precipitate formed and whether it formed immediately or took somewhat longer to become evident. In some cases these differences are needed to make a definite identification of an unknown.

An important part of the procedure for Part II is adding HNO$_3$ to see whether the precipitate formed will dissolve in acid. It is quite easy to distinguish between two ions when both give a precipitate with the same reagent, but one dissolves in acid and the other does not.

The 6M NH$_3$ is used to help identify precipitates formed with Ag$^+$. Some of these precipitates can dissolve as a result of the formation of the silver diammine ion, Ag(NH$_3$)$_2$$^+$. This reaction with NH$_3$ aids in their identification.

EXPERIMENTAL RESULTS

Part I: Qualitative Analysis of Group 2 Elements

Table 1

Reagents	0.1M Solutions of Group 2 Cations (As Nitrates)				
	Mg^{2+}	Ca^{2+}	Sr^{2+}	Ba^{2+}	Unknown #____
0.02M K$_2$CrO$_4$					
0.1M (NH$_4$)$_2$C$_2$O$_4$	COMPLETE IN YOUR NOTEBOOK	COMPLETE IN YOUR NOTEBOOK	COMPLETE IN YOUR NOTEBOOK	COMPLETE IN YOUR NOTEBOOK	COMPLETE IN YOUR NOTEBOOK
0.1M Na$_2$SO$_4$					
0.1M NaOH					

Part II: Qualitative Analysis of Selected Anions

Table 2

Reagents	0.1M Solutions of Anions (As Na Salts)				
	CO_3^{2-}	SO_4^{2-}	Cl^-	I^-	Unknown #___
1M HNO_3					
0.1M $Ba(NO_3)_2$					
1M HNO_3 added to precipitates	COMPLETE IN YOUR NOTEBOOK	COMPLETE IN YOUR NOTEBOOK	COMPLETE IN YOUR NOTEBOOK	COMPLETE IN YOUR NOTEBOOK	COMPLETE IN YOUR NOTEBOOK
0.1M $AgNO_3$					
1M HNO_3 added precipitates from $AgNO_3$					
6M NH_3 added to precipitates from $AgNO_3$					

ANALYSIS OF RESULTS

Part I: Qualitative Analysis of Group 2 Elements

1. Write net ionic equations for each combination in which a precipitate occurred.

2. State the identity of your unknown (along with its sample number). Give the reasoning you used to arrive at your conclusion.

Part II: Qualitative Analysis of Selected Anions

1. Write net ionic equations for each combination in which a precipitate formed or another reaction occurred with the addition of the first reagent.

2. Write net ionic equations for each situation in which the precipitate redissolved on the addition of HNO_3 or NH_3.

3. State the identity of your unknown (along with its sample number). Give the reasoning you used to arrive at your conclusion.

FOLLOW-UP QUESTIONS

1. Devise a sequence of reactions to follow (using filtering or centrifuging where necessary to remove precipitates) to identify an unknown containing two or more cations of Group 2 elements. If requested by your instructor, test this on an unknown solution containing two cations.

2. Devise a sequence of reactions to follow (using filtering or centrifuging where necessary to remove precipitates) to identify an unknown consisting of two or more of the anions tested in Part II. If requested by your instructor, test this on an unknown solution containing two anions.

3. Why are the reagents used to test for cations usually alkali metal salts or ammonium salts rather than salts of other metals?

4. Why are the reagents used to test for anions usually a nitrate of the cation that is reacting rather than other salts of that cation?

5. For fast and accurate identification of substances, major research or testing laboratories now use very sophisticated (and expensive!) equipment. Find out from a reference source the name of one of the instruments now used for analysis and briefly describe its method of operation. Be sure to note the reference you used to answer this question.

CONCLUSION

State in general terms the principles involved in developing a qualitative analysis scheme.

Factors That Affect Reaction Rates

For a given set of conditions, every chemical reaction occurs at a characteristic rate. Chemical engineers are often interested in discovering ways to increase the rates of slow reactions, particularly when they are important to industrial processes. In industry, the general goal is to produce a top-quality material as quickly, efficiently, and cheaply as possible under the constraints of environmental and safety considerations. The rate of a reaction is always expressed as the change in some measured quantity of the reactant (or product) used up (or produced) per unit of time. Some quantities suitable for such studies may be mass, concentration, or color. However, sometimes all that is required is a qualitative result, observing that one reaction is faster than another by noting which one occurs in a shorter time.

The rate of a chemical reaction is determined by a number of factors. Some reactions will take place very slowly under almost any conditions, while others are always extremely rapid. For most reactions, the rates can be affected by changing the conditions under which the reaction takes place.

In this experiment, you will examine the effects of five different factors on the rates of a variety of chemical reactions. Therefore, this experiment is divided into five parts. Each part varies only one condition: concentration of one reactant (Part I), temperature (Part II), surface area of one reactant (Part III), nature of reactants (Part IV), or presence of a catalyst (Part V). Each of these factors will have an effect on the reaction rate, which you will measure.

In Parts I and II of this experiment, magnesium metal will be reacted with hydrochloric acid. The products of this reaction are magnesium chloride and hydrogen gas. Since there is an excess of hydrochloric acid, the magnesium metal will be completely used up. If the time taken for the magnesium to react completely is measured, the rate can be calculated from the result. The factors studied for this reaction are concentration and temperature.

In Part III, you will add hydrochloric acid to two different forms of calcium carbonate, marble chips, and powdered calcium carbonate. In Part IV, you will observe how the nature of the reactants can affect the rate by reacting two different substances with the same chemical reagents. Finally, in Part V, you will observe the effect of adding a catalyst on the rate of a reaction.

OBJECTIVES

1. to observe and record the effect of reactant concentration on the rate of a reaction

2. to observe and record the effect of reactant temperature on the rate of a reaction

3. to observe and record the effect of reactant surface area on the rate of a reaction

4. to observe and record the effect of the nature of the reactants on the rate of a reaction

5. to observe and record the effect of the presence of a catalyst on the rate of a reaction

SUPPLIES

Equipment
4 beakers (250 mL)
4 test tubes (18 mm × 150 mm)
centigram balance
test-tube rack
graduated cylinder (25 mL)
Erlenmeyer flask (250 mL)
stirring rod
stopwatch or watch with second
   hand
thermometer
kettle or hot plate
ice
scissors
metric ruler
lab apron
safety goggles

Chemical Reagents
0.5M, 1.0M, 3.0M, and 6.0M HCl
magnesium ribbon
$CaCO_3$ chips (marble chips)
$CaCO_3$ powder
0.02M $KMnO_4$
0.1M $FeSO_4$ (freshly prepared)
0.1M $Na_2C_2O_4$
0.1M $MnSO_4$
3M H_2SO_4

PROCEDURE

CAUTION

The hydrochloric acid solutions are corrosive to skin, eyes, and clothing. Wash any spills and splashes with plenty of water. Call your instructor.

Part I: Effect of Concentration on Reaction Rate

1. Put on your lab apron and safety goggles.

2. Obtain 8 cm of magnesium ribbon from your instructor and record the given mass of 1.000 m of the ribbon in your copy of Table 1 in your notebook.

3. Cut the magnesium into 8 strips exactly 1.00 cm long. (Save 4 of them for Part II.)

4. Label four test tubes with the appropriate concentration of hydrochloric acid to be added (0.5M, 1.0M, 3.0M, and 6.0M).

5. Using a graduated cylinder, measure 10 mL of each of the concentrations of acid and place in the appropriate test tube.

6. For each of the four concentrations of HCl, place a 1 cm piece of magnesium in the test tube containing the acid. Start timing as soon as the magnesium comes into contact with the acid. In each case record the time, in seconds, it takes for all of the magnesium to react in your copy of Table 1. Do not calculate Reaction Rate in Table 1 until you perform the Analysis of Results when directed to do so by your instructor.

Part II: Effect of Temperature on Reaction Rate

1. Obtain four 250 mL beakers and make four 150 mL water baths of approximately 100°C, 50°C, 20°C, and 0°C. Use boiling water directly from a kettle or a hotplate for the first one and a mixture of boiling and room temperature water to obtain approximately 50°C in the second beaker. For the third, use room temperature water and for the fourth, add ice to room temperature water until the temperature is 0°C.

2. Place 10 mL of 1.0M hydrochloric acid into each of four test tubes. Place one test tube in each beaker and wait 3–4 min to allow the acid to reach the temperature of the water in each beaker.

3. Measure the temperature of the acid in the first test tube and record this value in Table 2. Then place a 1 cm piece of magnesium in the acid and record the amount of time necessary for the reaction to go to completion. Repeat for the other three temperatures. Again, do not calculate Reaction Rate in Table 2 until you perform the Analysis of Results.

Part III: Effect of Surface Area on Reaction Rate

1. Determine the exact mass of a $CaCO_3$ chip (marble chip) and transfer it to a 250 mL Erlenmeyer flask.

2. Using a watch or clock that shows seconds, note the time as you add 15 mL of 3M HCl to the flask.

3. Again note the time when the reaction mixture stops bubbling and the marble chip has dissolved. If there is still a portion of the chip left after 5 min, stop the reaction by pouring off the acid, rinsing the marble chip with water, and setting it aside to dry on a paper towel. Weigh it before you leave the laboratory. Record your results in your copy of Table 3.

4. Using a piece of weighing paper, determine the exact mass of about 0.75 g – 1.00 g of powdered calcium carbonate, $CaCO_3$, and transfer it to a 250 mL Erlenmeyer flask.

5. Using a watch or clock that shows seconds, note the time as you add 15 mL of 3M HCl to the flask.

6. Again note the time when the reaction mixture stops bubbling and the powdered $CaCO_3$ has dissolved. Record the elapsed time in your copy of Table 3.

7. Do not calculate Reaction Rate in Table 3 until you perform the Analysis of Results.

Part IV: Effect of the Nature of the Reactants on Reaction Rate

1. Place 3 mL of freshly prepared 0.1M $FeSO_4$ in a 13 mm × 100 mm test tube. Add 1 mL of 3M H_2SO_4, then add 5 drops of 0.02M $KMnO_4$, shaking after each drop by tapping the test tube.

2. Place 3 mL of 0.1M $Na_2C_2O_4$ in a 13 mm × 100 mm test tube. Add 1 mL of 3M H_2SO_4 and 5 drops of 0.02M $KMnO_4$, shaking after each drop by tapping the test tube.

CAUTION

Your thermometer is made of glass and breaks easily, leaving sharp edges that cut. Handle your thermometer gently. If your thermometer breaks, call your instructor. If it contains mercury, be aware that mercury liquid and vapor are very poisonous.

CAUTION

Sulfuric acid (H_2SO_4) is very corrosive. Do not get any on your skin, in your eyes, or on your clothing. Wash any spills or splashes with plenty of water, and call your instructor.

3. Compare the lengths of time taken for the purple color to disappear in each test tube. (If one or both do not react immediately, leave them in the rack and go on to Part V while you wait for the reaction to be completed.) Record your results in Table 4.

Part V: Effect of a Catalyst on Reaction Rate

1. In this part, you will be studying the same reaction as in Part IV, Step 2, but you will be using a catalyst. To each of two 13 mm × 100 mm test tubes, add 3 mL of 0.1M Na$_2$C$_2$O$_4$ and 1 mL of 3M H$_2$SO$_4$.

2. To only one of the test tubes, add 3 drops of 0.1M MnSO$_4$ as a catalyst.

3. Then to both tubes, add 5 drops of 0.02M KMnO$_4$.

4. Measure the time taken to reach a colorless solution in each case and record these times in Table 5. Do not calculate Reaction Rate in Table 5 until you perform the Analysis of Results.

5. Clean up and put away all materials, following the instructions for reagent disposal.

6. Before leaving the laboratory, wash your hands thoroughly with soap and water.

REAGENT DISPOSAL

Return any unused magnesium metal to the designated container. HCl solutions left in the test tubes after the reaction has finished (in Parts I and II) should be returned to another designated container for neutralization before being discarded down the sink. All other solutions may be washed down the sink with plenty of water. Left over marble chips can be disposed of in the garbage.

POST LAB CONSIDERATIONS

A chemical reaction occurs when the reacting particles have an effective collision that results in the formation of new particles. A simple collision is not enough — there also has to be sufficient energy involved in the collision for it to become effective and cause a reaction to occur. If the number of effective collisions can be controlled, then the rate of the reaction can be controlled. Some of the ways that can be used to change the number of collisions include changing the concentrations of the reactants or changing the surface area of the reactants. Temperature changes affect the speed of the molecules, and therefore the energy they contain. The higher the temperature, the higher the average kinetic energy. As a result, the temperature determines how effective a collision will be.

The effect of surface area can only be seen if the reaction is heterogeneous, that is, the reactants are in more than one phase. Examples would include a solid reacting with a solution (as in this case) or a liquid reacting with a gas.

A general statement that can be made concerning the comparison between the rates of different chemical reactions is that in most cases, reactions that require the breaking of covalent bonds are slower than ones which only involve electron transfer or occur as a result of electrostatic attraction between ions. The interpretation of the results of Part IV will be aided with a knowledge of what actual reactions are occurring. The reactions in Part IV are given by the net ionic equations:

$$5Fe^{2+}(aq) + MnO_4^-(aq) + 8H^+ \rightarrow 5Fe^{3+}(aq) + Mn^{2+}(aq) + 4H_2O(l)$$

$$\text{and } 2MnO_4^-(aq) + 5C_2O_4^{2-}(aq) + 16H^+(aq) \rightarrow 10CO_2(g) + 2Mn^{2+}(aq) + 8H_2O(l)$$

The second equation is also used in Part V in which Mn^{2+} is added as a catalyst. A catalyst speeds up a reaction by lowering the amount of energy required by the molecules in order to have an effective collision.

EXPERIMENTAL RESULTS

Part I: Effect of Concentration on Reaction Rate
Table 1

Mass of 1.00 m of Mg = g		Mass of 1.00 cm of Mg = g	
Concentration of HCl	Reaction Time (s)		Reaction Rate (g Mg/s)
0.5M			
1.0M	COMPLETE IN YOUR NOTEBOOK		COMPLETE IN YOUR NOTEBOOK
3.0M			
6.0M			

Part II: Effect of Temperature on Reaction Rate
Table 2

Temperature	Reaction Time (s)	Reaction Rate (g Mg/s)
Boiling = °C		
Hot Water = °C	COMPLETE IN YOUR NOTEBOOK	COMPLETE IN YOUR NOTEBOOK
Room Temp. = °C		
Ice Water = °C		

Part III: Effect of Surface Area on Reaction Rate
Table 3

Reactant	Mass CaCO$_3$ Reacted (g)	Reaction Time (s)	Reaction Rate (g CaCO$_3$/s)
CaCO$_3$ (marble) chip	COMPLETE IN YOUR NOTEBOOK	COMPLETE IN YOUR NOTEBOOK	COMPLETE IN YOUR NOTEBOOK
Powdered CaCO$_3$			

Part IV: Effect of the Nature of the Reactants on Reaction Rate
Table 4

Reactants	Reaction Time (s)	Reaction Rate (s^{-1})
Fe^{2+} + MnO$_4^-$ + H$^+$	COMPLETE IN YOUR NOTEBOOK	COMPLETE IN YOUR NOTEBOOK
C$_2$O$_4^{2-}$ + MnO$_4^-$ + H$^+$		

Part V: Effect of a Catalyst on Reaction Rate
Table 5

	Reaction Time (s)	Reaction Rate (s^{-1})
With Mn^{2+} Catalyst	COMPLETE IN YOUR NOTEBOOK	COMPLETE IN YOUR NOTEBOOK
Without Mn^{2+} Catalyst		

ANALYSIS OF RESULTS

Part I: Effect of Concentration on Reaction Rate

1. Calculate the average reaction rate in each case by determining the grams of magnesium used per second and record in Table 1.

2. On a sheet of graph paper, graph the reaction rate vs. concentration of HCl results from Part I.

3. Look at your results from Part I. Does doubling the concentration of hydrochloric acid double the reaction rate? Explain your answer in terms of collision theory.

4. Use your graph to predict the reaction rate and then calculate the reaction time for a 1 cm magnesium strip in 4.5M HCl solution, under the same conditions as used in Part I.

Part II: Effect of Temperature on Reaction Rate

1. Calculate the average reaction rate in each case by determining the grams of magnesium used per second and record in Table 2.

2. On another sheet of graph paper, graph the reaction rate vs. temperature results from Part II. Look at your results. Which reaction's rate was the fastest? Explain your answer in terms of collision theory.

3. Use your graph to predict the reaction rate and then calculate the reaction time for a 1 cm magnesium strip in $1.0M$ HCl solution, at a temperature of 75°C.

Part III: Effect of Surface Area on Reaction Rate

1. Calculate the average rate of reaction in each case from the mass of the $CaCO_3$ reacted divided by the time elapsed in seconds and record in Table 3. (Note that if not all the marble chip dissolved after 5 min, use the loss of mass of the chip divided by the 300 s elapsed.)

2. Look at your results from Part III. Which reaction had the slowest rate? Explain why, using collision theory.

Part IV: Effect of the Nature of the Reactants on Reaction Rate

1. Determine the rate for each reaction by taking the reciprocal of the time in s. Which reaction occurred at a faster rate?

2. Explain the reason for this result by comparing what is involved in changing Fe^{2+} to Fe^{3+} to what is involved in changing $C_2O_4^{2-}$ to $2CO_2$.

Part V: Effect of a Catalyst on Reaction Rate

1. In each reaction in this part, the $KMnO_4$ was the limiting reagent and the same amount was used each time. Determine the reaction rate therefore by simply taking the reciprocal of the time in seconds in each case and record the results in Table 5.

2. By what factor did the rate increase when a catalyst was used?

FOLLOW-UP QUESTIONS

1. Based on your results in Parts I, II, and III, which of the following sets of conditions do you expect to result in the fastest reaction?
   a. powdered $CaCO_3$, $2.0M$ HCl, and 50°C
   b. $CaCO_3$ chip, $6.0M$ HCl, and 25°C
   c. powdered $CaCO_3$, $6.0M$ HCl, and 50°C
   d. $CaCO_3$ chip, $2.0M$ HCl, and 50°C

2. Explain why you will be more successful in lighting a fire made from kindling wood than in lighting a log directly.

3. Explain why blowing on a smoldering fire may make it burn better.

4. Look up the meaning of the term "autocatalysis" in a reference source. Explain why this term would apply to the catalyzed reaction you studied in Part V.

5. Enzymes are catalysts made of protein, which are necessary for almost every reaction occurring in living cells. Find out why the rate of enzyme-catalyzed reactions increase with increasing temperature only up to about 37°C (body temperature), then decrease above that temperature.

CONCLUSION

State the results of Objectives 1, 2, 3, 4, and 5.

The Iodine Clock Reaction

It is very important for a chemist to understand the conditions that affect the rate of a chemical reaction. In chemical manufacturing processes, controlling the rate of a given reaction can make all the difference between an economical process and an uneconomical one.

In the previous experiment (11A) you investigated the principle that the rate of a reaction is determined by several factors, namely: concentration of reactants, temperature, surface area of reactants (for a heterogeneous reaction), nature of reactants, and the presence of a catalyst. In this experiment, you will carry out a different reaction, but you will again investigate the effect of the concentration of reactants (in Part I) and the temperature (in Part II) on the reaction rate.

This experiment involves a reaction that is sometimes called an *iodine clock* reaction. There are a number of different combinations of chemicals that give a reaction of this type. What happens, essentially, is that there are two different reactions: one in which iodine is produced (a slow reaction) and one in which the iodine produced in the first reaction is used up (a fast reaction). By carefully controlling the quantities of reactants, you can obtain a situation in which the reactant in the second reaction is used up first, allowing iodine to form at that point. At very low concentrations the iodine then combines with starch to suddenly give a deep blue-black color, at a time determined by the conditions used. Hence the term "iodine clock". The time elapsed from when the solutions were first mixed together until the point when the blue-black color appears is measured, and from this time measurement the rate of the reaction can be determined. You will alter the conditions of concentrations of reactants in Part I and temperature in Part II in order to determine their effect on reaction rate.

OBJECTIVES

1. to observe and record the effect of changing the concentration of a reactant on the rate of a reaction

2. to observe and record the effect of changing the temperature of a system on the rate of a reaction

SUPPLIES

Equipment

test-tube rack

2 beakers (100 mL)

2 graduated cylinders (10 mL)

8 test tubes (18 mm × 150 mm)

2 dropping pipets

thermometer

ice

4 beakers (250 mL)

electric kettle or hot plate

lab apron

safety goggles

stopwatch or other timing device

Chemical Reagents

Solution A: 0.020M KIO$_3$ (potassium iodate)

Solution B: 0.0020M NaHSO$_3$ (sodium bisulfite)

(also containing 4 g of starch and 12 mL of 1M H$_2$SO$_4$/L)

PROCEDURE

Part I: Effect of Concentration

1. Put on your lab apron and safety goggles.

2. Obtain in separate 100 mL beakers about 60 mL of Solution A (0.020M KIO$_3$) and 90 mL of Solution B (0.0020M NaHSO$_3$ containing H$_2$SO$_4$ and starch) and label the beakers.

3. In a 10 mL graduated cylinder place 10.0 mL of Solution A, using a dropping pipet, to obtain the volume as accurately as possible. Transfer the solution to an 18 mm × 150 mm test tube in a rack.

4. In the same manner measure out 10 mL of Solution B and transfer it to another test tube. Use a different graduated cylinder and dropping pipet than for Solution A and keep the same ones for each solution for subsequent parts of the procedure.

5. In order to measure the time needed for the reaction to occur you will need a watch or clock with a sweep second hand, or preferably a digital watch with a stopwatch function. One partner must record the time, while the other partner mixes the solutions. Mix the solutions in one of the two test tubes and record the time from the instant they first mix.

6. Very quickly pour the solution back and forth between the two test tubes three times to make sure they are thoroughly mixed, then wait for the completion of the reaction.

7. Record the time at the instant the deep blue-black color first appears.

8. In order to study the effect of changing the concentration of Solution A, half the class will be assigned the values 9.0 mL, 7.0 mL, 5.0 mL, and 3.0 mL, and the other half the values 8.0 mL, 6.0 mL, 4.0 mL, and 2.0 mL. In each instance, measure out the volume in the graduated cylinder and add enough water to make it up to the 10.0 mL mark. Then transfer each dilution of Solution A to a test tube and mix it with 10.0 mL of Solution B as before. For each, record the time taken for the color to appear in your copy of Table 1 in your notebook.

9. Record your results on the board in order to get class averages.

Part II: Effect of Temperature

1. In this part of the procedure you will keep the concentration constant and vary the temperature, both above and below room temperature. In order that the reaction times lie in a suitable range, Solution A will be at only half the concentration of the original solution.

2. Make up 2 sets of each of solutions of A and B, with 5.0 mL of Solution A and 5.0 mL of water in one set of four test tubes and 10.0 mL of Solution B in the other 4 test tubes.

3. Make 4 water baths (in 250 mL beakers) at temperatures of 5°C, 15°C, 25°C, and 35°C, or 10°C, 20°C, 30°C, and 40°C, depending on which set of temperatures your instructor assigns you. Use ice to obtain the temperatures below room temperature and hot water from a tap, kettle, or beaker on a hot plate to obtain the temperatures above room temperature. The beakers should be about two-thirds full, so that the solutions in the test tubes are well beneath the level of the water in the baths.

4. Place one test tube containing diluted Solution A and another containing Solution B in each water bath and leave them for 10 min to allow them to adjust to the temperature required.

5. Try to maintain the temperatures in the water baths within 0.5°C of the temperatures assigned by adding ice or hot water as required. This will make comparisons with other groups in the class more meaningful.

6. When the temperatures are at the correct value and the tubes have been in for enough time, mix each pair of solutions into one test tube and then pour back and forth three times. Then place the test tube back in the water bath. In Table 2, record the time elapsed from the instant the solutions are mixed to the instant the blue-black color first appears. Do this for each pair of solutions at each temperature.

7. Record your results on the board in order to get class averages.

8. Before leaving the laboratory, wash your hands thoroughly with soap and water.

CAUTION

Your thermometer is made of glass and breaks easily, leaving sharp edges that cut. Handle your thermometer gently. If your thermometer breaks, call your instructor. If it contains mercury, be aware that mercury liquid and vapor are very poisonous.

REAGENT DISPOSAL

All solutions remaining after each reaction may be safely rinsed down the sink with plenty of water. Your instructor will tell you what to do with the left over original solutions.

POST LAB CONSIDERATIONS

The blue-black color observed in Parts I and II occurs as a result of two separate reactions. Initially, the iodate ion, IO_3^-, reacts with the bisulfite ion, HSO_3^-, giving iodide ion, I^-, and sulfate ion, SO_4^{2-}, as follows:

$$IO_3^-(aq) + 3HSO_3^-(aq) \rightarrow I^-(aq) + 3SO_4^{2-}(aq) + 3H^+(aq)$$

The bisulfite ions are present in lower concentration and are therefore used up first. When this happens, the IO_3^- ions then react with I^- ions in the presence of H^+ ions to give molecular iodine, I_2:

$$IO_3^-(aq) + 5I^-(aq) + 6H^+(aq) \rightarrow 3I_2(aq) + 3H_2O(l)$$

In the presence of starch, iodine forms the intense blue-black color as a result of the iodine molecules being trapped in the long starch molecules. The appearance of this color indicates that the first reaction is complete and the second one has begun to take place.

The uncertainty in measuring the time taken for the reaction could easily be ±2 s unless you are very careful. Thus, the interpretation of results will be more meaningful if the class averages at a particular concentration are considered. Measuring the time taken for a reaction to be completed is not the same as measuring its rate, but there is an inverse relationship between them: rate is proportional to the reciprocal of time. Consequently, in interpreting the results you will calculate the rate in terms of reciprocal seconds (s^{-1}) and plot graphs of the rate against concentration or temperature.

EXPERIMENTAL RESULTS

Part I: Effect of Concentration

Table 1

Volume of KIO_3 (mL)	10.0	9.0	7.0	5.0	3.0
Time for reaction (s)		COMPLETE IN YOUR NOTEBOOK			

(If you were assigned the other values of 8.0, 6.0, 4.0, and 2.0, use these instead.)

Part II: Effect of Temperature

Table 2

Temperature (°C)	5.0	15.0	25.0	35.0
Time for reaction (s)		COMPLETE IN YOUR NOTEBOOK		

(If you were assigned the other values of 10.0°C, 20.0°C, 30.0°C, 40.0°C, use these instead.)

ANALYSIS OF RESULTS

Part I: Effect of Concentration

1. Calculate the concentration of KIO_3 in the final mixture for each of your dilutions. Remember that the original $[KIO_3]$ was $0.020M$ and that the original dilution, when mixed with 10 mL of Solution B, gave a total volume of 20 mL in each case.

2. Calculate the rate of reaction (in s^{-1}) for each case by taking the reciprocal of the time elapsed.

3. Plot a graph of your results, with rate plotted against $[KIO_3]$.

4. Repeat these calculations with the class averages and plot your results on the same sheet of graph paper as for Analysis 3. Remember to label your results and the class averages.

5. Considering any uncertainty in time for the reaction, what type of graph results?

6. Referring to the collision theory of reaction rates, state why you would expect the change of rate with change in concentration that you observed.

Part II: Effect of Temperature

1. Calculate the rate of reaction at each temperature (in s^{-1}) by taking the reciprocal of the time elapsed.

2. Calculate the factor by which the rate changed for each 10°C interval in temperature.

3. Plot a graph of your results, with rate plotted against temperature.

4. Repeat these calculations with the class averages, and plot your results on the same sheet of graph paper as for Analysis 3.

5. Referring to the collision theory of reaction rates, state why you would expect the change of rate with temperature that you observed.

FOLLOW-UP QUESTIONS

1. Different versions of the iodine clock reaction use different chemicals from those used here. From a reference source, find one other combination of chemicals that gives a reaction such as this one, in which iodine is suddenly formed after a certain time lapse. Be sure to quote the reference that you used.

CONCLUSION

State how the rate of a reaction is affected by (a) altering the concentration of reactants and (b) altering the temperature.

11C

Measuring Reaction Rate Using Volume of Gas Produced

The previous two experiments (11A and 11B) demonstrated the effect of various factors on the rate of a chemical reaction. In these experiments, the time required to complete the reaction was measured and a reaction rate was calculated from that quantity. In addition to finding the time required for a reaction to go to completion, chemists frequently need to know what the rate is at different times during a reaction, in order to monitor how the reaction is proceeding. This information is obtainable in a variety of ways. For instance, if a gas is produced in a closed container, then continuous monitoring of the pressure indicates the rate. If a color is produced or used up, monitoring of the color intensity with a spectrophotometer indicates the rate. If a gas is produced and allowed to escape from the system, the decrease in mass over various time intervals shows how the reaction is progressing. This latter method can easily be demonstrated with an electronic balance. When a flask containing hydrochloric acid is placed on the pan of an electronic balance and marble chips are dropped in, the decrease in mass with time gives a measure of the rate at which CO_2 is produced. Yet another method of monitoring the rate of a reaction involving gases is to measure the volume of gas produced by displacing water from a eudiometer (gas measuring tube). It is this latter method that will be used in this experiment.

Ordinary household bleach is an aqueous solution of sodium hypochlorite, NaClO, containing a little more than 5% NaClO by mass. The bleaching action is caused by the hypochlorite ion, ClO^-. Under normal circumstances the hypochlorite ion breaks down slowly to give oxygen gas and the chloride ion, Cl^-.

$$2ClO^-(aq) \rightarrow 2Cl^-(aq) + O_2(g)$$

To speed this reaction to a measurable rate a catalyst is required. In this experiment, the catalyst is provided by the addition of cobalt(II) nitrate solution to the bleach. A black precipitate of cobalt(III) oxide forms and acts as the catalyst for the decomposition of ClO^-. The volume of oxygen produced is measured at 30 s intervals by displacing water from a eudiometer. From the results, you can plot a graph of gas volume produced versus time and calculate the average rate of oxygen evolution in millilitres per minute. The experiment is repeated at other temperatures and concentrations of ClO^- and the effect of these changes on the rate is observed.

OBJECTIVES

1. to measure the volume of a gas produced from a reaction mixture at regular time intervals during the reaction

2. to interpret the results and obtain the overall rate of reaction

3. to observe how the rate changes at different temperatures and concentrations

---

SUPPLIES

Equipment

Erlenmeyer flask (250 mL)
one-hole rubber stopper (#6) with
    5 cm of glass tubing inserted
rubber tubing
eudiometer (50 mL)
buret stand and clamp
graduated cylinder (25 mL)
graduated cylinder (10 mL)

pneumatic trough
thermometer
source of hot water (tap or kettle)
ice
large beaker or other container
    for water bath
lab apron
safety goggles

Chemical Reagents

5.25% sodium hypochlorite solution (household bleach, fresh, no added
    detergent in it)
0.10M cobalt(II) nitrate, $Co(NO_3)_2$

PROCEDURE

1. Put on your lab apron and safety goggles.

2. Refer to Figure 11C-1 to help with understanding how to set up the apparatus.

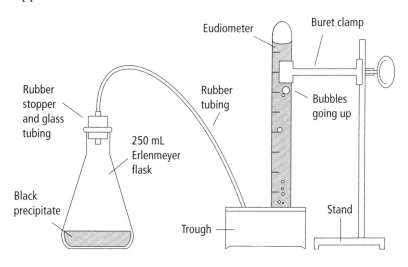

Figure 11C-1 *Set-up of the equipment for collection of gas*

3. Fill the eudiometer with water and invert it into the trough (half-filled with water), without letting any water come out. Hold it in the vertical position with the buret clamp attached to the stand.

4. Join the rubber tubing to the top of the glass tube which goes through the stopper on the flask. Place the other end into the neck of the eudiometer. (If your trough has an outside attachment for tubing, use that and position the eudiometer above the hole at the bottom of the trough.)

5. Measure 15 mL of bleach solution into the 25 mL graduated cylinder and pour it into the Erlenmeyer flask.

6. Measure 5 mL of 0.10M cobalt(II) nitrate solution into the 10 mL graduated cylinder.

7. Pour the cobalt nitrate solution into the flask and *immediately* place the stopper and tube on it. Record the time of mixing.

8. Note the formation of a black precipitate of cobalt (III) oxide, Co_2O_3. From now on you must swirl the flask gently but continually. This is necessary to dislodge bubbles of oxygen from the surface of the Co_2O_3 catalyst. If you stop swirling the rate decreases, so the amount of swirling must be kept uniform throughout this and subsequent steps of the procedure.

9. Record the total volume of oxygen that has collected in the eudiometer every 30 s until a volume of 50 mL has been obtained. Also record the actual elapsed time when the 50 mL mark is reached.

10. Repeat Steps 3 to 9, but have the reactants at a temperature of 10°C above room temperature before mixing them. You can accomplish this by placing both the flask with bleach and the graduated cylinder with cobalt(II) nitrate in a water bath for 10 min, then adding the cobalt(II) nitrate to the flask and putting it back into the water bath. Use hot water from a tap or kettle and adjust to the required temperature with cold water.

11. Repeat Step 10, but bring the reactants to a temperature 10°C below room temperature using ice.

12. Repeat Steps 3 to 9 at room temperature, but add 20 mL of water to the bleach solution before mixing, so that the overall concentrations are half of their original values.

13. Repeat Steps 3 to 9 at room temperature, but this time add 60 mL of water to the bleach solution before mixing, so that the overall concentrations after mixing are one quarter of their original values.

14. Repeat the experiment at other concentrations or temperatures if requested to do so by your instructor.

15. Clean up all your materials, following the instructions for reagent disposal.

16. Before you leave the laboratory, wash your hands thoroughly with soap and water.

REAGENT DISPOSAL

After collecting 50 mL of oxygen in each trial, pour the waste solution containing the black Co_2O_3 into the designated container.

POST LAB CONSIDERATIONS

The reaction in which the Co^{2+} ion reacts with the ClO^- ion is given by the equation:

$$2Co^{2+}(aq) + ClO^-(aq) + 2H_2O(l) \rightarrow Co_2O_3(s) + 4H^+(aq) + Cl^-(aq)$$

This reaction has to occur before the Co_2O_3 can start catalyzing the bleach, so do not be surprised if you find that no oxygen is given off during the first 30 s or 60 s.

When you plot your results, you may find the rate is not uniform. One cause might be that large bubbles come through just as you take a measurement. Another is the decreasing bleach concentration as the reaction proceeds. The trend relating reaction rate to changing temperature and concentration is nevertheless readily apparent.

EXPERIMENTAL RESULTS

Record your experimental results in five tables similar to the following. It is a good idea to copy them into your notebook before coming to the laboratory. Place them in such a way that they can be extended if necessary, as you do not know how many readings are required to reach 50 mL. It is possible that in some situations up to 20 readings may be needed (10 min) before the 50 mL mark is reached. Do not try to calculate the actual molarity of the bleach in the mixed solution. Record the concentration as full strength, half strength, or quarter strength in the table.

Conditions: Temperature = _____ Bleach Concentration = _____	Volume of O_2 (ml)
Time (s)	
0	
30	
60	
90	
⋮	

ANALYSIS OF RESULTS

1. Plot the graphs for each trial on a single sheet of graph paper, plotting volume of oxygen produced versus time elapsed. Label each graph with the conditions under which the results being graphed were obtained.

2. For each trial, calculate the overall rate of production of oxygen by dividing the volume of 50 mL by the time taken to produce that amount, in minutes. (The average rate is therefore expressed in millilitres per minute.)

3. Compare the calculated values of the rates with the temperatures used. By what factor does the rate change with a 10°C increase in temperature? By what factor does the rate change with a 10°C decrease in temperature?

4. Compare the calculated values of the rates at the different concentrations of bleach. By what factor does the rate change when the concentration of the bleach is halved? By what factor does the rate change when the concentration of the bleach is quartered?

FOLLOW-UP QUESTIONS

1. Bleach is made by the action of chlorine gas on sodium hydroxide, NaOH:

   $$Cl_2(g) + 2OH^-(aq) \rightarrow Cl^-(aq) + ClO^-(aq) + H_2O(l)$$

   However, if an acid is added to bleach, the process is reversed:

   $$Cl^-(aq) + ClO^-(aq) + 2H^+(aq) \rightarrow Cl_2(g) + H_2O(l)$$

   Why should you never mix bleach with any cleaner or other household product that may contain acid?

2. Special cleaning agents such as those used for cleaning mold and mildew off bathroom tiles may contain 10% sodium hypochlorite. Predict how the shape of the rate curve with this concentration differs from that of regular strength bleach.

CONCLUSION

State the results of Objectives 2 and 3.

Order of a Reaction

One of the factors that affect the rate of a reaction is the concentration of the reacting substances. When you double the concentration of a reactant you would expect to double the rate. However, for some reactions it is found that changing the concentration does not in fact change the rate at all, or may change it by a factor different from the concentration change factor. The reason for this can be explained by the fact that many reactions proceed by a sequence of steps (called the *reaction mechanism*) and the slowest step in this reaction mechanism is what determines the overall rate. This slowest step is called the *rate-determining step*. If one of the reactants does not appear in this rate-determining step, then it is not able to have any effect on the overall rate. In other reactions it may be found that doubling the concentration of a reactant makes the reaction rate greater by a factor of four. The rate, therefore, is proportional to the square of the concentration of this reactant. This can occur when two molecules of this reactant are involved in the rate-determining step.

Mathematically, these ideas can be expressed as follows:

Rate = $k[A]^x[B]^y[C]^z$ where k is called the *rate constant* for the reaction.

The exponents x, y, and z are referred to as the *order* of the reaction with respect to each of the reactants A, B, and C. The sum of these exponents, $x + y + z$ is called the *overall order* for the reaction. These quantities cannot be obtained by looking at the overall equation for the reaction, but must be obtained experimentally. Studying the results obtained in this way can provide useful information about the reaction mechanism.

The reaction to be studied in this experiment is between iodine and propanone (CH_3COCH_3). The overall equation is:

$$CH_3COCH_3(aq) + I_2(aq) \rightarrow CH_3COCH_2I(aq) + H^+(aq) + I^-(aq)$$

Furthermore, the reaction is catalyzed by hydrogen ions, formed from added HCl(aq). Note that changing the concentration of a catalyst is also a factor that changes the rate of a reaction.

Starch solution is added to make the presence of iodine much more visible. Starch forms a complex with iodine that is deep blue in color, even at very low concentrations. You will measure the time for this color to disappear, which will enable you to calculate the rate of the reaction. By measuring the rate at various combinations of concentrations of reactants, the order of the reaction can be determined.

OBJECTIVES

1. to determine the order of a reaction with respect to each of the reacting substances

2. to determine the overall order of a reaction

SUPPLIES

Equipment
4 beakers (100 mL)
4 graduated cylinders (10 mL)
stirring rod
water-soluble marker
lab apron
safety goggles
plastic gloves

Chemical Reagents
2.0M HCl
2.0M propanone (acetone),
CH_3COCH_3
0.010M I_2 (in 40% ethanol by
volume)
starch solution in a dropping
bottle

PROCEDURE

1. Put on your lab apron, safety goggles, and plastic gloves.

2. Obtain four 100 mL beakers, label them 1 through 4 with your water-soluble marker, and measure into each the volumes of reagents as listed in Table 1. Use a different 10.0 mL graduated cylinder for each, except for the starch solution. Mix the first four solutions together, then add the iodine solution last.

Table 1 Volumes of Reagents to be Mixed for Each Run

Run #	2.0M HCl	2.0M Propanone	Water	Starch Solution	0.010M I_2
1	20.0 mL	8.0 mL	0.0 mL	10 drops	4.0 mL
2	10.0 mL	8.0 mL	10.0 mL	10 drops	4.0 mL
3	20.0 mL	4.0 mL	4.0 mL	10 drops	4.0 mL
4	20.0 mL	8.0 mL	2.0 mL	10 drops	2.0 mL

3. As soon as the iodine solution is added to the mixture of the other four solutions, start timing, then stir the solution. Watch for the blue-black color of the starch-iodine complex to disappear. As soon as the color has disappeared, record in your copy of Table 2 the time elapsed since mixing.

4. When you have finished all four runs, submit your results in the manner directed by your instructor, in order to compare your results with other groups and obtain class averages.

5. Pour all solutions left over from the reactions down the sink with copious amounts of water.

6. Before leaving the laboratory, wash your hands thoroughly with soap and water.

REAGENT DISPOSAL

Any unused solutions should be returned to a designated waste container or flushed down the sink, as directed by your instructor.

CAUTION

The hydrochloric acid used in this experiment is corrosive to skin, eyes, and clothing. Wear a lab apron and safety goggles while performing this experiment. Any spills or splashes must be washed off your skin and clothing immediately, using plenty of water. Report any spills to your instructor.

The propanone (acetone) used here in an aqueous solution is a toxic chemical and care must be taken not to spill it on the skin or inhale it. Use with adequate ventilation. Plastic gloves must be worn in case of spills on the hands. If any is spilled on other areas of the body, rinse off immediately with copious amounts of water. Report to your instructor.

Iodine, used here in an alcohol solution, causes burns and is an irritant to eyes and skin. Care must be taken not to spill it on the skin or inhale it. If any is spilled, rinse off immediately with sodium thiosulfate solution, then plenty of water.

POST LAB CONSIDERATIONS

The volumes of solutions used in this experiment have been carefully chosen, with water added where necessary, to obtain situations where you can compare rates where just one of the reactants changes in concentration by a factor of two. If the effect on the rate is to change it by a factor of two, then the rate is proportional to the concentration of the reactant, and the order of the reaction, with respect to that reactant, is one. However, if changing the concentration of a reactant has no effect on the rate, the concentration of the reactant will not appear in the rate law expression and the order of the reaction, with respect to that reactant, is zero. If doubling the concentration of the reactant multiplies the rate by four, then the rate is proportional to the square of the concentration of the reactant. Some reactions have fractional orders but in this experiment the order should be 0, 1, or 2 for each reactant.

EXPERIMENTAL RESULTS

Table 2 Time Measured for Each Run and Class Averages

Run #	2.0M HCl	2.0M propanone	water	0.010M I$_2$	Time for color to disappear (s)	Time (class average) (s)
1	20.0 mL	8.0 mL	0.0 mL	4.0 mL		
2	10.0 mL	8.0 mL	10.0 mL	4.0 mL		
3	20.0 mL	4.0 mL	4.0 mL	4.0 mL		
4	20.0 mL	8.0 mL	2.0 mL	2.0 mL		

COMPLETE IN YOUR NOTEBOOK

ANALYSIS OF RESULTS

1. Using the following equation, calculate the rate for each run. Use either your own times or the class averages, as directed by your instructor.

$$\text{Rate (vol I}_2\text{/s)} = \frac{\text{volume of iodine solution used (mL)}}{\text{time for iodine color to disappear (s)}}$$

2. Using the following dilution factor formula, calculate the concentration of each reactant in the final solution mixture for each run. You may neglect the volume of the starch solution.

$$[\text{reactant}]_{\text{mixed}} = [\text{reactant}]_{\text{original}} \times \frac{\text{volume of reactant used}}{\text{total volume of final solution}}$$

3. Summarize your calculations by entering the results in the following table:

Table 3 Calculation Results Showing Concentrations of Solutions and Rate of Reaction

	[HCl]	[CH_3COCH_3]	[I_2]	Rate I_2 (mL/s)
Run 1				
Run 2	COMPLETE IN YOUR NOTEBOOK	COMPLETE IN YOUR NOTEBOOK	COMPLETE IN YOUR NOTEBOOK	COMPLETE IN YOUR NOTEBOOK
Run 3				
Run 4				

4. Choose the results in the two runs where the [HCl] is changed, keeping other concentrations the same. How does the rate change compare to the change in [HCl]? (Express both changes as ratios.) What is the order of the reaction with respect to HCl?

5. Choose the results in the two runs where the [CH_3COCH_3] is changed, keeping other concentrations the same. How does the rate change compare to the change in [CH_3COCH_3]? (Express both changes as ratios.) What is the order of the reaction with respect to CH_3COCH_3?

6. Choose the results in the two runs where the [I_2] is changed, keeping other concentrations the same. How does the rate change compare to the change in [I_2]? (Express both changes as ratios.) What is the order of the reaction with respect to I_2?

7. Write the rate law expression for the reaction.

8. What is the overall reaction order?

FOLLOW-UP QUESTIONS

1. Calculate the value of the rate in Run 1 by converting the units of (mL I_2)/s to (mol/L I_2)/s. Using this value and the concentrations of the other two reagents, calculate the value of the rate constant, k, by substituting in the rate law expression obtained in Analysis 7.

2. Using this value of the rate constant, calculate the rate expected if 20.0 mL of 2.0M HCl, 20.0 mL of 2.0M propanone, and 10.0 mL of 0.010M I_2 are all mixed, with 10 drops of starch solution present. At this rate, how long will it take before the blue-black color disappears?

CONCLUSION

State the results of Objectives 1 and 2.

Investigating Chemical Equilibrium

The chemical reactions you have studied to this point have proceeded to completion. However, many reactions proceed only to a state of *equilibrium*, where both reactants and products exist together. This results from some of the product molecules having sufficient energy to reform the reactants in a reverse reaction. A state of equilibrium is established when the rates of the forward and reverse reactions are equal. Although both reactions continue to occur, there is no net change in the observable properties (called *macroscopic* properties) such as concentration, pressure (for gases), or color intensity of a colored solution. In a reversible reaction, constant macroscopic properties (including temperature) indicate that equilibrium is present.

Any change to the conditions at equilibrium, such as concentration, pressure, or temperature, is said to produce a *stress* on the equilibrium. Le Chatelier's principle allows us to predict the effects of such a stress. The stress produces a shift in the system that attempts to counteract the imposed stress and a new equilibrium is established. The macroscopic properties of the system change, until they become constant once more as the new equilibrium is reached.

You will study five different equilibrium systems involving ions in solution. The first system, studied in Part I, is the conversion of the indicator bromcresol green from its blue form to its yellow form. Its structure is rather complex so the formula is simplified as HBcg. The extent to which the forward reaction is favored depends upon the concentration of hydrogen ions in solution:

$$HBcg \text{ (yellow form)} \rightleftharpoons Bcg^- \text{ (blue form)} + H^+$$
$$\text{"Acid"} \qquad\qquad\qquad \text{"Base"}$$

The second system (Part II) involves the light yellow iron(III) ion, Fe^{3+}, and colorless thiocyanate ion, SCN^-. They react together to form the complex ion $FeSCN^{2+}$ which exhibits a blood-red color:

$$Fe^{3+}(aq) + SCN^-(aq) \rightleftharpoons FeSCN^{2+}(aq)$$

The effect of changing the concentrations of the reactant ions will be studied.

The third system (Part III) involves the hydrated cobalt(II) ion, $Co(H_2O)_6^{2+}$, which can be converted to the chlorinated complex, $CoCl_4^{2-}(aq)$.

$$Co(H_2O)_6^{2+}(aq) + 4Cl^-(aq) \rightleftharpoons CoCl_4^{2-}(aq) + 6H_2O(l)$$
$$\text{Pink} \qquad\qquad\qquad\qquad \text{Blue}$$

The temperature of the system will be changed and the resultant effect on the position of equilibrium will be observed. This will enable a prediction to be made as to whether the reaction as written is exothermic or endothermic.

The fourth system (Part IV) involves the equilibrium between the yellow chromate ion, CrO_4^{2-}, and the orange dichromate ion, $Cr_2O_7^{2-}$. You will study the effect of adding H^+ and OH^- to this equilibrium and also the effect of adding Ba^{2+} to it.

The last system (Part V) involves an equilibrium between hydrated copper(II) ion, $Cu(H_2O)_4^{2+}$, and the tetramminocopper(II) ion, $Cu(NH_3)_4^{2+}$, in which the water molecules have been replaced with NH_3 molecules. The effect of acid and of NH_3 on this equilibrium will be examined.

OBJECTIVES

1. to recognize the macroscopic properties of five chemical systems at equilibrium

2. to observe shifts in equilibrium concentrations as stresses of concentration changes are applied to the systems

3. to observe a shift in equilibrium concentrations associated with a change in temperature

4. to explain the observations obtained by applying Le Chatelier's principle

SUPPLIES

Equipment
5 test tubes (13 mm × 100 mm)
test-tube rack
graduated cylinder (10 mL)
beaker (250 mL)
2 beakers (100 mL)
2 Erlenmeyer flasks (250 mL)
beaker tongs
hot plate
lab apron
safety goggles

Chemical Reagents
bromcresol green solution
0.01M HCl
0.01M NaOH
0.2M $FeCl_3$
0.2M KSCN
0.2M KCl
1M NaOH
$CoCl_2 \bullet 6H_2O$
6M HCl
0.1M K_2CrO_4
0.1M $K_2Cr_2O_7$
1M HCl
0.1M $Ba(NO_3)_2$
0.1M $CuSO_4$
1M NH_3

PROCEDURE

Part I: Equilibrium Involving Bromcresol Green

CAUTION

The hydrochloric acid and sodium hydroxide solutions are corrosive to skin, eyes, and clothing. Wash any spills and splashes with plenty of water. Call your instructor.

1. Put on your lab apron and safety goggles.

2. Obtain 2 clean, empty, dry 250 mL Erlenmeyer flasks. Add approximately 50 mL of water and 10 drops of bromcresol green solution to each flask. Record the color of this solution in your notebook.

3. To the first flask add a single drop of 0.01M HCl. Swirl the contents of the flask and continue the drop-by-drop addition until a definite color change is observed. The second flask will serve as a control. Compare the solution colors. Record the new color and the number of drops required for this change in your copy of Table 1 in your notebook.

4. Continue the drop-by-drop addition of 0.01M HCl to the first flask until a second color shift occurs. Compare with the control and record the new color change and number of drops required for this change in Table 1.

Copying the experiment is prohibited.   ©SMG Lab Books Ltd.

5. Now add 0.01*M* NaOH drop by drop in the first flask until a definite color change is observed. Record the color change and number of drops required in your data table.

6. Continue the drop-by-drop addition of 0.01*M* NaOH until the color changes again. Record the color change and number of drops required in Table 1.

Part II: Equilibrium Involving Thiocyanatoiron(III) Ion

1. Add 1 mL of 0.2*M* $FeCl_3$ to a 1 mL portion of 0.2*M* KSCN in a test tube. Note the color change as the reaction occurs.

2. Transfer the contents of the tube to a 250 mL beaker and add water to dilute the intensity of the color until the solution is light orange, to make subsequent changes easier to see.

3. Pour 5 mL of this solution into each of 5 separate test tubes labeled A to E. Nothing will be added to test tube A — it will serve as a control for comparison with the subsequent colors.

4. For each of the following reactions (Steps 5–8) record the results in your copy of Table 2. To record the "stress" involved, state which ion in the original equilibrium changed concentration and whether this change was an increase or a decrease.

5. To test tube B, add 10 drops of 0.2*M* KSCN.

6. To test tube C, add 10 drops of 0.2*M* $FeCl_3$.

7. To test tube D, add 10 drops of 0.2*M* KCl.

8. To test tube E, add 10 drops of 1*M* NaOH.

Part III: Equilibrium Involving Cobalt(II) Complexes

1. Place approximately 0.3 g of $CoCl_2 \bullet 6H_2O$ into each of two 100 mL beakers. Your instructor will have this amount displayed for a visual comparison. The exact mass is not important.

2. To the first beaker, add 10 mL of 6*M* HCl.

3. To the second beaker, add 10 mL of water. Note the colors of the solutions in each beaker. Record your observations in your copy of Table 3 in your notebook.

4. Gradually add water to the solution in the first beaker (containing the HCl) until a definite color change occurs. Record your observations in your copy of Table 3.

5. Place the first beaker on a hot plate and adjust the heat to gently warm. When a definite color change is observed, shut off the hot plate. Using beaker tongs, remove the beaker from the hot plate. Record the resulting color in Table 3.

6. Add approximately 50 mL of cold tap water to a clean 250 mL beaker. Carefully place the warm beaker and contents from Step 4 upright into this cold water bath. Record any additional changes in color intensity in Table 3.

CAUTION

Hydrated $CoCl_2$ is poisonous. Do not get it in your mouth; do not swallow any.

The heating of 6*M* HCl solution must take place within a fume hood.

Part IV: Equilibrium Involving Chromate and Dichromate Ions

1. Place 10 drops of $0.1M$ K_2CrO_4 and 10 drops of $0.1M$ $K_2Cr_2O_7$ in two different 13 mm × 100 mm test tubes.

2. Add to each, in alternation, $1M$ NaOH drop by drop until a color change occurs in one of the test tubes.

3. To the same test tubes add $1M$ HCl in the same manner until a color change is observed.

4. Repeat Steps 1 to 3, with two new test tubes, but add the $1M$ HCl first until a color change is observed, then add $1M$ NaOH. Record all your results in your copy of Table 4.

5. Place 10 drops of $0.1M$ K_2CrO_4 in a 13 mm × 100 mm test tube. Add 2 drops of $1M$ NaOH. Then add $0.1M$ $Ba(NO_3)_2$ solution drop by drop until a change is noted.

6. Add $1M$ HCl solution drop by drop to the test tube from Step 5 until a change occurs.

7. Place 10 drops of $0.1M$ $K_2Cr_2O_7$ in a 13 mm × 100 mm test tube. Add 2 drops of $1M$ HCl, then add 10 drops of $0.1M$ $Ba(NO_3)_2$ drop by drop.

8. Add $1M$ NaOH solution drop by drop to the test tube from Step 7 until a change is noted. Record all your results in Table 4.

9. Place 10 drops of $0.1M$ K_2CrO_4 in one test tube and 10 drops of $0.1M$ $K_2Cr_2O_7$ in another test tube. Add 10 drops of $0.1M$ $Ba(NO_3)_2$ to each. Observe the results and record them in Table 4.

Part V: Equilibrium Involving Copper(II) Complexes

1. Place 2 mL of $0.1M$ $CuSO_4$ in a 13 mm × 100 mm test tube.

2. Add 3 drops of $1M$ NH_3 and observe the result.

3. Continue adding $1M$ NH_3 until another change occurs.

4. Add $1M$ HCl drop by drop until a change occurs. Record your observations in your copy of Table 5.

5. Clean up all of your materials. Before you leave the laboratory, wash your hands thoroughly with soap and water.

POST LAB CONSIDERATIONS

The equilibrium system in Part I contains H^+ ions and therefore can be affected by the addition of any reagent changing the concentration of H^+. H^+ ions are present in acid solutions and OH^- ions are present in solutions of bases. Since H^+ will react with OH^- to form water, addition of a base affects this equilibrium by removing H^+ ions.

In Part II, the formation of $FeSCN^{2+}$ gave such an intense color that diluting the solution with water was necessary to enable small changes in the equilibrium to be observed more readily. In explaining your observations for this equilibrium, remember that spectator ions do not participate in the reaction.

In Step 8, a precipitate of $Fe(OH)_3$ was formed. In explaining your results, analyze how this reaction will affect the concentration of Fe^{3+} in the equilibrium solution.

For the reaction in Part III, recall that increasing the temperature of an equilibrium reaction favors the process which counteracts this change, that is, the endothermic direction. From your observations, you will be able to decide whether the forward or the reverse reaction is the endothermic one.

The equilibrium in Part IV can be represented by the equation:

$$2CrO_4^{2-}(aq) + 2H^+(aq) \rightleftharpoons Cr_2O_7^{2-}(aq) + H_2O(l)$$
$$\text{Yellow} \qquad\qquad\qquad \text{Orange}$$

The presence of $H^+(aq)$ in the equilibrium explains how it is that adding H^+ or OH^- is able to affect the position of this equilibrium. The other equilibrium involved in Part IV is the one in which Ba^{2+} ions react with CrO_4^{2-} ions to give solid $BaCrO_4$:

$$Ba^{2+}(aq) + CrO_4^{2-}(aq) \rightleftharpoons BaCrO_4(s)$$

Whether or not a precipitate could be observed here depends on the position of the first equilibrium involving CrO_4^{2-} and $Cr_2O_7^{2-}$.

The equilibrium in Part V initially involves the formation of OH^- ions in NH_3 solution:

$$NH_3(aq) + H_2O(l) \rightleftharpoons NH_4^+(aq) + OH^-(aq)$$

The OH^- ions then react with $Cu^{2+}(aq)$ to give a precipitate of $Cu(OH)_2$:

$$Cu^{2+}(aq) + 2OH^-(aq) \rightleftharpoons Cu(OH)_2(s)$$

When more NH_3 was added, NH_3 molecules replaced H_2O molecules in $Cu^{2+}(aq)$:

$$Cu(H_2O)_4^{2+}(aq) + 4NH_3 \rightleftharpoons Cu(NH_3)_4^{2+}(aq) + 4H_2O(l)$$

H^+ ions can react with NH_3 to give NH_4^+; therefore, the equilibrium shifts in response to this change.

EXPERIMENTAL RESULTS

Part I: Equilibrium Involving Bromcresol Green
Table 1

Initial Color of Bromcresol Green in Water			
Reagent Added	Stress	Color Change and No. of Drops Required	Direction of Equilibrium Shift
HCl (Step 3)			
more HCl (Step 4)	COMPLETE IN YOUR NOTEBOOK	COMPLETE IN YOUR NOTEBOOK	COMPLETE IN YOUR NOTEBOOK
NaOH (Step 5)			
more NaOH (Step 6)			

Part II: Equilibrium Involving Thiocyanatoiron(III) Ion
Table 2

Reagent Added	Stress	Color Observation	Direction of Equilibrium Shift
KSCN (test tube B)			
FeCl$_3$ (test tube C)	COMPLETE IN YOUR NOTEBOOK	COMPLETE IN YOUR NOTEBOOK	COMPLETE IN YOUR NOTEBOOK
KCl (test tube D)			
NaOH (test tube E)			

Part III: Equilibrium Involving Cobalt(II) Complexes
Table 3

Color of CoCl$_2$ + HCl		Color of CoCl$_2$ + H$_2$O	
	Stress	Color Observation	Direction of Equilibrium Shift
Step 4 (water added)			
Step 5 (heated)	COMPLETE IN YOUR NOTEBOOK	COMPLETE IN YOUR NOTEBOOK	COMPLETE IN YOUR NOTEBOOK
Step 6 (cooled)			

Part IV: Equilibrium Involving Chromate and Dichromate Ions
Table 4

		0.1M K$_2$CrO$_4$	0.1M K$_2$Cr$_2$O$_7$
Steps 1,2, and 3	Initial Color		
	1M NaOH added	COMPLETE IN YOUR NOTEBOOK	COMPLETE IN YOUR NOTEBOOK
	1M HCl added		
		0.1M K$_2$CrO$_4$	0.1M K$_2$Cr$_2$O$_7$
Step 4	Initial Color		
	1M HCl added	COMPLETE IN YOUR NOTEBOOK	COMPLETE IN YOUR NOTEBOOK
	1M NaOH added		

Copying the experiment is prohibited.

Steps 5 and 6		Initial Color	+ 1M NaOH	+ 0.1M Ba(NO₃)₂	+ 1M HCl
	0.1M K₂CrO₄	COMPLETE IN YOUR NOTEBOOK			

Steps 7 and 8		Initial Color	+ 1M HCl	+ 0.1M Ba(NO₃)₂	+ 1M NaOH
	0.1M K₂Cr₂O₇	COMPLETE IN YOUR NOTEBOOK			

Step 9		0.1M K₂CrO₄		0.1M K₂Cr₂O₇	
	Add 0.1M Ba(NO₃)₂	COMPLETE IN YOUR NOTEBOOK			

Part V: Equilibrium Involving Copper(II) Complexes

Table 5

	0.1M CuSO₄	+ 3 Drops NH₃	+ more NH₃	1M HCl Added
Appearance	COMPLETE IN YOUR NOTEBOOK			

ANALYSIS OF RESULTS

1. In Part 1, how would increasing the molarity of the NaOH solution from 0.01M to 0.1M affect the number of drops required for the observed color changes?

2. Apply Le Chatelier's principle to explain the results obtained when 1M NaOH was introduced into the iron(III) thiocyanate ion equilibrium system.

3. If the hydrated cobalt(II) ion complex were refrigerated, what would you predict as the color of the refrigerated solution?

4. Look at the equilibrium equation for the reaction involving the hydrated cobalt(II) ion complex. From your lab results, which reaction is endothermic? Cite evidence for your answer.

5. Predict how the addition of sodium chloride, NaCl, would affect the hydrated cobalt(II) ion equilibrium. Explain your prediction in terms of Le Chatelier's principle.

6. Write the balanced equation for the reaction of $Cr_2O_7{}^{2-}$ with OH^-.

7. Explain the reasons for the equilibrium shifts observed in Steps 1 to 4 of Part IV.

8. Compare the relative solubilities of $BaCrO_4$ and $BaCr_2O_7$.

9. Explain why no precipitate formed in $K_2Cr_2O_7$ in Step 7 of Part IV, while some did form in Step 9.

10. Explain the cause of the color change observed when HCl was added to the complex ion $Cu(NH_3)_4{}^{2+}$ in Part V.

FOLLOW-UP QUESTIONS

1. When Ag^+ ions are added to the red $FeSCN^{2+}$ ion in Part II, the color disappears and a white precipitate of $AgSCN$ forms. Explain why Fe^{3+} can be used as an indicator in a reaction to determine the concentration of an unknown solution of Ag^+ by reacting it with a solution of KSCN of known concentration.

2. A student discovers that after doing Part IV of this experiment, several of the test tubes are coated with a yellow precipitate that does not wash off easily. Devise a chemical method of removing this material.

CONCLUSION

1. State the effect on the position of an equilibrium if a change is made in the concentration of a reactant or product.

2. State the effect on the position of an equilibrium if a change is made in the temperature.

The Quantitative Relationship of a Reaction at Equilibrium

When chemical reactions are at equilibrium, both reactants and products are present, and as a result stoichiometric relationships assuming 100% completion do not apply. Chemists need to know how the concentrations of reactants and products are related to one another at equilibrium. This experiment will investigate that relationship.

In Experiment 12A you investigated the equilibrium reaction in which the iron(III) ion reacted with the thiocyanate ion to give the thiocyanatoiron(III) complex ion:

$$Fe^{3+}(aq) \quad + \quad SCN^-(aq) \quad \rightleftharpoons \quad FeSCN^{2+}(aq)$$

light yellow   colorless   blood-red

The $FeSCN^{2+}$ ion gives a deep blood-red color, which may appear orange in more dilute solutions. Here the reaction will be investigated quantitatively. In Part I, different initial concentrations of $Fe^{3+}(aq)$ will have $SCN^-(aq)$ added to them. In Part II, the equilibrium concentration of $FeSCN^{2+}(aq)$ will be measured by means of a spectrophotometer. From the results, the equilibrium concentrations of all three ions will be obtained and the results will be used to see whether any constant relationship exists among the values.

OBJECTIVES

1. to prepare various dilutions of Fe^{3+} and to react them with SCN^- ion

2. to measure the concentration of $FeSCN^{2+}$ ion produced by means of a spectrophotometer

3. to use the results to discover a constant mathematical relationship among the concentrations of reactants and products at equilibrium

SUPPLIES

Equipment

5 test tubes (18 mm × 150 mm)
test-tube rack
graduated cylinder (10 mL)
graduated cylinder (25 mL)
3 beakers (100 mL)
wash bottle

5 spectrophotometer tubes
  (cuvettes)
  (or 13 mm × 100 mm test tubes)
spectrophotometer
lab apron
safety goggles

Chemical Reagents

$0.200M$ $Fe(NO_3)_3$ (acidified)
$0.0020M$ KSCN

PROCEDURE

Part I: Reaction of SCN⁻ with Various Dilutions of Fe^{3+}

1. Put on your lab apron and safety goggles.

2. Obtain in separate 100 mL beakers about 20 mL of $0.200M$ $Fe(NO_3)_3$ and 30 mL of $0.0020M$ KSCN and label the beakers.

3. Place the 5 test tubes (18 mm × 150 mm) in a rack and label them A to E.

The flowchart below may help to clarify the dilution procedures that follow:

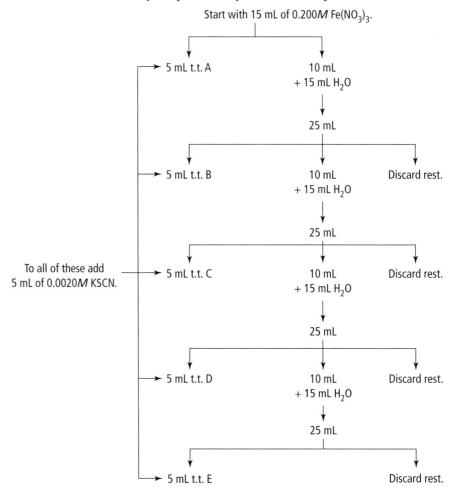

Start with 15 mL of $0.200M$ $Fe(NO_3)_3$.

5 mL t.t. A   10 mL + 15 mL H_2O

25 mL

5 mL t.t. B   10 mL + 15 mL H_2O Discard rest.

25 mL

To all of these add 5 mL of $0.0020M$ KSCN.   5 mL t.t. C   10 mL + 15 mL H_2O Discard rest.

25 mL

5 mL t.t. D   10 mL + 15 mL H_2O Discard rest.

25 mL

5 mL t.t. E   Discard rest.

4. Measure 5.0 mL of $0.200M$ $Fe(NO_3)_3$ in a 10 mL graduated cylinder and transfer it to test tube A.

5. Measure 10.0 mL of the $Fe(NO_3)_3$ solution into a 10 mL graduated cylinder. Transfer this to a 25 mL graduated cylinder, add water using a wash bottle to make it up to the 25.0 mL mark, then transfer it to a clean, dry beaker to mix.

6. Using your 10 mL graduated cylinder, transfer 5.0 mL of this diluted solution to test tube B. (If the cylinder is wet, rinse it with about 2 mL of your solution first.) Then measure 10 mL of the diluted solution, again in the 10 mL graduated cylinder, and pour it into the 25 mL cylinder (it can be wet). Make up to 25.0 mL with water using a wash bottle.

7. Repeat Step 6 with this new diluted solution, but place the 5.0 mL portion in test tube C, and continue similar dilutions of 10 mL to 25 mL to get 5.0 mL portions in test tubes D and E.

8. To each test tube add 5.0 mL of 0.0020M KSCN.

Part II: Measuring the Concentration of FeSCN^{2+} with a Spectrophotometer

1. If necessary, refer to the introduction to Experiment 10B to refresh your memory as to how the spectrophotometer should be set up and used. The wavelength for this experiment is 590 nm.

2. Obtain 5 cuvettes (spectrophotometer tubes) and place them in the rack. (Use clean scratch-free 13 mm × 100 mm test tubes if cuvettes are not available.) Transfer each of Solutions A to E to these tubes, first washing them with 2 mL of the solution if they are wet. Fill the tubes about three-quarters full.

3. Read the absorbance for each solution and record the value in your copy of Table 1 in your notebook. Note that for this experiment you will be calculating the concentration from your readings, so you must read absorbance rather than percent transmittance.

4. Before leaving the laboratory, wash your hands thoroughly with soap and water.

REAGENT DISPOSAL

Wash all contents of the tubes down the sink with plenty of water. Return any left over reactant solutions to the designated container, if directed to do so by your instructor.

POST LAB CONSIDERATIONS

The results that you have obtained in this experiment will now permit you to calculate the concentrations of each ion present at equilibrium. Your task will then be to determine whether a mathematical relationship exists among these concentration values.

In calculating [FeSCN^{2+}] in each test tube, some assumptions must be made. It is impossible to make up a set of test tubes of standard concentration of FeSCN^{2+} to compare against, since the equilibrium reaction will always come into play and the position of the equilibrium will shift on dilution of the mixture. For these reasons, no calibration graphs can be drawn, so you will have to assume that the absorbance measured is proportional to [FeSCN^{2+}].

In obtaining a standard concentration for comparison of results, you must assume that in test tube A, in which 0.200M Fe^{3+} is mixed with 0.0020M SCN$^-$, there is so much excess Fe^{3+} that essentially all the SCN$^-$ will be used up. You can therefore state that the initial [SCN$^-$] will be equal to the equilibrium [FeSCN^{2+}] in test tube A. This test tube then becomes the standard for the comparison of the absorbances measured in the experiment.

EXPERIMENTAL RESULTS

Table 1

Test Tube	Initial [Fe^{3+}]	Initial [SCN$^-$]	Absorbance
A			
B			
C	COMPLETE IN YOUR NOTEBOOK	COMPLETE IN YOUR NOTEBOOK	COMPLETE IN YOUR NOTEBOOK
D			
E			

(The initial [Fe^{3+}] and initial [SCN$^-$] can be calculated before you come to the laboratory. See Analysis of Results 1.)

ANALYSIS OF RESULTS

1. Calculate the initial [Fe^{3+}] and the initial [SCN$^-$] in each of the mixed solutions. Remember to account not only for the dilution factor for Fe^{3+} involved in each successive test tube (10 mL going to 25 mL), but also for the subsequent dilution of 5 mL to 10 mL for each ion when the solutions are mixed. As noted earlier, you could do these calculations before coming to the laboratory.

2. Calculate the equilibrium [FeSCN^{2+}] in each tube from the following equation:

$$[FeSCN^{2+}](\text{test tube } x) = [FeSCN^{2+}](\text{test tube A}) \times \frac{\text{Absorbance(test tube } x)}{\text{Absorbance(test tube A)}}$$

Note that the assumption that all the SCN$^-$ will be used up in test tube A implies that the equilibrium [SCN$^-$] = 0. This will give no meaningful results for any quantitative relationships in that test tube, but it does enable you to get meaningful results in the remaining four.

3. For test tubes B to E calculate the equilibrium [Fe^{3+}] and equilibrium [SCN$^-$] by subtracting the equilibrium [FeSCN^{2+}] from the initial [Fe^{3+}] and initial [SCN$^-$] respectively. (The mole ratio in the equation is 1:1:1.)

4. In order to see whether there is any mathematical relationship between these equilibrium concentrations, calculate the value of each of the following expressions for each of test tubes B to E. (Your instructor may suggest alternate or additional expressions to try.)

   a. $\dfrac{[FeSCN^{2+}][Fe^{3+}]}{[SCN^-]}$

   b. $\dfrac{[FeSCN^{2+}]}{[Fe^{3+}][SCN^-]}$

   c. $[Fe^{3+}][SCN^-][FeSCN^{2+}]$

   d. $\dfrac{[Fe^{3+}] + [SCN^-])}{[FeSCN^{2+}]}$

©SMG Lab Books Ltd.

5. Calculate the ratio of the largest value to the smallest value for each of the expressions (a) to (d) above. The expression that gives the smallest ratio will be the one that is most constant. It is unrealistic to expect any expression to give values which come out exactly the same, considering the assumptions that were made and the errors that will be present with so many volume measurement readings.

FOLLOW-UP QUESTIONS

1. The most constant expression in Analysis 5 is called the equilibrium constant expression and is given the symbol K_{eq}. Describe the form of the equilibrium constant expression (K_{eq}) in terms of the concentrations of reactants and products. How are these concentrations related?

2. With the new knowledge that this equilibrium constant relationship exists, explain why adding some more Fe^{3+} will cause the equilibrium $Fe^{3+}(aq) + SCN^-(aq) \rightleftharpoons FeSCN^{2+}(aq)$ to shift to the right, as predicted by Le Chatelier's Principle.

CONCLUSION

State your average value for the equilibrium constant for this reaction.

12C

Determination of a Solubility Product Constant

When an ionic solid dissolves in water, it dissociates to give the positive and negative ions in the same relative proportion that make up the solid. As more solid dissolves, the concentration of the ions naturally increases. This build-up of dissociated ions allows the reverse reaction (in which the ions crystallize out) to have a greater possibility of occurring. Eventually, a situation is reached in which the rate of dissolving is equal to the rate of crystallization. At this point, no more solid can dissolve, and the solution is said to be *saturated*. A state of equilibrium has been reached, which can be recognized by a constant color for the solution (if it is colored) or by a constant mass of solid left undissolved. The solubility product constant, K_{sp}, for an ionic solid is given by the product of the concentration of the ions, each raised to the power of the coefficients in the dissolving reaction. For instance, the K_{sp} for silver chloride, AgCl, is given by

$$K_{sp} = [Ag^+][Cl^-]$$

For a substance such as lead(II) iodide, PbI_2, the K_{sp} is given by

$$K_{sp} = [Pb^{2+}][I^-]^2$$

The K_{sp} expression gives the relationship between the ions in the saturated solution, and therefore their maximum possible concentration without causing precipitation. If solutions of suitable concentration of substances are available, it is possible to mix them to form a precipitate, then carry out appropriate dilutions until a point is reached at which no precipitate occurs. This process allows an approximate value to be determined for the K_{sp}. In this experiment, you will mix solutions of lead(II) nitrate and potassium iodide at a number of different dilutions and watch for the first situation in which no precipitate occurs. You will then be able to state the K_{sp} at room temperature as a range of values. The test tubes in which a precipitate did occur will then be heated until the precipitate dissolves, in order that you may determine the K_{sp} at different temperatures.

OBJECTIVES

1. to prepare a number of solutions of each of Pb^{2+} and I^-, of differing concentrations

2. to mix combinations of the above solutions and note whether a precipitate occurs

3. to obtain an approximate value of K_{sp} for PbI_2 at room temperature

4. to obtain the approximate value of K_{sp} for PbI_2 at temperatures higher than room temperature

SUPPLIES

Equipment

12 test tubes (18 mm × 150 mm)
2 test-tube racks
2 graduated cylinders (10 mL)
dropping pipet
water-soluble marker
thermometer
beaker (400 mL)

hot plate (or laboratory burner with ring stand, ring, and wire gauze)
2 beakers (100 mL)
stirring rod
lab apron
safety goggles

Chemical Reagents

0.010M Pb(NO$_3$)$_2$
0.020M KI

PROCEDURE

1. Put on your lab apron and safety goggles.

2. Obtain in separate 100 mL beakers about 40 mL of each of 0.010M Pb(NO$_3$)$_2$ and 0.020M KI and label the beakers.

3. Obtain twelve 18 mm × 150 mm test tubes and arrange them in two racks, each with 6 test tubes. Label each set A to F.

4. Into the first set of test tubes place 10.0 mL, 8.0 mL, 6.0 mL, 4.0 mL, 3.0 mL, and 2.0 mL of 0.010M Pb(NO$_3$)$_2$, respectively. Use your 10 mL graduated cylinder and get the precise amount by adding or subtracting drops with a dropper.

5. Add an amount of water to each tube to make the volume in each up to 10.0 mL (that is, 0.0 mL, 2.0 mL, 4.0 mL, 6.0 mL, 7.0 mL, and 8.0 mL, respectively).

6. Repeat Steps 4 and 5 with the test tubes in the second rack, using 0.020M KI instead of 0.010M Pb(NO$_3$)$_2$, using the second graduated cylinder.

7. Mix the contents of test tube A from the lead(II) nitrate set with the contents of test tube A from the potassium iodide set and replace the test tube in the rack.

8. Repeat Step 7 for each of the other 5 combinations.

9. Record in which test tubes a precipitate occurs in your copy of Table 1 in your notebook.

10. Add about 250 mL of water to a 400 mL beaker and place the beaker on a hot plate (or on a wire gauze on a ring clamp attached to a stand if a burner is used).

11. Place each of the test tubes which contain a precipitate in the beaker and begin heating slowly with the hot plate (or burner). (See Figure 12C-1.) Use a stirring rod to ensure that each precipitate is evenly distributed throughout the solution.

CAUTION

Lead(II) nitrate is very toxic. Do not get any in your mouth and do not swallow any. Avoid getting any on your skin since it can be absorbed. Wash away any spills or splashes with plenty of water. Call your instructor.

Figure 12C-1 *Heating test tubes containing PbI$_2$ precipitate*

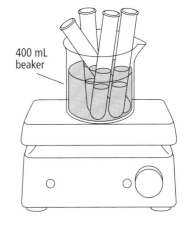

400 mL beaker

12. When the precipitate in each test tube dissolves, note the temperature of the water bath and record it in Table 1.

13. Before leaving the laboratory, wash your hands thoroughly with soap and water.

REAGENT DISPOSAL

Empty the contents of all test tubes into the designated waste container.

POST LAB CONSIDERATIONS

The K_{sp} expression for lead iodide, $K_{sp} = [Pb^{2+}][I^-]^2$, represents the equilibrium concentrations at the point where a precipitate just starts to form. When other concentration values are substituted into this expression it is called a *trial ion product* (or Trial K_{sp}). When this trial ion product exceeds the K_{sp} value, a precipitate should form until the equilibrium concentrations are reached. If the trial ion product is less than or equal to the K_{sp} value, no precipitate should form. If you note the temperature at which a precipitate dissolves, the trial ion product for that sample becomes the K_{sp} at that temperature.

EXPERIMENTAL RESULTS

Table 1

Test Tube	A	B	C	D	E	F
Vol. 0.010M $Pb(NO_3)_2$ (mL)	10.0	8.0	6.0	4.0	3.0	2.0
Vol. of water added (mL)	0.0	2.0	4.0	6.0	7.0	8.0
Vol. of 0.020M KI (mL)	10.0	8.0	6.0	4.0	3.0	2.0
Vol. of water added (mL)	0.0	2.0	4.0	6.0	7.0	8.0
Precipitate or no precipitate at room temperature						
Temperature at which precipitate dissolves (°C)						

COMPLETE IN YOUR NOTEBOOK

ANALYSIS OF RESULTS

1. For each of test tubes A to F calculate the $[Pb^{2+}]$ in the final mixed solution. In using the appropriate dilution factor, remember that the final volume in each case is the sum of the volumes of both the lead(II) nitrate and the potassium iodide, i.e., 20 mL.

Copying the experiment is prohibited.   ©SMG Lab Books Ltd.

2. Repeat for $[I^-]$ in the final mixed solution in test tubes A to F.

3. Calculate the value of the trial ion product for each of test tubes A to F (given by $[Pb^{2+}][I^-]^2$).

4. State the range of values in which your experimental K_{sp} must lie. (This will be between the trial ion product of the last test tube giving a precipitate and the trial ion product of the first test tube not giving a precipitate.)

5. From the results of Step 12 in Table 1, make up a new table showing the temperature, the K_{sp}, and the solubility in each case. (Since in each situation the $[I^-]$ was twice the $[Pb^{2+}]$, the solubility of PbI_2 is given simply by the $[Pb^{2+}]$ alone.)

6. What is the trend in the solubility as the temperature is increased?

7. Plot a graph of solubility (moles per litre) against temperature.

FOLLOW-UP QUESTIONS

1. If you were given a saturated solution of lead(II) iodide and asked to determine the K_{sp} of PbI_2 from it, how would you proceed?

2. Will lead(II) iodide be more or less soluble in a solution of $0.10M$ KI than it will be in pure water? Explain your answer.

3. After doing this experiment, a student finds that the test tubes have a coating of yellow lead(II) iodide on the inside which doesn't wash off easily. On the basis of your experimental results, suggest the best method for removing this coating.

4. Compare your K_{sp} value with that obtained from a chemical handbook/data booklet or other reference source. Cite your reference and suggest some reasons for any difference.

CONCLUSION

State the results of Objectives 3 and 4.

12D

Applications of Solubility Product Principles

There are many instances in which knowledge of solubility equilibria and solubility product values are important to a chemist. For example, a detailed scheme for identifying and separating a large number of different ions depends on a knowledge of K_{sp} values. Also, the common ion effect is often used to control the concentration of added reagents in order to exceed the K_{sp} for one ion and not another, thus effecting ion separation.

One aspect of solubility equilibria with which you may already be familiar is the topic of water hardness. Essentially, hard water is water that does not allow soap to lather well because metal ions such as Ca^{2+} and Mg^{2+} ions are present in the water. These Ca^{2+} and Mg^{2+} ions get into the water from the geological formations over which the water flows. Water found in limestone areas is more likely to be harder than water which contacts mainly granite. Thus, the problem of water hardness depends to a great extent on where you live.

The reason why hard water does not allow soap to form suds very well is that the Ca^{2+} and Mg^{2+} ions react with the stearate ion, $C_{17}H_{35}COO^-$ in soap forming an insoluble curd or scum. (Soap consists mostly of sodium or potassium stearates, the active cleaning compounds.) Thus, a lot of soap gets wasted when the stearate ions are precipitated by Ca^{2+} and Mg^{2+} before the soap can start to lather and help remove dirt.

There are two main types of hard water. Temporarily hard water contains $Ca(HCO_3)_2$ or $Mg(HCO_3)_2$, which can both be removed by boiling. Permanently hard water contains mainly sulfates and chlorides of Ca^{2+} and Mg^{2+}, which cannot be removed by boiling; other means must be used. In Parts I and II of this experiment, you will investigate temporarily and permanently hard water respectively, and investigate ways of removing the hardness.

One other important application of solubility equilibria and K_{sp} values is in analytical chemistry, in situations where the quantity of a dissolved ion needs to be determined. This is often done by precipitation, and in Part III of this experiment you will determine the [Cl⁻] in a sample of water (tap water, river water, lake water, or an unknown chloride solution) by titrating with a standard solution of silver nitrate. Sodium (or potassium) chromate can be used as an indicator. Since AgCl is less soluble than Ag_2CrO_4, it will be precipitated first. When all the chloride has been precipitated, Ag_2CrO_4 will be formed. It has a brick-red color (as opposed to white for the AgCl), so the first appearance of a brick-red color indicates that all the chloride has been precipitated.

OBJECTIVES

1. to demonstrate the formation of temporarily hard water, as well as how the hardness can be eliminated

©SMG Lab Books Ltd.

2. to demonstrate the effect of permanently hard water, as well as how the hardness can be eliminated

3. to determine the concentration of Cl^- in a water sample by titrating with standard $AgNO_3$

SUPPLIES

Equipment
Erlenmeyer flask (250 mL)
bunsen burner
ring stand
clamp
wire gauze
test-tube rack
8 test tubes (13 mm × 100 mm)
buret (50 mL)
stopper
pipet (25 mL) or
   graduated cylinder (25 mL)
2 beakers (250 mL)
filter funnel
lab apron
safety goggles

Chemical Reagents
saturated limewater (calcium
   hydroxide, $Ca(OH)_2$)
CO_2 supply
powdered pure soap or liquid
   soap
$0.4M$ $MgSO_4$
$0.4M$ $CaCl_2$
$2M$ Na_2CO_3
$0.100M$ $AgNO_3$
sample of water containing
   chloride ions
$0.10M$ Na_2CrO_4

PROCEDURE

Part I: Temporarily Hard Water

1. Put on your lab apron and safety goggles.

2. Set up three 13 mm × 100 mm test tubes in a rack and label them A to C.

3. In a 250 mL Erlenmeyer flask, obtain 25 mL of saturated limewater solution and record its appearance in your copy of Table 1.

4. Bubble CO_2 gas into the solution from the cylinder provided (or from the CO_2 gas generating flask) and record the appearance of the solution in Table 1. Keep bubbling until the precipitate which forms at first dissolves again and record the appearance of the resulting solution.

5. Pour off about 5 mL of this solution into a 13 mm × 100 mm test tube (A).

6. Set up the flask on the stand and heat with the bunsen burner until the solution has boiled for 5 min. Observe and record the result.

7. Pour 5 mL of the flask's contents into a second test tube in the rack (B). Discard the remaining contents.

8. Place 5 mL of distilled water into a third test tube (C).

9. To each test tube add enough powdered pure soap (or 1 drop of liquid soap) to cover the surface of the liquid.

10. Shake each test tube. Note the relative amount of lathering in each test tube and record your observations in your copy of Table 2.

Part II: Permanently Hard Water

1. Set up five 13 mm × 100 mm test tubes in a rack. Label them A to E and add the following to each:

   A: distilled water
   B: 4 mL of 0.4M MgSO$_4$
   C: 4 mL of 0.4M CaCl$_2$
   D: 4 mL of 0.4M MgSO$_4$ + 1 mL of 2M Na$_2$CO$_3$
   E: 4 mL of 0.4M CaCl$_2$ + 1 mL of 2M Na$_2$CO$_3$

2. To each add enough pure soap powder (or 1 drop of liquid soap) to cover the surface of the liquid. Note the appearance of each in your copy of Table 3.

3. Shake each test tube. In Table 3, record the relative amount of lathering in each test tube.

Part III: Determining the Chloride Ion Concentration in a Water Sample

1. Obtain approximately 100 mL of 0.100M silver nitrate solutions, AgNO$_3$, in a 250 mL beaker. (Your instructor may suggest more or less of this, depending on the amount of chloride in your samples to be tested and how many measurements you are to make.)

2. Set up the buret with its clamp and stand, and pour about 10 mL of AgNO$_3$ into it, using a filter funnel. Rinse back and forth (Use a stopper, not your finger!) and discard the rinsings through the tip into a 250 mL beaker. Use this beaker for all your silver compound wastes.

3. Refill the buret to the top and drain enough into your silver compound wastes beaker so that the tip is filled and free from air bubbles.

4. Your instructor will recommend using a 25 mL, 50 mL, or 100 mL sample of water, depending on the amount of chloride content in it. Transfer the specified amount to your Erlenmeyer flask, using either a 25 mL pipet or a graduated cylinder. Record the volume of the sample in your copy of Table 4.

5. Add 1 mL of 0.10M Na$_2$CrO$_4$ to the water sample and note the resulting color.

6. Record the initial volume reading on the buret in Table 4 and run the AgNO$_3$ solution into the flask, swirling all the time. You should notice that, although a white precipitate is produced, the solution stays yellow because of chromate ions present.

7. As the titration continues you will notice a reddish color begin to form which disappears as the swirling continues. Slow down the rate at which you are adding the AgNO$_3$ at this point, until you are adding it drop by drop. Stop at the point where the contents of the flask show the first sign of a reddish color that remains.

8. Read the final volume in the buret and calculate the volume used to precipitate all the Cl$^-$ ions. Record both figures in Table 4.

9. Empty the contents of the flask into your beaker containing silver compound wastes.

AgNO$_3$ is poisonous and is corrosive to skin and eyes. It will result in brown stains on skin if you spill any on yourself. If this occurs, wash with sodium thiosulfate solution, then with plenty of water. Call your instructor.

Na$_2$CrO$_4$ is poisonous, and is an irritant to skin and eyes. Do not get any on your skin. If you do, wash it off with plenty of water.

10. Repeat Steps 3 to 9 once or twice more, with either the same water sample or a different one, as directed by your instructor.

11. Wash your hands thoroughly with soap and water before leaving the laboratory.

REAGENT DISPOSAL

All the solutions from Parts I and II may be safely disposed of by being rinsed down the sink with copious amounts of water. Empty your beaker of silver compound wastes from Part III into the designated waste container. Return any unused silver nitrate solution to the container provided. Clean all glassware carefully.

POST LAB CONSIDERATIONS

Calcium carbonate, $CaCO_3$, is only very slightly soluble in water.

$$CaCO_3(s) \rightleftharpoons Ca^{2+}(aq) + CO_3^{2-}(aq)$$

$$K_{sp} = [Ca^{2+}][CO_3^{2-}] = 4.8 \times 10^{-9}$$

This means that the solubility is about $7 \times 10^{-5}M$ or 7×10^{-3} g/L. However, when CO_2 dissolves in water, another equilibrium is set up:

$$CO_2(g) + H_2O(l) \rightleftharpoons H_2CO_3(aq) \rightleftharpoons H^+(aq) + HCO_3^-(aq)$$

The $H^+(aq)$ from this equilibrium combines with the CO_3^{2-} from the $CaCO_3$ equilibrium, forming more HCO_3^-. The removal of the CO_3^{2-} causes the solubility equilibrium for $CaCO_3$ to move to the right; in other words, more $CaCO_3$ dissolves. Eventually a colorless solution of calcium bicarbonate, $Ca(HCO_3)_2$, forms. The dissolved Ca^{2+} ions cause the water to be hard because they can precipitate the stearate ions from soap.

If this solution of $Ca(HCO_3)_2$ is boiled, CO_2 gas comes out of the solution. The result is the shifting of all the equilibria back to the left and the consequent precipitation of $CaCO_3$. This process naturally removes the hardness from the water, as the Ca^{2+} ions have been removed from the solution by precipitation. Thus, this solution is classified as temporarily hard.

Note that $Ca(HCO_3)_2$ does not exist in the solid phase. If you try to boil off the water to obtain the solid, then $CaCO_3$ will be formed. The same result occurs if the solution is allowed to evaporate over a long period: CO_2 and H_2O are removed, and $CaCO_3$ is deposited. This process occurs within certain household appliances. For example, a kitchen kettle will develop an unwanted interior scaling of $CaCO_3$ after prolonged use. The same is true for hot water heaters and clothes irons.

The use of CrO_4^{2-} in Part III as an indicator in the titration with Ag^+ to determine $[Cl^-]$ is an interesting application of solubility product principles. What happens first is the $[Cl^-]$ precipitation with Ag^+. Here is how it works, using a 50 mL water sample.

concentrations in initial titration sample	$[Cl^-] = 0.020M$ (example)	$[CrO_4{}^{2-}] = 0.0020M$ (calculated)
precipitate with Ag^+	$AgCl(s)$	$Ag_2CrO_4(s)$
K_{sp} values	1.8×10^{-10}	1.1×10^{-12}
to begin precipitation	$[Ag^+] = 9.0 \times 10^{-9}M$	$[Ag^+] = 2.3 \times 10^{-5}M$

By examining the above values for $[Ag^+]$ required to begin precipitation you can see that

    a. AgCl will precipitate first and

    b. after Cl^- ions are removed, Ag_2CrO_4 starts to precipitate and a red color suddenly appears indicating the end point.

EXPERIMENTAL RESULTS

Record your data and observations in tables similar to the following. It would be a good idea to have these in your notebook before coming to the laboratory.

Part I: Temporarily Hard Water

Table 1

Appearance of limewater solution
Appearance when CO_2 initially bubbled in
Appearance when CO_2 bubbled in for a longer time

Table 2

Test Tube	Contents	Height of Lather
A	Unboiled solution	
B	Boiled solution	
C	Distilled water	

COMPLETE IN YOUR NOTEBOOK

Part II: Permanently Hard Water

Table 3

Test Tube	Contents	Appearance	Height of Lather
A	Distilled H_2O		
B	0.4M $MgSO_4$		
C	0.4M $CaCl_2$	COMPLETE IN YOUR NOTEBOOK	COMPLETE IN YOUR NOTEBOOK
D	0.4M $MgSO_4$ + 2M Na_2CO_3		
E	0.4M $CaCl_2$ + 2M Na_2CO_3		

Part III: Determining the Chloride Ion Concentration in a Water Sample

Table 4

[$AgNO_3$] =	Trial 1	Trial 2	Trial 3
Sample #			
Volume of water sample used (mL)			
Initial reading of $AgNO_3$ (mL)	COMPLETE IN YOUR NOTEBOOK	COMPLETE IN YOUR NOTEBOOK	COMPLETE IN YOUR NOTEBOOK
Final reading of $AgNO_3$ (mL)			
Volume of $AgNO_3$ used (mL)			

ANALYSIS OF RESULTS

Part I: Temporarily Hard Water

1. Explain the results that occurred when CO_2 was bubbled into the lime-water solution.

2. Explain the results that occurred when the solution was boiled.

3. In which test tube were the fewest soapsuds formed? Why?

Part II: Permanently Hard Water

1. State what happened in test tubes D and E when the Na_2CO_3 solution was added. Give equations for the reactions.

2. Explain the results of adding soap to each test tube and shaking.

Part III: Determining the Chloride Ion Concentration in a Water Sample

1. Write the net ionic equation for the reaction that occurred.

2. For each determination, do the following:
   a. Calculate the number of moles of Ag^+ used (from the volume required and molarity).
   b. Calculate the number of moles of Cl^- present (from the number of moles of Ag^+ and the balanced equation).
   c. Calculate the $[Cl^-]$ present in mol/L (from the number of moles of Cl^- and the volume used).
   d. Calculate the $[Cl^-]$ in parts per million (ppm). (This is the same as the number of milligrams of Cl^- per litre.)

FOLLOW-UP QUESTIONS

1. Limestone consists of calcium carbonate, $CaCO_3$. Use your understanding of the equilibria shown in the Post Lab Considerations to explain how limestone caves have been formed and why stalactites and stalagmites are often found in them. Use a reference book if necessary.

2. What is meant by the terms "kettle scale" and "boiler scale"?

3. A certain brand of automatic coffee machine has instructions saying "Important: With daily use this unit should be cleaned once a month with white vinegar." What is the reason for this instruction?

4. Why would it be a good idea, in an area with permanently hard water, to add some washing soda (Na_2CO_3) to the water in a washing machine before adding the laundry detergent?

5. In the 1960's and 1970's laundry detergents contained large amounts of trisodium phosphate (TSP, Na_3PO_4). The use of this chemical has now been cut back. Find out the reason for this change.

6. A 25.0 mL sample of seawater was found to require 152 mL of 0.10M $AgNO_3$ to precipitate all the chloride ion in a titration like that in Part III. Assuming that AgCl was the only substance precipitated, what is the $[Cl^-]$ in the seawater?

CONCLUSION

1. Describe how to eliminate temporary and permanent hardness of water.

2. Classify your water samples as being either high or low in chloride concentration and relate this to whether a sample was of fresh or salt water.

Introduction to Acids and Bases

By the 1500's chemists recognized that certain substances shared a common property — a sour taste. These substances possessed other characteristic properties as well. They were given the collective name of "acids" from the Latin word *acidus*, meaning sour. Another group of substances, called alkalis (or bases), was prepared from the ashes of wood. Bases had a slippery feel and were discovered to be effective cleaners.

When defining acids or bases, it is important to realize that there are two types of definitions — *operational* (or *laboratory*) definitions and *conceptual* definitions. An operational definition is a description of expected test results from a laboratory situation. A conceptual definition attempts to explain the operational definition. Tests for acidity and alkalinity are commonplace today in such fields as gardening and swimming pool maintenance. For example, specialized acid-base test kits are available to home gardeners who wish to monitor the acidity or alkalinity of their soil. One component of such kits is a chemical indicator solution which will show a characteristic color, depending on the conditions of acidity.

In Part I of this experiment, you will first test several unknown solutions of acids and bases and note some of their properties. The similarities of properties should enable you to write some operational definitions. Next, the identities of the unknown solutions will be revealed and you will attempt to write conceptual definitions of acids and bases. In the past, chemists proposed several conceptual definitions of acids and bases. Svante Arrhenius suggested what is certainly the most fundamental definition in the late 1800's. Arrhenius, one of Sweden's most famous chemists, was awarded the Nobel Prize in chemistry in 1903 for his work with ionic solutions. It is quite likely that your conceptual definitions of acids and bases in this experiment will be similar to those of Arrhenius.

Part II of this experiment involves acid-base tests of household products. From the results you obtain and the information provided, you will be asked to classify the household products according to your operational and conceptual definitions of acids and bases.

OBJECTIVES

1. to become familiar with a variety of typical laboratory tests for acids and bases

2. to develop operational definitions of acids and bases

3. to develop conceptual definitions of acids and bases

4. to test a variety of household products and classify them as acids or bases

SUPPLIES

Equipment
6 small test tubes
   (10 mm × 75 mm)
6 dropping pipets
microwells or spot plate or glass
   square (10 cm × 10 cm)

test-tube rack
lab apron
safety goggles

Chemical Reagents
set of 6 unknown solutions (acids
   or bases) labeled A–F
chemical indicators:
   phenolphthalein solution in a
   dropper bottle
   methyl orange solution in a
   dropper bottle

red litmus paper
blue litmus paper
magnesium ribbon (6 cm)
set of 6 household products
   (vinegar, Easy-Off® oven cleaner,
   household ammonia, lemon
   juice, 7-Up®, milk of magnesia)

PROCEDURE

Part I: Tests of Unknown Solutions

1. Put on your lab apron and safety goggles.

2. Place 2 or 3 drops of each solution of the six unknown acids or bases in separate wells of your microwells and add 1 or 2 drops of phenolphthalein solution. Record your results in your copy of Table 1 in your notebook.

3. Repeat Step 2 using methyl orange solution instead of phenolphthalein.

4. Repeat Step 2, but add a small piece of red litmus paper instead of the indicator solution.

5. Repeat Step 2, but add a small piece of blue litmus paper instead of the indicator solution.

6. Repeat Step 2, but use test tubes instead and add a small (about 0.5 cm) strip of magnesium.

Part II: Tests of Common Household Products

1. Repeat Part I for the household products provided by your instructor. Record the observations in your copy of Table 2 in your notebook.

2. Before leaving the laboratory, wash your hands thoroughly with soap and water.

REAGENT DISPOSAL

Rinse all chemicals from the microwells and test tubes with copious amounts of water. To avoid plugging the drain, remove the rinsed pieces of litmus paper and magnesium and place them in the designated waste container.

CAUTION

Remember, A to F are unknowns. Whether they are hazardous or not, it is always a good practice to minimize your contact with unknown chemicals. Some of these chemicals are corrosive to skin, eyes, and clothing. Wash away any spills or splashes with plenty of water.

The phenolphthalein indicator used in this experiment is toxic and flammable. Make sure there are no open flames in the vicinity.

POST LAB CONSIDERATIONS

You should be able to place each of the six unknown solutions into one of two groups, on the basis of Table 1. One property of acids is that they react with active metals such as magnesium. Knowing this, you will be able to determine which group is the acid group and which is the base group. In Part II, you may have noticed that in some instances some of the indicators did not react as you might have expected. For now, you can think of the indicators as having different "sensitivities" to acids and bases, the effect being that they will not always give positive results. As long as one of the tests showed a positive result and provided that you did not get any conflicting results, you can classify a solution on the basis of that one result.

In order to develop conceptual definitions, you will require more information about the solutions tested. Relevant information such as chemical formulas and electrical conductivity will be provided by your instructor at an appropriate time.

EXPERIMENTAL RESULTS

Part I: Tests of Unknown Solutions
Table 1

Unknown Solution	Chemical Indicators				Magnesium Metal
	Phenolphthalein	Methyl Orange	Red Litmus	Blue Litmus	
A					
B					
C					
D					
E					
F					

COMPLETE IN YOUR NOTEBOOK

Part II: Tests of Common Household Products
Table 2

Household Products	Chemical Indicators				Magnesium Metal
	Phenolphthalein	Methyl Orange	Red Litmus	Blue Litmus	
Vinegar					
Easy-Off® Oven Cleaner					
Household Ammonia					
7-Up®					
Lemon Juice					
Milk of Magnesia					

COMPLETE IN YOUR NOTEBOOK

ANALYSIS OF RESULTS

1. Examine the data in Table 1 and form groups of solutions on the basis of similar properties. Classify one of these groups as acids and the other as bases. (A hint was provided in the Post Lab Considerations.)

2. Write operational definitions for acids and bases based on the results of Part I of this experiment.

3. Using your results from Part II and your operational definition from Part I, classify the household products as acids or bases.

4. What, if any, general pattern exists with regard to the types of household products which are acids and those which are bases?

FOLLOW-UP QUESTIONS

1. a. Find out the chemical formula for each of the unknown solutions from your instructor and classify them as acids or bases.
   b. Write conceptual definitions of acids and bases.

2. a. Find out the chemical formulas of the active ingredients in the household products from your instructor and group them as acids or bases.
   b. How do your conceptual definitions explain your acid-base classifications of the household products?

3. a. Using a reference source, discover and write out the Arrhenius definitions of acids and bases. Be sure to cite the reference you used.
   b. How do the Arrhenius definitions compare to your conceptual definitions?

4. Acid rain contains varying amounts of sulfuric acid and/or nitric acid.
   a. Predict the test results you might expect if you were to test a sample of acid rain in this experiment.
   b. What should the chemical formulas of sulfuric acid and nitric acid have in common?
   c. Consult a reference source and write out the chemical formulas for sulfuric acid and nitric acid.

CONCLUSION

State the results of Objective 3.

Brönsted-Lowry Acid and Base Equilibria

In Experiment 13A you were introduced to the topic of acids and bases, and you learned that an acid gives off H^+ ions in solution and a base gives off OH^- ions in solution. These statements are the *Arrhenius* definitions for an acid and a base. They apply to aqueous ionic solutions.

Another pair of definitions for an acid and a base has been proposed to take into account the fact that not all acid-base reactions occur in aqueous solution; they can occur in other solvents as well. These definitions are known as the *Brönsted-Lowry* definitions, after the scientists who first proposed them. According to the Brönsted-Lowry theory, an acid is defined as a proton (H^+) donor and a base is defined as a proton acceptor. Another part of this theory reveals that when an acid and a base react together, they produce another base and another acid respectively. You can see that the Brönsted-Lowry definitions include the Arrhenius definitions, since H^+ is the same as a proton and OH^- reacts with (accepts) a proton (H^+) when they neutralize one another. Using HA to indicate an acid and B^- to indicate a base, the equation for a Brönsted-Lowry acid-base reaction can be shown as follows:

$$HA + B^- \rightleftharpoons A^- + HB$$
$$\text{acid} \quad \text{base} \quad \text{base} \quad \text{acid}$$

A pair of chemical species such as HA and A^- or HB and B^- is called a *conjugate acid-base pair*. (A^- is the conjugate base of HA and HA is the conjugate acid of A^-). If the reaction equilibrium shown above favors the products over the reactants, then HA must be a stronger acid than HB. (That is, HA has the greater tendency to donate protons.) Likewise, B^- is a stronger base than A^-. (B^- has a greater tendency to accept protons.)

An *acid-base indicator* is an example of a weak acid or base, but what makes it unique is that it has a conjugate base or acid which is a different color. The $[H^+]$ at which the color changes varies from one indicator to another; thus, indicators can be used to determine the $[H^+]$ in a solution.

In this experiment, you will use five different indicators which will be identified only by number. They will each be added to six unknown solutions containing a conjugate acid-base pair. Therefore, you will have eleven solutions to start with, including the indicators that are conjugate acid-base pairs. From the resulting thirty mixtures you will be able to deduce the relative strengths of all eleven as weak acids and arrange them in order of decreasing strengths of acids (or increasing strengths of conjugate bases).

OBJECTIVES

1. to obtain an understanding of the equilibria which involve acids and bases

CAUTION

The hydrochloric acid and sodium hydroxide solutions are corrosive to skin, eyes, and clothing. Wash any spills and splashes with plenty of water. Call your instructor.

CAUTION

Some of the unknowns in this experiment are strongly acidic or strongly basic. Treat them all as though they are corrosive to skin, eyes, and clothing. Wash any spills and splashes with plenty of water. Call your instructor.

CAUTION

Some of the indicators used in this experiment consist of flammable solutions. Make sure there are no open flames in the vicinity.

2. to observe the color changes that occur with a number of different acid-base indicators in several different solutions

3. to arrange all the Brönsted-Lowry acids involved in this experiment in order of decreasing strength

SUPPLIES

Equipment
microwells or spot plate
lab apron
safety goggles

Chemical Reagents
$1M$ HCl
$1M$ NaOH
6 solutions of different pH
(labeled HA_1/A_1^-, HA_2/A_2^-, etc., to HA_6/A_6^-)
5 different indicator solutions
(labeled HIn_1/In_1^-, HIn_2/In_2^-, etc., to HIn_5/In_5^-)

PROCEDURE

1. Put on your lab apron and safety goggles.

2. Place 2 drops of $1M$ HCl into each of 5 depressions in your microwells or spot plate.

3. Add 1 drop of each indicator solution separately to the HCl and record the color in your copy of Table 1 in your notebook. (These results give you the color of the acid form of each indicator.) Repeat Steps 2 and 3, using $1M$ NaOH instead of HCl. (The results give the color of the base form of each indicator.)

4. Repeat Steps 2 and 3 with the unknown solution HA_1/A_1^- and the five different indicators and continue the process with all the other unknown solutions until you have recorded the color in all 30 possible combinations of unknown solution with unknown indicator.

5. Wash your hands thoroughly with soap and water before leaving the laboratory.

REAGENT DISPOSAL

Rinse all chemicals down the sink with plenty of water.

POST LAB CONSIDERATIONS

The results with HCl and each indicator tell you what the color of the acid form of the indicator is, since HCl is a strong acid and will cause the indicator to accept a proton. The results with NaOH and each indicator tell you what the color of the base form of the indicator is, since NaOH is a strong base and will cause the indicator to donate a proton.

Copying the experiment is prohibited.   ©SMG Lab Books Ltd.

In order to interpret the results and deduce a list of acid strengths, consider the following example:

$$HA_1 + In_3^- \rightleftharpoons A_1^- + HIn_3$$

If in this combination the indicator HIn_3 is showing the color of its acid form, then HA_1 is a stronger acid than HIn_3 because HA_1 was able to donate a proton. In addition, In_3^- is a stronger base than A_1^-. On the other hand, if in the same example the mixture shows the color of the basic form of HIn_3, namely In_3^-, then HIn_3 is stronger than HA_1 and A_1^- is stronger than In_3^-. Note that the stronger acid and base always react to give the weaker acid and base.

You will often use indicators in subsequent experiments and some of them may be the same ones you used here. The important fact to realize about indicators is that they are weak acids just like any other weak acid and are therefore subject to equilibrium shifts. The only reason that indicators were used in this experiment was that, since the weak acid and conjugate base which constitute each indicator happen to have different colors, any equilibrium shifts were easy to identify.

CAUTION

Some of the indicators used in this experiment are toxic. Do not get any in your mouth, do not swallow any. Wash any spills and splashes with plenty of water.

EXPERIMENTAL RESULTS

Table 1

	HIn_1/In_1^-	HIn_2/In_2^-	HIn_3/In_3^-	HIn_4/In_4^-	HIn_5/In_5^-
HCl					
NaOH					
HA_1/A_1^-					
HA_2/A_2^-					
HA_3/A_3^-					
HA_4/A_4^-					
HA_5/A_5^-					
HA_6/A_6^-					

COMPLETE IN YOUR NOTEBOOK

ANALYSIS OF RESULTS

1. Make up another table like the one showing your results, but leave out HCl and NaOH. From your results, fill in each box with a statement about the relative strengths of the two acids involved; for instance, $HA_1 > HIn_3$ or $HIn_3 > HA_1$.

2. Arrange the eleven acids in a list, with the strongest at the top and weakest at the bottom. Then write an ionization equation for each by putting H^+ and the conjugate base on the right.

For example, $HA_1 \rightleftharpoons H^+ + A_1^-$.

Label each side of the list with a vertical arrow, one for increasing strength of acid and one for increasing strength of base.

FOLLOW-UP QUESTIONS

1. Your instructor will tell you the identity of the five indicators used in this experiment. Use a reference source to determine the pH range over which these particular indicators change color. Be sure to cite the reference you use.

2. The six unknown solutions were all at a whole number of pH units in the range 0–14. Try to work out the pH of each unknown solution. For some of them you may not be able to determine the pH exactly, but you should be able to narrow it down to a range of pH values.

3. One way of determining the pH of a particular solution is to use what is called a universal indicator, which consists of a mixture of different indicators that give a number of different color changes as the pH changes. From a reference source, find out the composition of a universal indicator. As usual, be sure to cite the reference you use.

CONCLUSION

State the results of Objective 3.

Copying the experiment is prohibited.

Acid-Base Titration

Titration is a very important laboratory technique which is used to determine the concentration of a wide variety of chemical substances. A standard solution (one of known molarity) is titrated against (reacted with) another solution in such a manner that the concentration of the second solution may be calculated from the results. The second solution is added to a known volume of the first solution by means of a buret, which allows the volume of solution delivered to the reaction vessel to be accurately determined. A chemical indicator is used to show when the reaction is complete.

Acid-base titrations involve a net reaction in which aqueous hydrogen ions and hydroxide ions react with one another to form neutral water molecules:

$$H^+(aq) + OH^-(aq) \rightleftharpoons H_2O(l)$$

This net process is called *neutralization*.

The indicator phenolphthalein will be used to show when the reaction is complete, at which point the number of moles of acid consumed equals the number of moles of base added. This point is called the *equivalence point*.

A titration is one of the most common analytical procedures performed by the chemist. We all depend upon chemical analysis and it is with this branch of chemistry that the average citizen is most likely to come into contact. Decisions involving large sums of money, or even life and death, depend upon the accuracy and speed of chemical analysis, whether in hospital lab testing, environmental pollution monitoring, or crime detection.

OBJECTIVES

1. to titrate a hydrochloric acid solution of unknown concentration with standardized 0.5*M* sodium hydroxide

2. to titrate an acetic acid solution (vinegar) with standardized 0.5*M* sodium hydroxide

3. to utilize the titration results to calculate the molarity of the hydrochloric acid and the molarity and percent composition of the vinegar

SUPPLIES

Equipment
suction bulb
volumetric pipet (10 mL)
buret (50 mL)
buret stand and clamp
Erlenmeyer flask (250 mL)
lab apron
safety goggles

Chemical Reagents
standardized NaOH solution
    (approx. 0.5M, known exactly)
unknown HCl solution
white vinegar (acetic acid
    solution, CH_3COOH)
phenolphthalein solution

PROCEDURE

Part I: Determining the Molarity of a Hydrochloric Acid Solution

The hydrochloric acid and sodium hydroxide solutions are corrosive to skin, eyes, and clothing. Wash any spills and splashes with plenty of water. Call your instructor.

1. Put on your lab apron and safety goggles.

2. Obtain about 50 mL of the hydrochloric acid solution of unknown concentration and about 100 mL of the standardized NaOH solution. Your instructor will provide you with the exact molarity of the NaOH. Record this value in your copy of Table 1 in your notebook.

3. Using a suction bulb, pipet 10.00 mL of the HCl solution into a 250 mL Erlenmeyer flask, after rinsing the pipet with a small amount of HCl first.

4. Add 3 drops of phenolphthalein solution.

The phenolphthalein indicator used in this experiment is toxic and flammable. Make sure there are no open flames in the vicinity.

5. Rinse a clean buret with approximately 15 mL of the standardized NaOH solution. Drain the buret and refill with standardized NaOH solution. Flush a small amount through the tip to remove any possible air bubbles. Clamp it into position with the buret clamp and stand. (See Figure 13C-1.) Record the initial reading of the buret in Table 1.

Figure 13C-1 *Set-up of buret and flask for titrating*

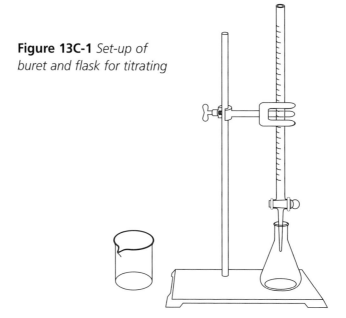

Copying the experiment is prohibited.   ©SMG Lab Books Ltd.

6. Gradually dispense some of the standardized NaOH solution into the flask, swirling constantly. Continue adding NaOH solution, watching the contents of the flask carefully for changes.

7. As the equivalence point approaches, a pinkish color is evident, which initially disappears with swirling. At this point, place a piece of white paper under the flask so that the pink color is more easily observed. When this color starts to take a little longer to dissipate, add the NaOH solution drop by drop. Stop the titration and take the reading on the buret when the solution remains pale pink for approximately 30 s. The most accurate end point to the titration is where the solution remains the faintest possible pink.

8. Repeat Steps 3 to 7 using a second 10.00 mL sample of the HCl. Knowing the volume required in your first titration enables you to be extra careful with the remaining ones. When you are within 1 mL of the previous value, add the NaOH a drop at a time, swirling after each drop. This lessens the likelihood of your overshooting the mark.

9. If the two values differ widely, it would be a good idea to do one more titration if you have time.

Part II: Determining the Percentage Composition of Vinegar

1. Obtain approximately 30 mL of white vinegar (acetic acid solution).

2. Using the same buret of NaOH as was used in Part I, do more titrations, but this time use 10.00 mL portions of vinegar instead of HCl. Follow exactly the same procedures as in Part I (Steps 3 to 9). Refill the buret as required. Record your observations in your copy of Table 2.

3. Wash your hands thoroughly with soap and water before leaving the laboratory.

CAUTION

The vinegar solution is mildly corrosive. Wash any spills and splashes with plenty of water.

REAGENT DISPOSAL

Mix any leftover acids and bases together to neutralize them and pour them down the sink with plenty of water. Do not return any solutions to their original containers.

POST LAB CONSIDERATIONS

During the HCl titration, the hydroxide ions liberated from the standardized NaOH solution reacted in a 1:1 ratio with the hydrogen ions from the HCl to form neutral water molecules. When the number of moles of both species were the same, the equivalence point was reached. Since we have the volume of a solution of known molarity, the number of moles of NaOH can be calculated as follows:

$$\text{Volume}_{NaOH} \text{ (L)} \times \text{Molarity}_{NaOH} = \text{Reactant Moles}_{NaOH}$$

From the balanced equation for the reaction:

$$\text{Reactant Moles}_{NaOH} = \text{Reactant Moles}_{HCl}$$

Knowing the volume of HCl used originally, the molarity of the HCl can be calculated from the formula:

$$\text{Molarity}_{HCl} = \frac{\text{Moles}_{HCl}}{\text{Volume}_{HCl}\ (L)}$$

In Part II, calculate the molarity of the acetic acid in vinegar in the same manner as shown for the HCl. In addition, calculate the percentage composition of the vinegar. This is given by:

$$\text{Percentage composition} = \frac{\text{mass solute}}{\text{mass solution}} \times 100\%$$

The mass of the acetic acid (CH_3COOH) is obtained from the number of moles times the molar mass. The mass of the solution is obtained from the measured volume of the solution times its density. For this experiment you may assume that the density of vinegar is 1.00 g/mL.

In both parts of this experiment, the acid and the base were in a 1:1 mole ratio. However, later you may encounter situations where this is not the case. For these the equivalence point is defined as the point at which the acid and base are in the mole ratio given by the coefficients in the balanced equation for the reaction.

EXPERIMENTAL RESULTS

Part I: Determining the Molarity of a Hydrochloric Acid Solution

Table 1 Volume of NaOH Needed to Neutralize 10.00 mL of Unknown HCl Solution

Molarity of NaOH = M	Trial 1	Trial 2	Trial 3 (if necessary)
Initial reading of buret (mL)			
Final reading of buret (mL)			
Volume of NaOH used (mL)			
Average volume of NaOH (mL)			

Part II: Determining the Percentage Composition of Vinegar

Table 2 Volume of NaOH Needed to Neutralize 10.00 mL of Vinegar

Molarity of NaOH = M	Trial 1	Trial 2	Trial 3 (if necessary)
Initial reading of buret (mL)			
Final reading of buret (mL)			
Volume of NaOH used (mL)			
Average volume of NaOH (mL)			

Copying the experiment is prohibited.

ANALYSIS OF RESULTS

Part I: Determining the Molarity of a Hydrochloric Acid Solution

1. Write out the balanced formula equation for the titration reaction of HCl(aq) with NaOH(aq).

2. Calculate moles of NaOH from the average volume used in Part I and the given molarity.

3. Calculate moles of HCl present originally.

4. Calculate the molarity of the HCl solution.

Part II: Determining the Percentage Composition of Vinegar

1. Write out the balanced formula equation for the titration reaction of CH_3COOH(aq) with NaOH(aq).

2. Calculate moles of NaOH from the average volume used in Part II and the given molarity.

3. Calculate moles of acetic acid present originally.

4. Calculate the molarity of the acetic acid solution.

5. Calculate the mass of acetic acid in 1.00 L of solution.

6. Calculate the percentage of acetic acid in the vinegar.

FOLLOW-UP QUESTIONS

1. While doing a titration, it is permissible to use a wash bottle to wash down any material that may have splashed higher up in the flask. This would appear to increase the volume of acid in the flask. Why will it have no effect on the results?

2. What was the reason for rinsing out the buret with NaOH solution before starting the titrations?

3. By law, vinegar must be not less than 4% by mass acetic acid. Did your sample meet this specification?

CONCLUSION

State the results of Objective 3.

13D

Hydrolysis — The Reaction of Ions with Water

When a base "neutralizes" an acid, the result of the reaction is the formation of a salt and water. You would expect, therefore, that a salt dissolved in water would be neither acidic nor basic; that is, its pH should be 7. However, some ions are known to undergo a reaction with water, in a process called *hydrolysis*. Salts are composed of positive ions (*cations*) and negative ions (*anions*). When a cation reacts with water, the process is called *cationic hydrolysis* and when an anion reacts with water, the process is called *anionic hydrolysis*. In both cases, the resulting solutions are either acidic or basic. In the case of some salts, both anion and cation hydrolyze and the resulting pH depends on which hydrolysis reaction predominates.

In this experiment, you will determine the pH of a large number of salt solutions in water. From the results you will deduce information about which ions have hydrolyzed. The type of hydrolysis is related to the relative strengths of the acid and base from which a given salt is formed. In addition, you will measure the pH of some salts of amphiprotic anions (anions which can either gain or lose a proton) and use the result to deduce which hydrolysis predominates, and consequently, whether $K_b > K_a$ or $K_b < K_a$. The pH of each solution will be determined by one of two methods: either adding some universal indicator solution or using small strips of universal indicator paper. The method used will depend on which type of indicator your instructor has available. A universal indicator is a mixture of several different indicators, which change color at different pH values, so that a sequence of color changes is observed over a large pH range. The sequence usually approximates the colors of the spectrum, with red at low pH, green near neutral, and blue or violet at high pH.

OBJECTIVES

1. to measure the pH of a large number of salts and identify those which undergo hydrolysis

2. to explain why hydrolysis occurs (or does not occur) in terms of the relative strengths of the acid and base from which a given salt is made and to write a net ionic equation for each hydrolysis

3. to deduce which is greater for some amphiprotic anions, their K_a value or their K_b value

SUPPLIES

Equipment
microwells or spot plate
lab apron
safety goggles

Chemical Reagents

0.1M solutions of each of the following in dropper bottles:

sodium chloride, NaCl
sodium acetate, NaCH$_3$COO
ammonium chloride, NH$_4$Cl
ammonium sulfate, (NH$_4$)$_2$SO$_4$
calcium nitrate, Ca(NO$_3$)$_2$
sodium carbonate, Na$_2$CO$_3$
sodium phosphate, Na$_3$PO$_4$
potassium bromide, KBr
potassium sulfate, K$_2$SO$_4$
ammonium oxalate, (NH$_4$)$_2$C$_2$O$_4$
ammonium acetate,
    NH$_4$CH$_3$COO

ammonium carbonate, (NH$_4$)$_2$CO$_3$
iron(III) sulfate, Fe$_2$(SO$_4$)$_3$
aluminum chloride, AlCl$_3$
potassium monohydrogen
    phosphate, K$_2$HPO$_4$
potassium dihydrogen
    phosphate, KH$_2$PO$_4$
sodium bicarbonate, NaHCO$_3$
potassium bisulfate, KHSO$_4$
sodium bisulfite, NaHSO$_3$
solutions of Fe$_2$(SO$_4$)$_3$, Al$_2$(SO$_4$)$_3$,
    and FeCl$_3$ that have been
    standing for some months
universal indicator solution or
    universal indicator paper

PROCEDURE

1. Put on your lab apron and safety goggles.

2. In the first depression in your microwells (or spot plate) place 2 drops of either distilled water or tap water (whichever was used to make up the solutions — your instructor will tell you which to use). This will act as a control since this water will be considered neutral.

3. To the water, add 1 drop of universal indicator solution or a 0.5 cm strip of universal indicator paper, as directed by your instructor.

4. Note the color given by the indicator. By consulting the color chart provided with the universal indicator, which correlates color with pH, estimate the pH of the water.

5. Add 2 drops of the first solution assigned to you from Table 1 in the Experimental Results to the next depression in your microwells, add indicator as before, and record the color and corresponding pH in the appropriate row in the table.

6. Continue Procedure 5 until you have investigated all 19 solutions shown in Table 1 and Table 2.

7. Your teacher will have on display some solutions of iron(III) chloride (or iron(III) sulfate) and aluminum sulfate that have been left standing for some weeks or months. Look at them carefully and record what you see.

8. Before you leave the laboratory, wash your hands thoroughly with soap and water.

CAUTION

Most of these solutions are poisonous, corrosive, or irritants. Wash any spills or splashes immediately with plenty of water. Call your instructor.

REAGENT DISPOSAL

Wash all solutions down the sink with copious amounts of water. Be careful not to let the small pieces of indicator paper block the sink; discard them in the garbage container.

POST LAB CONSIDERATIONS

You will most likely have found that the pH of the water alone was a little less than the expected value of 7, even if you used distilled water. This is caused by the dissolving of carbon dioxide from the air. Therefore, for this experiment, a solution showing the same pH as the water sample should be considered to be neutral, that is, neither ion hydrolyzed. Any pH higher than the value displayed by the water indicates basic hydrolysis.

Salts formed from a strong acid and a strong base do not undergo hydrolysis. Basic hydrolysis occurs if the salt is derived from a strong base and a weak acid. For example, consider a hypothetical weak acid HA. Its sodium salt will give Na^+ and A^- in solution. Weak acids must always satisfy the relationship between [HA], [H^+], and [A^-] as determined by the K_a expression and its corresponding value. When [A^-] is present in appreciable quantities in solution and non-ionized HA is not present at all, the K_a expression cannot be at its correct value. The position of the equilibrium must therefore shift, with the ion A^- combining with the H^+ from water to give non-ionized HA until the K_a value is satisfied. This process leaves OH^- behind and the solution becomes basic. For example, a solution of potassium fluoride is basic because the fluoride ion undergoes anionic hydrolysis as follows:

$$F^-(aq) + H_2O(l) \rightleftharpoons HF(aq) + OH^-(aq)$$

Acidic hydrolysis of the ammonium ion occurred in this experiment because ammonia is a weak base and salts of ammonia with strong acids will hydrolyze, giving acidic solutions:

$$NH_4^+(aq) + H_2O(l) \rightleftharpoons NH_3(aq) + H_3O^+(aq)$$

Some ammonium salts used in this experiment were formed from a weak acid and ammonia. In these, the pH you observed depended upon the relative strength of the acid compared to ammonia's strength as a base. You will do calculations to verify your results, by comparing the K_a of NH_4^+ with the calculated value of the K_b of the anion involved.

The other type of acidic hydrolysis involved metal ions having a small diameter and a high charge (3+). Such ions are strongly attracted to water molecules, and in fact form hydrated ions in which the metal ion itself is surrounded by (usually) six water molecules (ligands). The water molecules align themselves with the negative oxygen ends of the molecular dipoles oriented toward the positive metal ion. The attraction of the positive metal ion for the negative charge on the surrounding water molecules is so great that protons can be donated from the water molecules to give an acidic solution (pH less than 7). For example, the hydrated ion $Fe(H_2O)_6^{3+}$ can act as an acid:

$$Fe(H_2O)_6^{3+}(aq) + H_2O(l) \rightleftharpoons Fe(H_2O)_5OH^{2+}(aq) + H_3O^+(aq)$$

The K_a for this ionization is 6.0×10^{-3}, making $Fe(H_2O)_6^{3+}$ relatively strong as weak acids go, stronger than such weak acids as HF, HNO_2, and CH_3COOH. The ionization can proceed further, with $Fe(H_2O)_5OH^{2+}$ losing more protons, giving $Fe(H_2O)_4(OH)_2{}^{+}$, and eventually $Fe(H_2O)_3(OH)_3$. The latter is formed as a precipitate in solutions of Fe^{3+}(aq) that have been left standing for a long time.

The five substances in Table 2 are salts of sodium or potassium with an amphiprotic anion, that is, an anion which can donate or accept a proton. There are two possible reactions involving these ions, acidic hydrolysis or basic hydrolysis. Which of these two reactions will occur to the greater extent will depend upon the value of K_a for HB^- relative to K_b for HB^-. If the K_a is larger, the solution will be acidic, but if the K_b is larger, the solution will be basic. The pH that you measured for the solution will therefore indicate whether the K_a or the K_b is larger. (You will check your results by calculation.) K_a values can be obtained from a table of acid ionization constants. K_b can be calculated from the formula $K_b = \dfrac{K_w}{K_a}$, where $K_w = 1.00 \times 10^{-14}$. Here K_a refers to the acid ionization constant for the conjugate acid of the anion HB^-, namely H_2B.

EXPERIMENTAL RESULTS

Table 1

Solution	Color of Universal Indicator	pH	Acidic, Basic, or Neutral	Ion(s) That Hydrolyzed
NaCl				
$NaCH_3COO$				
NH_4Cl				
$(NH_4)_2SO_4$				
$Ca(NO_3)_2$				
Na_2CO_3				
Na_3PO_4				
KBr				
K_2SO_4				
$(NH_4)_2C_2O_4$				
NH_4CH_3COO				
$(NH_4)_2CO_3$				
$Fe_2(SO_4)_3$				
$AlCl_3$				

Table 2

Solution	Color of Universal Indicator	pH	Type of Hydrolysis (Acidic or Basic) That Predominates
K_2HPO_4			
KH_2PO_4			
$NaHCO_3$		COMPLETE IN YOUR NOTEBOOK	
$KHSO_4$			
$NaHSO_3$			

ANALYSIS OF RESULTS

1. Referring to both your experimental results and the Post Lab Considerations above, fill in columns 4 and 5 in Table 1 and column 4 in Table 2.

2. For each salt tested, state the acid and base from which it is obtained and whether the acid and base are strong or weak. Then write the net ionic equation for the hydrolysis, if any occurs.

3. Note that some (ammonium) salts are formed from a weak acid and the weak base NH_3. For these, write a net ionic equation for each ion, then state from your results which is stronger, the acid or the base. Verify your result by calculating the K_b for the anion (as outlined in the Post Lab Considerations) and comparing it to the K_a for NH_4^+.

4. The substances K_2HPO_4, KH_2PO_4, $NaHCO_3$, $KHSO_4$, and $NaHSO_3$ all have an amphiprotic anion, that is, one which can either gain or lose a proton. Write two net ionic equations for each ion, one in which a proton is removed (the ion is acting as an acid) and one in which a proton is accepted (the ion is acting as a base). For each of the substances, state which reaction occurred to the greater extent on the basis of your observations of the pH. Then, look up the K_a for each ion and calculate each ion's K_b. Compare these two results and verify that your calculations agree with your experimental observations.

5. What was the precipitate observed in solutions of Fe^{3+} salts that had been standing for a long time? Give equations showing how this precipitate is formed.

6. Repeat Analysis 5 for the precipitate in the Al^{3+} salts.

FOLLOW-UP QUESTIONS

1. Many plants do not grow well in soil that is too acidic. A certain gardener wishes to increase the nitrogen content of the soil and has available potassium nitrate, KNO_3, and ammonium sulphate, $(NH_4)_2SO_4$, both of which are common fertilizers. Which one would be better for keeping the soil near neutral?

2. The chemical sodium phosphate, Na_3PO_4, is sold in stores as TSP (trisodium phosphate). It is commonly used as a cleaning agent. Explain why it could be expected to be useful for such a purpose.

3. Some types of baking powder consist of sodium bicarbonate, $NaHCO_3$, and calcium dihydrogen phosphate, $Ca(H_2PO_4)_2$. Explain the function of the $Ca(H_2PO_4)_2$ in the baking powder.

4. The precipitate that eventually forms in solutions of Al^{3+} and Fe^{3+} salts removes these ions from the solution; therefore, the solution does not remain at the concentration at which it was originally made up. Suggest a material that could be added to the solution when it is initially prepared that would minimize the hydrolysis and therefore prevent precipitation. (Hint: Think of Le Chatelier's principle!)

5. The observation of the pH for iron(III) sulfate, $Fe_2(SO_4)_3$, can be explained in another manner. Given that the K_{sp} for $Fe(OH)_3$ is 2.6×10^{-39}, calculate the Trial K_{sp} for a $0.1M$ solution of Fe^{3+} in neutral water. How does it compare to K_{sp}? Will a precipitate form? What ion will be left in excess in the solution as a result?

6. Look at the equations that you have written for the hydrolysis of the NH_4^+ and CO_3^{2-} ions in $(NH_4)_2CO_3$. What two ions produced (one in each) will now react with one another? What effect will this have on the position of both equilibria?

7. It is very likely that in the First Aid kit in your laboratory there is a small vial containing ammonium carbonate. This vial is crushed when needed to revive anyone who has fainted. In light of your answer to Follow-Up Question 6, state what substance you think would be responsible for reviving the patient. (You may wish to experiment with this yourself. Ask your instructor if you may carefully waft the fumes from a bottle of solid ammonium carbonate towards your nose.)

CONCLUSION

Summarize in general terms, what types of salts undergo hydrolysis and what type of solution they produce.

13E

Acid-Base Trends of Metal and Non-Metal Hydroxides

Oxides of elements are commonly encountered on a daily basis. Metal oxides, for instance, are important substances because O_2, the molecular form of oxygen found in air, is readily available and reacts well with most metals. For example, rust (Fe_2O_3) results when metallic iron reacts with the oxygen in the air. Non-metal oxides also have an effect on people. Oxides of sulfur and nitrogen are produced by industrial processes and can act as serious air pollutants. Combining any element with oxygen can produce the oxide of that element. The reaction equation is often a simple equation similar to this:

$$X \quad + \quad O_2 \quad \rightarrow \quad XO$$
$$\text{element} \quad \text{oxygen} \quad \text{oxide}$$

The above equation has not been balanced, since the formula of the oxide will depend on the ion charge of the element.

Although the reaction is easy to describe, the preparation of oxides poses a few problems. For instance, it can be difficult or hazardous to prepare some of the more interesting oxides such as MgO and SO_2. Therefore, in this experiment you will be provided with the oxides already prepared. In Part I, you will prepare hydroxide solutions of four metal oxides by adding water to them, then test the solutions for acidic and basic properties. In Part II, you will receive two already prepared solutions of non-metal oxides and test them for acidic and basic properties. When an oxide reacts with water, a hydroxide is formed according to this general equation $XO + H_2O \rightarrow XOH$. Note that the equation has not been balanced. A summary of the elements in this experiment, their oxides, and hydroxide solutions appears below:

Element + Oxygen	→	Oxide	Oxide + Water	→	Hydroxide Solution
$2Mg$ + O_2	→	$2MgO$	MgO + H_2O	→	$Mg(OH)_2$
$2Ca$ + O_2	→	$2CaO$	CaO + H_2O	→	$Ca(OH)_2$
$2Zn$ + O_2	→	$2ZnO$	ZnO + H_2O	→	$Zn(OH)_2$
$4Al$ + $3O_2$	→	$2Al_2O_3$	Al_2O_3 + $3H_2O$	→	$2Al(OH)_3$
$2S$ + $3O_2$	→	$2SO_3$	SO_3 + H_2O	→	$SO_2(OH)_2$
N_2 + $2O_2$	→	$2NO_2$	$2NO_2$ + H_2O	→	$NO_2(OH) + NO(OH)$

Most of these are definitely acidic or definitely basic. But there are certain oxides and hydroxides (known as *amphoteric* oxides and hydroxides) which can react with both acids and bases. An additional task you will have in Part III of this experiment is to test some hydroxides for amphoteric behaviour.

OBJECTIVES

1. to test the acid-base properties of solutions of metal oxides

2. to test the acid-base properties of solutions of non-metal oxides

3. to determine what, if any, periodic trend exists in acid-base properties of oxide solutions

---

SUPPLIES

Equipment
10 test tubes (13 mm × 100 mm)
test-tube rack
4 rubber stoppers
2 dropping pipets
2 beakers (50 mL)
lab apron
safety goggles

Chemical Reagents
universal indicator solution
    or wide range pH paper
CaO powder
MgO powder
ZnO powder
Al_2O_3 powder
two prepared solutions (labeled A
    and B) of non-metal oxides
6M HCl
6M NaOH
0.1M Al(NO$_3$)$_3$

PROCEDURE

Part I: Preparing and Testing Solutions of Metal Oxides

1. Put on your lab apron and safety goggles.

2. Add a small amount of each of the four powdered oxides to separate, labeled test tubes.

3. Half-fill the test tubes with water, stopper them, and shake the contents for about 2 min. You will probably notice that slurries result, since the hydroxides formed here are only slightly soluble.

4. Add 2 or 3 drops of universal indicator solution to each slurry. (Wide-range pH paper can be used in place of universal indicator.) Record your results in a copy of Table 1 in your notebook.

Part II: Testing Solutions of Non-metal Oxides

1. Solution A is a hydroxide solution of an oxide of sulfur; Solution B is a hydroxide solution of an oxide of nitrogen. Half-fill two labeled test tubes with these solutions. Test both solutions with universal indicator solution as in Part I. Include these results in Table 1 as well.

Part III: Testing for Amphoteric Behavior

1. Shake each test tube thoroughly again, then divide each slurry that resulted in Part I into two portions by pouring half of the sample into a clean test tube.

2. Obtain about 10 mL of 6M HCl and 6M NaOH in separate small beakers, which have been labeled. Place a clean dropping pipet in each beaker.

3. Test one portion of each slurry by adding 6M HCl drop by drop. Shake the test tube occasionally as you add the acid. Continue adding acid and

CAUTION

The hydrochloric acid and sodium hydroxide solutions are corrosive to skin, eyes, and clothing. Wash any spills and splashes with plenty of water. Call your instructor.

shaking until no further changes occur. Note all changes in a table similar to Table 2 in your notebook. Pay close attention to what happens to the cloudiness of each slurry.

4. Test the other portion of each slurry by adding 6M NaOH drop by drop. Shake the test tube occasionally as you add the base and record any changes in Table 2.

5. As an additional confirmation of the behavior of $Al(OH)_3$, add 2 mL of 0.1M $Al(NO_3)_3$ to a test tube, then add 6M NaOH dropwise until a gelatinous precipitate of $Al(OH)_3$ is obtained. Divide the contents of the tube into two approximately equal portions. Add a small amount of water if the precipitate is too thick to flow easily.

6. To the first tube, add more 6M NaOH until a change occurs. Record the result in Table 3.

7. To the second tube, add 6M HCl until a change occurs. Record the result in Table 3.

8. Before you leave the laboratory, wash your hands thoroughly with soap and water.

REAGENT DISPOSAL

Pour all solutions and slurries into the designated waste container.

POST LAB CONSIDERATIONS

By studying your results, you will be able to determine which hydroxides are acidic, basic, neutral, or amphoteric. Then, by examining the periodic table and noting the positions of the elements from which the hydroxides formed, you can determine whether any acid-base trends exist.

At this point, you may think it odd that a hydroxide of an element can act as an acid. Although many hydroxides behave as bases, the Brönsted-Lowry definition of an acid merely requires that a substance donate protons in a reaction. Consider the following equations involving a hypothetical hydroxide:

As a base: $X - O - H \rightarrow X^+ + OH^-$

can *accept* a proton

As an acid: $X - O - H \rightarrow XO^- + H^+$

can *donate* a proton

EXPERIMENTAL RESULTS

Parts I and II: Preparing and Testing Solutions of Metal and Non-metal Oxides
Table 1

Hydroxide Solution Tested	Universal Indicator Results	Acidic, Basic, or Neutral
$Mg(OH)_2$		
$Ca(OH)_2$		
$Zn(OH)_2$	COMPLETE IN YOUR NOTEBOOK	COMPLETE IN YOUR NOTEBOOK
$Al(OH)_3$		
$SO_2(OH)_2$		
$NO_2(OH)$		

Part III: Testing for Amphoteric Behavior
Table 2

Hydroxide Solution Tested	Addition of Acid or Base	Universal Indicator Results		Other Changes
		Before	After	
COMPLETE IN YOUR NOTEBOOK	COMPLETE IN YOUR NOTEBOOK	COMPLETE IN YOUR NOTEBOOK		COMPLETE IN YOUR NOTEBOOK

Table 3

$Al(NO_3)_3$ + 6M NaOH	With more 6M NaOH added	With 6M HCl added
COMPLETE IN YOUR NOTEBOOK	COMPLETE IN YOUR NOTEBOOK	COMPLETE IN YOUR NOTEBOOK

ANALYSIS OF RESULTS

1. **a.** Write the formula for Solution A, $SO_2(OH)_2$, in a different, more familiar form.
   b. What is the acid name of this substance?
   c. Repeat for Solution B, $NO_2(OH)$.

2. Write chemical equations to explain how $Zn(OH)_2$ can react with an acid or a base.

3. Write chemical equations to explain how $Al(OH)_3$ can react with an acid or a base.

FOLLOW-UP QUESTIONS

1. **a.** Carbon dioxide gas, an oxide of carbon, is present in varying amounts in the atmosphere. Predict whether rainwater containing dissolved CO_2 would be acidic or basic.
   b. Consult a reference source to explain the effect of rainwater on limestone and marble (both $CaCO_3$). Be sure to cite the reference you used.

2. **a.** Consult a reference source to help you explain how acid rain is formed from the pollutants SO_2 and NO. Again, cite your reference.
   b. Lime (CaO) is sometimes used to neutralize the effects of acid rain. It can be dumped into affected lakes in order to raise the pH to acceptable levels. However, this rather drastic measure ignores the source of the problem. Find out some ways in which acid rain can be reduced at the source. Once again, be sure to cite any references that you use.

CONCLUSION

State the results of Objective 3.

Buffer Solutions of Weak Acids and Weak Bases

A buffer solution is a solution of special composition, which is able to resist changes in pH that occur if small amounts of acid or base are added. Many important chemical reactions, especially enzyme reactions, will occur only over a small range in pH. Investigating such reactions requires the use of buffer solutions to maintain the pH in that range.

In Part I of this experiment, you will investigate the effect of the buffering of an acetic acid solution on the rate at which the acid reacts with solid calcium carbonate. In Part II, you will use acid-base indicators to determine which substances can give rise to buffers and which cannot. In Part III, you will compare the relative abilities of two solutions at the same pH (one a prepared buffer, one unbuffered) to resist a change in pH when an acid or a base is added.

OBJECTIVES

1. to investigate the equilibria involving weak acids and bases, and how these equilibria may be altered

2. to discover the requirements for making a buffer solution

3. to determine the effectiveness of a buffer solution in neutralizing excess acid and base, in comparison with a non-buffered solution

SUPPLIES

Equipment
3 test tubes (18 mm × 150 mm)
3 test tubes (25 mm × 200 mm)
8 test tubes (13 mm × 100 mm)
test-tube rack
water-soluble marker
graduated cylinder (10 mL)
centimetre ruler
centigram balance
lab apron
safety goggles

Chemical Reagents
$3M$ acetic acid, CH_3COOH
sodium acetate, $NaCH_3COO$
calcium carbonate, $CaCO_3$
    (powder)
bromcresol green indicator
$0.1M$ HCl
$0.1M$ ammonia, NH_3
phenolphthalein indicator
ammonium chloride, NH_4Cl
sodium chloride, NaCl
buffer solution pH 7
$0.1M$ NaOH
NaCl solution (any molarity)

PROCEDURE

The acetic acid solution is mildly corrosive. Wash any spills and splashes immediately with plenty of water.

The hydrochloric acid solution is corrosive to skin, eyes, and clothing. Wash any spills and splashes off your skin and clothing immediately with plenty of water. Call your instructor.

The ammonia solution is mildly corrosive. Wash any spills and splashes immediately with plenty of water.

Phenolphthalein solution is flammable. Extinguish all flames in the area before using the solution.

Part I: Effect of a Common Ion on [H⁺] in a Weak Acid

1. Put on your lab apron and safety goggles.

2. Obtain three 18 mm × 150 mm test tubes in a rack and label them A, B, and C. Place 10 mL of $3M$ CH_3COOH in each.

3. Place 2 g of $NaCH_3COO$ in test tube B and shake to dissolve. Place 4 g of $NaCH_3COO$ in test tube C and shake to dissolve. You will use Solutions A, B, and C in Step 6.

4. Obtain three 25 mm × 200 mm test tubes and using a water-soluble marker make a mark on each 10 cm from the bottom.

5. Place 0.5 g of powdered $CaCO_3$ in the bottom of each large test tube.

6. Add Solution A to the first large test tube and shake quickly. Note the time in seconds it takes for the foam to rise to the 10 cm mark. Repeat with Solutions B and C. Record your results in your copy of Table 1 in your notebook.

Part II: Detecting Common Ion Effect with Indicators

1. Place 1 mL of $3M$ acetic acid in each of two 13 mm × 100 mm test tubes. Add water to half fill each test tube and then add 3 drops of bromcresol green indicator. Note the color in your copy of Table 2. Use a table of indicators to determine the range in which the pH of acetic acid must lie.

2. Add 0.5 g (a few crystals) of $NaCH_3COO$ as a source of the common ion CH_3COO^- to one of the test tubes and shake to dissolve. Record the color in Table 2 and estimate the range in which the pH must lie.

3. Repeat Steps 1 and 2 using fresh test tubes, but place 5 mL of $0.1M$ HCl instead of acetic acid and water, in both tubes, and add 0.5 g (a few crystals) of NaCl as a source of the common ion Cl^- to one of them.

4. Add 5 drops of $0.1M$ NH_3 solution to each of two small test tubes half full of water. Add 1 drop of phenolphthalein to each and note the color in Table 2. Use a table of indicators to determine the range in which the pH of ammonia must lie.

5. To one of the tubes, add a few small crystals of NH_4Cl, as a source of the common ion NH_4^+, and record any color change in Table 2.

6. Repeat Steps 4 and 5 using fresh test tubes, but place 5 drops of $0.1M$ NaOH in both tubes and add a few crystals of NaCl as a source of the common ion Na^+ to one of them.

Part III: Determining the Effectiveness of Buffers

1. Obtain 5 mL of NaCl solution in a 13 mm × 100 mm test tube. (Assume that the pH of the solution is 7.) Obtain 5 mL of the pH 7 buffer solution in a second 13 mm × 100 mm test tube. Add 2 drops of phenolphthalein indicator to each.

2. Add 0.1M NaOH solution drop by drop to each test tube. Count the number of drops required before a color change is observed and record it in Table 3.

3. Repeat Step 1, but add 2 drops of bromcresol green indicator instead of the phenolphthalein. Record your observations in Table 3.

4. Add 0.1M HCl solution drop by drop to each test tube. Count the number of drops required before a color change is observed and record it in Table 3.

5. Before leaving the laboratory, wash your hands thoroughly with soap and water.

REAGENT DISPOSAL

Rinse all solutions down the sink with plenty of water.

POST LAB CONSIDERATIONS

The reaction you observed in Part I is a reaction between calcium carbonate and the hydronium ions from the acid, according to the equation:

$$CaCO_3(s) + 2H^+(aq) \rightarrow Ca^{2+}(aq) + CO_2(g) + H_2O(l)$$

Since increased $[H^+]$ will lead to a faster rate (as shown by the time for the foam to reach a particular height), the measured time will give an indication of the $[H^+]$ present. This in turn relates to the equilibrium involving the non-ionized acetic acid molecules and the acetate ions which accompany the H^+.

In Part II, of the four solutions tested, two were acids (one weak and one strong) and two were bases (one weak and one strong). If a color change in the indicator occurred, it meant that an equilibrium must have existed and the common ion added was able to shift (change the position of) the equilibrium.

The buffer solution used in Part III contained a weak acid and its conjugate base in approximately equal concentrations. The results showed its effectiveness in minimizing the effect on pH when a strong acid or base was added. The buffer solution did this by means of the types of equilibrium shifts studied in Parts I and II.

EXPERIMENTAL RESULTS

Part I: Effect of a Common Ion on [H⁺] in a Weak Acid

Table 1

Solid Reagent	Solution Added	Time for Foam to Rise 10 cm (s)
$CaCO_3$	CH_3COOH	
$CaCO_3$	CH_3COOH + 2 g $NaCH_3COO$	COMPLETE IN YOUR NOTEBOOK
$CaCO_3$	CH_3COOH + 4 g $NaCH_3COO$	

Part II: Detecting Common Ion Effect with Indicators

Table 2

Solution	Indicator	Color	pH Range
CH_3COOH	bromcresol green		
$CH_3COOH + CH_3COO^-$	bromcresol green		
HCl	bromcresol green		
$HCl + Cl^-$	bromcresol green	*COMPLETE IN YOUR NOTEBOOK*	*COMPLETE IN YOUR NOTEBOOK*
NH_3	phenolphthalein		
$NH_3 + NH_4^+$	phenolphthalein		
NaOH	phenolphthalein		
$NaOH + Na^+$	phenolphthalein		

Part III: Determining the Effectiveness of Buffers

Table 3

Solution	Color change to phenolph-thalein by adding base	No. of drops of base to give color change	Color change to bromcresol green by adding acid	No. of drops of acid to give color change
NaCl Solution (Unbuffered assume pH 7)	*COMPLETE IN YOUR NOTEBOOK*	*COMPLETE IN YOUR NOTEBOOK*	*COMPLETE IN YOUR NOTEBOOK*	*COMPLETE IN YOUR NOTEBOOK*
pH 7 Buffer Solution				

ANALYSIS OF RESULTS

1. Which solution in Part I gave the slowest rate? Explain this result in terms of Le Chatelier's principle, as applied to the acetic acid ionization equilibrium.

2. Which of the two acids tested in Part II changed pH when a common ion was added? Explain why this result occurred.

3. Which of the two bases tested in Part II changed pH when a common ion was added? Explain why this result occurred.

4. Referring to your results in Part III, calculate the fraction of the volume of the buffer or the unbuffered solution that was required to cause the indicator to change color in each of the four situations studied. Assume that the volume of one drop is 0.05 mL.

FOLLOW UP QUESTIONS

1. Which of the following pairs of solutions will constitute a buffer?
   a. NH_3 and NH_4NO_3
   b. HNO_3 and $NaNO_3$
   c. KH_2PO_4 and K_2HPO_4
   d. KOH and KCl
   e. HNO_2 and $NaNO_2$

2. Blood must be maintained at a fairly constant pH of between 7.3 and 7.4. One of the principal buffers responsible for doing this consists of carbonic acid (H_2CO_3, from $CO_2(g)$ and H_2O) in equilibrium with the bicarbonate ion, HCO_3^-. If you breathe too deeply and rapidly, a condition known as hyperventilation may occur in which some muscles may become temporarily paralyzed because the pH of the blood becomes too high. Explain why the pH changes in this way and why the condition can be corrected by exhaling into a paper bag and then breathing the exhaled air in again.

CONCLUSION

State in general terms what types of substances are needed to make a buffer.

13G

Using a Primary Standard to Analyze Acid and Base Solutions

A common laboratory procedure is to determine the concentration of an acid or base solution by titrating it against a solution of known concentration. This experiment assumes that you already have experience in performing acid-base titrations, such as determining the concentration of acetic acid in vinegar, having been given a sodium hydroxide solution of known molarity. However, in this experiment you will have to standardize the NaOH yourself.

You will first have to prepare a solution of an acid of known concentration by weighing out a sample and making it up to a known volume in a volumetric flask. To be suitable for such a use, a substance must be very pure and stable. Also, it must not absorb water from the air. A chemical such as this is called a *primary standard*. Sodium hydroxide cannot be used as a primary standard because it is difficult to obtain 100% pure, it readily absorbs moisture from the air and reacts with the $CO_2(g)$ in the air. A common primary standard for acid-base titrations is oxalic acid, which occurs in the crystalline form as the dihydrate $H_2C_2O_4 \cdot 2H_2O$. This is the primary standard that you will use in Part I of this experiment. (It must be of analytical reagent purity.)

After preparing the solution of oxalic acid of known molarity, you will carry out a titration in order to determine the molarity of a NaOH solution (Part II). This standardized NaOH solution will have a variety of uses, such as determining the molar mass of an unknown solid acid (Part III) or the molarity of an unknown acid solution (Part IV). Keep in mind that, when performing titrations, it is important to make all measurements with as much accuracy as possible.

In this experiment, you will also have the opportunity to do some optional procedures, which you will design yourself (Parts V and VI).

OBJECTIVES

1. to prepare a standard solution of oxalic acid and use it to standardize an unknown sodium hydroxide solution

2. to determine the molar mass of an unknown solid acid by titration with standardized NaOH solution

3. to determine the pH and molarity of an unknown acid solution and calculate the K_a from the results

4. to analyze a variety of other unknown solutions by titration

SUPPLIES

Equipment

centigram balance
beaker (100 mL)
beaker (250 mL)
funnel
volumetric flask (250 mL)
Erlenmeyer flask (250 mL)
wash bottle
buret
pipet (25 mL)
suction bulb
pH meter or universal indicator
    paper or solution
stoppered bottle (500 mL)
ring stand
buret clamp
lab apron
safety goggles

Chemical Reagents

oxalic acid dihydrate crystals,
    $H_2C_2O_4 \cdot 2H_2O$
sodium hydroxide (NaOH)
    solution (approx. 0.1M)
phenolphthalein indicator
    solution
unknown solid acid
unknown weak acid solution

Reagents for Optional Procedures

soft drink
apple, lemon, or grapefruit juice
unknown HCl solution
household ammonia
limewater
bromcresol green indicator
solid sodium carbonate
antacid tablet

PROCEDURE

Part I: Preparing a Primary Standard Acid Solution

1. Before coming to the laboratory, calculate the mass of oxalic acid dihydrate, $H_2C_2O_4 \cdot 2H_2O$, that you will need to make up 250.0 mL of a 0.0500M solution.

2. Put on your lab apron and safety goggles.

3. Accurately determine the mass of an empty (clean and dry) 100 mL beaker and record it in Table 1 in your notebook.

4. Measure into the beaker the amount of oxalic acid that you have calculated you need and accurately determine the mass of the oxalic acid and the beaker. Record this figure in Table 1. Do not spend much time trying to get exactly the same mass as you calculated. The important thing is to record accurately the mass you do have and to calculate the molarity from this mass. For example, the mass you use may give the solution a molarity of 0.0496M. This is perfectly acceptable, provided that you use this figure in your calculations.

5. Dissolve the oxalic acid in water and pour the solution through a funnel into a 250 mL volumetric flask. Wash the beaker with water twice and add these washings to the flask. Now add water to the flask until the level is up to the mark. (Use a wash bottle as you get close to the mark.) Stopper the flask and shake to ensure that the solution is homogeneous. You now have your primary standard solution of oxalic acid.

Part II: Standardizing an Unknown NaOH solution

1. Obtain a 500 mL bottle with a stopper and fill it with NaOH solution of unknown molarity. Label it with your name and class.

2. Add about 15 mL of the NaOH solution to a buret through a funnel, rinse it back and forth, and then discard it through the tip into the sink.

3. Fill the buret with more NaOH solution and allow some to drain in order to remove any air bubbles in the tip. Remove the funnel.

4. Using the suction bulb on the end of your pipet, withdraw about 5 mL of oxalic acid, rinse it around in the pipet, and discard it. Then withdraw 25 mL of the standard oxalic acid solution and transfer it to a 250 mL Erlenmeyer flask. The correct volume is delivered when you have touched the tip of the pipet to the side of the flask. Do not blow through the pipet. (Note: Depending on the shape and size of your pipet and volumetric flask, you may have to transfer the oxalic acid first to a clean, dry beaker since the pipet will not reach deep enough into the volumetric flask.)

5. Add 3 drops of phenolphthalein solution to the acid in the Erlenmeyer flask.

6. Read the initial volume of NaOH in the buret as accurately as you can and record it in Table 2. Then open the valve on the buret. Allow the NaOH solution to run into the flask and swirl constantly to ensure thorough mixing.

7. After a time, you will notice a pink color that appears where the NaOH enters the liquid in the flask. When this color takes a longer time to disperse and disappear, slow down the rate of addition of NaOH until eventually you are adding it a drop a time. Stop the titration when the faintest possible pink color stays in the flask for about 20 s. Read the final volume of the NaOH in the buret and record it in Table 2. (The difference between the initial reading and the final reading represents the volume of NaOH required to neutralize the oxalic acid.)

8. If you are at all in doubt as to whether you have a pale pink color, take the reading anyway, then add one more drop. If the color immediately becomes much darker, the reading you took was probably the most accurate result. This is called the endpoint of the titration. Discard the solution down the sink.

9. Pipet another 25 mL sample of oxalic acid into the flask and again add 3 drops of phenolphthalein. Refill the buret (if necessary) and repeat the titration. Run in NaOH to within 1 mL of the volume needed in the first titration and then add the solution a drop at a time, swirling after each drop, until you get the faint pink endpoint. Repeat the titration until you have two readings that agree to within 0.1 mL.

10. Store your labeled bottle of standardized NaOH, in the location suggested by your instructor, until the next laboratory period, when Parts III and IV will be done.

CAUTION

Oxalic acid is poisonous. Always use a suction bulb rather than your mouth to withdraw the oxalic acid solution into the pipet.

Sodium hydroxide solution is corrosive to skin and clothing. Wash spills and splashes immediately with plenty of water. Inform your instructor.

Phenolphthalein is dissolved in a poisonous, flammable solvent.

You must assume that any unknowns are poisonous.

Part III: Determining the Molar Mass of an Unknown Solid Acid

1. Obtain a vial containing an unknown solid acid from your instructor. Record the identifying number or letter in Table 3.

2. Weigh out about 0.75 g of the solid acid into a clean, dry beaker and record the mass accurately in Table 3. It does not have to be exactly 0.75 g, as long as you know exactly how much you have.

3. Dissolve the acid in about 40 mL of water and transfer the solution to an Erlenmeyer flask. Rinse the beaker twice into the flask to ensure that all the acid solution is transferred. (The amount of water added does not affect the results.) Add 3 drops of phenolphthalein.

4. Run in NaOH from a buret as in Part II, measuring the volume required to reach the endpoint. Record this figure in Table 3.

5. Repeat Steps 2 to 4 until you get two readings in close agreement. (If you did not have exactly the same mass each time, check whether the results agree by determining the ratio of the volumes and comparing it with the ratio of the masses used. Alternatively, follow the calculations set out in the Analysis of Results section to determine the molar mass of the acid and see whether those results agree within experimental error.)

Part IV: Determining K_a for an Unknown Monoprotic Weak Acid

1. Obtain approximately 100 mL of the unknown weak acid provided. Record any identifying number or letter in Table 4, if more than one unknown is available.

2. Measure the pH of the solution. The most accurate way of doing this is with a pH meter, if one is available in the lab. If so, your instructor will give instructions on its use and calibration. Otherwise, use universal indicator paper or solution to determine the pH.

3. Use the suction bulb on your pipet to deliver a 25.00 mL portion of the unknown acid into an Erlenmeyer flask. (Rinse the pipet with the acid first.) Add 3 drops of phenolphthalein.

4. Titrate with your standard NaOH solution as you did in Parts II and III, until you get two results agreeing or until you run out of time.

OPTIONAL PROCEDURES

The following procedures are considered optional, to be done only if you are requested to do so by your instructor. Detailed instructions are not provided. It is hoped that from doing Parts I to IV you have developed a good understanding of the techniques and calculations required in acid-base titrations and can devise your own experiments. Choose a suitable indicator and check your procedure with your instructor before starting. It may be a good idea to get a rough estimate of the volumes required by measuring 10 mL portions with a graduated cylinder until an endpoint is reached, then determining from the results suitable volumes and concentrations to use with the more accurate buret.

Part V: Determining the Acid Concentration in Beverages

Many beverages are acidic. Determine the total concentration of acid in one or more of the following, as instructed: lemon juice, grapefruit juice, apple juice, or a colorless soft drink. Use your standard NaOH solution and phenolphthalein.

CAUTION

Hydrochloric acid is corrosive to skin and clothing. Wash spills and splashes immediately with plenty of water. Inform your instructor.

CAUTION

Ammonia, limewater, and washing soda solutions can irritate skin. Wash any spills off skin with water.

Part VI: Analyzing Other Solutions

Determine the concentration of the approximately $0.1M$ solution of HCl provided by titrating your standard NaOH into 25 mL portions of HCl, using phenolphthalein as an indicator. Then use this standardized HCl in any of the following procedures:

a. Determine the concentration of a household ammonia solution by titrating it with the HCl.

b. Determine the concentration of a saturated solution of limewater {calcium hydroxide, $Ca(OH)_2$} by titrating it with the standard HCl. Use the results to calculate K_{sp} for $Ca(OH)_2$.

c. Determine the number of molecules of water in washing soda or sal soda (hydrated sodium carbonate, $Na_2CO_3 \bullet xH_2O$) by titrating standard HCl against a known mass of the sodium carbonate dissolved in water.

d. Grind up a known mass of antacid tablet, add a measured volume of standardized HCl (enough to dissolve it), and determine how much HCl is left by titrating standard NaOH solution back into the flask. Calculate the amount of acid that is neutralized by the antacid.

Before you leave the laboratory, wash your hands thoroughly with soap and water.

REAGENT DISPOSAL

Wash solutions that are the end result of titrations down the sink with plenty of water. Your instructor will give you instructions on whether to save for possible reuse the standard solutions of oxalic acid, sodium hydroxide, and hydrochloric acid that are left over or to neutralize them and rinse them down the sink with copious amounts of water.

POST LAB CONSIDERATIONS

Oxalic acid is a diprotic acid. It can therefore release two hydronium ions when it reacts with a base such as sodium hydroxide. Make certain that you allow for this in your calculations.

In Part III, you may assume that the unknown solid acid is monoprotic unless you are told otherwise.

If you are asked to do Part VI (c), which involves washing soda, you should be aware of the fact that the crystals of hydrated sodium carbonate which make up washing soda tend to lose water on standing in the open air in a process known as efflorescence. The molar mass you determine may therefore not correspond to an exact whole number of molecules of water in the formula for the hydrated crystals of sodium carbonate.

EXPERIMENTAL RESULTS

Part I: Preparing a Primary Standard Acid Solution

Table 1

Calculated mass of oxalic acid dihydrate $H_2C_2O_4 \bullet 2H_2O$ (required for 250.0 mL of $0.0500M$ solution (g))	
Mass of beaker (g)	
Mass of beaker + oxalic acid (g)	
Mass of oxalic acid (g)	

Part II: Standardizing an Unknown NaOH Solution

Table 2 Volume of NaOH Needed to Neutralize 25.00 mL of Oxalic Acid

	Trial 1	Trial 2	Trial 3	Trial 4	Trial 5 (if necessary)
Initial reading of buret (mL)					
Final reading of buret (mL)					
Volume of NaOH required (mL)					
Average volume of NaOH (mL)					

Part III: Determining the Molar Mass of an Unknown Solid Acid

Table 3 Volume of NaOH Needed to Neutralize Known Mass of Unknown Solid Acid

Unknown Solid Acid #_____	Trial 1	Trial 2	Trial 3 (if necessary)
Mass of beaker (g)			
Mass of beaker + acid (g)			
Mass of acid (g)			
Initial reading of buret (mL)			
Final reading of buret (mL)			
Volume of NaOH used (mL)			

Part IV: Determining K_a for an Unknown Monoprotic Weak Acid

Table 4

Unknown Acid Solution #_____	Trial 1	Trial 2	Trial 3 (if necessary)
pH of unknown acid solution			
Initial reading of buret (mL)	COMPLETE IN YOUR NOTEBOOK	COMPLETE IN YOUR NOTEBOOK	COMPLETE IN YOUR NOTEBOOK
Final reading of buret (mL)			
Volume of NaOH used (mL)			

Since the following Parts are optional procedures in which you design your own experiment, you will also need to prepare tables for the data you will collect.

Part V: Determining the Acid Concentration in Beverages

Part VI: Analyzing Other Solutions

ANALYSIS OF RESULTS

Always write balanced equations for the reactions studied so that you are aware of the mole relationships to use in your calculations.

Part I: Preparing a Primary Standard Acid Solution

1. Calculate the mass of one mole of oxalic acid dihydrate, $H_2C_2O_4 \bullet 2H_2O$.

2. Calculate the number of moles in the measured mass of oxalic acid.

3. Calculate $[H_2C_2O_4 \bullet 2H_2O]$ when the mass in Procedure Part I, Step 1 is dissolved in 250.0 mL of solution.

Part II: Standardizing an Unknown NaOH Solution

1. Calculate the number of moles of oxalic acid in 25.00 mL of standard solution.

2. Calculate the number of moles of NaOH required to neutralize this amount of oxalic acid. (Remember that oxalic acid is diprotic.)

3. Using your average volume of NaOH required and the number of moles present as obtained above, calculate [NaOH] in the standardized solution in moles per litre. If your first titration result is somewhat larger than subsequent results, do not include it in calculating the average volume. (In the first titration students often overshoot the endpoint.)

Part III: Determining the Molar Mass of an Unknown Solid Acid

1. Calculate the number of moles of NaOH used in each titration.

2. Calculate the number of moles of unknown acid neutralized by this amount of NaOH. (Remember that the acid is monoprotic.)

3. Using the relationship

$$\text{molar mass} = \frac{\text{mass of substance (g)}}{\text{number of moles}}$$

calculate the molar mass of the unknown acid.

4. Repeat the calculation in Analysis 3 for each titration performed and calculate the average molar mass of the acid.

Part IV: Determining K_a for an Unknown Monoprotic Weak Acid

1. Calculate the $[H^+]$ in the unknown acid solution from the measured pH.

2. Calculate the average volume of NaOH required for the titration.

3. Calculate the number of moles of NaOH used to neutralize the acid. (This number is equal to the number of moles of acid, since the acid is monoprotic.)

4. Calculate the concentration of the acid from the relationship

$$\text{Molarity} = \frac{\text{number of moles}}{\text{volume (L)}}.$$

5. The K_a for a weak acid $HA \rightleftharpoons H^+ + A^-$ is given by the equation

$$K_a = \frac{[H^+][A^-]}{[HA]}.$$

Since for every molecule of HA that ionizes, one H^+ ion and one A^- ion are produced, $[H^+] = [A^-]$. Therefore, $K_a = \dfrac{[H^+]^2}{[HA]}$.

The [HA] term here represents the HA molecules left over after ionization has occurred; it should therefore be calculated by subtracting the $[H^+]$ from the total [HA] as obtained from the titration data. In many cases, however, you will find that allowing for this ionization does not make a significant difference to the answer.

Calculate the value of K_a for your acid as outlined in the above discussion.

Part V: Determining the Acid Concentration in Beverages

Part VI: Analyzing Other Solutions

These calculations are shown in outline only. Set out your own calculation procedure for whichever procedures you followed.

1. Calculate the concentration of acid in each beverage you tested.

2. Calculate the [HCl] from your titration data with NaOH. Then do whichever of the following is appropriate.
   a. Calculate the $[NH_3]$ in household ammonia.
   b. Calculate the $[Ca(OH)_2]$ in saturated $Ca(OH)_2$ solution and from these results calculate K_{sp} for $Ca(OH)_2$.
   c. Calculate the number of moles of $Na_2CO_3 \cdot xH_2O$ that must have reacted with the acid, then use the mass and number of moles to calculate the molar mass. From the result, determine the value of x in the formula $Na_2CO_3 \cdot xH_2O$ (that is, the number of molecules of water found in the formula for the hydrated crystal).

d. Calculate the number of moles of HCl used up by your mass of antacid and then convert this answer to the volume of $0.100M$ HCl used up by 1 g of antacid. Given that $0.100M$ HCl approximately represents stomach acid and that it has a density of 1.00 g/mL, calculate the mass of stomach acid neutralized by 1 g of antacid. (Note that this quantity includes the water in the solution as well as the acid itself.)

FOLLOW-UP QUESTIONS

1. A certain soft drink was analyzed and found to contain $0.080M$ H^+. Other ingredients of the drink include sugar or, in the diet form of the drink, an artificial sweetener. What property of this acid solution is overcome by using sugar or sweetener?

2. Every day, a manufacturing plant produces 8.0×10^3 L of NaOH waste of molarity $0.040M$. In order to comply with environmental regulations, this NaOH must be neutralized before being discharged as effluent. What mass of concentrated HCl will be required to neutralize it? ([HCl] = $12M$; density = 1.2 kg/L)

3. A sample of sodium hydroxide, NaOH, is known to have become contaminated with sodium carbonate, Na_2CO_3, by reaction with CO_2 in the air. A 1.00 g sample is titrated with $0.500M$ HCl and it is found that 48.6 mL of HCl are required for neutralization. Calculate the percentage by mass of Na_2CO_3 in the sample. (Hint: Let mass of $Na_2CO_3 = x$ g.)

4. Why would it be difficult to measure the concentration of acid in red wine or in a cola-type drink using the method in Part V? How could you overcome this difficulty?

5. There are some titrations in which the endpoint is obtained by measuring the electrical conductivity of the solution and watching for the point at which the conductivity is at a minimum. Such a titration is called an electrometric titration. An example is the reaction of $Ba(OH)_2$ solution with sulfuric acid, H_2SO_4. Write the net ionic equation for the reaction (remembering the solubility table) and then explain why the conductivity reaches a minimum.

CONCLUSION

1. State the molar mass of your unknown solid acid (and its sample number).

2. State the K_a of your unknown weak acid solution (and its sample number).

©SMG Lab Books Ltd.

Titration Curves

You have already performed a number of acid base titrations in earlier experiments (13C and 13G). You should therefore be well aware of the term *equivalence point*. This is the point where the number of moles of acid and base are in the stoichiometric ratio shown by the coefficients in the balanced equation. In this experiment, all reactions studied are in a 1:1 acid–base mole ratio. The focus of this experiment is to investigate how the pH of the acid–base mixture changes during the titration process. The rate of change of pH is very clearly seen if a graph is plotted for pH versus the volume of acid or base added as the titration proceeds. Such a graph is called a titration curve. These graphs can also be obtained by interfacing a pH meter with a computer.

In this experiment, you will obtain three titration curves by manually plotting your results. In Part I, the first curve's pH data will be theoretically obtained by calculation; it will be for a strong base titrated against a strong acid. It will be assigned as a pre-lab activity and will give you useful practice in titration calculations. In addition, it will enable you to see the relationship between pH and the volume of base added. In Part II, the second curve will be of the same type, but will be experimentally obtained using a buret to deliver the base solution and a pH meter to measure the pH. Finally, in Part III, the third curve, also experimentally obtained, will be for a strong base titrated against a weak acid and the shape of the curve will be compared to that for the strong acid.

A pH meter is an instrument with a wide variety of applications, ranging from the testing and monitoring of water quality to manufacturing processes and research. Meters vary in their construction and method of operation, but some general principles apply to all. A glass electrode is connected to the pH meter and inserted into the test solution. A voltage is then produced which is dependent on the pH of the solution. A needle on a scale or a digital readout gives the actual voltage obtained, but a scale showing the pH value directly is generally more useful. The meter must be set for the temperature and then calibrated by placing the electrode in one or more buffers of accurately known pH. Your instructor will give you specific details on the method of operation of the pH meter available to you.

OBJECTIVES

1. to calculate the pH at various stages of the titration of a strong base against a strong acid and plot the results on a graph

2. to measure experimentally the pH at various stages of the titration of a strong base against a strong acid and plot the results on a graph

3. to measure experimentally the pH at various stages of the titration of a strong base against a weak acid, plot the results on a graph, and compare the shape to that obtained in Objective 2

SUPPLIES

Equipment
pipet (25mL)
buret (50 mL)
buret stand and clamp
pH meter and electrode or pH
  probe and computer interface
beaker (150 mL)
suction bulb
glass stirring rod
lab apron
safety goggles

Chemical Reagents
0.100M NaOH
0.100M HCl
0.100M acetic acid, CH_3COOH
phenolphthalein solution or
  universal indicator solution

PROCEDURE

Part I: Calculated Titration Curve

In order to become acquainted with titration curves, perform the following calculations as a pre-lab activity.

1. Make a copy of Table 1 (Experimental Results) in your notebook.

2. Calculate the pH that results when 25.00 mL of 0.100M HCl is titrated with 0.100M NaOH solution run in from a buret, at each of the stages of volume of 0.100M NaOH added (in mL) as shown in Table 1.

   The calculations can be done in one of two ways: (a) Calculate the moles of acid or base left over, then divide by the total volume to get [H$^+$] (or [OH$^-$] if the titration has passed the equivalence point). (b) Since the concentrations used are identical, subtraction can give the volume of HCl or NaOH left over. The concentration of 0.100M then has to be reduced by multiplying by the dilution factor (volume unreacted divided by the total volume) to obtain [H$^+$] (or [OH$^-$] if beyond the equivalence point).

   Having now obtained the [H$^+$] or [OH$^-$], you can calculate the pH.

   For consistency and to allow comparison, calculate all your pH values to two decimal places.

   Record your calculated results in your copy of Table 1, Part I in your notebook.

3. Plot a graph of the results, with pH plotted against the volume of NaOH added.

Part II: Experimentally Obtained Titration Curve for NaOH against HCl

1. Put on your lab apron and safety goggles.

2. Set up and calibrate your pH meter according to your instructor's directions.

3. Using a suction bulb on your pipet, withdraw 25 mL of 0.100M HCl and transfer it to a 150 mL beaker. Remember to rinse your pipet with the HCl first.

4. Add 3 drops of phenolphthalein (or universal indicator solution) to the acid in order to observe the pH changes by means of a color change as well as with the pH meter.

CAUTION

The hydrochloric acid and sodium hydroxide solutions are corrosive to skin, eyes, and clothing. Wash any spills and splashes with plenty of water. Call your instructor.

5. Set up the buret in the clamp and stand and rinse it out with 10 mL of NaOH solution. Discard the rinsings through the tip.

6. Refill the buret with NaOH solution, allow some to drain through the tip to fill it, then adjust the volume to 0.00 mL. (This will make it easier to obtain a large number of volume readings.)

7. Place the electrode of the pH meter in the acid solution in the beaker and read the pH.

8. Run in as close as possible to 5.00 mL of NaOH solution, stirring the solution in the beaker constantly (with a stirring rod, not the electrode). You may wish to swirl your beaker as you have in previous titrations. (Do NOT use a magnet with a mixer.) Again read the pH.

9. Continue adding NaOH and recording the volume of NaOH added, with its related pH, under Part II of Table 1. Get as close as possible to the volume values for which you calculated the pH in Part I. The volume increments must become successively smaller as you approach the equivalence point. Be careful in this region, since the equivalence point will only be at 25.00 mL if both solutions were of precisely the same concentration, which may not be the case.

Part III: Experimentally Obtained Titration Curve for NaOH Against CH$_3$COOH

1. Rinse off the electrode for the pH meter before beginning the titration.

2. Repeat the Procedure in Part II, but titrate the NaOH against 0.100M CH$_3$COOH instead of HCl. Record all results under Part III of Table 1.

3. Clean up, following the instructions for reagent disposal.

4. Before leaving the laboratory, wash your hands thoroughly with soap and water.

REAGENT DISPOSAL

Wash all solutions formed as a result of titration down the sink with plenty of water. Return unused portions of original solutions to the container designated by your instructor.

POST LAB CONSIDERATIONS

When an acid and a base react together and neutralize one another, water is formed and a salt is left over in the solution. If the titration is between a strong acid and a strong base, then the salt which is present at the equivalence point will not undergo hydrolysis and the solution will be neutral. If the titration is between a strong base and a weak acid, then the salt which is present at the equivalence point will undergo anionic (basic) hydrolysis, producing OH$^-$ ions. Therefore, the pH at the equivalence point will be on the basic side of neutral; that is, it will be greater than 7. If the titration is between a weak base and a strong acid, then the salt present at the equivalence point will undergo cationic (acidic) hydrolysis, producing H$_3$O$^+$. The pH at the equivalence point will therefore be on the acidic side of neutral, that is, less than 7. By studying the titration curves, you can determine which indicator can be used for each type of titration in order to get a color change in the vertical portion of the graph on either side of the equivalence point. The transition point of the indicator should match the equivalence point of the titration as closely as possible.

EXPERIMENTAL RESULTS

Remember to do the calculations for Part I before coming to the laboratory. Show your calculations in your report, as well as recording the values in the table.

Table 1

PART I		PART II		PART III	
(25.00 mL 0.100M HCl) Calculated Values		(25.00 mL 0.100M HCl) Experimental Values		(25.00 mL 0.100M CH_3COOH) Experimental Values	
Volume of 0.100M NaOH (mL)	pH	Volume of 0.100M NaOH (mL)	pH	Volume of 0.100M NaOH (mL)	pH
0.00					
5.00					
10.00					
15.00					
20.00					
22.00					
24.00					
24.50					
24.80					
24.90					
24.95					
24.99					
25.00					
25.01					
25.05					
25.10					
25.20					
25.50					
26.00					
28.00					
30.00					
40.00					
50.00					

COMPLETE IN YOUR NOTEBOOK   COMPLETE IN YOUR NOTEBOOK

ANALYSIS OF RESULTS

1. Plot a graph of pH versus the volume of NaOH solution added for each set of results from Parts II and III.

2. State three differences in appearance between the graph in Part II (strong acid) and that in Part III (weak acid).

3. In Part I, for the addition of 0.02 mL (less than half a drop), by how much did the pH change between 24.99 mL and 25.01 mL?

4. In Parts II and III, what was the largest pH change you observed when only one drop was added?

5. The equivalence point in an acid-base titration is found at the middle of the most vertical portion on a titration curve. Find the value of the pH at this point for the graphs in Parts II and III.

6. Explain the reason for the difference between the equivalence points for strong and weak acids, as shown by your answer to Analysis 5.

FOLLOW-UP QUESTIONS

1. Sketch the shape of the titration curve if $0.100M$ HCl were run from a buret into 25.00 mL of $0.100M$ NaOH.

2. Use a table of indicators to select all the indicators which would be acceptable for use in your titration of a strong acid with a strong base.

3. Why is phenolphthalein the best indicator to use for titrating a strong base with a weak acid?

4. From your graph for Part III, read the pH at the point where half the acetic acid has been neutralized. (This corresponds to the point where half the volume of the NaOH required for neutralization has been added.) Calculate the $[H_3O^+]$ that corresponds to this pH. How does this concentration compare to the K_a for acetic acid? Explain this result by referring to the K_a expression for acetic acid.

CONCLUSION

State three differences between the titration curve from Part II and the titration curve from Part III.

EXPERIMENT

14A

Oxidation-Reduction Reactions of Elements and Their Ions

Oxidation is the process whereby electrons are lost by a chemical species (an atom, molecule, or ion). Conversely, *reduction* is the process whereby electrons are gained by a chemical species. Before electrons can be added to a chemical species, they must be removed from another chemical species; therefore, the processes of oxidation and reduction must occur together. The overall reaction is called an *oxidation-reduction reaction* or, in shorter form, a *redox reaction.*

You have already encountered a number of redox reactions in earlier experiments; for instance, reactions in which a metal reacts with an acid, giving positive ions of the metal and hydrogen gas. The reaction between magnesium and hydrogen ions to give magnesium ions and hydrogen gas is a good example of a redox reaction:

$$Mg(s) + 2H^+(aq) \rightarrow Mg^{2+}(aq) + H_2(g)$$

The reaction consists of two distinct parts, which can be written as separate reactions, each involving electrons. These are called *half-reactions.*

$$Mg(s) \rightarrow Mg^{2+}(aq) + 2e^- \qquad \text{(oxidation — loss of electrons)}$$
$$2H^+(aq) + 2e^- \rightarrow H_2(g) \qquad \text{(reduction — gain of electrons)}$$

The magnesium brings about reduction of H^+ to H_2, so it is called the *reducing agent.* The H^+ brings about oxidation of Mg to Mg^{2+} and therefore is called the *oxidizing agent.*

The overall equation for the reaction is obtained by adding the equations for the two half-reactions in such a way that the electrons cancel out. (This may mean that one or both of the equations for the half-reactions must be multiplied by some number to make the electrons involved in the oxidation and reduction numerically equal.) Note that the oxidizing agent is the species which itself becomes reduced in the process and the reducing agent is the species which itself becomes oxidized in the process. Because the reaction proceeds in the direction shown, it can be concluded that magnesium is a stronger reducing agent than H_2 and that H^+ is a stronger oxidizing agent than Mg^{2+}.

In Part I of this experiment, you will examine reactions between metals and aqueous solutions of ions of other metals. Then in Part II, you will investigate some reactions between free halogen molecules and aqueous solutions of ions of other halogen elements. From your results you will be able to arrange the equations for the reduction half-reactions in sequence from the strongest oxidizing agent to the weakest. This arrangement will show that any oxidizing agent on the left will be able to react with any reducing agent on the right that is lower on the list. Such a list can be expanded with other experimental results and is very useful for predicting whether or not a reaction will proceed.

OBJECTIVES

1. to investigate various combinations of metals with metal ions and discover which combinations undergo redox reactions

2. to investigate various combinations of the halogen elements chlorine, bromine, and iodine with the related halide salts and discover which combinations undergo redox reactions

3. to list all the reduction half-reactions studied in such a way that the halogen elements and metal ions are arranged in decreasing order of strength as oxidizing agents

SUPPLIES

Equipment

20 test tubes (13 mm × 100 mm)
test-tube rack
steel wool or emery paper
water-soluble marker
rubber stoppers (size 00)
lab apron
safety goggles

Chemical Reagents

$0.1M$ $Cu(NO_3)_2$
$0.1M$ $Zn(NO_3)_2$
$0.1M$ $Mg(NO_3)_2$
$0.1M$ $Pb(NO_3)_2$
small strips of copper, zinc,
    magnesium, and lead
$0.1M$ $NaCl$
$0.1M$ $NaBr$
$0.1M$ NaI
chlorine water
bromine water
iodine (50% ethanol solution)
n-heptane
$0.1M$ $AgNO_3$ and silver metal strips
    (for instructor demonstration)

PROCEDURE

Part I: Reactions between Metals and Metal Ions (Cu, Zn, Mg, Pb, and Ag)

1. Put on your lab apron and safety goggles.

2. Obtain 3 small strips of each metal (Cu, Zn, Mg, and Pb) and rub each with steel wool or emery paper to remove surface corrosion and reveal the shiny surface underneath. Rinse with water.

3. Place the strips in separate 13 mm × 100 mm test tubes (12 in all) and use your water-soluble marker to identify which metal is in each tube.

4. To each of the 3 test tubes containing copper metal, add in turn about 3 mL (one third of a test tube) of a $0.1M$ solution of the nitrate of each of the other metals. (It is not necessary to try to react copper metal with its own nitrate, $Cu(NO_3)_2$.)

5. Repeat with the other three metals, until you have all 12 possible combinations of metals with the nitrates of the others. Label all the combinations. Record your observations in Table 1 in your notebook.

CAUTION

The metal nitrate solutions used in this experiment are poisonous. Do not get any in your mouth and do not swallow any.

6. Your instructor will display an additional 8 combinations, consisting of silver metal (Ag) with nitrates of Cu^{2+}, Zn^{2+}, Mg^{2+}, and Pb^{2+}, and $0.1M$ $AgNO_3$ with each of Cu, Zn, Mg, and Pb. Observe which combinations show evidence of reaction and record your results in Table 1.

7. In some of the combinations you prepared, a metal will be produced from the positive ion in solution. Note that the metal may be very finely divided and may therefore appear as a black powder. The color and luster of metals are apparent only when the crystals formed are somewhat larger. Any change in the appearance of a metal or a solution will therefore indicate that a reaction has occurred. Some reactions are slower than others are, so leave the test tubes in the rack and take a final look at the results after doing Part II.

Part II: Reactions Between Halogens and Halide Ions

The bromine and iodine solutions which are used and which may be produced in this part of the procedure sometimes appear similar in color at certain concentrations. The purpose of Steps 1 and 2 in this part is to demonstrate a way of distinguishing between the two substances Br_2 and I_2. Note that no reaction occurs — the effect seen is simply a selective solubility for the Br_2 and I_2 out of the aqueous phase into the n-heptane phase.

1. Place 3 mL of bromine water, $Br_2(aq)$, in a test tube and add 1 mL of n-heptane. Stopper and shake vigorously. Note that the heptane and the water solution do not mix. You will be able to tell which is the heptane layer by observing which layer has the smaller volume. Note the color of the n-heptane and record it in Table 2 in your notebook.

2. Repeat Step 1 with 3 mL of the I_2 in 50% ethanol solution. Again record the color of the heptane layer.

3. To 3 mL of $0.1M$ NaBr and 3 mL of $0.1M$ NaI in separate test tubes, add 1 mL of chlorine water. Observe any changes, then to each add 1 mL of heptane, stopper the tube, and shake. Observe the color of the heptane layer and record what you see in Table 2.

4. Repeat Step 3, but use 1 mL of bromine water with $0.1M$ NaCl and $0.1M$ NaI.

5. Repeat Step 3, but use 1 mL of iodine solution in 50% ethanol with $0.1M$ NaCl and $0.1M$ NaBr.

6. Now make final observations of the results for Part I to check for any further changes.

7. Before leaving the laboratory, wash your hands with soap and water.

CAUTION

The n-heptane used in Part II is highly flammable and its vapors are hazardous if inhaled. Make sure there are no open flames in the laboratory. Avoid breathing the fumes. Do not get any on your skin. If you do, call your instructor.

CAUTION

The solutions of chlorine water, bromine water, and iodine in 50% ethanol are very poisonous and corrosive. Avoid breathing their fumes. Do not get any on your skin. If you do, rinse your skin with the sodium thiosulfate solution which your instructor has available for any such emergencies, then with plenty of water.

REAGENT DISPOSAL

Part I: Return all solutions and metals from Part I to the designated container. DO NOT pour the solutions or the small pieces of metal down the sink.

Part II: Pour the solutions from Part II into the designated beaker, which contains a solution of sodium thiosulfate. The sodium thiosulfate can react with unchanged chlorine, bromine, and iodine, which could otherwise be hazardous.

POST LAB CONSIDERATIONS

Note that for every combination of element and ion there is a combination in which the element and ion are reversed. For example, you will have the Cu/Zn^{2+} combination and the Zn/Cu^{2+} combination. Only one of these will react. If the reaction occurred, the conclusion is that the metal ion in the reactant (or in Part II, the halogen molecule) is a stronger oxidizing agent than the other metal ion (or halogen molecule) produced during the course of the reaction.

EXPERIMENTAL RESULTS

Part I: Reactions Between Metals and Metal Ions (Cu, Zn, Mg, Pb, and Ag)
Table 1

Reactants (Metal + Metal Ion)	Observations	Reaction (Yes or No)	Ion that is the Stronger Oxidizing Agent
$Cu + Zn^{2+}$			
$Cu + Mg^{2+}$			
$Cu + Pb^{2+}$			
$Zn + Cu^{2+}$			
$Zn + Mg^{2+}$			
$Zn + Pb^{2+}$			
$Mg + Cu^{2+}$			
$Mg + Zn^{2+}$			
$Mg + Pb^{2+}$	COMPLETE IN YOUR NOTEBOOK	COMPLETE IN YOUR NOTEBOOK	COMPLETE IN YOUR NOTEBOOK
$Pb + Cu^{2+}$			
$Pb + Zn^{2+}$			
$Pb + Mg^{2+}$			
$Ag + Cu^{2+}$			
$Ag + Zn^{2+}$			
$Ag + Mg^{2+}$			
$Ag + Pb^{2+}$			
$Cu + Ag^{+}$			
$Zn + Ag^{+}$			
$Mg + Ag^{+}$			
$Pb + Ag^{+}$			

Part II: Reactions Between Halogens and Halide Ions

Table 2

Halogen	Color of aqueous layer	Color of n-heptane layer
Bromine	COMPLETE IN YOUR NOTEBOOK	COMPLETE IN YOUR NOTEBOOK
Iodine		

Reactants (Halogen + Halide Ion)	Observations	Reaction (Yes or No)	Halogen that is the Stronger Oxidizing Agent
$Cl_2 + Br^-$			
$Cl_2 + I^-$			
$Br_2 + Cl^-$	COMPLETE IN YOUR NOTEBOOK	COMPLETE IN YOUR NOTEBOOK	COMPLETE IN YOUR NOTEBOOK
$Br_2 + I^-$			
$I_2 + Cl^-$			
$I_2 + Br^-$			

ANALYSIS OF RESULTS

1. Write a balanced equation for the reduction half-reaction of each metal ion. Then arrange the equations in order of decreasing strength of these ions as oxidizing agents. (This is the same as saying "decreasing ease of reduction of the ion.")

2. Write a balanced equation for the reduction half-reaction of each halogen molecule and then arrange the equations in order of decreasing strength of these molecules as oxidizing agents.

3. Other experiments have determined that Ag^+ is a stronger oxidizing agent than I_2, but a weaker oxidizing agent than Br_2. Also, I_2 is a stronger oxidizing agent than Cu^{2+}. Using this information, put all the half-reaction equations together in one list, from strongest oxidizing agent to weakest.

4. For every instance in which a reaction did occur, write the balanced overall redox equation by adding together two half-reaction equations, one for the oxidizing agent and one for the reducing agent (by reversing one from the list). In some instances you will have to multiply the half-reaction equation by an appropriate number in order to make the number of electrons equal, so that they cancel out.

FOLLOW-UP QUESTIONS

1. On the basis of the results of this experiment, state whether you would expect a redox reaction to occur spontaneously in each of the following situations. Give the balanced equation if a reaction does occur.
   a. Br_2 and Pb
   b. I^- and Zn^{2+}
   c. Cl_2 and Cu
   d. I_2 and Mg

2. What would happen to sterling silver jewellery (an alloy of 92.5% Ag and 7.5% Cu) if it were exposed to fumes of bromine?

3. Some laboratory waste pipes used to be made of lead. What would happen if waste Cu^{2+} solutions were allowed to go down such pipes?

4. To remove Cu^{2+} wastes from a solution before discharging it down the sink, steel wool (an alloy of iron) can be added. This produces copper metal on the steel wool. The solid copper can then be disposed of safely. Is iron a stronger or a weaker reducing agent than copper?

CONCLUSION

1. State whether halogens are generally oxidizing or reducing agents and give the periodic trend you observed.

2. State whether metals are generally oxidizing or reducing agents.

14B

Redox Titrations Involving Iodine

Redox reactions are involved in a wide variety of techniques for quantitative analysis of chemical substances. The methods for calculating the amounts of substances involved in these reactions (expressed either as mass in grams or as the volume of a solution of known molarity) will have been introduced to you in your studies of stoichiometry. The balanced equations for many of these redox reactions are complex and must be obtained either by adding balanced half-reaction equations or by using the oxidation number method.

A substance that is often used in quantitative redox reactions is iodine, I_2. It is easily formed by oxidizing I^-, but the reaction can be reversed just as easily, so a wide variety of reactions can involve I_2 as a reactant or product. In addition, it gives a characteristic deep blue color with starch solution even when it is in very low concentrations, making it easy to determine when the I_2 is all used up or when it begins to form. Starch is therefore used as the indicator in these reactions.

In Part I of this experiment, you will prepare a solution of potassium iodate (KIO_3) of known concentration. This solution makes a good primary standard in redox titrations, since it is stable and can be obtained very pure. In Part II, known volumes of this solution will have excess H^+ and I^- added and a reaction will occur in which I_2 is produced in a quantity determined by the moles of KIO_3 present initially. A solution of sodium thiosulfate, $Na_2S_2O_3$, of unknown concentration will then be titrated into the solution, which will react with the I_2. Starch will be added when most of the I_2 has reacted with $S_2O_3^{2-}$ and the titration will be continued until the blue color disappears. The concentration of the $Na_2S_2O_3$ solution can now be calculated. This solution can be used to determine the amount of I_2 in other solutions. In Part III, the $[Cu^{2+}]$ in a solution will be determined by adding I^-, which reduces Cu^{2+} to Cu^+ in copper(I) iodide, CuI, and is oxidized to I_2 in the process. In Part IV, the amount of vitamin C in a sample will be determined by analyzing it with a standard I_2 solution.

OBJECTIVES

1. to prepare a solution of potassium iodate, KIO_3, of known molarity

2. to standardize a solution of sodium thiosulfate, $Na_2S_2O_3$, by titrating it against standard KIO_3 (with excess I^-, H^+)

3. to determine the molarity of Cu^{2+} in an unknown sample by reacting it with I^- and titrating the liberated I_2 with standard $S_2O_3^{2-}$

4. to use a standard I_2 solution to determine the mass of ascorbic acid (vitamin C) in a juice sample or a vitamin tablet

 ©SMG Lab Books Ltd.

SUPPLIES

Equipment

centigram balance
3 beakers (100 mL)
beaker (250 mL)
funnel
wash bottle
volumetric flask (250 mL)
buret (50 mL)
pipet (25 mL)
Erlenmeyer flask (250 mL)
graduated cylinder (10 mL)
bottle (500 mL) with stopper
suction bulb
mortar and pestle
lab apron
safety goggles

Chemical Reagents

solid potassium iodate, KIO_3
1M potassium iodide, KI
1M sulfuric acid, H_2SO_4
sodium thiosulfate solution
   ($Na_2S_2O_3$ approx. 0.12M)
starch solution
copper(II) sulfate solution
   ($CuSO_4$, unknown
   concentration)
iodine in potassium iodide
   solution (I_2/KI)
250 mg or 300 mg vitamin C
   tablets
orange or other citrus juice

PROCEDURE

Part I: Preparing a Standard Potassium Iodate Solution

1. Before coming to the laboratory, calculate the mass of KIO_3 required to make up 250 mL of a 0.0200M solution of KIO_3.

2. Put on your lab apron and safety goggles.

3. Accurately measure the mass of a clean, dry 100 mL beaker and record it in your copy of Table 1 in your notebook.

4. Place solid KIO_3 in the beaker until you have approximately the mass calculated in Step 1. Record the actual mass accurately in Table 1.

5. Dissolve the KIO_3 in water and pour the solution through a funnel into a 250 mL volumetric flask. Rinse the beaker twice and add the rinsings to the flask.

6. Add water until the level of the solution is up to the mark, stopper the flask, and shake it thoroughly to make the solution homogeneous.

Part II: Standardizing a Sodium Thiosulfate Solution

1. Transfer the standard KIO_3 solution to a clean, dry 250 mL beaker.

2. Obtain in 100 mL beakers approximately 50 mL each of 1M KI, 1M H_2SO_4, and starch solution. Label each beaker.

3. Using a suction bulb on your pipet, withdraw 25.00 mL of the KIO_3 solution and transfer it to a 250 mL Erlenmeyer flask, touching the tip to the side of the flask to ensure that the correct volume is delivered.

4. Add to the flask containing the KIO_3 solution approximately 5 mL of 1M KI and 5 mL of 1M H_2SO_4. These are excess amounts, so precise measurement is not required. Use a 10 mL graduated cylinder for adding the

CAUTION

Potassium iodate solution is poisonous. Do not get any in your mouth and do not swallow any. Always use a suction bulb on your pipet.

CAUTION

Sulfuric acid solution is very corrosive. Wash any spills or splashes on skin or clothing with plenty of water. Call your instructor

KI and H_2SO_4. (You will notice that a brown precipitate is formed at first and that it dissolves again to give a clear brown solution. This behaviour is characteristic of iodine, I_2.) The amount of precipitate formed is determined by the moles of KIO_3 originally present. The iodine will now be made to react with sodium thiosulfate solution, $Na_2S_2O_3$, in order to determine the molarity of the $Na_2S_2O_3$.

5. Fill a 500 mL bottle with the approximately $0.12M$ $Na_2S_2O_3$ solution provided and label it with your name. Use solution from this bottle for all subsequent parts of the experiment requiring $Na_2S_2O_3$ solution.

6. Add about 10 mL of this solution to the buret, rinse, and discard. Fill the buret with $Na_2S_2O_3$, then open the valve briefly to allow some to drain through the tip.

7. Determine the initial buret reading and record it in Table 2.

8. Run the $Na_2S_2O_3$ solution into the flask, swirling constantly, until the brown color has faded to a light yellow. Add approximately 5 mL of starch solution and continue adding the $Na_2S_2O_3$ drop by drop until the blue-black color disappears. Note that the endpoint is a very precise one and that it is therefore important not to add the starch too soon. Take the reading on the buret and record it in Table 2.

9. Repeat Steps 3 to 8 until you obtain consistent results. You now have enough data to calculate the molarity of the $Na_2S_2O_3$ solution when you later perform your Analysis of Results.

Part III: Determining the Concentration of an Unknown Solution of Copper(II) Sulfate

CAUTION

Copper(II) sulfate solution is poisonous. Do not get any in your mouth and do not swallow any.

1. Obtain in a beaker approximately 100 mL of the unknown $CuSO_4$ solution provided. Write down its identifying letter or number if more than one unknown is provided.

2. Using a suction bulb, withdraw into a pipet 25.00 mL of the $CuSO_4$ solution and transfer it to a 250 mL Erlenmeyer flask. Remember to rinse the pipet with the solution first.

3. Add 10 mL of $1M$ KI solution to the $CuSO_4$. Use a graduated cylinder; a precise volume is not required.

4. The cloudy brown material produced in the flask consists of brown I_2 solution and a precipitate of white copper(I) iodide, CuI. The iodine can now be titrated with $Na_2S_2O_3$. The CuI does not interfere with this reaction.

5. Take the initial reading on the buret and record it in Table 3. Run the solution into the flask until the brown color has faded to a light yellow. Add 5 mL of starch solution, then add $Na_2S_2O_3$ drop by drop until the blue-black color disappears. Take the final reading on the buret and record it in Table 3. (A light-colored precipitate of CuI will remain.)

6. Repeat Steps 2 to 5 once or twice more until consistent results are obtained. You now have enough data to calculate the molarity of Cu^{2+} and therefore, the molarity of the $CuSO_4$ solution. These calculations can be done later during Analysis of Results.

Part IV: Determining the Amount of Vitamin C (Ascorbic Acid) in a Sample

1. Obtain in a 250 mL beaker about 200 mL of the solution of iodine (in potassium iodide) (I_2/KI) provided. You will need to standardize it by completing Steps 2 to 5 before doing the rest of Part IV.

2. Using a suction bulb, withdraw 25.00 mL of the iodine solution into a pipet and transfer it to a 250 mL Erlenmeyer flask.

3. Refill the buret with the standardized $Na_2S_2O_3$ solution, take the initial reading, and record it in Table 4.

4. Run the $Na_2S_2O_3$ solution into the flask until the brown color of the I_2 fades to a pale yellow, add 5 mL of starch solution, and continue the titration *dropwise* until the dark blue color just disappears. Again take the final reading on the buret and record it in Table 4.

5. Repeat Steps 2 to 4 until consistent results are obtained. You now have enough data to calculate the molarity of the I_2 solution when you later perform your Analysis of Results.

6. Discard the $Na_2S_2O_3$ solution remaining in the buret, wash the buret with water, then rinse it with the I_2 solution. Discard this, then fill the buret again with I_2, and drain some to refill the tip.

7. Obtain a 250 mg (or 300 mg) tablet of vitamin C (ascorbic acid), grind it with a mortar and pestle, and place the powder in a 250 mL Erlenmeyer flask. Add 5 mL of starch solution.

8. Take the initial reading of the I_2 solution in the buret and record it in Table 5. Then allow it to run into the flask. Swirl constantly, watching for the first appearance of the characteristic dark blue color, which stays even after swirling. Again take the final reading on the buret and record it in Table 5.

9. Repeat Steps 7 and 8 until consistent results are obtained if requested to do so.

10. Obtain a sample of orange or other citrus juice (or other fruit juice to which vitamin C has been added). Using a graduated cylinder, measure out 100 mL of the juice and pour it into a 250 mL Erlenmeyer flask. Add 5 mL of starch solution.

11. Take the initial reading of the I_2 solution in the buret and record it in Table 6. Then allow it to run into the flask. Swirl constantly, watching for the first appearance of the characteristic dark blue color, which stays even after swirling. Again take the final reading on the buret and record it in Table 6.

12. Repeat, using another sample of another juice if requested to do so by your instructor.

13. Before leaving the laboratory, wash your hands thoroughly with soap and water.

CAUTION

Iodine causes burns and is a strong irritant to eyes and skin. If any is spilled on your skin, wash first with sodium thiosulfate solution, then with plenty of water.

REAGENT DISPOSAL

Rinse solutions that are left over in the flask after the titrations down the sink with copious amounts of water. If requested to do so by your instructor, return any leftover solutions of KIO_3, $Na_2S_2O_3$, KI, and I_2/KI solutions to their designated containers.

POST LAB CONSIDERATIONS

In order to calculate the results for this experiment, you will need to work out the balanced overall redox equation for each reaction that is occurring, then use the mole relationships in the equation to relate reacting quantities.

The balanced half-reactions occurring in this experiment are as follows:

Production of I_2 from KIO_3, KI, H_2SO_4:	$2IO_3^- + 12H^+ + 10\ e^- \rightarrow I_2 + 6H_2O$ $2I^- \rightarrow I_2 + 2e^-$
Standardization of $Na_2S_2O_3$:	$2S_2O_3^{2-} \rightarrow S_4O_6^{2-} + 2e^-$ $I_2 + 2e^- \rightarrow 2I^-$
Production of I_2 from Cu^{2+} by I^-:	$Cu^{2+} + I^- + e^- \rightarrow CuI$ $2I^- \rightarrow I_2 + 2e^-$

You need not show an equation for the reaction of vitamin C (ascorbic acid, $C_6H_8O_6$) with I_2. They react in a 1:1 mole ratio.

The deep blue-black color formed by starch and iodine is very useful in a variety of situations. Its formation is not really a chemical reaction — the iodine molecules just happen to fit closely inside the long spiralling starch molecule and interact strongly with it. The combination is unstable above 50°C. You encountered this blue-black color in an earlier experiment on rates of reactions. It is interesting to note that here you are using starch to test for the presence of iodine, but in food chemistry the reverse occurs, iodine solution is used to test for the presence of starch. You may have performed such a test in an earlier science course.

Note that iodine is only slightly soluble in water, but does dissolve well if I^- ions are present. The reaction that occurs is $I_2 + I^- \rightarrow I_3^-$. However, the complex I_3^- breaks down very readily when any chemical is present that can react with I_2 (such as $S_2O_3^{2-}$) and the solution therefore acts as though it were a solution of I_2.

EXPERIMENTAL RESULTS

Part I: Preparing a Standard Potassium Iodate Solution
Table 1 Preparing a Standard KIO_3 Solution

Calculated mass of potassium iodate, KIO_3, required for 250.0 mL of 0.0200M solution (g)	
Mass of beaker (g)	
Mass of beaker + KIO_3 (g)	
Mass of KIO_3 (g)	

Copying the experiment is prohibited.   ©SMG Lab Books Ltd.

Part II: Standardizating a Sodium Thiosulfate Solution

Table 2 Volume of $Na_2S_2O_3$ Needed to React with Iodine from 25.00 mL of KIO_3

	Trial 1	Trial 2	Trial 3	Trial 4 (if necessary)
Initial reading of buret (mL)				
Final reading of buret (mL)		*COMPLETE IN YOUR NOTEBOOK*		
Volume of $Na_2S_2O_3$ required (mL)				
Average volume of $Na_2S_2O_3$ (mL)				

Part III: Determining the Concentration of an Unknown Solution of Copper(II) Sulfate

Table 3 Volume of $Na_2S_2O_3$ Needed to React with Iodine from 25.00 mL of $CuSO_4$

Unknown $CuSO_4$ Solution # _____	Trial 1	Trial 2	Trial 3	Trial 4 (if necessary)
Initial reading of buret (mL)				
Final reading of buret (mL)		*COMPLETE IN YOUR NOTEBOOK*		
Volume of $Na_2S_2O_3$ required (mL)				
Average volume of $Na_2S_2O_3$ (mL)				

Part IV: Determining the Amount of Vitamin C (Ascorbic Acid) in a Sample

Table 4 Volume of $Na_2S_2O_3$ Needed to React with 25.00 mL of I_2 Solution

	Trial 1	Trial 2	Trial 3	Trial 4 (if necessary)
Initial reading of buret (mL)				
Final reading of buret (mL)		*COMPLETE IN YOUR NOTEBOOK*		
Volume of $Na_2S_2O_3$ required (mL)				
Average volume of $Na_2S_2O_3$ (mL)				

Table 5 Volume of I_2 Needed to React with Ascorbic Acid (Vitamin C)

Mass of Vitamin C in Tablet = _____ mg

	Trial 1	Trial 2	Trial 3	Trial 4 (if necessary)
Initial reading of buret (mL)				
Final reading of buret (mL)		*COMPLETE IN YOUR NOTEBOOK*		
Volume of I_2 required (mL)				
Average volume of I_2 (mL)				

Table 6 Volume of I$_2$ Needed to React with Juice

	Trial 1	Trial 2	Trial 3	Trial 4 (if necessary)
Type of juice				
Volume of juice (mL)				
Initial reading of buret (mL)				
Final reading of buret (mL)		COMPLETE IN YOUR NOTEBOOK		
Volume of I$_2$ used (mL)				

ANALYSIS OF RESULTS

Part I: Preparing a Standard Potassium Iodate Solution

1. Calculate the concentration of KIO$_3$ solution formed when you dissolved your calculated mass of KIO$_3$ in water and made the volume up to 250.0 mL.

2. Calculate the number of moles of KIO$_3$, and therefore of IO$_3^-$, in 25.00 mL of this solution.

Part II: Standardizing a Sodium Thiosulfate Solution

1. Work out the overall redox equation for the reaction of IO$_3^-$, I$^-$, and H$^+$ to give I$_2$.

2. Work out the overall redox equation for the reaction of S$_2$O$_3^{2-}$ and I$_2$ to give S$_4$O$_6^{2-}$ (tetrathionate ion) and I$^-$.

3. State the relationship between moles of IO$_3^-$ and moles of S$_2$O$_3^{2-}$ working through moles of I$_2$.

4. From this relationship and the number of moles of KIO$_3$ in 25.00 mL of solution, calculate the number of moles of S$_2$O$_3^{2-}$ with which the KIO$_3$ reacts.

5. Knowing the average volume and the number of moles of S$_2$O$_3^{2-}$ used, calculate the [S$_2$O$_3^{2-}$].

Part III: Determining the Concentration of an Unknown Solution of Copper (II) Sulfate

1. Work out the overall redox equation for the reaction: Cu^{2+} + I$^-$ → CuI(s) + I$_2$.

2. Recalling from Part II the relationship between moles of I$_2$ and moles of S$_2$O$_3^{2-}$ and using the equation in Analysis 1 above, state the relationship between moles of Cu^{2+} and moles of S$_2$O$_3^{2-}$.

3. From the average volume (from Part III) and the known concentration (from Part II) of S$_2$O$_3^{2-}$ used, calculate the number of moles of S$_2$O$_3^{2-}$ used.

4. Calculate the number of moles of Cu^{2+} originally present.

5. Calculate [Cu^{2+}] in the original sample from the number of moles and volume used.

Part IV: Determining the Amount of Vitamin C (Ascorbic Acid) in a Sample

1. Calculate the number of moles of $S_2O_3^{2-}$ used from the average volume used and the molarity from Part II.

2. Calculate the number of moles of I_2 present, using the relationship obtained in Part II.

3. Calculate $[I_2]$ from the number of moles used and the volume in litres.

4. From the average volume of I_2 solution used in the vitamin C titration, calculate the number of moles of I_2 required to react with the vitamin C.

5. Recalling that it was stated in the Post Lab Considerations that vitamin C and I_2 react in a 1:1 mole ratio and that vitamin C (ascorbic acid) has the formula $C_6H_8O_6$, calculate the mass in milligrams of vitamin C present.

6. Compare your result with the rated amount of vitamin C for that tablet and calculate the percentage deviation between your result and the rated amount.

7. In the same manner, calculate the number of milligrams of vitamin C in 100 mL of each juice sample tested.

FOLLOW-UP QUESTIONS

1. Vitamin C was oxidized by iodine in this experiment. By referring to a table of standard reduction potentials, explain why the vitamin C content of foods is decreased on exposure to air.

2. A chemist who wishes to analyze a sample of hydrated copper(II) nitrate finds that when a sample with a mass of 1.08 g is dissolved in water and excess KI solution is added, 34.9 mL of $0.128M$ $Na_2S_2O_3$ are required to react with the liberated iodine. What is the number of moles of water per mole of copper(II) nitrate in the hydrated crystal?

3. A sample of apple juice states on the label "Contains no less than 35 mg/100 mL of ascorbic acid (vitamin C)." A 25.00 mL sample was titrated with $0.00800M$ I_2 solution and found to require 6.55 mL until the starch indicator turned blue. Does this sample meet the stated concentration?

CONCLUSION

State the results of Objectives 3 and 4.

Redox Titrations Involving the Permanganate Ion

A common laboratory oxidizing agent is the permanganate ion, MnO_4^-, which is usually provided by the compound potassium permanganate, $KMnO_4$. It is especially useful for quantitative redox reactions because the permanganate in solution is an intense purple color, but when reduced all the way to the 2+ state in Mn^{2+} becomes virtually colorless, thereby acting as its own indicator. A sample of a reducing agent can therefore be titrated with $KMnO_4$ solution and the faint purple color that remains even after the solution is swirled makes the completion of the reaction apparent. You may think that $KMnO_4$ will not be highly accurate in showing the completion of the reaction, since it must be left over to be seen as a purple color. However, its color is very intense; the $0.020M$ solution you will be using is a very dark purple and its color can still be detected when 1 mL of the solution is added to 2 L of water, that is, when $[MnO_4^-] = 1.0 \times 10^{-5}M$. This figure represents only 0.05% of the original concentration, which is certainly accurate enough for most situations.

Potassium permanganate is obtainable in analytical reagent quality, so a solution of it can be made up to an accurate concentration from a known mass of crystals. However, the solution should be freshly prepared because after a time, any potassium permanganate solution decomposes to a certain extent and a brown coloration of MnO_2 appears on the side of the container.

The Mn in the permanganate ion has an oxidation number of 7+; in the manganese(II) ion it has an oxidation number of 2+. It still has other common oxidation states; 6+ in the manganate ion (MnO_4^{2-}), which is green, and 4+ in manganese dioxide, which is brown. In order to make sure that all the permanganate ion is reduced completely to Mn^{2+} and not some other state, you must follow the instructions in the experiment carefully. In Part I of this experiment, you will look in a qualitative way at the conditions which result in these different compounds, before you go on to use $KMnO_4$ quantitatively in Parts II, and III. In Part II you will determine the $[Fe^{2+}]$ in an unknown solution (or the molar mass of an unknown iron compound), then in Part III you will determine the concentration of a solution of hydrogen peroxide, H_2O_2. Your instructor will provide you with a solution of potassium permanganate of known concentration.

OBJECTIVES

1. to determine the conditions under which $KMnO_4$ is reduced completely to Mn^{2+}

2. to determine the $[Fe^{2+}]$ in an unknown solution (or the molar mass of an unknown compound containing Fe^{2+})

3. to determine the $[H_2O_2]$ in a solution of hydrogen peroxide

SUPPLIES

Equipment

buret (50 mL)	test-tube rack	centigram balance
stand	beaker (250 mL)	medicine dropper
buret clamp	beaker (100 mL)	filter funnel
Erlenmeyer flask (250 mL)	pipet (25 mL)	safety goggles
3 test tubes (18 mm × 150 mm)	suction bulb	lab apron
	graduated cylinder (10 mL)	

Chemical Reagents

standard solution of $KMnO_4$ (approx. 0.02M)

0.050M sodium sulfite, Na_2SO_3

3M sulfuric acid, H_2SO_4

6M sodium hydroxide, NaOH

unknown Fe^{2+} solution or unknown solid containing Fe^{2+}

hydrogen peroxide solution (approx. 3 %)

PROCEDURE

Part I: Preliminary Investigation of $KMnO_4$ as an Oxidizing Agent

1. Put on your lab apron and safety goggles.

2. Obtain in a 250 mL beaker about 150 mL of the solution of $KMnO_4$ provided. Note its concentration.

3. Obtain three 18 mm × 150 mm test tubes and place them in the rack. To each add 1 mL of the $KMnO_4$ solution.

4. Next, to one test tube add 2 mL of 3M H_2SO_4, to the second add 2 mL of water, and to the third add 2 mL of 6M NaOH.

5. To each test tube, add 2 mL of 0.050M Na_2SO_3. Record your observations in your copy of Table 1 in your notebook.

Part II: Determining the Concentration of a Solution of Fe^{2+}

1. Using the filter funnel, pour about 15 mL of $KMnO_4$ solution into your buret. Rinse and discard.

2. Fill up the buret with the $KMnO_4$ and allow some to drain in order to fill the tip. Read the volume.

3. Obtain about 85 mL of unknown Fe^{2+} solution from your instructor. Use a 100 mL beaker. Write down any identifying letter or number if more than one unknown is provided.

4. Using a suction bulb on your pipet, withdraw about 5 mL of the Fe^{2+} solution and rinse inside the pipet with it. Discard. Refill the pipet to the 25 mL mark with more Fe^{2+} solution and transfer to a 250 mL Erlenmeyer flask.

5. Add 10 mL of 3M H_2SO_4 to the flask, then allow the $KMnO_4$ solution to run into the flask, swirling constantly.

CAUTION

Potassium permanganate ($KMnO_4$) solution is a strong irritant and will stain skin and clothing. Wash any spills with plenty of water

3M H_2SO_4 is very corrosive and will damage skin and clothing. Wash any spills with plenty of water and notify your instructor.

6M NaOH is very caustic and will damage skin and clothing. Wash any spills with plenty of water and notify your instructor.

Sodium sulfite Na_2SO_3 is a strong irritant to skin. Wash any spills with plenty of water.

6. When the purple color starts to take a longer time to dispense, slow down the addition of the $KMnO_4$ until you add it a drop at a time. Record the volume in the buret when the faint purple color first stays in the flask.

7. Repeat once or twice if necessary, to obtain consistent results. Record your observations in your copy of Table 2.

8. If instead of using an unknown solution you are instructed to use a particular mass of an unknown solid containing Fe^{2+}, then measure the mass accurately, dissolve the solid in about 30 mL of water, add 10 mL of $3M$ H_2SO_4, and carry out the titration in the same manner as described above.

Part III: Determining the Concentration of an H_2O_2 Solution

1. Obtain in a clean, dry test tube about 5 mL of hydrogen peroxide (H_2O_2) solution, labeled 3% or "10 volume." (This is the type available in drug stores as an antiseptic.)

2. Obtain a clean, dry 250 mL flask and measure its mass.

3. Using a medicine dropper, place 20 to 30 drops of hydrogen peroxide in the flask (about 1 mL to 1.5 mL) and again measure the mass.

4. Add about 30 mL of water and 10 mL of $3M$ H_2SO_4.

5. Read the volume of $KMnO_4$ in the buret (after refilling if necessary), then run the solution in as before to the first appearance of a pale purple color. Record the volume in your copy of Table 3.

6. Repeat 1 or 2 more times, as necessary, to obtain consistent results. Record all observations in Table 3.

7. Before you leave the laboratory, wash your hands thoroughly with soap and water.

REAGENT DISPOSAL

Place any unused solutions of $KMnO_4$ and Fe^{2+} in the designated waste containers. Solutions left in the flask after the titrations may safely be rinsed down the sink with copious amounts of water.

POST LAB CONSIDERATIONS

In order to calculate the results for this experiment, you first need to work out the balanced overall redox equation for each reaction. Then, you will use the mole relationships in each equation to relate the quantities that are reacting.

The following are the half-reactions occurring in this experiment:

Reduction of MnO_4^-:

In acid:	$MnO_4^- + 8H^+ + 5e^- \rightarrow Mn^{2+} + 4H_2O$
In neutral solution:	$MnO_4^- + 4H^+ + 3e^- \rightarrow MnO_2 + 2H_2O$
In base:	$MnO_4^- + e^- \rightarrow MnO_4^{2-}$
Oxidation of SO_3^{2-}:	$SO_3^{2-} + H_2O \rightarrow SO_4^{2-} + 2H^+ + 2e^-$
Oxidation of Fe^{2+}:	$Fe^{2+} \rightarrow Fe^{3+} + e^-$
Oxidation of H_2O_2:	$H_2O_2 \rightarrow O_2 + 2H^+ + 2e^-$

Remember that the titrations in Parts II and III were done in acidic solution.

EXPERIMENTAL RESULTS

Part I: Preliminary Investigation of KMnO$_4$ as an Oxidizing Agent

Table 1 Preliminary Investigation of KMnO$_4$ as an Oxidizing Agent

Type of Solution	Color	Ion or Molecule Present
Acidic (3M H$_2$SO$_4$)		
Neutral (water)	COMPLETE IN YOUR NOTEBOOK	COMPLETE IN YOUR NOTEBOOK
Basic (6M NaOH)		

Part II: Determining the Concentration of a Solution of Fe^{2+}

Table 2 Volume of KMnO$_4$ to React with 25.00 mL of Fe^{2+} Solution

Unknown # , [KMnO$_4$] = M	Trial 1	Trial 2	Trial 3 (if necessary)
Initial volume of KMnO$_4$ (mL)			
Final volume of KMnO$_4$ (mL)	COMPLETE IN YOUR NOTEBOOK	COMPLETE IN YOUR NOTEBOOK	COMPLETE IN YOUR NOTEBOOK
Volume of KMnO$_4$ required (mL)			
Average volume (mL)			

(If you used a solid Fe^{2+} unknown, add a row indicating the mass used.)

Part III: Determining the Concentration of an H$_2$O$_2$ Solution

Table 3 Volume of KMnO$_4$ to React with H$_2$O$_2$ Solution

[KMnO$_4$] = M	Trial 1	Trial 2	Trial 3 (if necessary)
Mass of empty flask (g)			
Mass of flask + H$_2$O$_2$ (g)			
Mass of H$_2$O$_2$ (g)	COMPLETE IN YOUR NOTEBOOK	COMPLETE IN YOUR NOTEBOOK	COMPLETE IN YOUR NOTEBOOK
Initial volume of KMnO$_4$ (mL)			
Final volume of KMnO$_4$ (mL)			
Volume of KMnO$_4$ used (mL)			

ANALYSIS OF RESULTS

Part I: Preliminary Investigation of KMnO$_4$ as an Oxidizing Agent

1. Write the overall redox equation for MnO_4^- reacting with SO_3^{2-} to give Mn^{2+} and SO_4^{2-} in acidic solution.

2. Write the overall redox equation for MnO_4^- reacting with SO_3^{2-} to give MnO_2 and SO_4^{2-}. (This occurred in neutral solution, but H^+ ions will appear in the final equation.)

3. Write the overall redox equation for MnO_4^- reacting with SO_3^{2-} to give MnO_4^{2-} and SO_4^{2-} (in basic solution).

4. Explain why titrations using permanganate are performed in acid solution.

Part II: Determining the Concentration of a Solution of Fe^{2+}

1. Write the balanced overall redox equation for MnO_4^- reacting with Fe^{2+} in acid solution to give Mn^{2+} and Fe^{3+}.

2. From the average volume of MnO_4^- used and the molarity of the solution provided by your instructor, calculate the number of moles of MnO_4^-.

3. Using the mole relationship given by the balanced equation, calculate the number of moles of Fe^{2+} used.

4. Calculate the $[Fe^{2+}]$ from the number of moles and the volume of the solution (in litres). (If you used a solid sample, calculate the molar mass or percent of Fe instead, as directed by your instructor.)

Part III: Determining the Concentration of an H$_2$O$_2$ Solution

1. Write the balanced overall redox equation for MnO_4^- reacting with H_2O_2 in acid solution to give Mn^{2+} and O_2.

2. For the first titration, calculate the number of moles of MnO_4^- from the volume and the molarity.

3. Using the mole relationship given by the balanced equation, calculate the number of moles of H_2O_2 oxidized and convert to grams using the molar mass of H_2O_2.

4. Using the calculated mass of H_2O_2 above and the mass of the solution from Table 3, calculate the percent of H_2O_2 in the solution.

5. Repeat Analysis 2 to Analysis 4 for each of the other titrations performed and average your answers for the percent of H_2O_2 in the solution.

FOLLOW-UP QUESTIONS

1. A bottle containing a standard solution of KMnO$_4$ is found to have brown stains on the inside. Why will this KMnO$_4$ be of no further use for quantitative experiments?

2. Hydrogen peroxide is usually labeled 3%, meaning 3 g/100 mL. Assuming that the solution has a density of 1 g/mL, what is the percent deviation between your calculated concentration and the stated 3% figure?

3. Hydrogen peroxide breaks down easily to give water and oxygen as follows:

$$2H_2O_2(aq) \rightarrow 2H_2O(l) + O_2(g)$$

Bottles of hydrogen peroxide are sometimes labeled as 10 volume as well as 3%. This means the volume of oxygen that can be liberated is 10 times the volume of the solution. Remembering that 1 mol of gas occupies 22.4 L at STP, calculate the volume of oxygen at STP that could be produced from 1 L of a 3% solution. Is 10 L a good approximation to your answer?

4. Many different materials can catalyze the breakdown of H_2O_2. (If your dropper is not clean, you may find bubbles of oxygen forming in the dropper!) However, high temperature alone can cause sufficient pressure to build up because of released oxygen to explode a glass container. For this reason, hydrogen peroxide is usually purchased in plastic bottles, which often have a venting cap to allow gas to escape. Under what conditions should hydrogen peroxide be stored?

CONCLUSION

State the results of Objectives 2 and 3.

14D

Electrochemical Cells

Electrochemical cells are extensively used in our society. They come in many shapes and sizes and have many applications. For instance, motor vehicles have electrochemical cells in the form of storage batteries that are used to start the engine. Another type of electrochemical cell, the dry cell, is commonly used to provide electrical energy for such things as flashlights, toys, watches, calculators, and smoke alarms. An increasingly common electrochemical cell, the fuel cell, has recently received much attention because of its use in electric powered motor vehicles. Cars running on fuel cells have zero harmful emissions; in fact their only emission is water vapour.

Although the types of electrochemical cells are varied, the operation of all types is based on the same principle — spontaneous redox reactions. The chemistry involved is the same as that for a redox reaction between species in the same container. However, an electrochemical cell is set up so that the reacting species are not permitted to come in contact with each other. Electrons are transferred from one species to another by means of an external circuit. In this external circuit, the energy of the electrons is "tapped" or put to work, to illuminate a light bulb, for instance.

In this experiment, you will construct laboratory models of three electrochemical cells: a zinc-lead cell in Part I, a lead-copper cell in Part II, and a zinc-copper cell in Part III. In Part IV, you will investigate the effect of changing solution concentration on cell voltage. Although your cells will not look like those commonly used, they should enable you to understand the theory of the operation of electrochemical cells better. Before beginning this experiment, you should take the time to review in your textbook the terminology and theory associated with electrochemical cells.

OBJECTIVES

1. to become familiar with the construction and operation of electrochemical cells

2. to predict the reactions and voltages that should result

3. to construct three electrochemical cells and measure their voltages

4. to observe the effect of non-standard conditions on voltage

SUPPLIES

Equipment
2 beakers (150 mL)
U tube
cotton batting
2 wire leads with clips
voltmeter (0 V-3 V D.C.)
steel wool
lab apron
safety goggles

Chemical Reagents
metal strips (copper, zinc, lead)
0.5M copper(II) nitrate
   ($Cu(NO_3)_2$) solution
0.5M zinc nitrate
   ($Zn(NO_3)_2$) solution
0.5M lead(II) nitrate
   ($Pb(NO_3)_2$) solution
0.5M potassium nitrate
   (KNO_3) solution
1.0M sodium sulphide
   (Na_2S) solution

PROCEDURE

Part I: Making a Zinc-Lead Cell

1. Put on your lab apron and safety goggles.

2. Obtain 80 mL each of zinc nitrate and lead(II) nitrate solution in separate 150 mL beakers. Label these beakers so that you do not get them confused.

3. Prepare a salt bridge by filling a glass U tube with potassium nitrate solution and plugging both ends with a small clump of cotton batting. Do not allow air to become trapped in the tube. Carefully invert the U tube and place it in the two beakers, as shown in Figure 14D-1.

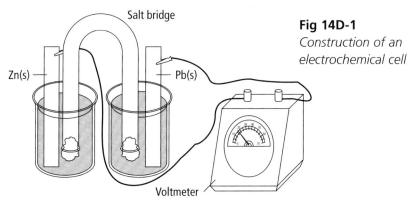

Fig 14D-1
Construction of an electrochemical cell

4. Obtain a zinc strip and a lead strip, clean the surfaces with steel wool and a paper towel, and rinse them in water. Place the zinc strip in the zinc nitrate solution and the lead strip in the lead(II) nitrate solution.

5. Connect a voltmeter to the zinc-lead cell as in Figure 14D-1. Connect the leads so that a positive reading results on the voltmeter. Record the measured voltage as soon as the circuit is connected. As described in Experimental Results, make a labeled sketch of your electrochemical cell.

6. While the cell is operating, consult a table of standard reduction potentials and decide at which cell oxidation is occurring. Label this half-cell as the anode on your sketch. Before you label the other cell the cathode, first convince yourself that your cell has all the chemical species needed for a redox reaction.

7. Indicate the direction of electron flow (from anode to cathode) on your diagram.

8. Use the table of standard reduction potentials to calculate the theoretical standard state voltage that should result in a zinc-lead cell.

9. Before dismantling the cell, observe the effect of removing the salt bridge or any electrode.

10. Take the cell apart and save the zinc and lead solutions and the electrodes for Parts II and III of the experiment.

11. Dismantle the salt bridge, following the instructions for reagent disposal.

Part II: Making a Lead-Copper Cell

1. Obtain 80 mL of copper(II) nitrate solution in a 150 mL beaker. Also obtain a copper strip.

2. Prepare a new salt bridge to avoid contaminating the half-cell solutions.

3. Use the Procedure from Part I to construct and study a lead-copper cell. Here, place the lead strip in the lead(II) nitrate and the copper strip in the copper(II) nitrate. Remember to record all the observations and sketch your lead-copper cell.

Part III: Making a Zinc-Copper Cell

1. In this part you will construct a zinc-copper cell, using the Procedure from Part I. This time you will place the zinc strip in the zinc nitrate and the copper strip in the copper(II) nitrate. You will need to prepare a new salt bridge. Record all observations and sketch your zinc-copper cell.

2. Disconnect the voltmeter and save the zinc-copper cell for Part IV.

Part IV: The Effect of Solution Concentration on the Cell Voltage of a Zinc-Copper Cell

Check with your instructor. Your instructor might choose to demonstrate Part IV in a fume hood.

1. Reconnect the zinc-copper cell from Part III and record the initial voltage in a copy of Table 1 in your notebook.

2. Slowly add 40 mL of $1M$ sodium sulfide (Na_2S) solution to the zinc nitrate solution and wait for a few minutes. Record your observations, as well as the new voltage, in Table 1.

3. Repeat Step 2 with the copper half-cell.

4. Before leaving the laboratory, wash your hands thoroughly with soap and water.

CAUTION

Sodium sulfide is corrosive; in solution it reacts with acids to form H_2S gas, which has an offensive odor and is poisonous. Part IV should thus be done only under well-ventilated conditions.

REAGENT DISPOSAL

Use tweezers to remove the cotton plugs from the salt bridge and place them in the designated container. Rinse the KNO_3 solution from the salt bridge down the sink with copious amounts of water. The $Pb(NO_3)_2$ solution should not be contaminated so it can be poured back into its original container. The remaining $Zn(NO_3)_2$ and $Cu(NO_3)_2$ solutions cannot be re-used; they now contain S^{2-} ions and should be poured into the designated waste container. Return any remaining Na_2S solution to its bottle.

POST LAB CONSIDERATIONS

In any operating electrochemical cell, there will be a net redox reaction with oxidation taking place at the anode and reduction at the cathode. The specific oxidation and reduction reactions for a cell can be determined by examining a table of standard reduction potentials. Consider the following example of a magnesium-copper cell using solutions of magnesium nitrate and copper(II) nitrate.

Anode (oxidation)	$Mg(s) \rightarrow Mg^{2+} + 2e^-$;	$E° = +2.37$ V
Cathode (reduction)	$Cu^{2+} + 2e^- \rightarrow Cu(s)$;	$E° = +0.34$ V
Overall	$Cu^{2+} + Mg(s) \rightarrow Mg^{2+} + Cu(s)$;	$E°_{cell} = +2.71$ V

These half-reactions were chosen as a pair so that the overall cell voltage would be positive. If the reverse reactions had been chosen, then the cell voltage would have been -2.71 V, representing a non-spontaneous reaction uncharacteristic of electrochemical cells.

Once the anode and cathode reactions have been determined, all the other aspects of cell operation, such as direction of electron flow and cation/anion migration fall into place.

The results in Part IV, which involve the addition of Na_2S, are properly explained by using the Nernst Equation which is usually discussed in more advanced studies of electrochemical cells. However, for our purposes we can relate the voltage effects of changing half-cell concentrations to the "shifting" concepts of Le Chatelier's principle. Even though a chemical equilibrium does not exist in the operating cell, the voltage of the cell changes as though "shifts" were occurring in the overall redox reaction. The key to interpreting these "shifts" is to examine a table of solubilities to identify decreases in ion concentration that result from precipitate formation.

You may have noticed that the measured voltage is usually less than the theoretical voltage. Some internal resistances of the cell can account for this effect. For example, the salt bridge offers a resistance to the flow of ions, thereby decreasing the voltage. Also, the non-standard concentrations used in your cells will contribute to lower voltages.

Part I: Making a Zinc-Lead Cell

Part II: Making a Lead-Copper Cell

Part III: Making a Zinc-Copper Cell

For each cell you constructed, you should have a labeled sketch similar to Figure 14D-2. All solutions and electrodes, and the anode, cathode, and the direction of electron flow should be labeled in each. Also, the measured voltage should be recorded for each cell.

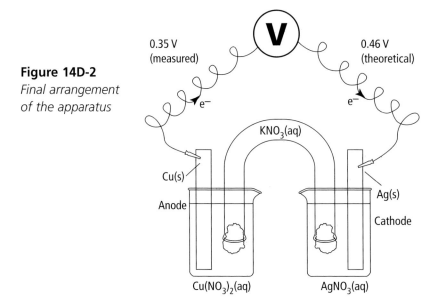

Figure 14D-2
*Final arrangement
of the apparatus*

0.35 V
(measured)

0.46 V
(theoretical)

e^-

e^-

$KNO_3(aq)$

$Cu(s)$

Anode

$Ag(s)$

Cathode

$Cu(NO_3)_2(aq)$

$AgNO_3(aq)$

Part IV: The Effect of Solution Concentration on the Cell Voltage of a Zinc-Copper Cell

Table 1

	Observations	Voltage
Initial Voltage		
Adding Na_2S to the Zn half-cell	COMPLETE IN YOUR NOTEBOOK	COMPLETE IN YOUR NOTEBOOK
Adding Na_2S to the Cu half-cell		

ANALYSIS OF RESULTS

1. For each cell you constructed, write the equations for the following:
   a. the anode half reaction
   b. the cathode half reaction
   c. the overall cell reaction
   Calculate the theoretical standard state cell voltage.

2. a. When Na_2S was added to the Zn half-cell, what precipitate formed?
   b. What change in voltage occurred?
   c. Referring to Le Chatelier's principle, explain why this voltage change occurred.

3. a. When Na_2S was added to the Cu half-cell, what precipitate formed?
   b. What change in voltage occurred?
   c. Referring to Le Chatelier's principle, explain why this voltage change occurred.

4. What effect did removing the salt bridge have on the operation of each electrochemical cell? Explain.

5. In Parts I, II, and III, how did your measured voltages compare to the theoretical voltages? Was there any general pattern?

FOLLOW-UP QUESTIONS

1. Design and draw a diagram of an electrochemical cell that has a magnesium anode and a theoretical standard state voltage of +3.17 V. Label the diagram as you did those in this experiment.

2. Explain why you should not expect an electrochemical cell to operate for an unlimited period of time.

3. Illustrate the migration of all anions and cations in a zinc-copper cell by drawing a labeled diagram of such a cell. What general statement can you make concerning the directions of flow of anions and cations?

4. Predict which ions, Cu^{2+} or Zn^{2+}, should migrate into the salt bridge in Follow-Up Question 3. How could you test your prediction?

5. Predict the voltage reading of a zinc-copper cell when the cell reaction reaches equilibrium.

CONCLUSION

State the results of Objective 3.

14E

Electrolytic Cells

In the experiment on electrochemical cells (14D), you assembled apparatus and reagents so that spontaneous redox reactions occurred and produced electrical energy. Here, a chemical change produced electrical energy. Electrolytic cells involve processes opposite to those in electrochemical cells; that is, electrolytic cells require an external source of electrical energy (a battery or D.C. power supply) that "forces" a non-spontaneous redox reaction to occur. In electrolytic cells, electrical energy produces a chemical change.

Electrolytic cells are important to the chemical process industries involved in the production of pure metals and gases. Another application of electrolytic cells is in the protection and beautification of metals by silver plating or chrome plating.

Although all electrolytic cells are similar in their assembly, they vary as to how complex it is to interpret the reactions that take place. For example, a cell having more chemical species capable of reacting is more complicated, with respect to determining which species react, than a cell having fewer chemical species. In order to classify electrolytic cells according to such complexities, it is convenient to describe them as Type 1, Type 2, or Type 3 cells. A Type 1 cell contains unreactive electrodes (usually carbon or platinum) and a molten salt. This type of cell is awkward to operate in a school laboratory since molten salts require extremely high temperatures. A Type 2 cell also contains unreactive electrodes, but the substance to be electrolyzed is part of an aqueous ionic solution. A Type 3 cell is the most complicated cell with regard to interpreting its operation. It contains not only an aqueous ionic solution, but also reactive electrodes.

In this experiment, you will construct and operate both Type 2 and Type 3 electrolytic cells. In Parts I and II, you will carry out experiments involving the electrolysis of KI and $ZnSO_4$ solutions respectively. Then in Part III, you will copper plate a metal object such as a key – remember to bring a suitable object to the laboratory for this part.

For each cell, it will be helpful if you can identify the anode and cathode in advance. In electrolytic cells, the electrodes are determined by the external power supply, which has two terminals, one positive and one negative. Since the negative terminal has a surplus of electrons, it will provide this surplus to any electrode to which it is connected. This electrode consequently becomes the cathode of the electrolytic cell, since reduction can occur only where there is a supply of electrons. By identifying the anode and cathode in advance, you will be able to make appropriate observations at each electrode.

Before beginning this experiment, you should take the time to review the terminology and theory associated with electrolytic cells.

OBJECTIVES

1. to electrolyze a KI solution using carbon electrodes

2. to electrolyze a $ZnSO_4$ solution using carbon electrodes

3. to copper plate a metal object

4. to interpret the products of each electrolytic cell with anode and cathode half-reactions

SUPPLIES

Equipment
U tube
ring stand
buret clamp
2 beakers (250 mL)
electrode holder
2 cylindrical carbon electrodes
1 copper electrode (strip)
copper wire (bare)
6 V battery or D.C. power supply
2 wire leads with alligator clips
steel wool or sand paper
lab apron
safety goggles

Chemical Reagents
1.0M KI
1.0M $ZnSO_4$
1.0M $CuSO_4$
phenolphthalein solution

CAUTION

The solutions used in this experiment are poisonous. Wash off any spills with water and dry with a paper towel.

PROCEDURE

As a matter of habit, you should clean all electrodes before and after each use. Use the piece of steel wool (or sand paper) to remove any surface coatings and then wipe the electrodes clean with paper towel.

Part I: Electrolysis of 1.0M KI

1. Put on your lab apron and safety goggles.

2. Fill a clean U tube with 1.0M KI solution, so that the solution level is about 2.0 cm from the top. Add 5 drops of phenolphthalein to each side of the tube.

3. Place a cylindrical carbon electrode in each side of the U tube and clip a wire end to each electrode. (See Figure 14E-1.) Do not allow the metal ends of the wire leads to contact the solution.

4. Connect the wire leads to a 6V battery or D.C. power supply. Observe what happens at each electrode during the next several minutes. Record your observations in your copy of Table 1 in your notebook while the cell is operating. Use a table of standard reduction potentials to determine the anode and cathode half-reactions.

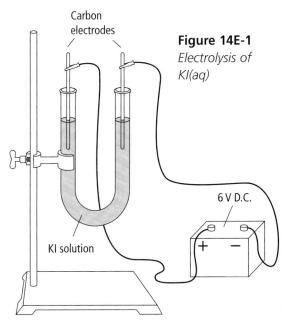

Carbon electrodes

Figure 14E-1
Electrolysis of KI(aq)

6 V D.C.

KI solution

5. Disconnect the wire leads, first from the power supply, then from the electrodes.

6. Clean up your apparatus, following the reagent disposal instructions.

Part II: Electrolysis of 1.0*M* ZnSO₄

1. Obtain 150 mL of 1.0*M* $ZnSO_4$ solution in a clean 250 mL beaker.

2. Place an electrode holder on this beaker and insert a cylindrical carbon electrode in each side of the holder. Connect a wire lead to each electrode. (See Figure 14E-2.)

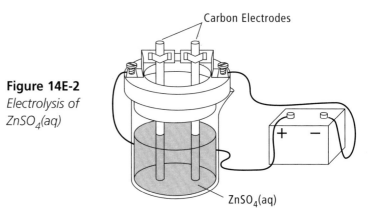

Carbon Electrodes

Figure 14E-2
Electrolysis of ZnSO₄(aq)

ZnSO₄(aq)

3. Repeat Steps 3, 4, and 5 from Part I, but record all observations in Table 2. Do not operate the cell longer than 5 min to 10 min, as the carbon electrodes will probably start to flake apart due to a physical, rather than chemical, process.

Part III: Copper Plating

1. Obtain 200 mL of 1.0*M* $CuSO_4$ solution in a clean 250 mL beaker.

2. You should have selected a metal object to be plated, such as a coin or a key. Prepare the object for plating by polishing it with steel wool. The idea is to remove any surface film such as oxides or finger grease, so that the copper plating will adhere more effectively. After cleaning the object, avoid touching it with your fingers.

3. Place an electrode holder on a second, empty beaker. Insert a strip of copper metal into one side of the electrode holder.

4. Use the piece of bare copper wire to suspend the metal object from the other terminal of the electrode holder. (See Figure 14E-3.) Ensure that the metal object is completely below the 200 mL mark on the beaker.

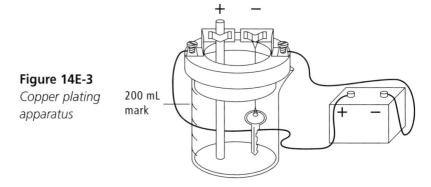

Figure 14E-3
Copper plating apparatus

200 mL mark

Copying the experiment is prohibited.

5. Using a wire lead, connect the object to be plated to the NEGATIVE terminal of the power supply. Connect the copper electrode to the POSITIVE terminal and turn on the power supply. Finally, pour the 200 mL of $CuSO_4$ solution into the cell. Observe what happens at each electrode over the next several minutes and record your observations in Table 3 while the cell is operating.

6. Disconnect the wire leads, first from the power supply, then from the electrodes.

7. Remove both electrodes from the solution. Rinse the object, then pat it dry with a paper towel. You may wish to try polishing the plated surface with a fine abrasive such as chalk dust.

8. Clean up, following the reagent disposal instructions.

9. Before leaving the laboratory, wash your hands thoroughly with soap and water.

REAGENT DISPOSAL

Rinse the KI solution from the U tube down the sink with copious amounts of water. You can return both the $ZnSO_4$ solution and the $CuSO_4$ solution to the containers provided by your instructor.

POST LAB CONSIDERATIONS

The products of electrolysis can be predicted by using a table of standard reduction potentials. Analysis of the anode and cathode half-reactions listed should provide support for your experimental observations.

The half-reactions in Parts I and III are straightforward and easy to determine. However, to determine the half-reactions for Part II, you may need to review the concept of overpotential.

EXPERIMENTAL RESULTS

It would be useful to have these data tables ready in your notebook before you come to the laboratory.

Part I: Electrolysis of 1.0*M* KI

Table 1 Electrolysis of 1.0*M* KI (Carbon Electrodes)

Electrode	Observations	Half-Reactions
Anode	COMPLETE IN YOUR NOTEBOOK	COMPLETE IN YOUR NOTEBOOK
Cathode		

Part II: Electrolysis of 1.0M ZnSO$_4$

Table 2 Electrolysis of 1.0M ZnSO$_4$ (Carbon Electrodes)

Electrode	Observations	Half-Reactions
Anode	COMPLETE IN YOUR NOTEBOOK	COMPLETE IN YOUR NOTEBOOK
Cathode		

Part III: Copper Plating

Table 3 Copper Plating

Electrode	Observations	Half-Reactions
Anode	COMPLETE IN YOUR NOTEBOOK	COMPLETE IN YOUR NOTEBOOK
Cathode		

ANALYSIS OF RESULTS

1. For Part I, how do the anode and cathode half-reactions explain your observations?

2. For Part II, how do the anode and cathode half-reactions explain your observations?

3. In Part II, what anode and cathode half-reactions would occur if the over-potential effect did not exist?

4. For Part III, how can you explain your observations at (a) the anode and (b) the cathode?

5. In Part III, predict what might happen if the metal object to be plated were placed in the CuSO$_4$ *before* the power was connected.

FOLLOW-UP QUESTIONS

1. The electrolytic cell in Part I produces reactions similar to those in a chlor-alkali industrial plant, where an NaCl solution is electrolyzed by means of unreactive electrodes.
   a. Predict the anode and cathode half-reactions for a chlor-alkali plant.
   b. Suggest a reason why it would be unwise to simulate the chlor-alkali process in Part I of this experiment.
   c. What common acid is often manufactured as a byproduct at chlor-alkali plants? (Hint: Examine the products of electrolysis.)

2. If the over potential effect did not exist, which common electroplating process would be impossible? Why?

3. In the electrorefining of copper, highly pure copper metal is produced at the cathode.

a. Consult a reference book, then draw a labeled diagram to illustrate an electrolytic cell capable of refining copper. Identify the materials used for the anode, cathode, and electrolytic solutions.

b. Give two reasons why impurities in the anode do not contaminate the cathode.

4. A $1.0M$ Na_2SO_4 solution is to be electrolyzed in a U tube containing carbon electrodes. Before electrolysis begins, bromthymol blue indicator solution is added to the colorless solution and the color is adjusted to green (neutral). Predict the colors that will result at each electrode and support your predictions with anode and cathode half-reactions.

5. When a $ZnSO_4$ cell such as the one in Part II is operated in industry, the $[Zn^{2+}]$ is one critical factor for an efficient recovery of $Zn(s)$. If the $[Zn^{2+}]$ in the cell drops below a certain level, another substance starts to be reduced at the cathode.

a. What undesirable reduction half-reaction occurs?

b. What practical problems could result if this were allowed to happen?

CONCLUSION

State the results of Objective 4.

SUGGESTIONS FOR FURTHER INVESTIGATION

Part III.A: Copper Plating, Quantitative

The copper plating can be performed in a quantitative manner and your instructor may wish you to do this. The following procedural steps correspond to those in Part III.

2a. Measure the mass of the dry object to be plated before placing it in the electrolytic cell. Record this value in your own designed Table 4.

5a. Place a milliammeter in the circuit in series with the cell. Measure and record both the current passing through the cell and the length of time in seconds for which it passes.

7a. When the plating is complete and the object is dry, measure and record its mass.

ADDITIONAL ANALYSIS OF RESULTS

1. Determine the following values by calculation:
   a. mass of copper deposited.
   b. moles of copper deposited
   c. moles of electrons involved
   d. quantity of electrons passed (coulombs)
   e. number of coulombs/mole of electrons

14F

Corrosion of Iron

Iron is the fourth most abundant element by mass in the earth's crust (after oxygen, silicon, and aluminum) and therefore, it is the second most abundant metal. However, since it is much easier to obtain from its ores than aluminum, iron is the most widely used structural metal. Most iron is used in making steel, which is an alloy of iron with carbon, and in some types of steels, with other elements as well. The wide range of products made from steel includes all types of vehicles, machinery, pipelines, bridges, and reinforcing rods and girders for construction purposes, to name but a few.

Unfortunately, however, iron has one major drawback: under certain conditions it can corrode or rust. If rusting is allowed to continue unchecked, the iron can eventually corrode completely away. Many millions of dollars are lost annually in replacing items (such as cars) which have been destroyed by corrosion. It is clearly very important to prevent waste of this magnitude by any available means.

The purpose of this experiment is to acquaint you with the process of corrosion and to demonstrate how it can be prevented or slowed.

OBJECTIVES

1. to expose iron nails to a wide variety of conditions involving access to air, water, acidity, and other materials

2. to deduce from the results the factors which hasten the corrosion process

3. to deduce from the results the factors which retard or prevent the corrosion process from occurring

SUPPLIES

Equipment
12 test tubes (18 mm × 150 mm)
test-tube rack
rubber stoppers
steel wool
beaker (250 mL)
water-soluble marker
kettle or hotplate
hammer (1 per class)
small piece of scrap wood
lab apron
safety goggles

Chemical Reagents
11 iron nails (approx. 5 cm long)
paint thinner or other solvent
galvanized iron nail
0.05M NaCl
0.05M HCl
0.05M NaOH
zinc strip (approx. 1 cm × 1 cm)
magnesium ribbon (5 cm long)
copper wire (5 cm long)
lubricating grease
(optional) 0.1M $K_3Fe(CN)_6$

PROCEDURE

1. Put on your lab apron and safety goggles.

2. Obtain 11 iron nails. Clean them with steel wool and place them in a 250 mL beaker. Pour paint thinner or another solvent over them to remove any oil or grease. Agitate, then pour off the solvent and return it to the waste container provided by your instructor. After this, try to handle the nails as little as possible.

3. Place one iron nail in each of 11 test tubes. Place the galvanized iron nail in the final test tube. Label the test tubes 1 to 12 with your water-soluble marker.

4. Vary the conditions in each test tube by carrying out the following operations. (Use enough water or solutions to cover each nail, unless otherwise specified.)
   #1 Add water.
   #2 Add water, but only enough to cover half the nail.
   #3 Add 0.05M NaCl solution.
   #4 Add 0.05M HCl solution.
   #5 Add 0.05M NaOH solution.
   #6 Do not add anything – just stopper the test tube.
   #7 Add water that has been boiled for 5 min (in a kettle or on a hotplate) to remove any dissolved air. Fill the test tube to the top and stopper it.
   #8 Attach the nail to the small piece of zinc by using a hammer to drive the nail through the zinc. (Place a piece of scrap wood underneath to protect your bench!) This should provide good contact between the zinc and the iron. Place in the test tube and add water.
   #9 Wrap the nail with a piece of magnesium ribbon as tightly as possible to ensure good contact. Place in the test tube and add water.
   #10 Wrap the nail with a piece of copper wire as tightly as possible to ensure good contact. Place in the test tube and add water.
   #11 Smear a small amount of lubricating grease to completely cover the bottom half of the nail. Place in the test tube and add water.
   #12 This test tube contains the galvanized iron nail. Add water.

5. Check whether any changes occur before the end of the period and record them in your copy of Table 1 in your notebook. Then label the test-tube rack with your name and class and place it in the area designated by your instructor.

6. Before leaving the laboratory, wash your hands thoroughly with soap and water.

7. After two or three laboratory periods, examine your test tubes and record any changes in Table 1.

8. On the day designated by your instructor, make your final observations and record them in your table.

9. On the final day, after making all other observations, remove the nail from test tube 11 and wipe the grease off with a paper towel. Observe the surface of the nail to see whether any corrosion has occurred and if so, where.

CAUTION

Paint thinner is flammable. Make sure there are no burner flames in the laboratory. Do not breathe the fumes.

CAUTION

The hydrochloric acid and sodium hydroxide solutions are corrosive to skin, eyes, and clothing. Wash any spills and splashes with plenty of water.

10. If no rust has formed in test tube 4 and if you are requested to do so by your instructor, add a small amount of potassium hexacyanoferrate(III) solution ($K_3Fe(CN)_6$) and observe the result.

REAGENT DISPOSAL

Rinse the liquids from the test tubes down the sink with plenty of water. Be careful not to let the nails go down the sink. Place the leftover nails and other metals in the designated container.

POST LAB CONSIDERATIONS

The corrosion of iron is a redox reaction in which iron is initially oxidized to Fe^{2+}:

$$Fe \rightarrow Fe^{2+} + 2e^-$$

The oxidizing agent is oxygen gas, which in the presence of hydrogen ions becomes reduced to water:

$$O_2 + 4H^+ + 4e^- \rightarrow 2H_2O$$

The Fe^{2+} ion itself is unstable and it can be oxidized to Fe^{3+} by the same half-reaction involving oxygen:

$$Fe^{2+} \rightarrow Fe^{3+} + e^-$$

As you can see, the half-reaction involving oxygen uses up H^+ ions; therefore, the solution becomes basic because OH^- ions are left behind. Both $Fe(OH)_2$ and $Fe(OH)_3$ are virtually insoluble, so a precipitate forms. What you see as rust in the test tube is mostly $Fe(OH)_3$. Rust that forms on objects exposed to the open air may lose some water from $Fe(OH)_3$ and is often assigned the formula $Fe_2O_3 \bullet xH_2O$, where the amount of water attached can vary with the conditions.

A precipitate may not have occurred in the test tube containing the HCl, since, with the larger amount of H^+ present, the amount of H^+ used up by the oxygen was not sufficient to make the solution basic. Evidence for the fact that some iron had actually dissolved was obtainable by adding some $K_3Fe(CN)_6$ solution, if you were asked to do so. A blue color would have indicated the presence of Fe^{2+} ions.

When iron is attached to another metal that can be oxidized more readily (that is, to a metal which is a stronger reducing agent than the iron), the electrons provided by this metal travel to the iron and force it to act as a cathode in the process. Since iron is forced to accept electrons, it cannot corrode, as corrosion involves giving off electrons. This method of preventing corrosion is called cathodic protection.

EXPERIMENTAL RESULTS

Table 1

Test Tube	Contents	First Observation	Second Observation	Final Observation	Amount of Corrosion Compared to Test Tube #1 (more, less, same)
1	Water				
2	Half water, half air				
3	0.05M NaCl				
4	0.05M HCl				
5	0.05M NaOH				
6	Air				
7	Boiled water (no air)				
8	Fe nail + Zn, water				
9	Fe nail + Mg, water				
10	Fe nail + Cu, water				
11	Grease on nail, water				
12	Galvanized nail, water				

COMPLETE IN YOUR NOTEBOOK

ANALYSIS OF RESULTS

1. Compare the results observed in test tubes 1, 2, and 7. In which test tube did the greatest amount of corrosion occur? In which did the least corrosion occur? What chemical is therefore necessary for corrosion?

2. Compare the results observed in test tubes 1 and 6. What substance in addition to the one from Analysis 1 is necessary for corrosion?

3. Compare the results observed in test tubes 3, 4, and 5. In which test tube was the amount of corrosion the greatest? In which was the amount of corrosion the least? What ion is therefore responsible for hastening the corrosion process?

4. **a.** Using a table of reduction potentials, write down the half-reactions for O_2 reacting with $1M$ H^+ to give H_2O and for O_2 reacting with $10^{-7}M$ H^+ to give H_2O, along with their E° values. Which of these half-reactions will occur to the greater extent?

   b. Write the two balanced overall redox equations for iron reacting with each of $1M$ H^+ and $10^{-7}M$ H^+ to give Fe^{2+}. Give the overall E° value for both reactions..

5. Write the balanced overall equation for Fe^{2+} reacting with O_2 and H^+ to give Fe^{3+} and water. Again, work out both overall E° values, one for $1M$ H^+ and one for $10^{-7}M$ H^+.

6. Write the net ionic equation for the reaction between Fe^{3+} and the OH^- ions left in solution which gives $Fe(OH)_3$.

7. Compare the results observed in test tubes 8, 9, and 10. Which metal(s) seemed to slow the corrosion process? Which metal(s) hastened corrosion? Do the results agree with the relative position of these four metals in the reduction potential table?

8. On the basis of your understanding of the factors involved in corrosion, explain the result in test tube 11.

9. Galvanized iron nails such as the one in test tube 12 are made by dipping the iron nail into molten zinc to coat them with a layer of zinc. Explain the result observed in this test tube.

FOLLOW-UP QUESTIONS

1. Blocks of magnesium (called *sacrificial anodes*) are connected at intervals to underground pipelines or to hulls of ships, to prevent corrosion of the iron. However, they have to be replaced periodically because they oxidize. Explain the chemical reasoning for this procedure.

2. Using a reference source, find out why objects that are galvanized (coated with zinc) do not need to have the zinc replaced, even though it is more active than the iron. Cite the reference you use.

3. Name some objects made of galvanized iron, other than nails, which you have in or around your home.

4. Explain why the salts put on roads in winter to melt ice can hasten the corrosion of a car if they are not thoroughly washed off.

5. Corrosion can be prevented by keeping air and water away from iron. Some ways of doing this are plating the iron with another metal that does not corrode (as in the chrome plated bumpers, etc., on a car) or painting the iron. However, these methods cannot always be used. For instance, gardeners should protect their gardening tools from rusting when stored in an outside tool shed over the winter, but cannot plate or paint them. What method of protecting gardening tools would you suggest?

6. What is stainless steel? Consult a reference source to obtain the composition of an example. Again, cite the reference you use.

7. Copper does not react with $1M$ H^+ to give Cu^{2+} and H_2, since the E° for the reaction is negative. However, if a strip of copper is half submerged in $1M$ HCl in a test tube, after a few days a blue color (indicating Cu^{2+}) is seen in the solution, showing that a reaction has occurred. Explain this result. Write an overall redox equation for the reaction and calculate its E°. (Your instructor may demonstrate this reaction to you or you may want to try it yourself. Ask permission first.)

CONCLUSION

State the results of Objectives 2 and 3.

Making Models of Some Carbon Compounds

The term structure in chemistry refers to the way in which the atoms of a molecule are joined together. Chemists can often predict the physical and chemical properties of a substance if its structure is known; hence, it is important to find a way of representing that structure. In two dimensions, the most common representations are the electron-dot (Lewis) formula, in which all the valence electrons of the atoms are shown, and the structural formula, in which bonding pairs of electrons are shown by a single line and non-bonding electrons are usually left out. These are useful up to a point, but as the molecules get more complex it is important to show the three-dimensional nature of the molecule. This is where ball-and-stick, ball-and-spring, or space-filling models help in the visualization.

Substances having the same molecular formula but a different structural formula are said to be *isomers* of one another; they are exhibiting *isomerism*. Two categories will be considered here, *structural isomers* and *geometric isomers*.

Carbon compounds often give rise to a number of different structural isomers because the carbon atoms can combine with each other in a variety of ways, including chains and ring structures (cyclic compounds). For example, the hydrocarbon butane, C_4H_{10}, may exist with its four carbon atoms linked in a straight chain of four or in a branched chain consisting of three carbons in a row, with the fourth attached to the central carbon.

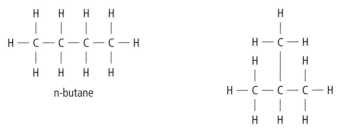

Other types of structural isomers occur when the carbon skeleton is identical, but the position of a functional group attaches to the carbon skeleton at different positions. Note the placement of the OH group in each of the following isomers of propanol:

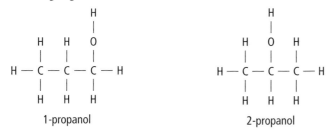

Sometimes, the two structural isomers may belong to two totally different classes of compounds, even though they have the same molecular formula. As a result they may have very different physical and chemical properties. For example, the following two isomers with molecular formula C_3H_8O belong to two different classes of compound, one in which the oxygen atom is attached to a hydrogen atom (an alcohol) and one in which the oxygen is attached between two carbon atoms (an ether):

1-propanol

methoxyethane (methyl ethyl ether)

Geometric isomerism occurs in some molecules having at least one double bond. The sequence for the atoms and bonds in the molecule is the same for each isomer, but there is a different orientation of the atoms or groups attached to the carbon atoms in the double bonds. Since rotation about a double bond is restricted, the parts of the molecule on either side of the double bond remain in fixed positions. In order to have this type of isomerism, each carbon atom in the double bond must have two different groups attached to it. The compound 1,2-dichloroethene exhibits this kind of isomerism:

cis-1,2-dichloroethene
(both chlorines are on the same
side of the double bond)

trans-1,2-dichloroethene
(the two chlorines are on opposite
sides of the double bond)

Before doing this experiment, if necessary, refresh your memory as to the number of bonding sites for each atom by referring back to Experiment 9B (Model Building With Covalent Molecules).

OBJECTIVES

1. to construct molecular models of some simple organic substances and to represent these structures with electron-dot and structural formulas

2. to construct molecular models of more complicated organic substances illustrating different types of isomers and represent them with structural formulas

SUPPLIES

Equipment
molecular model kit

Copying the experiment is prohibited.   ©SMG Lab Books Ltd.

PROCEDURE

1. Using the type of molecular model kit your instructor has made available to you, construct models for each of the following alkanes. Then, in your notebook, draw the structural formula and electron-dot formula for each molecule.
   a. methane CH_4
   b. ethane C_2H_6
   c. propane C_3H_8

2. Construct models for all structural isomers you find for each of the following compounds. Draw the structural formulas for all isomers and name them.
   a. butane C_4H_{10}
   b. pentane C_5H_{12}
   c. hexane C_6H_{14}
   d. cyclohexane C_6H_{12}

3. Construct models for all structural isomers of butene, C_4H_8. Draw the structural formulas for all isomers and then name them. Remember to consider the possibility of geometric isomerism.

4. Construct models for all structural isomers of propyne, C_3H_4, and butyne, C_4H_6. Draw the structural formulas for all isomers and then name them.

5. Construct models for all structural isomers of hexanol, $C_6H_{13}OH$, which have a straight chain of six carbon atoms. Identify the position of the OH group, draw the structural formulas for all isomers, and name them.

6. Construct models for the following structural isomers which have the same molecular formula, C_2H_6O. Observe how the different placement of the oxygen atom makes a big difference to the structure. Draw the structural formula for each isomer.
   a. ethanol C_2H_5OH
   b. methoxymethane (dimethyl ether) CH_3OCH_3

POST LAB CONSIDERATIONS

It can be seen that even with relatively simple molecules, there are often many structures possible. The IUPAC system for naming organic compounds was introduced so that there would be no confusion as to the name of a compound of a particular structure. Your instructor will give you the rules you will need for the classes of compounds you study. Once you know the rules, the structural formula can be written from the name and vice versa. Many common names for chemicals are in fact shortened versions of their IUPAC names. For instance, the insecticide DDT takes its name from shortening the longer name **d**ichloro**d**iphenyl**t**richloroethane. (Actually the correct IUPAC name is even longer: 1,1-bis(4-chlorophenyl)-2,2,2-trichloroethane!) Likewise the common name for the herbicide 2,4-**d**ichlorophenoxyacetic acid is 2,4-D.

EXPERIMENTAL RESULTS

Your observations in this experiment may be recorded in table form. However, it will be difficult to prepare the table for Steps 2, 3, 4, and 5 in advance as you do not know how many structures there are for each substance. Just list the compound and then draw all of the structures you find for that compound.

ANALYSIS OF RESULTS

1. How many isomers did you find for each of the following alkanes?
   a. methane
   b. ethane
   c. propane
   d. butane
   e. pentane
   f. hexane

2. Can cyclopentane (C_5H_{10}) be considered an isomer of pentane? Explain.

3. Look at your structures for pentane. How many different molecules can be made of pentene, C_5H_{10}, by replacing a C–C single bond with a C=C double bond? (Consider the possibility of geometric isomerism.)

FOLLOW-UP QUESTIONS

1. Look at the following four molecules, write the molecular formula for each one, and compare the formula. Assume a general hydrocarbon with no double or triple bonds or ring structures has the formula C_nH_{2n+2}. Based on what you observed about the formulas of the four molecules, give a set of rules that allow you to predict the number of hydrogen atoms involved in a general hydrocarbon when (a) one or more double bonds is present, (b) one or more triple bonds is present, and (c) one or more ring structures is present.

A $H-C\equiv C-CH_2-CH_2-CH_2-CH_3$ **B** $CH_2=CH-CH=CH-CH_2-CH_3$

C
$$CH_2 - CH$$
$$CH_2 \qquad CH$$
$$CH_2 - CH_2$$

D
$$CH_2 \quad CH_2$$
$$CH_2 \quad C$$
$$CH_2 \quad CH_2$$

2. Use a reference source to research what trans fatty acids are, how they arise, and what possible health risks may result from ingesting them. Cite the reference source you use.

CONCLUSION

Explain why there is such a huge number of organic compounds.

Preparation of Esters

Esters are a group of organic compounds best known for their interesting odors and flavors. Many natural odors and flavors were discovered to be esters and therefore, many synthesized esters are used in perfumes and foods.

An ester has the functional group $-\overset{\overset{\displaystyle O}{\|}}{C}-O-$, which is also known as an ester link. In the laboratory, an ester is usually formed from the reaction of a carboxylic (organic) acid and an alcohol, giving an ester and water as the products. This is an example of a condensation reaction, in which two molecules link up by the elimination of a small molecule between them; in this case, water.

We can write a general equation for the formation of esters as follows:

$$R-\overset{\overset{\displaystyle O}{\|}}{C}-O-H \; + \; H-O-R' \; \rightarrow \; R-\overset{\overset{\displaystyle O}{\|}}{C}-O-R' \; + \; H-O-H$$

$$\text{acid} \qquad\qquad \text{alcohol} \qquad\qquad \text{ester} \qquad\qquad \text{water}$$

Here, R and R' represent any alkyl group, of general formula C_nH_{2n+1}. Examples would be methyl (CH_3-), ethyl (C_2H_5-), or propyl (C_3H_7-). R and R' can also represent any aryl group (one that contains a benzene ring) such as phenyl (C_6H_5-). The first part of the name of an ester is derived from the alkyl or aryl group of the alcohol used and the second part is from the carboxylic acid, using the ending -oate. As an example, if ethyl alcohol (ethanol) combines with propanoic acid, the resulting ester is named ethyl propanoate. The aroma of oranges is attributed to octyl ethanoate (formed from octanol and ethanoic acid) and apricots have an aroma because of the presence of pentyl butanoate (formed from pentanol and butanoic acid).

The reaction between the alcohol and acid is rather slow at room temperature. In order to speed it up and get an appreciable yield in the time available, you will use a temperature of about 60°C and add sulfuric acid to act as a catalyst in the reaction. In this experiment, you will prepare four esters and carefully smell them to see if there are any odors you recognize.

OBJECTIVES

1. to synthesize several esters and to try to identify the odor of each

2. to write the chemical equations for the formation of each ester using structural formulas

SUPPLIES

Equipment

4 test tubes (18 mm × 150 mm)
water-soluble marker
test-tube rack
dropping pipet
centigram balance
hot plate
2 beakers (250 mL)
2 graduated cylinders (10 mL)
thermometer
lab apron
safety goggles
plastic gloves

Chemical Reagents

methanol
ethanol
1-propanol
glacial acetic acid (ethanoic acid)
butanoic acid
salicylic acid
concentrated sulfuric acid, H_2SO_4

CAUTION

Concentrated sulfuric acid is a powerful oxidizing agent and dehydrating agent. If mixed incorrectly with the other chemicals used in this experiment a fire can result. If added to a small amount of water, a large temperature rise can occur, which can result in severe burns. Follow the directions exactly.

All of the acids used in this experiment are corrosive to skin, eyes, and clothing. Wear a lab apron, safety goggles, and plastic gloves while performing this experiment. Any spills or splashes must be washed off your skin and clothing immediately, using plenty of water. Report any spills to your instructor.

PROCEDURE

1. Put on your lab apron, safety goggles, and gloves.

2. Label the four test tubes 1 to 4 with your water-soluble marker and place them in the test-tube rack.

3. Into the appropriate test tube, pour the correct amount of the alcohol and add the corresponding carboxylic acid as indicated in Table 1 below. Your instructor may suggest alternative or additional combinations depending on the chemicals available. (Use the centigram balance to measure the solid salicylic acid). Add 4 drops of concentrated sulfuric acid to each test tube.

Table 1 Reagents for Preparation of Esters

Test Tube	Carboxylic Acid	Alcohol
1	1 mL acetic acid	1 mL ethanol
2	1 mL acetic acid	1 mL 1-propanol
3	1 g salicylic acid	1 mL methanol
4	1 mL butanoic acid	1 mL ethanol

4. Put about 150 mL of water in a 250 mL beaker. Place the test tubes in the water and heat the water on a hot plate to a temperature of about 60°C. Leave the test tubes in the hot water bath for 15 min. (Do not use a bunsen burner as the alcohol vapors are flammable.)

5. Cool the test tubes by immersing them in cold water in another beaker.

6. Add 5 mL of water to each of the test tubes.

7. Carefully note the odor of the contents of each of the test tubes in your copy of Table 2 in your notebook. Hold the test tube about 30 cm away from your nose and gently waft the vapors toward your nose without

inhaling deeply. Each of the odors should be somewhat familiar to you. Alternatively, the contents of the test tube may be poured into a beaker half full of water and the odor above it detected carefully.

8. Dispose of all materials following the reagent disposal instructions.

9. Before leaving the laboratory, wash your hands thoroughly with soap and water.

REAGENT DISPOSAL

Any remaining concentrated H_2SO_4 must first be diluted before disposal. To dilute, slowly add the acid to at least ten times its volume of water in a beaker. If requested by your instructor, place the diluted acid in the designated waste container. All other liquids can be rinsed down the sink with copious amounts of water.

POST LAB CONSIDERATIONS

The reason for adding water to the contents of the test tube is to separate the esters from the reactants used. Esters are soluble in alcohol, but insoluble in water, and they generally have a density less than that of water, enabling them to separate and float to the top of the liquid mixture. This makes the detection of the odor more reliable.

To obtain a better understanding of the chemical changes that occur, you must write the balanced equations for these reactions using structural formulas. The structures of the alcohols and carboxylic acids used in this experiment are as follows:

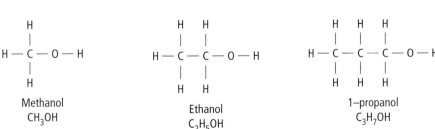

Acetic Acid (Ethanoic Acid)
CH_3COOH

Salicylic Acid (2-hydroxybenzoic acid)
HOC_6H_4COOH

Butanoic Acid
C_3H_7COOH

Methanol
CH_3OH

Ethanol
C_2H_5OH

1–propanol
C_3H_7OH

EXPERIMENTAL RESULTS

Table 2 Odors of Esters

Test Tube	Name of Ester Formed	Odor
1		
2	COMPLETE IN YOUR NOTEBOOK	COMPLETE IN YOUR NOTEBOOK
3		
4		

ANALYSIS OF RESULTS

1. Using structural formulas, write the equations for the reactions that occurred in each of the test tubes.

2. Name the ester formed in each of the test tubes.

FOLLOW-UP QUESTIONS

1. What is the name of the ester formed from each of the following combinations?
   a. ethanol and hexanoic acid
   b. methanol and pentanoic acid

2. What combination of alcohol and acid will form the following esters?
   a. hexyl octanoate
   b. methyl butanoate

3. Use a reference source to find two other esters that are used as flavorings. Cite the reference source you used.

4. The ester methyl salicylate is also known as "oil of wintergreen." Name some commercial products that contain this substance.

5. Salicylic acid is both an acid and an alcohol, and can also form an ester with its –OH functional group and an acid. Draw the structural formula for the ester formed when the –OH group of salicylic acid links up with acetic acid (ethanoic acid). It should be called salicyl acetate, but usually goes by the name acetyl salicylic acid (sometimes abbreviated as ASA). What is it used for?

6. Use a reference source to identify the chemicals involved in the manufacture of the synthetic fiber, polyester. Explain how these chemicals permit the formation of a long chain of molecules joined by ester links. Cite the reference source you used.

7. Acid was used in this experiment to promote the formation of the ester, but if the base sodium hydroxide is added to an ester, the reverse process occurs and the ester undergoes hydrolysis (reaction with water) to reform its original alcohol and acid. Write the equation for the hydrolysis of the ester n-propyl butanoate, $CH_3CH_2CH_2COOCH_2CH_2CH_3$.

CONCLUSION

Make a list of the odors you were able to detect and the ester responsible for that odor.

15C

Preparation of a Soap

The term "detergent" refers to any substance with strong cleansing power. Detergents are commonly classified as either soaps or synthetic detergents. Synthetic detergents are prepared from synthetically produced chemicals, whereas soaps are prepared from natural fats and oils. (The word "soap" has its roots in a Latin word meaning "animal fat.")

The history of soap making can be traced back 5000 years to the Middle East, where it was discovered that treating fat with alkali resulted in a substance with cleansing and healing powers. In fact, for many centuries soap was used medicinally only, in the treatment of skin wounds. Soap making remained relatively primitive until the 16th century, when techniques that produced a purer soap were developed. The reaction that produces soap is called *saponification*.

In more precise terms, soaps are salts of mixed fatty acids. Today they are prepared by reacting fats (which are esters) with alkali solutions such as sodium hydroxide or potassium hydroxide. For example, stearin, an ester, is a principal component of animal fat. It is the glycerol (1,2,3–propanetriol) ester of stearic acid, glyceryl tristearate, or stearin.

Stearin, when heated with sodium hydroxide, is broken down into glycerol and sodium stearate, a soap:

Copying the experiment is prohibited.

In a typical commercial process, a sodium hydroxide solution is added slowly and intermittently to a molten mixture of fats and oils. High temperature and good mixing are maintained by passing steam through the mixture. After a time, the fat is broken down to form an emulsified mixture of soap, glycerol, and unreacted NaOH. At this point an NaCl solution is added, which causes the soap to separate as a curd and float to the top of the mixture. In the final stages, perfumes, colorings, antiseptics, and other ingredients are added as necessary.

In Part I of this experiment, you will prepare a soap by reacting a fat with a fairly concentrated NaOH solution. Unlike the commercial process, ethanol will be added to help speed up the reaction. The ethanol serves as a solvent to bring the reacting materials into closer contact so that the procedure can be conducted in one laboratory period. Then in Part II, you will test your soap, a commercial soap, and lard for solubility, sudsing, and acidity.

OBJECTIVES

1. to prepare soap by saponification

2. to compare the results of tests on the soap prepared in the experiment and a soap prepared commercially

SUPPLIES

Equipment
beaker (250 mL)
2 beakers (150 mL)
water-soluble marker
pan (such as a dissecting tray)
3 wooden splints
glass stirring rod
hot plate
heat resistant mat
beaker tongs or crucible tongs
plastic spoon
test-tube rack
3 test tubes (16 mm × 150 mm)
metric ruler
lab apron
safety goggles

Chemical Reagents
lard, fat, or oil
commercially prepared bar of
    soap
saturated NaCl solution
neutral litmus paper or universal
    indicator solution
6M NaOH
ethanol (denatured)
distilled water

PROCEDURE

Part I: Saponification

1. Put on your lab apron and safety goggles.

2. Obtain a 150 mL beaker and using a water-soluble marker, label it "NaCl(aq)".

3. Place about 60 mL of saturated NaCl solution in this beaker and heat it on a hot plate (set at "high") until the solution just begins to boil. Set the solution aside on a heat resistant mat and save it for Step 9. Label a second 150 mL beaker "H_2O", place 100 mL of distilled H_2O in it, and set it aside as well.

4. Place about 15 g of fat (lard) in a 250 mL beaker. Heat the lard over the hot plate (set at "medium") until it melts. Stir the fat carefully with a glass stirring rod while it is melting. Be prepared to remove the beaker from the heat should overheating occur. Record the time of melting, as well as your observations, in your copy of Table 1 in your notebook.

5. Remove the beaker from the heat, then carefully and slowly pour 25 mL of ethanol into the molten lard. Stir the mixture and resume heating on "medium".

6. Slowly pour 25 mL of 6*M* NaOH solution into the mixture in a thin steady stream, stirring constantly and slowly. (Rapid addition or fast stirring may cause the fat to separate from the mixture.)

7. Continue to heat the mixture slowly and stir it regularly for the next 10 min or 15 min, until no evidence of fat globules remains. Occasionally, you will need to add distilled water (from the 150 mL beaker) to maintain a constant volume of mixture. Record the time at which no fat remains, as well as your observations, in Table 1. Turn off the hot plate.

8. Place some cold tap water in a tray for a cold water bath. Set the 250 mL beaker containing the mixture in the cold water bath and then add 40 mL of distilled water to the mixture while stirring it.

9. Allow the mixture to cool for several minutes in the cold water bath and then slowly add the 60 mL of warm NaCl solution from Step 3. Stir the mixture while adding the NaCl solution. In Table 1, record the time at which soap begins to form, as well as your observations.

10. The soap should now be visible as curds on the top of the mixture. Use a plastic spoon to scoop off a sample of soap and place it on a piece of paper towel that has been folded several times.

11. Save your soap sample for Part II. Clean up the rest of your apparatus according to the reagent disposal instructions.

Part II: Laboratory Tests

1. Label 3 test tubes A, B, and C with a water-soluble marker and place them in a test-tube rack.

2. Use separate wooden splints to add a small sample of each of the following substances to the test tubes: a sample of lard to test tube A, a sample of your lab soap to test tube B, and a sample of commercially prepared soap to test tube C.

3. Half-fill each test tube with distilled water and perform the following tests. *Solubility and Sudsing*: Place your thumb over the end of each test tube and shake vigorously for 15 s. Note how well each substance dissolves and, if sudsing occurs, measure the height of the suds that form. Record

your results in your copy of Table 2.

Acidity: Test the resulting water mixtures with neutral litmus paper or universal indicator solution and record your results in Table 2.

4. Clean up according to the reagent disposal instructions.

5. Before leaving the laboratory, wash your hands thoroughly with soap and water.

REAGENT DISPOSAL

For Part I, the solution that remains after the soap has been removed contains glycerol, NaCl, and NaOH. It can be washed down the drain with plenty of warm water.

For Part II, pour both the contents of test tube A and the solid soap into the designated waste container. The contents of the other test tubes can be rinsed down the sink with copious amounts of water.

POST LAB CONSIDERATIONS

Different kinds of fats and oils combined with different basic solutions produce different kinds of soaps. Soaps containing shorter carbon chains (10 to 12 carbons) are generally more soluble than those containing longer carbon chains (16 to 18 carbons). Also, soaps prepared from potassium hydroxide are usually more soluble than those prepared from sodium hydroxide.

In the days before sodium hydroxide was commercially available, soap makers relied exclusively on potash (K_2CO_3) as the source of their basic solution. The potash consisted of wood ash prepared in an iron pot. When potash is dissolved in hot water, a strong basic solution of KOH is produced.

In this experiment you may have noticed that the curds of soap were originally suspended in a thick, viscous liquid. This liquid was glycerol. Commercial hard soap is separated from the glycerol, formed into shapes, then aged for several weeks. In soft soaps (those sold in pump dispensers), the glycerol is not separated from the soap.

EXPERIMENTAL RESULTS

Part I: Saponification

Table 1

Time	Ingredient(s) added	Observations
about 10 rows needed	COMPLETE IN YOUR NOTEBOOK	

Part II: Laboratory Tests

Table 2

Test	Lard	Lab soap	Commercial soap
Apparent solubility in water			
Height of suds (cm)			
Neutral litmus paper test			

COMPLETE IN YOUR NOTEBOOK

ANALYSIS OF RESULTS

1. Describe the soap you prepared.

2. The soap you prepared is likely to be harsh on the skin. Why?

3. In Part II, what properties of your soap were similar to those of a commercially prepared soap?

FOLLOW-UP QUESTIONS

1. **a.** What practical problem might you encounter if you were to filter your final mixture to recover your soap?
   b. Suggest some solutions to this problem.

2. One popular brand of hand soap is made from a mixture of palm oil and olive oil. What do you think is the name of that brand of soap?

3. Soft soaps in pump dispensers are common in homes. State three criteria necessary to making a soft soap. (Refer to the Post Lab Considerations.)

4. During World War II, military manufacturing companies were very interested in the by-product of soap, glycerol (glycerin). Find out what it was used for.

CONCLUSION

State the results of Objective 2.

Oxidation of Alcohols

One of the amazing features of organic chemistry is the tremendous number of organic compounds which can react in a variety of ways to form new organic compounds. As a result, the number of organic compounds which can be synthesized in the laboratory is limitless. Many of the materials people take for granted today are a result of organic synthesis reactions. Some of the most familiar synthetic compounds include nylon, Teflon, rayon, polyester, and a variety of plastics. Since the molecules of these synthetics are quite complex in structure, it is preferable to study synthesis reactions involving simpler molecules first.

One typical method of synthesis involves the process of oxidation. Oxidation, as it applies to organic molecules, usually involves the addition of an oxygen atom or the removal of hydrogen atoms, or both. Oxidation reactions can be carried out by reacting organic compounds either with oxygen or with oxidizing agents such as potassium dichromate ($K_2Cr_2O_7$).

In the three parts of this experiment, three alcohols, methanol, ethanol, and 2-propanol, will undergo separate oxidation reactions to form new organic compounds. Alcohols can be classified as primary or secondary depending on where the hydroxyl (OH) group is attached to the carbon chain. Primary alcohols have their hydroxyl groups attached to the end carbon, whereas secondary alcohols have their hydroxyl groups attached to an intermediate carbon on the chain.

When each of the above alcohols is oxidized, the products of oxidation can be identified by characteristic odors.

OBJECTIVES

1. to investigate different methods of carrying out oxidation reactions

2. to oxidize primary and secondary alcohols

3. to identify the synthesized organic compounds by comparing their odors with those of known samples

SUPPLIES

Equipment
3 test tubes (16 mm × 150 mm)
test-tube rack
graduated cylinder (10 mL)
medicine dropper
bare copper wire (22 gauge)
lab burner
crucible tongs
metric ruler
beaker (250 mL)
lab apron
safety goggles

Chemical Reagents
methanol
ethanol
2-propanol
methanal sample
propanone sample
3M sulfuric acid
0.1M potassium dichromate
    solution

CAUTION

You should always detect odors with caution. Hold the test tube half an arm's length away from your nose. Waft the odor toward your nose with your hand, sniffing cautiously.

Figure 15D-1 *Apparatus for the oxidation of methanol*

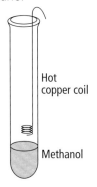

Hot copper coil

Methanol

PROCEDURE

Part I: Simple Oxidation of Methanol

1. Put on your lab apron and safety goggles.

2. Place about 3 mL of methanol in a clean test tube. Observe and record its odor in your copy of Experimental Results in your notebook.

3. Obtain a 30 cm length of bare copper wire. Make a coil at one end by wrapping the wire around a pencil 6 times; use the rest of the wire as a handle. Lower the coil into the test tube to just above the surface of the methanol and bend the handle over the edge of the test tube so that the coil is suspended above the methanol. (See Figure 15D-1.)

4. Hold the bent handle of the wire in a pair of crucible tongs and heat the coil in a burner flame for a few minutes.

5. Remove the hot coil from the flame, then immediately reinsert it in the test tube. Observe both the appearance of the copper coil and – cautiously – any odors produced during the process.

6. Compare the odor produced with the odor of methanal and propanone and record your observations in your notebook.

7. Clean up, following the instructions for reagent disposal. Save your copper coil for Part III.

Part II: Oxidation of Ethanol

1. Place 3 mL of $0.1M$ $K_2Cr_2O_7$ solution in a test tube, then add 3 mL of $3M$ sulfuric acid.

2. Obtain a 2 mL sample of ethanol and note its odor. Add the sample of ethanol to the contents of the test tube.

3. Set the test tube upright in a beaker containing hot tap water. Record any color changes that occur during the next 5 min. (Cr^{3+}(aq) ions have a characteristic green color.)

4. Compare the odor produced with the odors of methanal and propanone and record your observations.

5. Clean up, following the reagent disposal instructions.

Part III: Oxidation of 2-Propanol

1. Repeat Part I, using 2-propanol instead of methanol.

2. Clean up all materials following the reagent disposal instructions.

3. Before leaving the laboratory, wash your hands thoroughly with soap and water.

CAUTION

$3M$ sulfuric acid is corrosive to the skin, eyes, and clothing. When handling it wear safety goggles and a lab apron. Wash spills and splashes off your skin and clothing immediately, with plenty of water. Notify your instructor of any spills.

CAUTION

Most of the organic liquids used in this experiment are poisonous and flammable. Therefore, do not get any in your mouth and keep them away from open flames.

REAGENT DISPOSAL

Collect all liquids in the designated waste container(s).

POST LAB CONSIDERATIONS

The reaction in Part I involved the oxidation of a primary alcohol, methanol, by the removal of hydrogen atoms from the methanol molecule.

The reaction in Part II also involved the oxidation of a primary alcohol, ethanol, during which hydrogen atoms were removed from the ethanol molecule. Ethanal, whose odor is similar to that of methanal, was produced. The color change was merely an indication of a change in the oxidizing agent as $Cr_2O_7^{2-}$ ions (orange) changed to Cr^{3+} ions (green).

The alcohol in alcoholic beverages is ethanol. Upon being consumed, it is absorbed into the bloodstream and slowly metabolized by the body. However, a small amount of it is vaporized from the blood into the lungs. The subsequent ethanol concentration in the exhaled air can be related to that in blood. One type of "breathalyzer" used by police to detect drinking drivers utilizes a reaction similar to the one carried out in Part II of this experiment. The breathalyzer contains an acid solution of potassium dichromate solution. When a deep breath is exhaled through it, the ethanol in the exhaled air is oxidized to ethanal by the dichromate ion.

$$3CH_3CH_2OH + Cr_2O_7^{2-} + 8H^+ \rightarrow 3CH_3C{\overset{\displaystyle \diagup O}{\underset{\displaystyle \diagdown H}{}}} + 2Cr^{3+} + 7H_2O$$

| ethanol | orange color | | ethanal | green color |

An instrument measures the degree to which the intensity of the orange color is reduced and the results are registered on a dial which is calibrated to read blood-alcohol concentration.

The reaction in Part III was similar to that in Part I; however, since a secondary rather than a primary alcohol was oxidized, an entirely different class of organic compound was produced.

EXPERIMENTAL RESULTS

Part 1: Simple Oxidation of Methanol
Table 1

Odor of methanol	
Appearance of copper coil during the reaction	COMPLETE IN YOUR NOTEBOOK
Odor after the reaction	

Part II: Oxidation of Ethanol
Table 2

Odor of ethanol	
Color changes during the reaction	COMPLETE IN YOUR NOTEBOOK
Odor after the reaction	

Part III: Oxidation of 2-Propanol
Table 3

Odor of 2-propanol	
Odor after the reaction	COMPLETE IN YOUR NOTEBOOK

ANALYSIS OF RESULTS

1. Parts I and II involved the oxidations of methanol and ethanol.
   a. On the basis of comparing odors, what was the product of the oxidation of methanol?
   b. What was the product of the oxidation of ethanol?
   c. Therefore, which type of organic compound forms as a result of the oxidation of a primary alcohol?

2. Part III involved the oxidation of 2-propanol.
   a. On the basis of comparing odors, what was the product of the oxidation of 2-propanol?
   b. Therefore, which type of organic compound forms as a result of the oxidation of a secondary alcohol?

Copying the experiment is prohibited.

3. Structural formulas are useful in explaining differences between organic compounds.
   a. Compare the structural formulas of methanol and methanal, and comment on the differences between them.
   b. Compare the structural formulas of ethanol and ethanal, and comment on the differences between them.
   c. Compare the structural formulas of 2-propanol and propanone, and comment on the differences between them.

FOLLOW-UP QUESTIONS

1. Consult a reference source to find a common name and use for methanal.

2. Consult a reference source to find a common name and use for propanone.

3. Wine contains the alcohol, ethanol. Sometimes a wine will spoil and develop a vinegary taste. Explain how this can happen.

CONCLUSION

Summarize the results of Objectives 1, 2, and 3.

15E

Synthesis, Purification, and Analysis of an Organic Compound

The substance you will be preparing in this experiment is a very common drug which goes by the chemical name of acetylsalicylic acid, often abbreviated to ASA. In many parts of the world it goes by the common name aspirin, but in some countries the term "aspirin" is still the registered trade mark of the drug manufacturer.

For hundreds of years extracts of willow bark have been used in many countries for a variety of medicinal reasons. Scientists in the 19th century were able to isolate salicylic acid from these extracts and determined it was the active ingredient. Unfortunately it has an unpleasant bitter taste and causes stomach upset. Around 1900 it was discovered that if the –OH group of the salicylic acid is acetylated (replacing –H with –COCH$_3$ — an acetyl group), these problems are alleviated to a large extent. ASA is now used on a very large scale worldwide as an analgesic (to reduce pain), as an antipyretic (to reduce fever), and as an anti-inflammatory agent (to reduce swelling).

Salicylic acid has two functional groups attached to adjacent carbon atoms in a benzene ring, an alcohol functional group (–OH) and a carboxylic acid functional group (–COOH). When substituents are located on adjacent atoms in this way, the arrangement is referred to as the ortho- position. In fact, salicylic acid can be called ortho-hydroxybenzoic acid (abbreviated as o-hydroxybenzoic acid).

In this experiment, you will esterify the –OH group in the salicylic acid, using concentrated sulfuric acid as a catalyst. The reaction is shown by the following equation:

| Salicylic Acid | Acetic Anhydride | Acetylsalicylic Acid ("ASA" or "aspirin") | Acetic Acid |

The experiment will be done over three days, with the synthesis on the first day, purification on the second day, and final weighing and analysis on the third day. If resources or time are limited, your instructor may decide to do this as a demonstration.

OBJECTIVES

1. to synthesize acetylsalicylic acid from acetic anhydride and salicylic acid

2. to recrystallize the product from an ethanol solution

3. to test the product by comparing it chemically to a commercial preparation of ASA and to free salicylic acid (the starting material)

4. to calculate the percent yield of the product

SUPPLIES

Equipment
centigram balance
Erlenmeyer flask (125 mL)
beaker (400 mL)
2 beakers (100 mL)
2 graduated cylinders (10 mL)
ring stand
buret clamp
hot plate
heat resistant mat
thermometer
stirring rod
filter paper
vacuum filtration apparatus
plastic teaspoon
watch glass
water-soluble marker
lab apron
safety goggles

Chemical Reagents
salicylic acid crystals
acetic anhydride
concentrated sulfuric acid (in a plastic dropper bottle, one per class)
toluene
crushed ice
ethanol
$0.05M$ FeCl$_3$ solution

Salicylic acid can sometimes cause a skin rash if you get the powder on your hands, so be careful and wash your hands after handling this chemical.

You must be absolutely certain of exactly what you are doing in this experiment and follow all safety precautions without failure. The chemicals used can cause severe skin and eye damage if not handled properly. DO **NOT** WEAR CONTACT LENSES WHEN USING THE ACETIC ANHYDRIDE! **YOU MUST WEAR SAFETY GOGGLES AT ALL TIMES!**

PROCEDURE

Part I: Synthesis of ASA (Day 1)

1. Put on your lab apron and safety goggles.

2. Weigh a clean, dry 125 mL Erlenmeyer flask. Then place about 3 g of salicylic acid into the flask and record the exact mass of the salicylic acid and flask together in your copy of Table 1 in your notebook. Your instructor will show you approximately what 3 g looks like.

3. (Note: Steps 3 to 10 must be done in a fume hood.) Make a hot water bath by heating 200 mL of tap water to boiling in a 400 mL beaker on a hot plate.

4. Using the 10 mL graduated cylinder provided, measure out 5 mL of acetic anhydride in the fume hood and record this value in Table 1. Pour the acetic anhydride over the salicylic acid in the Erlenmeyer flask and add 3 drops of concentrated sulfuric acid (catalyst) to the mixture.

5. Set up a ring stand and buret clamp to hold the Erlenmeyer flask above the hot water bath. (See Figure 15E-1.) Place a thermometer in the flask.

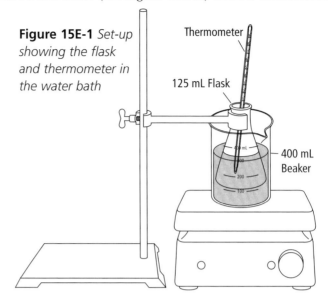

Figure 15E-1 *Set-up showing the flask and thermometer in the water bath*

6. Carefully lower the clamp and flask into the water bath until the flask is about 2 cm submerged. **Note**: Do not let ANY WATER get into the flask or the reaction will be ruined.

7. Heat the mixture and stir it occasionally with a stirring rod. Use the thermometer to monitor the temperature and when the temperature reaches 80°C – 90°C, remove the flask from the hot water bath. Place the flask on a heat resistant mat and allow the mixture to cool for 10 min.

8. While you are waiting for the mixture to cool, set up a single-flask vacuum filtration system. Also, use the graduated cylinder provided to measure out 10 mL of toluene and keep the toluene in the fume hood until it is needed.

9. If crystals have not formed after 10 min of cooling, put the stirring rod in the solution and deliberately scratch the bottom of the flask several times. This should cause crystals to start forming.

10. Break up the crystalline mass with the stirring rod and slowly add, with stirring, the 10 mL of toluene. Continue stirring the mixture around in the toluene to help extract and remove the unreacted salicylic acid.

11. (Note: The remaining procedures may be done at your bench.) Wet a piece of filter paper with a few drops of toluene and vacuum filter the reaction mixture. As soon as the product is free from toluene, wash the product with 2 mL of ice water (made by putting some crushed ice in cold water) and suck the product more or less dry. The purpose of the water is to destroy any left over acetic anhydride.

12. Using a water-soluble marker, label a 100 mL beaker with your name and class, weigh the beaker, and record its mass in Table 2. Scrape the crude product into the beaker and place the beaker in the assigned storage location until next day.

13. Clean up all of your equipment.

14. Before leaving the laboratory, wash your hands thoroughly with soap and water.

Part II: Purification of the ASA (Day 2)

1. Put on your lab apron and safety goggles.

2. Weigh the beaker and crude product from the previous day and record this value in Table 2. The crude product still contains some impurities such as salicylic acid. You will purify the ASA by recrystallizing it from a mixture of ethanol (CH_3CH_2OH) and water. ASA is soluble in ethanol but quite insoluble in water.

3. Put 9 mL of ethanol in a graduated cylinder. Add 6 mL of the ethanol to your crude ASA and stir to dissolve. If a clear solution is not produced after stirring for a minute, add another 1 mL of ethanol and stir. Repeat this addition up to a total of 9 mL if necessary. If there is still some undissolved solid, gently heat the solution on a hot plate (CAUTION: FIRE HAZARD from the ethanol!) until the solid has completely dissolved. Do NOT boil the solution.

4. Add 18 mL of hot water (90°C – 100°C) to the solution. If a solid separates at this point, warm the solution on a hot plate until the solid dissolves. Cover the beaker with a watch glass and set it aside on a heat resistant mat to cool slowly.

5. By the time the solution has cooled almost to room temperature you should be able to see a crop of ASA crystals. If crystals have not formed by the time the solution is cool, scratch the bottom of the beaker with a stirring rod several times to help induce crystallization.

6. Filter the crystals using vacuum filtration and scrape them into the previously-weighed beaker labeled with your name and class. Once again, store the beaker until next day.

Part III: Analysis for Purity of the ASA (Day 3)

1. Determine and record the mass of the beaker containing the recrystallized ASA which was stored after the previous class.

2. Use a plastic teaspoon to add a small portion of your ASA (enough to form a pile which could fit inside this "O") to a second 100 mL beaker for analysis. Dissolve in about 5 mL of water and then add 3 drops of $0.05M$ iron(III) chloride solution with stirring. Record your observations in Table 3. Wash out the analysis beaker.

3. Repeat Step 1 but with a similar-sized portion of commercial ASA. Record your observations.

4. Repeat the test with a similar-sized portion of free salicylic acid (that is, the starting chemical) and again record your observations.

CAUTION

Ethanol is flammable. Make sure there are no open flames in the vicinity.

REAGENT DISPOSAL

Any solid prepared ASA, commercial ASA, and salicylic acid may be disposed of in the waste basket. Place any unused ethanol as well as the toluene/water mixture extracted in the vacuum flask in the designated waste container for organic liquids. There should be no acetic anhydride or concentrated sulfuric acid left over in any of your containers as the full amount you used was taken directly from the dispensing bottle.

POST LAB CONSIDERATIONS

The balanced chemical equation for this synthesis reaction is:

$$C_7H_6O_3 + (CH_3CO)_2O \rightarrow C_9H_8O_4 + CH_3COOH$$

You will need to use this to calculate the theoretical yield.

The test using iron(III) chloride solution is to test for the presence of a phenolic hydroxyl group. Phenol is the compound C_6H_5OH in which the –OH group is attached directly to a benzene ring. Therefore, any organic compound in which there is an –OH group attached to a benzene ring is called a phenolic compound and the –OH group is called a phenolic hydroxyl group. By examining the structure of salicylic acid shown in the introduction, you can see that it is a phenolic compound. Iron(III) chloride gives a purple color in the presence of a phenolic group and it therefore enables us to distinguish between ASA and free salicylic acid.

EXPERIMENTAL RESULTS

Part I: Synthesis of ASA (Day 1)

Table 1

Mass of 125 mL Erlenmeyer flask (g)	COMPLETE IN YOUR NOTEBOOK
Mass of 125 mL Erlenmeyer flask + salicylic acid (g)	
Volume of acetic anhydride used (mL)	

Part II: Purification of the ASA (Day 2)

Table 2

Mass of 100 mL beaker (g)	COMPLETE IN YOUR NOTEBOOK
Mass of 100 mL beaker + crude ASA (g)	
Mass of 100 mL beaker + recrystallized ASA (g)	

Part III: Analysis for Purity of the ASA (Day 3)

Table 3

$FeCl_3(aq)$ added to:	Resulting Color
recrystallized ASA	COMPLETE IN YOUR NOTEBOOK
commercial ASA	
free salicylic acid	

ANALYSIS OF RESULTS

1. Calculate the mass of salicylic acid used as the starting material and convert it to moles.

2. Calculate the mass of acetic anhydride used as the starting material (density of the liquid is 1.082 g/mL) and convert it to moles.

3. Which substance is the limiting reagent?

4. Calculate the theoretical mass of ASA which should be produced.

5. Calculate the actual mass of recrystallized ASA which was produced.

6. Calculate the percent yield for the reaction.

7. Based on the $FeCl_3$ test, is your sample of ASA pure? Explain.

FOLLOW-UP QUESTIONS

1. A bottle of ASA tablets which has been opened for some time appears to smell of vinegar. What reaction do you think has occurred? (Hint: Recall the process of hydrolysis of an ester in Follow-Up Question 7 in Experiment 15B.) Are the tablets safe to ingest?

2. Write the balanced equation for the reaction which might have occurred.

CONCLUSION

State the results of Objective 4.

SUGGESTIONS FOR FURTHER INVESTIGATION

There are two possibilities for further investigation that your instructor may wish you to perform. The first is to determine the melting point of the ASA and compare the value you obtain to the known melting point. The closer these two values agree, the purer your sample. Your instructor will give you details as to how to carry out this determination.

The second possible method for assessing the purity of the product is to do an acid-base titration in order to determine the molar mass of ASA. You have already learned the required skills for this determination in Experiments 13C and 13G. In this case, however, the ASA can not be titrated directly with NaOH as ASA does not dissolve well enough in water. The procedure involves a back titration. Completely dissolve the ASA in a carefully measured volume of standard NaOH solution and then titrate with standard HCl solution to determine the amount of NaOH left over. This is called a back titration. If your instructor asks you to carry out this determination, you will be responsible for designing your own experiment, choosing appropriate volumes, concentrations, and indicators.

16A

Predictions Involving Precipitation, Acid-Base, and Redox Reactions

The scientific method involves three major phases. The first consists of making observations (doing experiments). Second, as a result of these experiments, relationships may become apparent and theories are put forward to explain these relationships. The third phase involves testing the theory. This is usually done by making predictions as to the outcome of an experiment and then performing the experiment to test the prediction.

At this point in your study of chemistry, you have been exposed to a large body of chemical knowledge, but you have not often been asked to predict a result. In this experiment you will have a chance to do so.

In Part I of this experiment, you will look at a large number of chemical combinations as a pre-lab activity and you will draw on your knowledge of precipitation reactions, acid-base reactions, and redox reactions in order to come up with a predicted result for the reaction. In the few situations where no reaction is possible, your prediction will be "no reaction."

In Part II, you will then perform the investigations and see whether your predictions were correct. If you do not predict a given result correctly, you will have to reassess your prediction and try to explain what happened.

In Part III, the reactions are somewhat more complex, so you will simply perform the investigations and attempt to explain the results.

OBJECTIVES

1. to predict the results of a large number of chemical reactions of different types

2. to perform investigations in order to test the predictions

3. to carry out a number of other reactions and interpret their results

SUPPLIES

Equipment
20 test tubes (13 mm × 100 mm)
test-tube rack
lab apron
safety goggles

Chemical Reagents

$0.1M$ $Ca(NO_3)_2$

$0.1M$ Na_2CO_3

phenolphthalein

saturated $Ba(OH)_2$ (about $0.1M$)

$0.2M$ H_2SO_4

$0.1M$ KI

$1M$ H_2SO_4

3% H_2O_2

$0.1M$ $Zn(NO_3)_2$

$0.1M$ NH_3

$6M$ HCl

$0.02M$ $KMnO_4$

$0.1M$ $FeCl_3$

$0.1M$ $Fe_2(SO_4)_3$

$0.1M$ $AgNO_3$

$0.1M$ KBr

$0.2M$ Na_2SO_3

$0.1M$ $K_2Cr_2O_7$

$0.5M$ Na_2CO_3

$1M$ HNO_3

$0.1M$ K_2SO_4

$0.1M$ $BaCl_2$

$0.1M$ $MgSO_4$

$0.1M$ $(NH_4)_2SO_4$

$0.1M$ $FeSO_4$

household bleach (NaClO)

starch solution

$0.1M$ $Cr(NO_3)_3$

$1M$ NaOH

PROCEDURE

Part I: Predicting Experimental Results

1. As a pre-lab activity, predict whether or not a reaction will occur in each of the following situations. Justify your predictions on the basis of E° values, solubility tables, etc. The relative amounts are not important for your prediction; they are put in as a guide for the investigations in which you will test your predictions.

   a. To 2 mL $0.1M$ $Ca(NO_3)_2$, add 2 mL $0.1M$ Na_2CO_3.

   b. To 2 mL of saturated $Ba(OH)_2$, add 1 drop of phenolphthalein, then 2 mL of $0.2M$ H_2SO_4.

   c. To 2 mL $0.1M$ KI, add 1 mL of $1M$ H_2SO_4, then 2 mL of 3% H_2O_2.

   d. To 2 mL of $0.1M$ $Zn(NO_3)_2$, add 2 mL of $0.1M$ NH_3.

   e. To 2 mL of $6M$ HCl, add 2 drops of $0.02M$ $KMnO_4$.

   f. To 2 mL $0.1M$ KI, add 2 mL of $0.1M$ $FeCl_3$.

   g. To 2 mL of $0.1M$ KBr, add 2 mL of $0.1M$ $FeCl_3$.

   h. To 2 mL of $0.2M$ Na_2SO_3, add 1 mL of $1M$ H_2SO_4, then 10 drops of $0.1M$ $K_2Cr_2O_7$.

   i. To 2 mL of $0.5M$ Na_2CO_3, add 2 mL of $1M$ HNO_3.

   j. To 2 mL of $0.1M$ $AgNO_3$, add 2 mL of $0.1M$ KBr.

   k. To 2 mL of $0.1M$ K_2SO_4, add 2 mL of $0.1M$ $FeCl_3$.

   l. To 2 mL of $0.1M$ Na_2CO_3, add 2 mL of $0.1M$ $BaCl_2$, then 1 mL of $1M$ HNO_3.

   m. To 2 mL of $0.1M$ $MgSO_4$, add 2 mL of $0.1M$ KI.

   n. To 2 mL of $0.1M$ $(NH_4)_2SO_4$, add 2 mL of saturated $Ba(OH)_2$.

   o. To 2 mL of $0.1M$ $FeSO_4$, add 1 mL $1M$ H_2SO_4, then 10 drops of $0.1M$ $K_2Cr_2O_7$.

   p. To 2 mL of $0.1M$ Na_2SO_3, add 1 mL $1M$ H_2SO_4, then 10 drops of $0.02M$ $KMnO_4$.

   q. To 2 mL of $0.1M$ $Fe_2(SO_4)_3$, add 2 mL of saturated $Ba(OH)_2$, then 1 mL of $1M$ HNO_3.

Part II: Confirming Predictions Experimentally

1. Put on your lab apron and safety goggles.

2. Using 13 mm × 100 mm test tubes and estimating volumes rather than actually measuring quantities, carry out all the investigations listed in Part I, (a) to (q). (2 mL is about one-fifth of the depth of a 13 mm × 100 mm test tube or a 2 cm depth; 1 mL is one-tenth the depth of a 13 mm × 100 mm test tube or a 1 cm depth.) Watch for color changes, cloudiness (indicating precipitate), the productions of gases, and the production of odors. Do not be biased by your predictions; record what you actually see.

Part III: Further Examples of Redox Reactions

1. To 2 mL of $0.1M$ KI, add 5 drops of starch solution; then add bleach (sodium hypochlorite, NaClO) until a color change is observed. Continue adding the bleach until a second color change is observed.

2. To 2 mL of $0.1M$ $Cr(NO_3)_3$, add $1M$ NaOH drop by drop, until the precipitate dissolves again. Finally, add 3 mL 3% hydrogen peroxide, H_2O_2.

3. To 2 mL of $0.1M$ $K_2Cr_2O_7$, add 1 mL of $1M$ H_2SO_4. Then add 3 mL of 3% H_2O_2.

4. Wash your hands thoroughly with soap and water before leaving the laboratory.

REAGENT DISPOSAL

Place the contents of test tubes containing chromium compounds, barium compounds, and silver compounds in separate designated waste containers. The contents of all other test tubes may be rinsed down sink with plenty of water.

POST LAB CONSIDERATIONS

The reactions predicted in Part I and subsequently carried out in Part II are relatively straightforward, so you should have had good success in predicting your results. For Part III, however, some explanations are required. In Step 1, the blue color characteristic of I_2 with starch should have been seen to form and then disappear again. The ClO^- is an oxidizing agent and is able to oxidize I^- to I_2, but it can also oxidize the I_2 to a higher oxidation state of +5 in IO_3^-. This reaction occurs in basic solution, since NaClO solution will be basic by hydrolysis.

The color changes you observed in the remainder of Part III would indicate that the Cr in Step 2, with an oxidation number of +3 (in $Cr(OH)_4^-$), was oxidized to +6 (CrO_4^{2-}), but the Cr in Step 3, with an oxidation number of +6 (in $Cr_2O_7^{2-}$), was reduced to the green Cr^{3+}. In both cases the reagent added was hydrogen peroxide. This shows that H_2O_2 (which has an oxidation number of –1) can either act as an oxidizing agent (becoming H_2O, in which the oxygen has an oxidation number of –2) or act as a reducing agent (becoming O_2 gas, with an oxidation number of 0). Note that for the oxidation of Cr^{3+} a basic solution was required, but the reduction of Cr from the +6 state had to occur in an acidic solution.

EXPERIMENTAL RESULTS

Your observations in this experiment are best not put in table form, as some experiments have more observations to be made than others, and a table restricts the amount of information you record. For each experiment, just describe everything you saw and state whether your observations agree with your predictions. If you did not predict correctly, try to explain what happened and why.

ANALYSIS OF RESULTS

1. For each situation in Part II in which a reaction occurred, write the net ionic equation and state what type of reaction it is (precipitation, acid-base, or redox). If the reaction was a redox reaction, also calculate its E°.

2. On the basis of the additional information given in the Post Lab Considerations, write equations for the half-reactions occurring in each step of the Procedure in Part III, then combine them to give the overall equation for each reaction. Remember that Steps 1 and 2 occurred in basic solution, but Step 3 occurred in acidic solution.

3. Calculate the E° for the reaction in Step 3 of Part III. (The other two steps may not have E° values listed in a typical table of standard reduction potentials.)

FOLLOW-UP QUESTIONS

1. Why is it more difficult to predict whether a redox reaction will proceed than it is to predict whether either an acid-base or a precipitation reaction will proceed?

2. Some redox reactions having positive predicted E° values do not actually occur. What factor(s) could be responsible?

CONCLUSION

Make a statement as to the amount of success you had in predicting the correct results of the chemical reactions listed in Part I.

16B

Molar Mass by Freezing Point Depression

The temperature at which a substance changes state (melting, freezing, boiling) at standard conditions is a definite fixed quantity, characteristic of that substance. However, if a second substance is mixed with the original substance, the change of state temperature of the original gets altered. This is particularly important when dealing with aqueous solutions. For example, dissolving a solute in water causes the freezing point to be lowered, as the molecules of water have more difficulty aligning with each other to form a pure crystal. On the other hand, the boiling point of an aqueous solution is higher than the boiling point of pure water. In this experiment, you will measure the depression of the freezing point of three different solutions.

When a pure substance like water freezes, the temperature stays constant throughout the phase change. However, with a solution, the temperature continues to drop as more water freezes and is removed from the solution, making the remaining solution more concentrated. (In a similar manner, the boiling point of a solution continues to rise as more water evaporates.) In addition, when a solution freezes, *supercooling* often occurs. This is a situation in which the temperature briefly drops below the freezing point, then rises slightly when the crystals actually form. The temperature you need to record is not the lowest temperature reached, but the temperature at which the ice crystals first start forming. (Refer to the sketch graphs in Figure 16B-1.)

Figure 16B-1
Sample Results

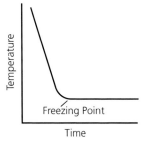

The concentration of a solution used in freezing point depression experiments must be expressed in molality, not molarity. The molality of a solution is the number of moles of solute added to 1 kg of solvent. The symbol used for molality is a small case m, italicized: *m*. The freezing point depression of a solute (ΔT) is given by the equation:

$$\Delta T = K_f \times m \times i$$

where K_f is the freezing point depression constant (°C/*m*),

m is the molality of the solution,

and i is the number of particles (molecules or ions) produced by one molecule of the solute.

After measuring the freezing point of water, the three solutions for which you will measure the freezing point depression are 1 m sucrose, 1 m NaCl, and an unknown. You will first determine the K_f for water from the freezing point depression observed with a 1 m solution of sucrose. Then you will use the value of K_f to determine i, the number of particles produced by a molecule of sodium chloride, NaCl. Finally, you will determine the molality of a solution of an unknown molecular solute and from that, the molar mass of the solute.

OBJECTIVES

1. to determine K_f (the freezing point depression constant) for water using a 1 m sucrose solution

2. to determine the number of particles produced by one molecule of NaCl from the freezing point depression of a 1 m solution of NaCl

3. to determine the molar mass of an unknown molecular solid

SUPPLIES

Equipment

large styrofoam cup
4 test tubes (18 mm × 150 mm)
thermometer (preferably –30°C to
    +50°C) or temperature probe
centigram balance
beaker (100 mL)
beaker (250 mL)
2 stirring rods
test-tube rack
crushed ice
lab apron
safety goggles

Chemical Reagents

1.00 m sucrose (sugar, $C_{12}H_{22}O_{11}$)
    solution
1.00 m sodium chloride (table
    salt, NaCl) solution
unknown molecular solid
sodium chloride (NaCl) crystals
distilled water

CAUTION

Your thermometer is made of glass and can easily break, leaving sharp edges that cut. Handle your thermometer gently. Do not use it to crush or stir ice. If your thermometer breaks, call your instructor. If it contains mercury, be aware that mercury liquid and vapor are very poisonous.

PROCEDURE

1. Put on your lab apron and safety goggles.

2. Obtain approximately 20 mL of NaCl crystals in a 100 mL beaker and add it to a large styrofoam cup half-filled with crushed ice. Stir to mix the contents.

3. Measure the temperature of the ice/salt mixture and proceed with the next step when the temperature is –10°C or lower.

4. Obtain 4 test tubes, label them 1 to 4, and place them in a test-tube rack.

5. Add distilled water to test tube 1 until it is about one-third full and place it in the ice/salt mixture. Stir constantly and periodically lift the test tube out enough to observe the contents. When ice crystals are seen beginning to form, insert the thermometer and measure the temperature of

the test tube contents to obtain the freezing point of water. Record this value in your copy of Table 1 in your notebook.

6. Add 1.00 *m* sucrose solution to test tube 2 until it is about one-third full and place it in the ice/salt mixture. Proceed as in Step 5 to measure and record the temperature at which crystals of ice are first seen to form in the sucrose solution.

7. Repeat using the 1.00 *m* solution of sodium chloride, NaCl, in test tube 3.

8. Make up your own solution of the unknown solid by weighing an empty 250 mL beaker, placing approximately 100 mL of water in it, and weighing again. Add the unknown solid until you have added approximately 20 g and again record the exact mass of the beaker and contents.

9. Stir until the solid has dissolved, then pour some into test tube 4 until it is approximately one-third full. Proceed to measure and record the freezing point of the solution as before. Make sure the temperature of the ice/salt mixture is still approximately –10°C and add more ice if necessary.

10. Pour all left over solutions down the sink and wash your hands before leaving the laboratory.

REAGENT DISPOSAL

All leftover solutions and the salt/ice mixture may be safely washed down the sink with plenty of water.

POST LAB CONSIDERATIONS

You may find when you calculate the result for the number of particles (ions) in the NaCl solution that it is not as high as you might predict it be and this is to be expected. In ionic solutions there is a certain amount of interionic attraction and formation of ion pairs that leads to less dissociation of the neutral compound than there would be if there were no interaction. Chemists use the term *activity* to represent the effective concentration of an ion in a solution, but a further discussion of this topic is beyond the scope of this experiment.

The depression of the freezing point has many practical applications. The antifreeze used in a car's cooling system is a solution of ethylene glycol (1,2-ethanediol) in water. If pure water were used, the expansion that occurs when water turns to ice would cause serious damage to the engine in winter conditions. It is necessary to keep the antifreeze in the engine in summer as well, because it also increases the boiling point and prevents the engine coolant from boiling over at high operating temperatures. Windshield washing fluid contains cleaning agents, but also usually has methanol added to lower the freezing point of the solution.

In areas where winter temperatures cause ice and snow to make driving conditions difficult, several different kinds of salts are sometimes spread on the roads. This lowers the freezing point and allows the snow and ice to melt. However, this is only useful if the temperature is just a few degrees below 0°C. Below about –10°C salt will not help.

EXPERIMENTAL RESULTS

Table 1

Freezing point of water (test tube 1)	
Freezing point of 1.00 m sucrose (test tube 2)	
Freezing point of 1.00 m NaCl (test tube 3)	*COMPLETE IN YOUR NOTEBOOK*
Mass of empty beaker	
Mass of beaker + water	
Mass of beaker + water + unknown solid	
Freezing point of unknown's solution (test tube 4)	

ANALYSIS OF RESULTS

1. Calculate the freezing point depression (ΔT, in °C) for the sucrose solution. Using the equation $\Delta T = K_f \times m \times i$, calculate K_f for water. Note that the molality of the sucrose solution is 1.00 m and that sucrose dissolves as a complete molecule, giving i the value of 1.

2. Using the same equation, calculate the value of i for NaCl from the freezing point depression (ΔT) observed for NaCl and the K_f value calculated in Analysis 1. Remember that the molality of the NaCl was 1.00 m.

3. The unknown solid dissolves as a complete molecule, giving i the value of 1. Using the ΔT for the unknown, and the K_f value calculated in Analysis 1, calculate the molality of the unknown's solution.

4. Using the mass of the unknown solid and the mass of the water used in making the solution, express the concentration in terms of grams of solid per 1000 g of water.

5. Calculate the molar mass of the solid from the mass per 1000 g of water and the molality.

FOLLOW-UP QUESTIONS

1. A sample of sea water was analyzed and found to be 0.47 m for the NaCl content. Disregarding other minerals that may be present, calculate the freezing point of this sample of sea water.

2. The substance mercury(I) nitrate was originally thought to have the formula $HgNO_3$, but is now known to be $Hg_2(NO_3)_2$ because the mercury(I) ion has the formula Hg_2^{2+}. Freezing point depression data provided some of the evidence for this discovery. What value for i would be obtained for a 1 m solution based on the formula $HgNO_3$?

3. Salt (NaCl) can result in corrosion problems on cars and bridges in areas where it is used to de-ice roads. Use a reference source to find out what other chemicals are now sometimes used instead, with their advantages and disadvantages. Cite the reference source you used.

4. Calculate the freezing point of 1 *m* acetic acid.

CONCLUSION

State the results of Objectives 1, 2, and 3.

Identifying a Volatile Liquid by Determining its Molar Mass

A volatile liquid is one that readily turns to vapor at relatively low temperatures. The term *vapor* is often used to describe the gaseous form of a substance which exists as a solid or liquid under ordinary conditions. One of the simplest methods of measuring the molar mass of a volatile substance is to use the ideal gas law in what is associated with the Dumas method, devised by Jean-Baptiste Dumas (1800–1884).

The concept of the mole had not yet been developed in Dumas' day. He computed molar masses (or rather, relative molecular weights) of certain liquids on the basis of relative gas (vapor) densities. Dumas correctly reasoned that the molar mass of a vapor relative to hydrogen was equal to the density of the vapor divided by the density of hydrogen gas under comparable conditions.

In modern chemistry, molar mass is ultimately determined by dividing the mass of a sample by its number of moles (g/mol). The mass of a sample is simply determined by weighing the sample, whereas the number of moles (n) of gas can be obtained now through the ideal gas equation:

$n = PV/RT$

In this experiment, you will trap a gas sample in a flask of known volume. To do this you will place a small amount of volatile liquid in a flask and heat the flask in a hot water bath. The liquid inside the warmed flask will completely vaporize and will be allowed to reach equilibrium with the room air pressure. Thus, the following variables will be measured:

1. volume (V) of the gas will be equal to the volume of the flask

2. temperature (T) of the gas will be directly measured

3. pressure (P) of the gas will be equal to room pressure

Since R is the known Universal Gas Constant (8.31 kPa·L/mol·K) the value of n can then be calculated. Once again, $n = PV/RT$.

By carefully measuring the mass (m) of the gas in the flask, the molar mass of the gas can be calculated from:

Molar mass = m/n (g/mol)

In this experiment, you will be working with an unknown sample of one of several volatile liquids. By determining your unknown liquid's molar mass you will be able to use this property to identify it.

OBJECTIVES

1. to determine the molar mass of an unknown volatile liquid by measuring properties of its vapor

2. to identify the unknown liquid based on its molar mass

SUPPLIES

Equipment

centigram balance
Erlenmeyer flask (250 mL)
two-hole stopper with capillary
   tubing and thermometer
   (preassembled by instructor)
large beaker (1000 mL)
graduated cylinder (250 mL)

graduated cylinder (25 mL)
ring stand
thermometer clamp
buret clamp
hot plate
lab apron
safety goggles

Chemical Reagents

unknown volatile liquid

PROCEDURE

1. Put on your lab apron and safety goggles.

2. Obtain a clean, dry 250 mL Erlenmeyer flask and a pre-made rubber stopper assembly. The stopper assembly consists of a two-hole stopper with a piece of glass capillary tubing and a thermometer inserted. (See Figure 16C-1.)

Figure 16C-2 *Prior to heating the flask*

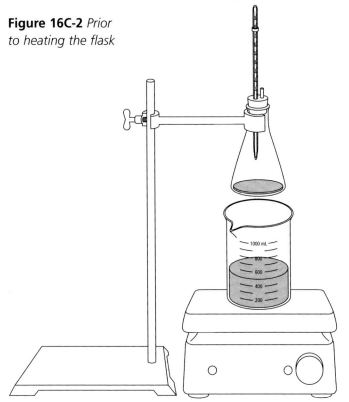

3. Insert the stopper assembly in the flask and place a small piece of tape on the top of the thermometer for later use. Weigh this combined apparatus and record this initial mass in your copy of Experimental Results. Also record the temperature of the air inside the flask (room temperature).

4. Set up a hot plate to heat a 1000 mL beaker that is half-filled with warm water.

5. Obtain about 5 mL of an unknown volatile liquid sample in a 25 mL graduated cylinder and record its identifying sample letter. Add this 5 mL of the liquid to your flask and replace the stopper assembly.

6. Set up a ring stand with buret clamp to hold your flask assembly well above the water. See Figure 16C-2 and note the arrangement of the ring stand. Make sure the flask is secure in the clamp.

7. Lower the clamp as far as possible so that the flask is as low as possible inside the beaker. Do not allow the flask to touch the sides of the beaker. You will now need to add more warm water to the beaker so that most of the flask is submerged (900 mL mark on the beaker).

8. Turn on the hot plate to medium heat to begin creating a hot water bath that will, in turn, heat the flask assembly. Remember, the vapor being formed in the flask is volatile and flammable so there must be **no open flames** in the area. Furthermore, it is helpful if you place a black (dark) background behind the tip of the tube to better observe the liquid and vapor that will escape.

9. Carefully observe the temperature inside the flask as it rises during heating. At some stage you will note that this rise in temperature "stalls" for a period of time (it remains unchanged). During this temperature stall, observe the contents of the flask carefully and you will notice that the volatile liquid in the flask has started boiling before the water in the beaker does. (Recall what volatile means.)

10. It is important to continue heating until all of the volatile liquid has vaporized. By observing the temperature carefully you will be able to note when the liquid has completely vaporized, since the temperature will start rising again after the stall. Also, periodically place a small piece of paper towel over the capillary tip to help indicate that vapor is escaping. (The paper towel will become wet as the escaping vapor condenses.) Wait for the combined evidence of the recommencing temperature rise (5°C above stall) and dry paper towel to indicate that all the liquid has vaporized and that all excess vapor has left the flask. Record the temperature now as the final temperature of the vapor. At this point, turn off the hot plate, lift the flask assembly above the water bath, and quickly dry any liquid from the tip of the capillary tube and cover it with your piece of tape. Hold the tape in place for about 30 s to ensure that the capillary tube is sealed. Dry the outside of the flask and you should notice that no liquid remains inside the flask.

11. Prepare a cold water bath by carefully replacing the hot water in the beaker with cold tap water. Arrange the apparatus as shown in Figure 16C-3 with the flask immersed in the cold water. Watch the thermometer and allow the flask to cool to room temperature (5 to 10 min). During cooling, once again observe the flask's contents and watch for evidence of the vapor condensing inside the flask.

12. Once again raise the flask above the water bath and dry the water from the outside of the flask, then weigh the combined flask, sealed stopper assembly, and condensed vapor. Do not record this value yet! Since air was in the flask for the initial weighing you must allow air to re-enter the flask at room temperature for a final weighing. Remove the flask assembly from the balance and listen very carefully while you slowly remove the tape. Place the tape back on the thermometer and, once again, weigh the flask assembly and record this final value.

CAUTION

Any unknown volatile liquids used in this experiment should be considered to be poisonous and flammable.

CAUTION

Inserting glass tubing and thermometers into rubber stoppers can be very dangerous. This activity should be left to your experienced instructor.

Figure 16C-3
Cooling the flask to room temperature

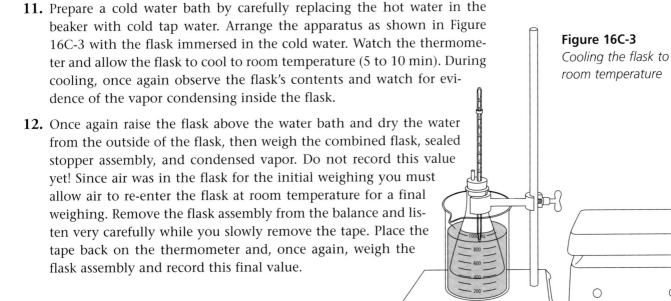

13. Remove the stopper assembly and discard the condensed vapor as described by the reagent disposal instructions.

14. Measure the volume occupied by the vapor in the flask by the following method. Fill the flask with water so that when the stopper assembly is reinserted, the capillary tube is filled with water. Carefully remove the stopper assembly, taking care to not spill any water. Measure the flask's water volume by pouring the water into a 250 mL graduated cylinder followed by a 25 mL graduated cylinder. Record the combined volume as the volume that was occupied by the vapor in the flask.

15. Record the barometric (room) pressure.

16. Put away all of your equipment and then wash your hands thoroughly with soap and water before leaving the laboratory.

REAGENT DISPOSAL

The unknown volatile liquid should be poured into a waste container in the fume hood.

POST LAB CONSIDERATIONS

In Dumas' era a similar experiment would have been conducted but with slightly different treatment of data. For instance, Dumas would have calculated the vapor density of the gas formed by dividing the gas mass (which is equal to the condensed vapor mass) by the flask's volume, thus obtaining a value expressed in grams per litre. This value would naturally be referenced to a specific pressure and temperature. Next, Dumas would compare this vapor density to a relative standard such as hydrogen gas and in so doing would also determine a relative formula mass. Dumas would never have described his findings as molar masses since the mole concept had not yet been developed.

In many cases a pure substance's property such as molar mass can be used to "fingerprint" or identify that substance. In this experiment, you will be provided with a limited number of possible liquids with which to match the molar mass that you have determined. Otherwise, more properties would be required to narrow your process of identification.

EXPERIMENTAL RESULTS

Unknown sample ____

Room temperature (°C)

Initial mass (flask + stopper assembly) (g)

Final mass (flask + stopper assembly + condensed vapor) (g)

Final temperature of vapor (°C)

Volume occupied by vapor in flask (mL)

Barometric (room) pressure (kPa)

ANALYSIS OF RESULTS

1. Use the ideal gas equation, as described in the introduction, to calculate the number of moles (n) of vapor that were present in the flask when heating was stopped. First, remember to ensure all measured variables (P, V, and T) are expressed in their appropriate units. Remember that the temperature must be on the Kelvin scale.

2. From your data, determine the mass of the condensed vapor that was present in the flask.

3. Calculate the molar mass of the condensed vapor (unknown volatile liquid).

4. Obtain the chemical formulas of the possible unknown solutions from your instructor. Calculate the theoretical molar masses for each one.

5. Based on the molar mass you experimentally obtained, what is the identity of your unknown volatile liquid?

FOLLOW-UP QUESTIONS

1. Calculate the volume of your vapor sample at STP.

2. Calculate the vapor density (at STP) in grams per litre for your vapor sample.

3. Using the now known identity of your volatile liquid, calculate its theoretical vapor density at STP. (Hint: Assume you have 1 mol of vapor at STP. First determine its mass in grams and its volume in litres.)

4. Compare the theoretical vapor density to the vapor density you determined in Follow-Up Question 2. Remember, comparing vapor densities in Dumas' day provided a means of comparing relative masses of gases before the development of the mole.

5. Explain how your "stall" temperature could also be used to identify your unknown volatile liquid.

CONCLUSION

State the results of Objectives 1 and 2.

16D

Gravimetric Analysis: Phosphorus Content in Fertilizer

Simply stated, gravimetric analysis means analysis by weighing. Gravimetric analysis is a laboratory technique which is concerned with determining how much of one or more components is present in a particular sample. For example, gravimetric analysis might answer the question of how much nitrogen is in a bag of fertilizer. A gravimetric analysis typically involves first dissolving a sample, then precipitating one of its components, and finally, recovering this precipitate to be weighed.

Modern analytical laboratories tend towards using more advanced, automated techniques rather than relying on the traditional manual gravimetric ones. However, a general chemistry laboratory should provide experiences in traditional methods of analysis to develop the skills and techniques required to learn to operate more state-of the-art analytical equipment.

In this experiment, you will carry out a gravimetric analysis of a sample of commercial fertilizer for its phosphorus content. You may have noticed that most fertilizers and plant foods have three numbers such as 10–6–8 on their labels. These numbers represent three essential components of a complete fertilizer. They mean that the fertilizer will contain at least 10% nitrogen (in the form of N), 6% phosphorus (expressed as P_2O_5), and 8% potassium (expressed as K_2O). Anything else in the fertilizer consists of materials such as fillers and dyes, although good quality fertilizers will contain other essential trace elements as well. Plants depend on nitrogen for leaf and stem growth, phosphorus for root development and blooms, and potassium for roots and general vigor.

Fertilizer companies follow an historic standard in which the elements P and K are expressed as P_2O_5 and K_2O even though these chemicals are not present as such. This means that 100 kg of 20–20–20 fertilizer contains 20% or 20 kg of elemental nitrogen, 20 kg of P_2O_5, and 20 kg of K_2O, with the rest being other materials. By applying the percentages of P and K in these compounds, it is apparent that only 8.8 kg of P and 16.6 kg of K are present. Thus, if the same label were expressed in elemental terms, it would read 20–8.8–16.6.

A sample of complete fertilizer (with its three numbers known) will be dissolved in water and the phosphorus will be precipitated as a compound, recovered, and weighed. In water, the predominant phosphorus-containing species in your fertilizer sample is HPO_4^{2-}, which will be precipitated according to the net ionic equation:

$$5H_2O(l) + HPO_4^{2-}(aq) + NH_4^+(aq) + Mg^{2+}(aq) + OH^-(aq) \rightarrow MgNH_4PO_4 \bullet 6H_2O(s)$$

At the end of the experiment, the precipitate, magnesium ammonium phosphate hexahydrate, will be dried and weighed. Working with this mass and your understanding of stoichiometry, you will be able to work backwards through the reaction and calculate the mass of P in the reactants. The mass of P can then be expressed as % P and % P_2O_5.

OBJECTIVES

1. to use gravimetric analysis to determine the % P in a sample of fertilizer

2. to determine the % P_2O_5 and compare this value to a given value

SUPPLIES

Equipment
2 beakers (250 mL)
stirring rod
centigram balance
filtering apparatus
wash bottle
lab apron
safety goggles

Chemical Reagents
0.5*M* magnesium sulfate
   ($MgSO_4 \bullet 7H_2O$)
2.0*M* ammonia solution (NH_3)
a complete fertilizer (such as
   soluble plant food)

CAUTION

Ammonia vapor is very irritating and in high concentrations can even be debilitating or lethal. Avoid contact with skin and clothing. Wash any spills with plenty of water

PROCEDURE

Part I: Removing the Phosphorus by Precipitation (Day 1)

1. Put on your lab apron and safety goggles.

2. Obtain a 250 mL beaker and weigh it on a centigram balance. Record this value in your copy of Table 1 in your notebook.

3. Set the centigram balance to an additional 4.00 g, then add fertilizer to the beaker until you are very close to this amount. Measure the mass of the beaker and fertilizer accurately. Record the mass in your copy of Table 1 in your notebook.

4. Add 50 mL of distilled water to the beaker and use a stirring rod to stir the sample for 3 min to completely dissolve the fertilizer.

5. Add 50 mL of 0.5*M* $MgSO_4 \bullet 7H_2O$ to the beaker and stir.

6. Add 150 mL of 2.0*M* NH_3 slowly while stirring. A white precipitate of $MgNH_4PO_4 \bullet 6H_2O(s)$ should start to form. Allow this mixture to sit for about 15 min to complete the precipitation.

7. Set up a filtering apparatus with a second 250 mL beaker. (See Figure 16D-1.) Obtain a piece of filter paper and use a pencil to label it with your name. Weigh and record the mass of the filter paper in Table 1. Properly fold and place the filter paper in the filter funnel.

8. Slowly add the contents of the original beaker into the filter paper and rinse out the beaker with a wash bottle. When the filtering is complete, rinse the precipitate in the filter paper with a small quantity of water from the wash bottle.

9. When the filter paper has drained, carefully remove it from the funnel and place it on a piece of folded paper towel. Put the filter paper and towel in the assigned storage location to dry overnight.

Figure 16D-1 *Filtering apparatus*

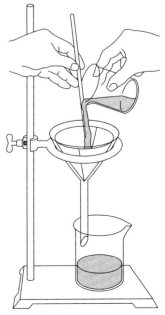

10. Put away all of your equipment and follow the reagent disposal instructions.

11. Wash your hands thoroughly with soap and water before leaving the laboratory.

Part II: Weighing the Precipitate (Day 2)

1. Obtain your filter paper with precipitate, $MgNH_4PO_4 \cdot 6H_2O(s)$, from the storage location and weigh it. Record this value in Table 1.

2. Put away all of your equipment and follow the reagent disposal instructions.

3. Wash your hands thoroughly with soap and water before leaving the laboratory.

REAGENT DISPOSAL

Rinse all solutions down the sink with copious amounts of water. Place the precipitate and filter paper in the designated waste container.

POST LAB CONSIDERATIONS

The data that you have collected will allow you to calculate the mass of P in your sample of fertilizer. Then to calculate % P use the following formula:

$$\% \text{ P} = \frac{\text{mass of P reacted}}{\text{mass of fertilizer sample}} \times 100\%$$

Furthermore, since the moles of P reacted are double the moles of P_2O_5 in the sample, the mass of P_2O_5 can also be determined. You will then be able to calculate % P_2O_5 and compare this value to the value that is provided by the fertilizer company. Again,

$$\% \text{ P}_2\text{O}_5 = \frac{\text{mass of P}_2\text{O}_5}{\text{mass of fertilizer sample}} \times 100\%$$

EXPERIMENTAL RESULTS

Table 1

Mass of beaker (g)	
Mass of beaker + fertilizer (g)	
Mass of filter paper (g)	
Mass of filter paper and $MgNH_4PO_4 \cdot 6H_2O(s)$ (g)	

ANALYSIS OF RESULTS

1. Using your results from Table 1, determine the mass of the fertilizer you used and the $MgNH_4PO_4 \cdot 6H_2O$ precipitate you produced.

2. First calculate the molar mass of $MgNH_4PO_4 \cdot 6H_2O$, then determine the moles of $MgNH_4PO_4 \cdot 6H_2O$ that were produced.

3. Refer to the balanced equation in the introduction and use the appropriate mole ratios to calculate the moles of HPO_4^{2-} that reacted.

4. Based on the moles of HPO_4^{2-} that reacted, determine the number of moles of P that reacted, then convert this value to grams of P reacted.

5. Calculate % P in your fertilizer sample. (Consult the Post Lab Considerations.)

6. From the moles of P that reacted, determine the moles of P_2O_5, then grams of P_2O_5 that were in your original sample.

7. Calculate the % P_2O_5 in your fertilizer sample and compare this value to the value provided by your instructor.

FOLLOW-UP QUESTIONS

1. Chemists rely on gravimetric analysis to regularly monitor chemicals that may affect our environment. What is the meaning of the term *eutrophication*? How do fertilizers and certain laundry detergents contribute to the eutrophication of rivers and lakes? Consult a reference source for this question.

2. Sterling silver is an alloy (metal mixture) of 92.5% Ag and 7.5% Cu. A chemist uses gravimetric analysis to determine the silver content of a 4.05 g "silver" charm from a bracelet. Two reactions are used in the analysis:

   Reaction 1: The charm is completely reacted with nitric acid to form a solution containing $AgNO_3$.

   Reaction 2: NaCl(aq) is added to the solution to precipitate all the Ag^+ as AgCl(s). (No other metal ions are precipitated.)

   The resulting AgCl(s) is dried and weighed and its mass is recorded as 4.41 g. What is the percentage of silver in the charm and should this charm be classified as sterling silver?

CONCLUSION

State the results of Objectives 1 and 2.

16E

Preparation and Testing of a Coordination Compound (Complex Salt)

Coordination compounds are typically formed from transition metals. A coordination compound usually has two parts: a complex ion with a transition metal ion in its center and counter ions to neutralize the charge of the complex ion so that the resulting compound has no net charge. The metal ion is bonded to either polar neutral molecules such as H_2O or NH_3, anions such as Cl^-, CN^- and, many others, or a combination of both. One example of a coordination compound is $[Co(NH_3)_5Cl]Cl_2$ written in the form [complex ion]counter-ions. Another example is the compound $K_3[Fe(CN)_6]$. Here the Fe^{3+} ion is complexed by six CN^- ions, so that the resulting ion has a 3– charge. This necessitates three K^+ ions to act as the counter ions. The NH_3, Cl^-, and CN^- in the previous two compounds are called ligands and bond by donating a lone pair of electrons to the central metal ion. In Lewis acid-base chemistry, the ligand behaves as a Lewis base (donates a lone pair) and the metal ion behaves as an acid (accepts a lone pair) and together they form a coordinate covalent bond. This type of bonding is different from normal covalent bonding in which each atom supplies one electron.

Unlike the ligands mentioned above, some ligands contain more than one atom with a lone pair that can bond to a central metal ion. Such ligands are called chelating agents (from Greek, chela, for claw). As a result of the multiple coordinate covalent bonds that form, chelating agents bind very tightly to metal ions and can be used to "claw" unwanted metals from where they may be harmful. One example of a chelating agent is ethylene diamine tetra acetate, EDTA, which is easily manufactured. Chelation therapy uses chelating agents such as EDTA to detoxify the human body of certain metal ions. A key principle of chelation therapy is that the metal ion bound to the chelating agent becomes chemically inert. The resulting coordination compounds, called *chelates*, are then expelled by the body in the urine. It should be noted that, although chelation therapy has been used since the 1940s, its efficacy for the treatment of disease is still controversial in the medical community.

Biological compounds often have central metal ions with rather complicated organic structures complexed to them. Examples are hemoglobin (with Fe^{3+} at the center), chlorophyll (with Mg^{2+} at the center), and Vitamin B-12 or cyanocobalamin (with Co^{3+} at the center).

In this experiment a coordination compound, specifically a hydrated complex salt, will be synthesized. In this case, the complex ion will be the anion in the salt. The name of this salt is potassium tris(oxalato)ferrate(III) trihydrate and its chemical formula is $K_3[Fe(C_2O_4)_3] \bullet 3H_2O$. The oxalate ion, $C_2O_4^{2-}$ is the coordinating agent and each ion has two coordinating positions. It is said to be bidentate ("two-toothed").

The method of preparing this particular complex salt was chosen so that the number of reactants would be kept to a minimum. By starting with $FeCl_3$ and $K_2C_2O_4$, all the chemical species are present to create a crystalline product. First, the Fe^{3+} ions react with $C_2O_4^{2-}$ to form the complex ion $Fe(C_2O_4)_3^{3-}$. Second, the $Fe(C_2O_4)_3^{3-}$ complex crystallizes out with K^+ ions to form the hydrated complex salt crystals, $K_3[Fe(C_2O_4)_3] \cdot 3H_2O$. A more detailed description of this sequence is provided in the Post Lab Considerations.

OBJECTIVES

1. to observe the synthesis of the complex salt potassium tris(oxalato)ferrate(III) trihydrate

2. to test the resulting chelating effect on the Fe^{3+} ion

SUPPLIES

Equipment
centigram balance
hot plate
2 beakers (150 mL)
graduated cylinder (25 mL)
stirring rod
tweezers
2 medicine droppers
filtering apparatus
tray for 3 cm deep ice water bath
    (one or two per class)
wash bottle
aluminum foil
lab apron
safety goggles

Chemical Reagents
iron(III) chloride hexahydrate
    crystals, $FeCl_3 \cdot 6H_2O$
potassium oxalate monohydrate
    crystals, $K_2C_2O_4 \cdot H_2O$
0.1M potassium thiocyanate
    solution, KSCN

CAUTION

$FeCl_3 \cdot 6H_2O$ is harmful if swallowed, inhaled, or absorbed through the skin. Wash off any spills on skin or clothing with plenty of water

CAUTION

$K_2C_2O_4 \cdot H_2O$ is poisonous and corrosive. Wash off any spills on skin or clothing with plenty of water

PROCEDURE

Part I: Synthesis of the Complex Salt (Day 1)

1. Put on your lab apron and safety goggles.

2. Obtain a clean dry 150 mL beaker and, near the top of the beaker, use a felt marker to label this beaker "A" along with your name. Obtain a centigram balance, then weigh beaker A and record this mass in your copy of Experimental Results. Now, weigh out about 3.0 g of $FeCl_3 \cdot 6H_2O$ into beaker A, but record the obtained mass accurately. Add 15 mL of water and stir until the crystals have dissolved. Set aside this beaker on a piece of white notepaper for later.

3. Obtain a second 150 mL beaker, labeled "B" as well as your name, then weigh and record its mass. Weigh out about 12.0 g of $K_2C_2O_4 \cdot H_2O$ into beaker B and record the mass. Add 20 mL of water to the beaker and use a hot plate (set on medium) to heat the mixture. Stir until the solid dissolves

and heat until you see vapor condensing inside the beaker. Continue heating for 3 min, but do not allow the solution to boil. Carefully remove beaker B from the hot plate and pour its contents into beaker A (which is still sitting on the white paper). A color change should occur immediately. Record your qualitative observations in your copy of Experimental Results.

4. Place beaker A in a shared tray (with other lab groups) of ice and water so that about one third of the beaker is submerged. Crystals should begin to form but sometimes crystal growing can be tricky. Crystals need an irregular surface on which to grow so you may need to lightly scratch the inside bottom of the beaker with a stirring rod to initiate crystallization. About 20–30 min of cooling is required for the crystals to finish forming.

5. Carefully decant (pour off) the solution (called the *supernatant*) from beaker A into beaker B without losing any of the crystals. Cover beaker B with a fitted piece of aluminum foil to prevent contamination from dust in the air and place it in the assigned storage location. You will test the supernatant next day.

6. Add 25 mL of water to beaker A and heat gently on the hot plate while stirring to dissolve the crystals. This redissolving in clean water should improve the purity of the crystals that will be produced. Remove the beaker from the hot plate and allow it to cool for 5 min.

CAUTION

KSCN can cause minor skin irritations. Wash off any spills on skin or clothing with plenty of water.

7. This product will slowly decompose when exposed to light so it should be stored in a dark location. Cover beaker A with a fitted piece of aluminum foil, then store your beaker in the assigned location to allow the crystals to reform overnight. If the crystals form slowly and undisturbed, large crystals will be obtained. Otherwise, small crystals will result.

8. Before leaving the lab, wash your hands thoroughly with soap and water.

Part II: Recovering the Complex Salt and Testing the Chelating Effect on the Fe^{3+} Ion (Day 2)

1. Put on your lab apron and safety goggles.

2. Obtain both beakers from the storage location and set up a filtering apparatus. Filter the contents of beaker A to recover the crystals. Use a wash bottle to rinse all of the crystals from the beaker onto the filter paper.

3. When the filtering is complete, leave the filter paper containing crystals in the funnel for now. Dispose of the filtrate by washing it down the sink with plenty of water.

4. Obtain a glass square and place it on a piece of white notepaper. Use tweezers to place a few crystals of the original $FeCl_3 \cdot 6H_2O$ on the left section of the glass square.

5. Use a clean medicine dropper to place a drop of the supernatant solution, $K_3[Fe(C_2O_4)_3] \cdot 3H_2O(aq)$, from beaker B on the middle section of the glass square.

6. Use clean tweezers to place a few crystals of your complex salt ($K_3[Fe(C_2O_4)_3] \cdot 3H_2O$) on the right section of the glass square.

7. Rinse out beaker B with plenty of water, then put about 5 mL of $0.1M$ KSCN solution in it along with a clean medicine dropper. Use the

Copying the experiment is prohibited.   ©SMG Lab Books Ltd.

dropper to add one drop of KSCN solution to each of the three samples on the glass square. Record your results.

8. Before leaving the lab, wash your hands thoroughly with soap and water.

REAGENT DISPOSAL

Rinse all solutions down the sink with copious amounts of water. Place all solids in the designated waste container or store them for later use as directed by your instructor.

POST LAB CONSIDERATIONS

The preparation of this particular complex salt can be described by the following two step mechanism:

Step 1 $Fe^{3+}(aq) + 3C_2O_4^{2-}(aq) \rightarrow Fe(C_2O_4)_3^{3-}(aq)$ {complex anion}

Step 2 $3K^+(aq) + Fe(C_2O_4)_3^{3-}(aq) + 3H_2O(l) \rightarrow K_3[Fe(C_2O_4)_3] \bullet 3H_2O(s)$

To obtain the final product (complex salt), the solution was cooled to promote the formation of the emerald green crystals of $K_3[Fe(C_2O_4)_3] \bullet 3H_2O$.

One of the important features of a complex salt is its ability to bind a metal ion in the middle of its structure and render it inert. As stated in the introduction, an application of this is found in chelation therapy. Since the bound ion in your complex salt is the Fe^{3+} ion, a simple test for free Fe^{3+} can be conducted. Free Fe^{3+} ions (light yellow) are known to react with SCN^- ions to form a blood-red product according to:

$Fe^{3+}(aq) + SCN^-(aq) \rightarrow FeSCN^{2+}(aq)$
yellow   colorless   red

Evidence of the chelation of the Fe^{3+} ion would be a negative test with SCN^- ions, thus a blood-red color will <u>not</u> appear.

EXPERIMENTAL RESULTS

Table 1

Material Weighed	Mass (g)
Beaker A + $FeCl_3 \bullet 6H_2O$	
Beaker A	
Calculated mass of $FeCl_3 \bullet 6H_2O$ used	
Beaker B + $K_2C_2O_4 \bullet H_2O$	
Beaker B	
Calculated mass of $K_2C_2O_4 \bullet H_2O$ used	

Qualitative observations

Part I: Synthesis of the Complex Salt (Day 1)

Complex salt formation

Part II: Recovering the Complex Salt and Testing the Chelating Effect on the Fe^{3+} Ion (Day 2)

KSCN(aq) added to $FeCl_3 \cdot 6H_2O$(s)

KSCN(aq) added to supernatant, $K_3[Fe(C_2O_4)_3] \cdot 3H_2O$(aq)

KSCN(aq) added to complex salt crystals, $K_3[Fe(C_2O_4)_3] \cdot 3H_2O$(s)

ANALYSIS OF RESULTS

1. All of the original Fe^{3+} should have reacted if the other reactants were in excess.
   a. Refer to the Post Lab Considerations and write the balanced overall reaction for the complex salt formation.
   b. From the mass of $FeCl_3 \cdot 6H_2O$ used (Table 1), determine the moles of Fe^{3+} available to react.
   c. Refer to your balanced equation and determine the moles of $C_2O_4^{2-}$ required. How many grams of $K_2C_2O_4 \cdot H_2O$ would be needed? Compare this value to the mass of $K_2C_2O_4 \cdot H_2O$ that you actually used, then decide whether or not you provided an excess amount of $C_2O_4^{2-}$.
   d. What experimental evidence do you have that tells you which of Fe^{3+} ions or $C_2O_4^{2-}$ ions were present in excess?

2. The complex salt in this experiment was formed in stages or steps.
   a. Write the chemical formula for the complex salt prepared in this experiment.
   b. Write the formula for the complex ion in the salt.
   c. What element provides the counter ions for this salt?

3. The main purpose of chelation is to bind a metal ion so that it becomes chemically unreactive. What do the results of the KSCN testing indicate about the chelating effect on the Fe^{3+} ion?

FOLLOW-UP QUESTIONS

1. Compounds containing oxalate ions are added to automobile radiators to remove rust. Suggest a general explanation for the process involved.

2. In the introduction, the complex salt, $[Co(NH_3)_5Cl]Cl_2$, is mentioned. There are a number of other related amine complexes of $CoCl_3$, namely $[Co(NH_3)_6]Cl_3$, $[Co(NH_3)_4Cl_2]Cl$, and $[Co(NH_3)_3Cl_3]$. When the chloride ion is part of the complex ion, it does not undergo the usual reactions of the chloride ion. Design an experiment that will enable you to differentiate amongst the structures shown above.

CONCLUSION

State the results of Objective 2.

Measuring Liquid Volumes

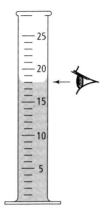

Chemists use several different types of apparatus for measuring liquid volumes. All of these devices are graduated, but it is important to note that there are two methods of graduation. Some are graduated to contain (TC) a certain volume of liquid, and some are graduated to deliver (TD) a certain volume. In fact, the letters TC or TD are often labeled on the apparatus so that you will know how the scales were calibrated. Any scale must be carefully examined so that all the calibrations are understood. In particular, determine what volume is represented by each marked unit, so that intermediate volumes between the markings can be estimated as accurately as possible. Furthermore, when reading a scale you must ensure that you look on a level line at the scale, as in Figure A1-1. Also, you will notice that the top surface of a liquid usually forms a depression called a *meniscus*. Always read the bottom of the meniscus.

Figure A1-1 *When reading a scale such as this, take care to have a level line of sight.*

Three specialized volumetric devices will now be described:

1. A *volumetric flask* is used whenever a specific liquid volume is required, mostly when making up solutions. The flask is graduated with a line etched around the neck of the flask at the appropriate position and is labeled TC. If a 1.0 L volumetric flask is being used to prepare 1.0 L of an aqueous solution, the technique is to dissolve the solute in about 750 mL of water first, then add water until it exactly reaches the 1.0 L mark. The very last portion should be added dropwise either from a wash bottle or a dropping pipet. The final step is then to shake the flask to make the solution homogeneous. (See Figure A1-2.)

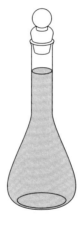

Figure A1-2 *A volumetric flask.*

2. A *pipet* is designed to measure and deliver volumes of liquids that are usually 25.0 mL or less. Pipets, then, are graduated TD. Some pipets are like volumetric flasks in that they only have one calibration and are used for only one specific volume. These are called *volumetric pipets*. Other pipets may be graduated. The graduations on these need to be studied carefully, as some are graduated from the top down, some from the bottom up, and some do not have to be drained all the way out to get the required volume.

Do not try to fill a pipet by placing the neck in your mouth and sucking the liquid in. This is dangerous as many liquids are poisonous or corrosive. You should always use a rubber suction bulb to draw the liquid into the pipet. (Your instructor may suggest an alternate device instead of the rubber bulb.) When draining the pipet into a flask, do not blow the liquid out; instead, allow the liquid to drain at its own rate. Touch the tip of the pipet against the side of the flask to get the last few drops of liquid out. Note however that a small amount will always remain. This is supposed to stay in the tube at the bottom of the pipet, as it is calibrated to deliver the correct amount in this manner. See Figure A1-3 for the steps involved in obtaining and transferring a specific volume with a pipet. Practise your pipetting technique with water before using a pipet in an experiment.

Figure A1-3 *Using a volumetric pipet.*

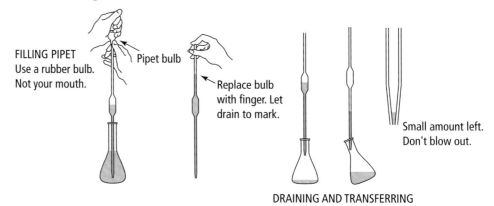

3. A *buret* is used for dispensing variable volumes of liquids, therefore it is calibrated TD. (See Figure A1-4.) There are a variety of valves available on burets, so you should familiarize yourself with the type in your laboratory. Always rinse your buret first with with the solution to be used, so that your solution does not become diluted by any water inside the buret. (Be sure to run a small amount of solution through the tip as part of the rinsing process to fill the tip and remove any air bubbles.) When using your buret, carefully pour the solution into the top using a small beaker and then adjust the initial TD reading to zero. Each time a volume is dispensed, it is not necessary to refill the buret to zero, since the volume dispensed can be determined by difference. However, if it is apparent that dispensing a similar volume for a second reading will take the level beyond the graduations at the bottom of the buret, it is better to refill before starting. Never allow the liquid to drain below the last graduation of the buret, because you will be unable to take readings in this region. As with the pipet, the last drop of liquid hanging from the tip can be retrieved by touching the flask to the tip of the buret. Once the experiment has been completed, the buret should be cleaned with a soap solution and then rinsed out with water.

Figure A1-4 *Using a buret.*

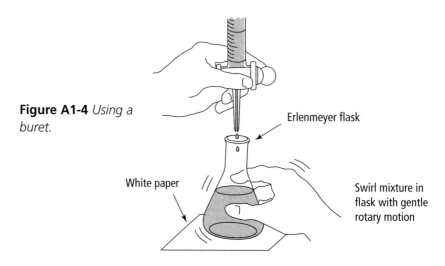

Charges of Some Common Ions

Positive Ions (Cations)		Negative Ions (Anions)	
aluminum	Al^{3+}	acetate	CH_3COO^-
ammonium	NH_4^+	bromide	Br^-
barium	Ba^{2+}	carbonate	CO_3^{2-}
cadmium	Cd^{2+}	hydrogen carbonate, bicarbonate	HCO_3^-
calcium	Ca^{2+}	chlorate	ClO_3^-
chromium(II), chromous	Cr^{2+}	chloride	Cl^-
chromium(III), chromic	Cr^{3+}	chlorite	ClO_2^-
cobalt	Co^{2+}	chromate	CrO_4^{2-}
copper(I), cuprous	Cu^+	dichromate	$Cr_2O_7^{2-}$
copper(II), cupric	Cu^{2+}	fluoride	F^-
hydrogen, hydronium	H^+, H_3O^+	hydroxide	OH^-
iron(II), ferrous	Fe^{2+}	hypochlorite	ClO^-
iron(III), ferric	Fe^{3+}	iodate	IO_3^-
lead	Pb^{2+}	iodide	I^-
lithium	Li^+	nitrate	NO_3^-
magnesium	Mg^{2+}	nitrite	NO_2^-
manganese(II), manganous	Mn^{2+}	oxalate	$C_2O_4^{2-}$
mercury(I), mercurous	Hg_2^{2+}	hydrogen oxalate	$HC_2O_4^-$
mercury(II), mercuric	Hg^{2+}	perchlorate	ClO_4^-
nickel	Ni^{2+}	permanganate	MnO_4^-
potassium	K^+	phosphate	PO_4^{3-}
scandium	Sc^{3+}	monohydrogen phosphate	HPO_4^{2-}
silver	Ag^+	dihydrogen phosphate	$H_2PO_4^-$
sodium	Na^+	sulfate	SO_4^{2-}
strontium	Sr^{2+}	hydrogen sulfate, bisulfate	HSO_4^-
tin(II), stannous	Sn^{2+}	sulfide	S^{2-}
tin(IV), stannic	Sn^{4+}	hydrogen sulfide, bisulfide	HS^-
zinc	Zn^{2+}	sulfite	SO_3^{2-}
		hydrogen sulfite, bisulfite	HSO_3^-
		thiosulfate	$S_2O_3^{2-}$

Atomic mass values have been rounded to the first decimal place for ease of calculation. If more accurate values are required, use the periodic table in Appendix 4.

Element	Symbol	Atomic Number	Atomic Mass	Element	Symbol	Atomic Number	Atomic Mass
Actinium	Ac	89	(227)	Europium	Eu	63	152.0
Aluminum	Al	13	27.0	Fermium	Fm	100	(253)
Americium	Am	95	(243)	Fluorine	F	9	19.0
Antimony	Sb	51	121.8	Francium	Fr	87	(223)
Argon	Ar	18	39.9	Gadolinium	Gd	64	157.2
Arsenic	As	33	74.9	Gallium	Ga	31	69.7
Astatine	At	85	(210)	Germanium	Ge	32	72.6
Barium	Ba	56	137.3	Gold	Au	79	197.0
Berkelium	Bk	97	(249)	Hafnium	Hf	72	178.5
Beryllium	Be	4	9.0	Hassium	Hs	108	(265)
Bismuth	Bi	83	209.0	Helium	He	2	4.0
Bohrium	Bh	107	(262)	Holmium	Ho	67	164.9
Boron	B	5	10.8	Hydrogen	H	1	1.0
Bromine	Br	35	79.9	Indium	In	49	114.8
Cadmium	Cd	48	112.4	Iodine	I	53	126.9
Calcium	Ca	20	40.1	Iridium	Ir	77	192.2
Californium	Cf	98	(251)	Iron	Fe	26	55.8
Carbon	C	6	12.0	Krypton	Kr	36	83.8
Cerium	Ce	58	140.1	Lanthanum	La	57	138.9
Cesium	Cs	55	132.9	Lawrencium	Lr	103	(257)
Chlorine	Cl	17	35.5	Lead	Pb	82	207.2
Chromium	Cr	24	52.0	Lithium	Li	3	6.9
Cobalt	Co	27	58.9	Lutetium	Lu	71	175.0
Copper	Cu	29	63.5	Magnesium	Mg	12	24.3
Curium	Cm	96	(247)	Manganese	Mn	25	54.9
Darmstadtium	Ds	110	(271)	Meitnerium	Mt	109	(266)
Dubnium	Db	105	(260)	Mendelevium	Md	101	(256)
Dysprosium	Dy	66	162.5	Mercury	Hg	80	200.6
Einsteinium	Es	99	(254)	Molybdenum	Mo	42	95.9
Erbium	Er	68	167.3	Neodymium	Nd	60	144.2

Element	Symbol	Atomic Number	Atomic Mass	Element	Symbol	Atomic Number	Atomic Mass
Neon	Ne	10	20.2	Seaborgium	Sg	106	(263)
Neptunium	Np	93	(237)	Scandium	Sc	21	45.0
Nickel	Ni	28	58.7	Selenium	Se	34	79.0
Niobium	Nb	41	92.9	Silicon	Si	14	28.1
Nitrogen	N	7	14.0	Silver	Ag	47	107.9
Nobelium	No	102	(254)	Sodium	Na	11	23.0
Osmium	Os	76	190.2	Strontium	Sr	38	87.6
Oxygen	O	8	16.0	Sulfur	S	16	32.1
Palladium	Pd	46	106.4	Tantalum	Ta	73	180.9
Phosphorus	P	15	31.0	Technetium	Tc	43	(98)
Platinum	Pt	78	195.1	Tellurium	Te	52	127.6
Plutonium	Pu	94	(242)	Terbium	Tb	65	158.9
Polonium	Po	84	(209)	Thallium	Tl	81	204.4
Potassium	K	19	39.1	Thorium	Th	90	232.0
Praseodymium	Pr	59	140.9	Thulium	Tm	69	168.9
Promethium	Pm	61	(147)	Tin	Sn	50	118.7
Proctactinium	Pa	91	(231)	Titanium	Ti	22	47.9
Radium	Ra	88	(226)	Tungsten	W	74	183.8
Radon	Rn	86	(222)	Uranium	U	92	238.0
Rhenium	Re	75	186.2	Vanadium	V	23	50.9
Rhodium	Rh	45	102.9	Xenon	Xe	54	131.3
Rubidium	Rb	37	85.5	Ytterbium	Yb	70	173.0
Ruthenium	Ru	44	101.1	Yttrium	Y	39	88.9
Rutherfordium	Rf	104	(257)	Zinc	Zn	30	65.4
Samarium	Sm	62	150.4	Zirconium	Zr	40	91.2

Based on $^{12}_{6}C = 12.0000$. Masses in parentheses are the mass numbers of the most stable or best known isotope.

PERIODIC TABLE OF ELEMENTS
(based on $^{12}_{6}C = 12.0000$)

Key:
- 29 — Atomic number
- Cu — Symbol
- Copper — Name
- 63.546 — Atomic mass

TRANSITION METALS

1 (IA)	2 (IIA)	3 (IIIB)	4 (IVB)	5 (VB)	6 (VIB)	7 (VIIB)	8 (VIII)	9 (VIII)	10 (VIII)	11 (IB)	12 (IIB)	13 (IIIA)	14 (IVA)	15 (VA)	16 (VIA)	17 (VIIA)	18 (VIIIA)
1 H Hydrogen 1.008																	2 He Helium 4.0026
3 Li Lithium 6.941	4 Be Beryllium 9.012											5 B Boron 10.81	6 C Carbon 12.0011	7 N Nitrogen 14.0067	8 O Oxygen 15.9994	9 F Fluorine 18.998	10 Ne Neon 20.179
11 Na Sodium 22.9898	12 Mg Magnesium 24.305											13 Al Aluminum 26.9815	14 Si Silicon 28.0855	15 P Phosphorus 30.974	16 S Sulfur 32.06	17 Cl Chlorine 35.453	18 Ar Argon 39.948
19 K Potassium 39.098	20 Ca Calcium 40.08	21 Sc Scandium 44.956	22 Ti Titanium 47.88	23 V Vanadium 50.942	24 Cr Chromium 51.996	25 Mn Manganese 54.938	26 Fe Iron 55.847	27 Co Cobalt 58.933	28 Ni Nickel 58.69	29 Cu Copper 63.546	30 Zn Zinc 65.39	31 Ga Gallium 69.72	32 Ge Germanium 72.59	33 As Arsenic 74.92	34 Se Selenium 78.96	35 Br Bromine 79.904	36 Kr Krypton 83.80
37 Rb Rubidium 85.467	38 Sr Strontium 87.62	39 Y Yttrium 88.905	40 Zr Zirconium 91.224	41 Nb Niobium 92.906	42 Mo Molybdenum 95.94	43 Tc Technetium (98)	44 Ru Ruthenium 101.07	45 Rh Rhodium 102.906	46 Pd Palladium 106.42	47 Ag Silver 107.87	48 Cd Cadmium 112.41	49 In Indium 114.82	50 Sn Tin 118.71	51 Sb Antimony 121.75	52 Te Tellurium 127.60	53 I Iodine 126.905	54 Xe Xenon 131.29
55 Cs Cesium 132.905	56 Ba Barium 137.34	57 La Lanthanum 138.906	72 Hf Hafnium 178.49	73 Ta Tantalum 180.948	74 W Tungsten 183.85	75 Re Rhenium 186.207	76 Os Osmium 190.2	77 Ir Iridium 192.22	78 Pt Platinum 195.08	79 Au Gold 196.967	80 Hg Mercury 200.59	81 Tl Thallium 204.383	82 Pb Lead 207.2	83 Bi Bismuth 208.980	84 Po Polonium (209)	85 At Astatine (210)	86 Rn Radon (222)
87 Fr Francium (223)	88 Ra Radium (226)	89 Ac Actinium (227)	104 Rf Rutherfordium (257)	105 Db Dubnium (260)	106 Sg Seaborgium (263)	107 Bh Bohrium (262)	108 Hs Hassium (265)	109 Mt Meitnerium (266)	110 Ds Darmstadtium (271)								

Lanthanide series

58 Ce Cerium 140.12	59 Pr Praseodymium 140.908	60 Nd Neodymium 144.24	61 Pm Promethium (145)	62 Sm Samarium 150.36	63 Eu Europium 151.96	64 Gd Gadolinium 157.25	65 Tb Terbium 158.925	66 Dy Dysprosium 162.50	67 Ho Holmium 164.930	68 Er Erbium 167.26	69 Tm Thulium 168.934	70 Yb Ytterbium 173.04	71 Lu Lutetium 174.96

Actinide series

90 Th Thorium 232.038	91 Pa Protactinium 231.036	92 U Uranium 238.029	93 Np Neptunium (237)	94 Pu Plutonium (244)	95 Am Americium (243)	96 Cm Curium (247)	97 Bk Berkelium (247)	98 Cf Californium (251)	99 Es Einsteinium (252)	100 Fm Fermium (257)	101 Md Mendelevium (258)	102 No Nobelium (259)	103 Lr Lawrencium (260)

Masses in parentheses are the mass numbers of the most stable or best-known isotope.